"This riveting history of the anti-Nazi resi[...] dinary portrait of two people—a Jewish w[...] man—who fought Hitler and also fell in l[...] diaries, and letters of Eva Lewinski and Otto Pfister, their three children have written the account of their parents' efforts to undermine Nazism as they risked their lives in Germany, France, and Belgium. An intimate story about Germans *and* Jews opposing the same horrific enemy, this book adds a whole new dimension to Holocaust literature. This is a moving love story and an important history made human at the grassroots level."

—Marion A. Kaplan, author of *Between Dignity and Despair: Jewish Life in Nazi Germany*

"Eva Lewinski and Otto Pfister courageously devoted themselves, over a period of years, to combating Nazism, while carefully nurturing a deep, life-sustaining love for one another. Their intermingled life stories, ably contextualized by the authors of this book, provide readers with a moving, richly documented, real-life drama, lovingly presented and thoroughly researched."

—Jack Jacobs, author of *Jews and Leftist Politics: Judaism, Israel, Antisemitism, and Gender*

"Their courage, resourcefulness, love, and unending optimism against all odds are thrilling. This is the American story of the mid-twentieth century."

—Tom Brokaw, author of *The Greatest Generation*

"The authors have done a superb job in supplementing their parents' letters and diaries using their own rigorous research, and the story progresses in a way that is historically interesting and emotionally satisfying."

—Susan Elisabeth Subak, author of *Rescue and Flight: American Relief Workers Who Defied the Nazis*

"This is a book for every student and every teacher. I had the privilege of being one of Eva's high school students from 1969–1971, and our friendship continued. As she wrote, she 'related to kids' because she liked and respected them. She inspired us to learn, and she responded to me and other teens from her deep well of experience. She nurtured every interest in the bigger things in life: purpose, service to others, and appreciation for the anchors of nature, spirit, music, poetry. At the time, I did not know much detail about her remarkable early life with Otto. But how we all benefited! I am grateful that this history has been told and will be preserved. I am deeply touched and inspired."

—Carol Larson, President and CEO, David and Lucile
Packard Foundation


"*Eva and Otto* is a moving story of resistance and love told largely through the correspondence of Eva Lewinski and Otto Pfister. It provides a rare view into what it can mean personally to dedicate oneself wholeheartedly to a struggle against tyranny. Eva and Otto's love for each other sustained them as they suffered long separations, danger, and imprisonment to fulfill their mission. Their longing to marry and create a family existed in tension with the rigorous ethic of the tightly knit resistance group of which they were a part and their commitment to carrying out anti-Nazi activities until Hitler was defeated. The extraordinary job that Eva and Otto's children have done in tracking down the documents needed to tell their parents' story also illuminates a little-known chapter in the history of the fight to rid the world of Nazism."

—John F. Sears, former Executive Director of the Franklin and Eleanor
Roosevelt Institute

# Eva & Otto

# Eva & Otto

## Resistance, Refugees, and Love in the Time of Hitler

Tom, Kathy, and Peter Pfister

Purdue University Press • West Lafayette, Indiana

**Library of Congress Cataloging-in-Publication Data**

Names: Pfister, Thomas L., 1948- author. | Pfister, Katherine D., 1946-
author. | Pfister, Peter J., 1948- author.
Title: Eva and Otto : resistance, refugees, and love in the time of Hitler
/ Tom Pfister, Kathy Pfister, Peter Pfister.
Identifiers: LCCN 2019026491 (print) | LCCN 2019026492 (ebook) |
ISBN 9781557538819 (paperback) | ISBN 9781612496153 (epub) |
ISBN 9781612496146 (pdf)
Subjects: LCSH: Political refugees--United States--Biography. | Pfister,
Eva Lewinski, 1910-1991. | Pfister, Otto, 1900-1985. | Anti-Nazi
movement--Germany--Biography. | Anti-Nazi movement--France--
Biography. | United States. Office of Strategic Services--Officials and
employees--Biography. | World War, 1939-1945--Secret service-
-United States. | Refugees--Government policy--United States. |
World War, 1939-1945--Refugees--United States. | Internationaler
Sozialistischer Kampfbund--History.
Classification: LCC D809.U5 P45 2020  (print) | LCC D809.U5
(ebook) | DDC 940.54/86730922--dc23
LC record available at https://lccn.loc.gov/2019026491
LC ebook record available at https://lccn.loc.gov/2019026492

*To our parents,*
*for the precious writings they preserved,*
*for the sacrifices they made for others, including us,*
*and for the lessons that can be learned from their lives*

*You have decided, and so have I, to go the hard way, to do what we think was our duty. And even though we realize only too well that our individual action does not change the course of things one way or the other . . . , we did individually all that we could. And we did it as one which makes us very, very rich. . . . I think we can say, without being pretentious, that we do not have to be ashamed of ourselves.*

—Eva's letter to Otto on December 24, 1944, reflecting on their years of resistance work

*A few words about my visit with Mrs. Roosevelt. That I, an unknown refugee, should be able to enter the White House; that the wife of the President would receive me, shake my hand with great warmth, listen to what I had to say, ask questions, and then promise to try to help—that was perhaps one of the most profound experiences that I ever had.*

—Eva recalling her meeting with Eleanor Roosevelt in the White House on December 27, 1940, seeking help with the rescue of other anti-Nazi political refugees

*Now, let's go for a little walk, you and I. I take your hand, and we walk through the streets of Marseille which have seen your eyes—sad like on the photo that you left for me, but infinitely good.*

—Otto's letter from Marseille to Eva in New York on November 8, 1940

# Contents

# Preface

This is a true story about German opposition and resistance to Adolf Hitler as revealed through the early lives of Eva Lewinski Pfister (1910–1991) and Otto Pfister (1900–1985). We—Tom, Kathy, and Peter—are the three grown children of Eva and Otto and the authors of this book. Our parents chose to dedicate their early lives to helping others in the most challenging of historical circumstances. We wrote this book because we believe that their story is important. We feel privileged to share it.

In 1979, our parents gave us a 130-page unpublished memoir titled "To Our Children." Eva described it as "an attempt to give you an overview of your family background" and noted that it was "mostly written by Eva with Otto's additions and help." Otto died in 1985 and Eva in 1991. They left a unique treasure by preserving papers written as the events in this book unfolded: Eva's handwritten diaries, hundreds of pages of correspondence to each other, and documents pertaining to their anti-Nazi work and efforts to obtain emergency U.S. visas for themselves and others. We carefully stored these papers at Tom's house in an old wooden cabinet that had been crafted by Otto's hands.

After Eva's death, the three of us wrote a short memorial book to preserve some of the thoughts we expressed about them in small gatherings with family and close friends. Since that time, we often thought about writing something more comprehensive about their early years. But we were busy with our lives and families, and this remained a project for the future.

Kathy ignited our work on this book in the summer of 2011, when she began to make plans with her husband Neil for a trip to France to trace the steps that Eva had taken after the German blitzkrieg began in

May 1940. Peter and Tom found the idea of Kathy's trip compelling and decided to go along. Peter's wife Bonnie and Tom's son Franklin joined Kathy and Neil. In the months before the trip, we immersed ourselves in our parents' papers. Most were originally written in German, some in French. At various times during and after her work on the 1979 memoir, Eva had translated some portions of her diaries and correspondence into English. Having studied in Germany in college, Peter and Tom began to undertake the task of translating other letters, diaries, and documents.

As we considered how best to tell this story, we quickly agreed that we should rely heavily on our parents' writings. Their own words offer unique contemporaneous insights into the events and times. But we also decided that their words would be most meaningful if presented along with a careful examination of the historical context. This required research.

We reviewed records from a number of archives in America and Germany. We also requested records under the Freedom of Information Act (FOIA) from previously secret files of the U.S. Office of Strategic Services (OSS), the FBI, and the State Department. Our research revealed astonishing new information that we had not learned from our parents. And the records we obtained from our FOIA requests, some of which were released for the first time, exposed new information about the roles of U.S. government agencies and officials in rescuing some refugees threatened by Hitler, including our parents, and turning away so many others.

Our experience working closely together on this book was one of the most gratifying aspects of the project. After an early exchange of preliminary drafts of different sections written by each of us, we decided that the story needed to be presented in one voice. Tom volunteered to be the primary writer of the many subsequent drafts of all chapters, and Kathy and Peter are grateful to him for taking on that role. Over the course of seven years, we met more than a dozen times—in Los Angeles and Ventura (hosted by Tom), Amherst (hosted by Kathy), and Berkeley (hosted by Peter). In those meetings, we shared proposed outlines, discussed the results of our research, and reviewed and edited drafts of chapters. Our work triggered vivid memories of our parents.

We also had numerous marathon evening conference calls—usually lasting two or three hours—in which we discussed revisions of drafts of chapters that had been prepared by Tom for Kathy and Peter to review.

Following the calls, Tom revised the drafts, incorporating the agreed-upon changes, and sent them back to Kathy and Peter for further review and discussion in the next call. Reflecting Kathy's dedication, one of our conference calls took place in late December 2018, at her request, while she was still in an acute care rehabilitation facility following difficult spine surgery.

We made a number of trips. In addition to our journey to southern France in 2011, Peter and Tom visited archives together in the United States and Germany. In 2018, we agreed to donate our parents' papers to the U.S. Holocaust Memorial Museum in Washington, D.C., so they can be preserved and made available for future research. On May 9, 2018, the three of us made an unforgettable trip to the museum (along with Kathy's husband Neil, Peter's wife Bonnie, and Tom's daughter Eliza) and personally delivered the first portion of our parents' papers.

We have made every effort to tell our parents' story truthfully, without embellishing or oversimplifying it. In quoting our parents' words, we made a few minor modifications in punctuation and phrasing without annotation in the interest of clarity. Most of the translations of Eva and Otto's quoted writings are from the original German into English, and we have noted the few instances when the translation is from the original French. Of course, some judgments are always necessary in the process of translating. Quotations from Eva and Otto's 1979 memoir and from the correspondence between them in 1944–1945 are in the original English unless otherwise noted.

# Prologue

They met in Paris in 1935 at Le Restaurant Végétarien des Boulevards at 28 Boulevard Poissonnière. Eva left a description of this first encounter with Otto in a diary entry five years later on March 15, 1940. The diary entry, like so many thereafter, was directed to Otto, who had been separated from her by the sweep of historical events. Eva wrote:

> That evening, just five years ago. I was sitting at the cash register, looked sadly, disappointed, into the emptiness of the many faces in front of me. I was looking—for how long already—for the sign of a human being. Nobody there. At about 9 p.m., the door opens quickly. With long, hasty, but not nervous steps, a tall fellow enters, goes to a group of young people, sits down with them, after a warm greeting. You are that person. Something moves me; there is a human being. I can, I have to, follow your conversation. I become happier, as I hear you talk about idealistic philosophy, about Kant, about mystics, and . . . about Rilke, with deep inner involvement. Your back is towards me, you can't see me. I feel close to you.
>
> It is getting late. You are getting up, come to the register. You pay. Then, for the first time, your eyes see me, your look is open and great. In a sudden movement you shake hands with me, the strange, sad, shy girl, and you leave. Barely is the door shut, when you open it again and stand in front of me. "N'est-ce pas, vous aussi, vous connaissez Rilke? [Isn't it true, you also know Rilke?]" "I love him," I believe I replied, and gave you

my hand again, in deep happiness. That night, I dreamt about you; I was no longer alone.

What had brought that strange, sad, shy girl to this vegetarian restaurant in Paris? And who was that tall fellow with a look that was open and great? Who were these two human beings who shared an interest in idealistic philosophy and Kant and a love for the poet Rainer Maria Rilke and who made a fateful connection that night in 1935?

The paths that Eva and Otto took separately and together after they met—as Germans who resisted Hitler and as political refugees in Europe and America—are the primary focus of this story. But first we must examine the different paths they took before they met.

# PART I.

## EVA'S PATH TO 28 BOULEVARD POISSONNIÈRE

*A person needs calm to develop. My, our generation's misfortune is that it did not have time to mature.*

—EVA'S DIARY ENTRY IN PARIS, JANUARY 1, 1935

# 1. Childhood in Goldap (1910–1926)

Eva was born in 1910 in Goldap, a small town in East Prussia, where she lived until the age of sixteen. With only about 10,000 inhabitants at the time, Goldap was "in the flat lake country that is called Masuren, with many woods, wide fields and ranches, but no mountains."[1] East Prussia, then a province in the northeastern part of Germany, was divided between Russia and Poland after World War II. Goldap is now in Poland.

Eva's father, Louis Lewinski, had two young sons, Erich and Ernst, when his first wife died of cancer. He then married Charlotte Rosenkranz, and they had four children together: Eva, Rudi, Hans and Ruth. Louis's and Charlotte's parents had come to Germany from Poland to escape the persecution of the Jews there. Eva recalled that her grandparents "observed the customs of the Jewish religion, but rather liberally; and their children were educated within the framework of German culture." She also noted: "A few of my mother's brothers and sisters married non-Jewish Germans, a decision that was rather unusual at that time."

Louis Lewinski was a respected citizen of Goldap. He successfully operated a shop facing the large market square in the center of town in which he sold clothing, material, furs, and household linens. Eva's family lived in a flat above the store.

When Eva was about four years old, World War I broke out. In the first days of the war, Goldap experienced a wave of anti-Semitism. "As happens very often," Eva later recalled, "war creates fear and hysteria. In our little town, so immediately threatened by the Russian troops, the hostility was directed against the Jews. It was felt that they did not really belong—were subject perhaps to foreign influence—were probably enemies of Germany, spies for the foreign invaders." This deeply affected Eva's family:

> Under this suspicion, all Jewish men in our little town (there were perhaps twelve) were arrested and put into jail. For our family, this was an absolute tragedy, an attack on my father's integrity, a nightmare. He stayed in jail for a few days; my mother, accompanied by Erich, spent days and nights on the footsteps of the official's office, trying to convince him what a horrible error had been made. We were told that during those days in prison, our father did not sleep, barely ate, and his heart hurt constantly. When he was released—no accusations, no apologies—he was a broken man.

Shortly after her father's release from prison, the entire civilian population of Goldap was forced to flee from the advancing Russian troops. Eva was bundled up with other families in a hay wagon because trains did not run any more. They arrived in Königsberg (now Kaliningrad), where her paternal grandmother lived and gave them shelter. Eva was told that this shelter was unlawful because Königsberg was a fortress, and civilian refugees were not permitted. She hid with her younger brother Hans "under a big comforter in a big bed, told not to make a sound when the soldiers patrolled, looking for refugees. It was cold, and dark—we had no gas or other light." Supper was "a slice of dark bread with turnip marmalade."

Eva's youngest brother Rudi was born while the family was in hiding in Königsberg. Shortly after Rudi's birth, her family was able to return to Goldap in the spring of 1917. All of the houses had been burned, so they lived in temporary barracks placed in the middle of the market square. The town slowly began to recover. The family store was reopened, Eva's oldest brother Erich left school to join the German Army, and Eva began school. "The war went on; we were poor, did not have much to eat. But there were good feelings in our family; mother and father were close, and all we kids were loved." Eva recalled her father's compassion: "From time to time he would bring in a stranger who had come to the store, or to the synagogue, and who had nobody in town. So he shared our dinner, and mother washed his shirt; and once in a while, when the stranger's shirt was not more than rags, father took his own shirt off, asked mother to wash it and to give it to the stranger."

One of Eva's warmest childhood memories was walking to her first day of school with her father: "I was terribly shy, afraid of facing a new world. My father who did not talk much must have sensed my feelings. I was dressed, ready to go the few blocks to school. He takes my hand, and walks with me to school. I have never forgotten the beautiful feeling of being safe, and loved by this strong, sad man who was my father."

But soon after that, when Eva was not yet eight years old, her father died of a heart attack. She later recalled the trauma of that loss:

> The strongest memory of these few years is of the last evening we saw our father, on Christmas Eve 1917. That afternoon, he did not want to get up from his nap (which he needed every day because of his impaired health). So, after supper, we all gathered around his bedside, sang, played games, and were very happy—mother very big—six weeks later, Ruth was to be born. And suddenly it all ended. He began coughing, turned quite white, we were quickly taken out, stayed with friends during the next few days. And on the morning of December 27, he died, having never regained consciousness.

Eva's mother never left her husband's bedside. After his death, she shielded Eva and her siblings from seeing their father on his deathbed and removed a black ribbon that someone had placed in Eva's hair. Eva recalled that "we children did not go to the funeral which many, many townspeople attended—he had been loved by many. Mother wanted us to remember him as he had been alive and loving, not as he was put into his grave."

Eva's family struggled to make ends meet after her father's death. The family's store was sold, but the funds from the sale barely covered the outstanding bills. Her older brothers, Erich and Ernst, were away at war, and her younger sister Ruth was born six weeks after her father's death. Eva was then the oldest of the children at home, not quite eight years old. Hans was six, Rudi three. It was impossible for her mother to get a job. Eva's uncles, aunts, and friends in Goldap helped out by inviting them to dinner periodically. Her mother cooked for boarders they took into their home and made "fine lace handkerchiefs until late into the night" that she was able to sell.

When Eva was about twelve years old, she pitched in by taking on a job tutoring a young student. "This was during the inflation years . . . I got paid only once in money (it was a proud feeling!); when we realized that the next morning the money had so devalued that it did not buy anything, my pupil's parents then paid me in goods—flour, sugar, eggs, bread; and that helped."

Although it was a difficult time, they were grateful for what they had. "We never went to bed hungry," Eva recalled, "although we were no doubt undernourished. Our clothes were always neat and ironed." Eva was especially grateful that despite their financial struggles, her mother paid for piano lessons. "Music was important to her: she had a beautiful voice, and belonged to a choral group 'Die Blaue Schleife' [the Blue Ribbon], where her warm alto was much appreciated. For her, music was just a necessary part of education." Eva's piano lessons and her mother's passion for music instilled in Eva a love of music that would later sustain her in the darkest of times. She also had access to good schooling. "Mother was extremely grateful that we, as fatherless and fairly bright children, got a scholarship to the academic high school which at that time charged tuition."

Apart from the incident at the beginning of the war that had so deeply hurt her father, Eva's family was generally liked and accepted as part of a small minority of Jews in their town. But when Eva was a child in school, she had her first encounter with "cruel, cutting, painful prejudice":

> Suddenly, one morning at recess . . . I find myself ignored by everyone, and I am completely alone. I can't understand what could have happened—no fight, no argument; as late as yesterday, we all had laughed and had had fun together. Back in the classroom, again nobody talks. But on my desk is the meanest cartoon I had ever seen, depicting the ugly, bad Jew who destroys the trusting, good German. Then the snickering starts until the teacher comes in; anti-Semitic rhymes, sneering, total rejection.

Eva was comforted by her mother: "I don't remember how I got through that day. But I will never forget how mother, when I told her sobbingly what had happened, put her arms around me and said that that's the way people were from time to time, and that one could not fight it; and all one could do was to feel and stay much more closely together in one's love for another, and then no-one could really hurt you. I don't know why or how, but it helped." Eva further recalled that "in a few days, the ugly feelings at school subsided; they had at that time not really taken hold of the children's minds, and we went on as before."

Following her father's death, Eva developed a special relationship with her mother. "During those childhood years after father's death, mother and I were very close. I was the oldest one at home—the two older boys Erich and Ernst away at war; and naturally, I became mother's comfort, and she shared her loneliness and her concerns with me, the child that had to grow up too fast. I did not mind this, as I remember." Eva later recognized her "real lack of maturity and of understanding" in this relationship:

> One instance stands out clearly in my memory. The war was going badly. Erich was at the Western Front, terribly young and vulnerable. Mail came rarely, and with great delays. One morning, Mutti brings in joyfully a letter from Erich from the front, written with much love, and full of hope. We read it together; Mutti is so happy. And then I say, looking at the date at the top of the letter: "But, Mutti, he wrote that three weeks ago. Then all was well. But in the meantime, he could well have been killed." Never will I forget the expression of shock in mother's eyes, at this exercise in cruel logic.[2]

Other family members became concerned that Eva's relationship with her mother was too "adult," too serious. They urged her mother to keep an emotional distance from Eva. The impact of this adjustment on Eva was harsh and lasting. "Soon the moment came when our good friends in Goldap, and uncles and aunts in Insterburg, realized that I did not act as a child my age should, and that mother ought to do something about it. She did—and suddenly I was expelled from our relationship of sharing happiness and sorrow, and I was asked to be a happy, carefree child as were all the others my age. This did not work at all—I resented it terribly, and it set the stage for many feelings of unhappiness, of withdrawal, and of reaching out to other older people for friendship and understanding."

Education in a high school for girls in Goldap would not lead to entry into a university. "So, instead of sending me away to a bigger city which offered high schools for girls preparing them for university study," Eva later explained, "something very rare for that time happened: a unique exception was made, and I was admitted at the all-boys' Gymnasium (academic high school), the first, and at that time only, girl at that school."

The Jewish children in Eva's school did not participate in religious education classes because the school was Protestant. Instead, they attended religion classes after school with the local rabbi. "There, we were supposed to learn some Hebrew, study the Old Testament, and generally be trained and reinforced in our religious beliefs." But Eva was unable to accept his religious teaching. She later explained that she and the other students "absolutely despised the rabbi," an immigrant from Poland who did not speak German well and "did not know how to handle a bunch of sharp, critical kids." She recalled that "when we asked questions about the content of some bible stories which we could not accept at face value, because many of them went against laws of science and logic, he was not able to interpret them as to their real meaning. Instead he got angry, and red in the face." Eva later reflected:

> It was, looking back and remembering, really an ugly situation; and in my "know-it-all," pretty intolerant, mind, it was enough to convince me that religion, in the sense of belonging to a church, was not for me. Since I had just read somewhere that at the age of thirteen, a child may legally decide to leave the church into which he was born, I made an especially big show of what he considered to be insolence (and no doubt it was) by asking one of those theological questions which he could not answer. He turned red again, raised his voice, and told me to leave the room. Whereupon I rose . . . and said that that was fine with me; since I had recently turned thirteen, I had not planned to ever return anyway, because I was going to declare my departure from the religion.
>
> I never went back, and how my poor mother was able to live this down, I don't know. Eventually, the shock of all the good people in our little town subsided, and I was re-accepted in the fold of family and friends—though I, from then on, did not any longer participate in any religious observance; I would have felt a hypocrite had I done it. When I wanted and needed

to feel close to God, I would explain, I would go out into the woods, into nature, hear music—there, my religious feelings would be genuine.

Later when Eva was nearly fifteen years old, she was suddenly rejected, without explanation, by her best friend at school, Ilse, because of Eva's Jewish heritage. Eva responded by beginning her first diary. The entries were written in pencil, in old Gothic German script, and cover the period 1925–1926. In her first entry, on January 22, 1925, she wrote:

For quite some time I have had the idea to start a diary, to account in these pages what goes on in my inner and outer life. But something always came up that kept me from doing it. Also, as long as I thought I had a girlfriend to whom I could confide everything, the urge for a diary was not that great. Now, however, when I have become aware that I was in error as to her friendship, I have nothing left but these pages, and I will confide to them everything that moves me.

Nobody can understand how it hurts to have lost Ilse for whom I cared so much, and still do. What beautiful hours we spent with each other! It is so great to have a human being who completely understands you. I had always yearned for a real friend, and when I finally thought I had found her, how happy I was! I believed that she cared for me also, and if that is so, then she cannot so completely ignore me now. I do understand that it must not always have been easy for her to have a Jewish girl for a friend. But that she does not talk to me about that openly, that she avoids—I'd almost say cowardly—every occasion for a talk—that hurts the most.

Mutti came home today; the pleasure about her return was of course not as great as usual because I was so depressed about Ilse. Mutti probably does not know how much I love her, because I am not the kind of person who can show easily what she feels.

Eva's relationship with her Jewish heritage and her views about religion were complex. She would soon decide to devote her life to the fight against Nazism as a member of an unusual political group that rejected all forms of formal religion in favor of a Kantian-based philosophy of ethical activism. As she later explained,

> Much later, when the persecution of the Jews had become deadly, when I had to leave Germany, . . . when our family was spread all over because of anti-Semitism and persecution, when some of them perished in the concentration camps, I had different thoughts about my rebellion as a child. I felt deep loyalty to all those suffering and persecuted because they were Jews, and knew I was one of them—on what level: race, culture, history, identification? I could not ever clarify. Definitely not on the level of the religious dogma, the crux of which—the chosen people theory—I just cannot accept. Yet, I never could quite get rid of a certain feeling of guilt whenever I thought of my decision to break ties with the Jewish religion.

Eva's independent early reflections about life were not limited to her thoughts about religion. Her diary entry on December 2, 1925, reveals much about the search of this fifteen-year-old girl for self-awareness and her deep interest in personal relationships. She wrote: "I wonder if human beings continue to develop, or if there is a point in life where things come to a standstill." She observed that her older brother Erich was "today an enthusiastic Social Democrat and agnostic," but in his earlier wartime letters—which she had just reread—Erich had written "of his devotion to Judaism to which he would forever remain loyal, and of his belief in the necessity of an autocratic government, since people are not mature enough for self-government." Eva wondered, "How ever did this deep change in his beliefs occur? Who knows for how much longer he will be a Social Democrat? Perhaps other influences might push him into an opposite direction!"

On August 18, 1926, with a mix of excitement and trepidation, Eva revealed to her diary that she had made a decision about the next big step in her young life:

> I really racked my brain these last months as to what I should do when I am finished with school. I did not find an answer, and this uncertainty contributed to my general feeling of unhappiness. Now I know what I am going to do. Nobody told me

I had to, the decision was totally mine, and I believe I did the right thing. Briefly, come Easter I will be able to study in a foreign country. That this will be possible is due only to Erich. He has done so much for me that I just cannot thank him enough. Barely 16 years old, and I will already be able to get to know foreign lands, customs and people! This is a prospect that could not be any better. And yet, I know that it will not be easy for me to feel at home with strangers. I am, although I often give the appearance of being withdrawn and independent, someone who needs much love, and so I will probably suffer a lot and will not be able to talk to anyone about it. Well, time will tell, and perhaps I will find there, where I expect it least, someone who understands me.

And in a diary entry on November 28, 1926, Eva struggled with the fact that she had matured too soon:

Loneliness is painful. I realize that more and more often in spite of my youth. And when I get together with people of my own age, I have nothing to say. . . . How I would like to be just like a child, how I would like not to know all the things I do know!

If only the time were near where real life begins. I am longing for work that will completely absorb and satisfy me, and where there would be no time for sadness. Who knows if time will bring fulfillment to these expectations!

Eva could not have imagined how the future would challenge the fulfillment of her expectations.

## 2. Study in France and at the Walkemühle (1926–1932)

At the end of 1926 at the age of sixteen, Eva and her family left their home in Goldap and moved to Kassel, a midsize town with an active cultural life not far from Frankfurt in central Germany where her oldest brother Erich had become a lawyer. For a short time Eva worked in Erich's law office to acquire clerical skills, and in the spring of 1927 she went to Nancy, France, as an exchange student to study at the university and perfect her knowledge of French.

While living with a French family, Eva quickly overcame some initial difficulties with the language. She was not comfortable, however, with her host family, finding them narrow-minded, and she rebelled against their conservative views. She also fell in love with another exchange student, "deeply, immaturely, felt very guilty about it, and ran away from it, and from all the feelings that it had stirred up."[1]

Despite the trauma of this relationship and the conflict with her host family, Eva's experience of living and studying in France would have enormous value in her later life. "What I had gained during that period in France," she later reflected, "was not any kind of growth in terms of self-knowledge. But my French was now really good, and I also had learned to love and to know a lot about French literature, philosophy, and history—a fact which some years later became a life saver in a very critical situation, and which continued to be helpful all through my life."

After her year of study in France, Eva returned home to Kassel, Germany, in 1928. She felt that the time had come for her to make some "far-reaching decisions" about the further course of her life. She decided not to return to France to continue her studies at the university and instead "to join a philosophical-political group of idealists led by a Kantian Professor of Philosophy, Leonard Nelson, who had laid the scientific, philosophical foundation for a moral obligation to political activism." This group, which her brother Erich had previously joined, was the Internationaler Sozialistischer Kampfbund (ISK).[2] Eva's brother Erich suggested, and Eva agreed, that she should become a personal assistant to Leonard Nelson. Eva's decision to become involved with the ISK would transform her life for the next twenty years.

Not much has been written in English about the history of the ISK.[3] Leonard Nelson (1882–1927), a pacifist and idealistic professor of philosophy at the University of Göttingen, had initially founded the predecessor of the ISK in 1917 under the name Internationaler Jugend-Bund (International Youth League, IJB). Nelson's work drew from the teachings of post-Kantian philosopher Jakob Friedrich Fries (1773–1843). The IJB did not fit within the philosophical and political frameworks of either the German communist youth organization, which banned its members from joining the IJB in 1922, or the German social democratic youth organization from which the IJB was expelled in 1925. After 1925, the IJB became the independent socialist splinter group known as the ISK. Based on Nelson's teachings, the ISK sought to educate an elite group of ethical leaders who would, by their active political involvement and personal example, help improve the human condition.

Eva described the unusual commitments required to become an active member of the ISK:

> You had to pledge your life to it. Also, your lifestyle had to change in accordance with the predominance of the political obligation: no personal wealth; life of utmost simplicity; no marriage or other family ties; vegetarianism; rejection of church directed dogmas. In case of conflict, personal ties had to be severed, and in order to be able to do this when it was required, strenuous character education with severe personal demands had to be accepted. The educational maxim was: utter honesty; follow the golden rule, or, as it was rather expressed, the maxim of the Kantian philosophy of Ethics and Justice: When there is conflict, not to do unto others what you would not want them to do unto you.

Eva later explained why she joined the ISK at that time:

To understand the situation then: We lived in Germany under the Weimar Republic, a relatively short period of Parliamentary Democracy, squeezed between the reign of absolute Monarchy under the Kaiser until 1918, and the terror rule of Hitler which started in 1933. During these fifteen years, the men and women in the Weimar Republic tried to make democracy work in Germany. But there were too many odds against them which made their attempts doomed to failure: a desperate economic situation with unemployment reaching hopeless proportions, and with little or no chance for a member of the working class to make a decent living for himself and for his children, leave alone to rise into a higher strata of society. There were also the effects of a lost war, with feelings of frustration fanned into exaggerated nationalism and desire for revenge.

It is true that the situation did not always look hopeless during those years: For the first time in German history, a member of the working class had become President: Friedrich Ebert. Many men and women of good will—and many of humble beginnings—were members of the Reichstag, and tried to pass good legislation. And there were organizations outside of the government that had high aspirations to create a better world, thinking they had answers to the most burning problems, and feeling that, if only enough people would devote their lives to the causes of peace and justice, they could not help but make progress, and avoid the specter of impending disaster.

Yet, Ebert, and all the other people who tried so hard, had to fight against non-acceptance, against apathy, against lack of democratic traditions, against economic and national misery, against violent outbursts from radical groups of the left and of the right. And shortly after Ebert's death in 1925, an ardent traditional monarchist, former General under Kaiser Wilhelm, Paul von Hindenburg, was elected President of the Republic. Slowly, but irrevocably, he moved the nation from one crisis to another, and finally towards the election of Adolf Hitler as Chancellor. Elected through the disintegrating democratic process, he very quickly abolished every remaining vestige of democracy that had been so painfully built up during the years of the Weimar Republic, and established the rule of terror.

Eva described the idealistic duty motivating her decision: "Feeling that the country—and perhaps mankind—was sliding towards catastrophe (hunger, violence, curtailment of freedom, war), we were convinced that it was everyone's sacred duty to do whatever he or she could do to stop this crazy slide. We were convinced that there were more good people than bad, and if only all the good people would join forces, give up the comforts of their own lives, do their duty, then right had a chance to win over wrong." Eva later admitted that this was "naive, perhaps, knowing nothing about power politics; yet understandable if one agrees with the thought that one should follow one's own conscience." Eva was willing to accept the enormous sacrifices of this commitment:

> So I decided: *not* to continue my studies at the University, *not* to train myself and look for a rewarding and well paying job so that I could make a good life for myself, and start helping out mother financially; to reject the thought of personal happiness such as love, marriage, children. And instead to devote my life to the struggle for what is right.

Encouraged by her older brother Erich, Eva took an initial step in her commitment to the ISK by agreeing to work for Leonard Nelson as his personal assistant. That arrangement, however, did not last long. "This first step was too big for me to handle. I was quite young, and the utter loneliness in the house of this brilliant man was more than I could take." When her brother Ernst returned home on leave from his work with a German engineering firm in South Africa, he strongly objected to Eva's decision to become involved in the ISK, and she seized on the opportunity to leave Nelson: "Ernst very strongly impressed on me that I had no right to do what I was doing, but that, if I did not want to continue my studies, I had to get a job and help support mother and the children. I was quickly convinced, said good-bye to Nelson, and went to Dortmund, to work in the record store of one of Ernst's friends."

For the next few months, Eva held a position as a sales clerk in the record shop. Unknown to her when she took the job, Ernst had arranged the position for her and had initially paid her salary in the hope that she would abandon her political activism and "life of self-denial" with the ISK. When Eva discovered this and learned that Ernst had hoped that she and his unmarried friend would grow to like each other and that she would lead the kind of life that he envisioned for her, she felt be-trayed and quit the job immediately. This episode, along with historical events, would put an end to communications between Eva and Ernst for many years.

Eva was now ready to turn back and commit herself fully to the ISK, and she agreed to become a student at the ISK's special country school called the Walkemühle. This began a period of her life that she later confessed was "most difficult to describe." Though her years at the Walkemühle were positive in many respects, they were extremely neg-ative in others. On one hand, "those three years . . . were invaluable in terms of what I learned about myself." But on the other, they were "ter-ribly and, in retrospect, unnecessarily, painful—so much so that at the end of the three years, I almost died—and that is to be taken literally."

The Walkemühle was, as Eva described it, "an international Liberal Arts College created by Leonard Nelson that was attended by young peo-ple (not all Germans) who had decided to accept the rigorous training of character and intellect which would prepare them to take an active part in the political life of their countries." In addition to this college, the Walkemühle also taught preschool and elementary school students who had been entrusted by their parents (most of whom believed in Nelson's philosophy) to receive the best possible education. "The school was small, in the heart of rural, fairly backwards, Germany. Our instructors were educators of renown, philosophers, mathematicians, economists, historians; also shop teachers, and a wonderful old gardener whom we all loved." Eva noted that there were also "many other great people on the staff who not only did their work in house and kitchen, but were friends and educators as well."

The director of the Walkemühle, Minna Specht, had an enormous impact on Eva. Eva described her as "one of the leading educators of our time, and the most beautiful, creative woman I ever had the fortune to know. She was the close friend and co-worker of Leonard Nelson; and she was also loved by all who ever had any prolonged contact with her." Specht's work at the Walkemühle would end when the Nazis shut the school down in 1933. She would then move the school with the young children first to Denmark and then to England.[4]

The ISK's rigorous education at the Walkemühle involved, in essence, training students to find ethical solutions to human problems through rigorous application of reason and Socratic dialogue. Eva explained:

The Walkemühle. COURTESY OF AdsD/FRIEDRICH-EBERT-STIFTUNG.

All of us who were there were chosen, and we accepted to spend three years of rigid training willingly, if not really knowingly. Character and mind were to be trained, helped to be honest, independent, and strong. Intellectually, that meant that we had no typical college education there. All courses were held entirely in the Socratic Method, where we students, in small groups, started out with a question in a given subject matter, and tried to find solutions, in rigorous self and mutual examination and questioning—the instructor not providing any answers, only making certain that we did not stray, and that no glib statement remained unsupported or unchallenged. We were to experience—and we did—that honest answers towards truth could be found by ourselves, not based on any outside dogmatic authority. The morning sessions were devoted to these discussions. In the afternoons, everyone wrote detailed minutes of the morning work from which he or she developed the questions to be handled the following morning.

A very difficult process, slow, painstaking; but rewarding, and one that gave confidence in the potential of one's own reason. It was never easy, but went rather well in studies of math where truth was objective, not shaded by emotions. Economics, history, was possible also. Philosophy much harder, and inter-personal relations . . .

"Interpersonal relations," Eva later observed, "were not overtly handled at all." The students at the Walkemühle knew from the outset that they were expected to train themselves to be independent of emotional ties. Help was offered to the students only in an impersonal way, but it was not without warmth. Leonard Nelson's father was "loved by all, a frail, old gentleman, with all the grace and culture of a totally different life-style, who had accepted ours, yet added to it the rich warmth which was part of his nature." "Vater Nelson," as he was called, "had wonderful records, was a great musician, and played the piano beautifully—some-times he and Minna Specht would play duets for us. The evenings which we all spent once a week in his living room, were filled with music and reading (I remember especially Van Gogh's Letters to his brother Theo. They were read beautifully by Gustav Heckmann, our Math teacher, and outstanding leader in Socratic conversations, and they opened a new world for me.)"

Eva studying at the Walkemühle in 1929.

The students could never discuss their individual feelings, and Eva had intense feelings of guilt for having promised not to have any contact whatsoever with her mother during those three years—even though her mother lived only a short distance from the Walkemühle. Eva acknowledged that she and other students had freely decided to accept such restrictions and expected them to be difficult. But they believed that they would grow from coping with their pain. "This was a lot easier in theory than in reality," Eva recalled, "and I did not grow, I only hurt, especially also from being aware that my decision was unbelievably painful for my mother."

Eva's guilt about cutting off all contact with her mother was not the only emotion she suppressed. "Other feelings began to stir in me, as was natural: for a special younger girl towards whom I felt deep friendship and understanding; for a boy with whom I would have loved, and sometimes did, to talk alone, and walk, and go on bike hikes, and just feel his presence." The consequence of being unable to talk with anyone about the "growing turmoil" within her was nearly fatal:

> The feeling of guilt grew and grew and became overwhelming, guilt at not being able to live up to my promise, at being a failure. With what we know now, it was not surprising that I became ill, very ill. Nothing organic, it appeared; I did not become irrational in my behavior either; I just could no longer eat, or if I did, keep food down. So I became very weak, and discovered that this was perhaps the only way out: being too ill, no demands which I could not meet, could be made upon me, nor could I make them upon myself. I gradually became free of guilt.
>
> It must have been a frightening experience for all around me who cared: to see me slip away. First at school, then at home. Now I could go home, be loved and cared for by mother, and Erich and [his wife] Herta, staying in the beautiful little room which belonged to my sister Ruth—bright, red furniture, flowers, love and care surrounding me. In my memory, this was a rather soft, nice time for me—no pain, just gently floating in a warm world without inner conflicts.
>
> They tried what they could, especially Erich, to get me out of it: doctors, hospital, diagnosis that I had to go on a meat

broth diet if I wanted to live. I refused; for ethical reasons I was a vegetarian, and I would have put myself outside the circle of my friends, if I had followed that diet—that I could and would not do. The local doctors did not know what else to do.

Eva's brother Erich saved her life. "In his despair and overwhelming desire to bring me back to living," Eva recalled, "Erich found a vegetarian doctor in Switzerland, with psychiatric orientation: Dr. Bircher-Benner." Erich's wife Herta took Eva to Switzerland, leaving Erich and their little child behind "in a demonstration of love that I can never forget." The treatment was successful. "In Zurich, I slowly was guided back, helped to see my guilt feelings for what they really were, helped to accept life and nature and emotion for something real and good, and not to be ashamed of. I learned some degree of self-understanding, and as I did, I started to get well."

# 3. Anti-Nazi Work in Germany (1932–1933)

After her study at the Walkemühle and her recovery in Switzerland, Eva moved to Essen, a city in the central part of Germany's Ruhr region. She held a number of small jobs while devoting most of her time and strength to political work with the Internationaler Sozialistischer Kampfbund (ISK) in its fight against the rise of Hitler.

These were hard years with high unemployment in Germany. Most jobs that Eva held were temporary: waiting tables, cleaning, secretarial work in a department store. She was able to earn enough money to eat and pay the rent and was proud when her salary "made it possible to save some money, and to take gifts home for mother and the children: Hans, Rudi, and Ruth." But the primary purpose of these jobs was to allow her to engage in her work with the ISK: "The main thrust in these years was the desperate, rather naive, attempt to help stem the tide of Nazism." The ISK "tried with all its might to get all people of good will together to form a united front against the Nazis."[1]

Eva recalled how the ISK, "with tremendous efforts . . . guided in Berlin by Willi Eichler . . . launched a daily paper *Der Funke* (the Spark) in addition to the monthly magazine which had existed for a long time."[2] Eva and other ISK members in Essen were primarily involved "in the daily selling of the paper in the streets, at corners, in pubs, in front of factories, from house to house—on Sundays also in the country to which we rode on our bikes."

> I will never forget the exhausted look on face and body of the coal miners, when they came out of the pits: pale, covered with dust, with no spring in their walk. I don't forget the tenements

23

where they lived, the children. In pubs, I often ran into prostitutes who would buy my paper—perhaps not to read it, but because I was a young girl, alone? And especially I don't forget the physical fear that I experienced when I would walk back and forth on the sidewalk in front of a big store, calling out: "Der Funke! Unite against the Nazis!" And when walking, or rather marching, behind me, would be uniformed storm troopers—would they trip me, would they thrust a knife? Plain, cold fear; but one walked on. It was frightening—one did not often see a young girl alone at that time, doing political work.

Members of the small ISK group in Essen also participated actively in political discussions: "asking annoying questions in local Nazi meetings; giving talks in small towns and villages at trade union or cultural gatherings, at our own group meetings." As Eva recalled, "It seemed important to repeat over and over again that only in joining ranks could the Nazi threat be overcome." They experienced hostility and threats at the Nazi meetings, but Eva never encountered physical violence.

The ISK continued to have fundamental philosophical and political disagreements with the German Communist Party (KPD) and remained split from the major German socialist party, the German Social Democratic Party (SPD). Despite such differences, the ISK recognized the urgent need for unity among these parties in seeking to prevent Hitler from taking power. In 1932, the ISK reached out to the KPD and the SPD to unite in an attempt to prevent the Nazis from gaining control of Germany in the Reichstag election of July 1932. Eva recalled that the ISK's "Dringender Appell für die Einheit" (Urgent Appeal for Unity) was the "last vital, desperate attempt of the ISK to try blocking the Nazis' ascent to power."

Eva explained that this appeal was made "to everyone, members of the Socialist and Communist Parties, of the Trade Unions, the Independents," to finally create a united labor front to resist Hitler. "Wherever possible, we put big posters on billboards, and our small local groups organized meetings where more people and organizations were encouraged to support this appeal by signing." The appeal was also published in the ISK's newspaper, *Der Funke*, and in placards posted throughout Berlin. Signatories to the appeal included ISK leaders Willi Eichler and Minna Specht; scientists Albert Einstein, Franz Oppenheimer, Emil Gumbel, and Arthur Kronfeld; writers Kurt Hiller, Erich Kästner, Heinrich Mann, Ernst Toller, and Arnold Zweig; and artist Käthe Kollwitz.

The appeal was obviously too little too late, and any subsequent overt opposition to the Nazis quickly became very dangerous. The ISK made the same appeal against Hitler prior to the federal election in March 1933 but with fewer signatories. Soon after the placards appeared, writer Heinrich Mann and artist Käthe Kollwitz who had signed the appeal were forced by the Nazis to withdraw from the Akademie der Künste (Art Academy).[3] Eva noted: "As history tells us, all these efforts, no matter how visible and logical, did not accomplish the desired results. The two political parties of the German Left went into the final elections separately, as hostile competitors; they were defeated, and after Hitler's victory, their leaders were arrested, killed, or exiled; the organizations were dissolved, the reign of terror took over, and those active members who survived were forced underground."

Shortly after his appointment as chancellor by President Paul von Hindenburg on January 30, 1933, Hitler outlawed all opposing political parties. He used the Reichstag fire on February 27, 1933, as the basis for an emergency decree the following day that allowed him to suspend civil liberties and to raid the offices of the KPD and arrest Communist Party members. He then pushed through the Enabling Act on March 23, 1933, that essentially gave him dictatorial powers. The SPD and various socialist splinter parties and groups who had opposed Hitler, including the ISK, were banned and compelled to work underground or in exile.[4]

The final days before Hitler embarked on his reign of terror against all opponents forced drastic changes in Eva's life. "What I had done politically had certainly not been important in the general range of things; but I had nevertheless been too visible to be ignored." Search warrants and warrants for arrest of political opponents were issued. Eva made a quick farewell trip to Kassel to see Erich, her mother, and her younger siblings, Hans, Rudi and Ruth. "I can't go home anymore—my place had been searched, and I must go into hiding."

At the same time, Erich, Herta and their son Theo barely escaped with their lives to Switzerland. The Gestapo questioned Eva's mother and her other siblings about Erich's escape and searched their apartment but took no further action against them. Eva lived in hiding for a short time with friends in a neighboring city.

As she planned her escape from Germany, Eva also struggled with the prospect of parting from an ISK colleague, Rudi Lieske, with whom she had developed a close relationship. Eva recalled that her ISK group in Essen had been so committed to stopping Hitler's thrust to power that "there was room for nothing else." But this was not quite true:

> The work and friendship with Rudi that gradually turned into love sustained him and me during these years. Yet, neither he nor I at any time held any hope that this love could continue, that there would ever be conditions where we could just live together, work, be happy, have children—all these wishes that were very strong in me, were assumed to be totally impossible of fulfillment.

Hitler's assumption of power in 1933 eliminated any hope about a future with Rudi. Eva needed to escape from Germany. Her colleagues determined that in view of her knowledge of French, she would be most useful in the anti-Nazi fight with ISK members in exile in Paris. Other ISK members, both Jewish and non-Jewish, would remain to fight Hitler in small underground groups in Germany in coordination with the Paris group. Eva would later determine, after intense emotional struggle, that her close relationship with Rudi could not survive as he remained in Germany and she worked with the ISK in Paris.

In preparing for her escape, Eva took her passport to the police station in Essen to ask for the exit permit that was necessary to leave Germany. However, the police refused and seized her passport based on a new ordinance requiring the confiscation of all passports of Jews. While staying with friends in Cologne (registered at one address and living at another), Eva devised a scheme to get her passport back. She asked a friend to send her a postal money order to the Central Post Office in Cologne. When she went to pick it up, she was asked for her identification. "I said regretfully that my passport was being held in Essen, for technical reasons, and what was I to do? I really needed that money!"

The postal official expressed sympathy and regret, but without identification he could not give Eva the money. "So I asked if he could perhaps give me a slip of paper stating that I needed the passport in order to receive the money that was being held for me. He was glad to comply, and I had the beautiful slip, with signature and stamp, which I sent to the local Police Station in Essen." Eva then waited. "It did not take long: One morning, the lady (a friend) at whose house I was registered came in . . . pale and a little shaking. That morning, a police constable had rung her doorbell, asked if I lived there. . . . She said, with great fear for herself and for me, that I did, but that I was not home. Well, the man said, he could just as soon have her take care of it. And he handed her my passport that she now held out to me! I can tell you—it seemed a beautiful document!"

A few days later, Eva was on a train to the Saar area—then a small internationally governed country between Germany and France that one could enter without legally leaving Germany. From there, she took another train into France and was on her way to Paris. "Friends told me later that my ploy was discovered, and that I was accused in an article in the Essen paper. I never saw the article; it was supposed to have said something about 'Jewish girl cheating authorities of passport.'"

Eva's flight to France in 1933 to escape the Nazi threat not only separated her from Rudi, her first real love, but also pulled her apart from most of her family. Eva's brother Erich had been an attorney in Kassel, Germany, when Hitler took over in 1933. In addition to participating in the ISK's anti-Nazi activities (such as distributing *Der Funke* and other ISK publications), Erich had represented individuals and groups who were prosecuted for resisting the Nazis. He often clashed in court with the infamous Nazi attorney (and later judge) Roland Freisler.[5] As one of Hitler's early targets, Erich barely escaped from Kassel on March 23, 1933, evading Nazi storm troopers by slipping out through a back door as they entered his office. A friend drove him to Frankfurt that day while he hid with his wife Herta and young son Theo under a blanket on the floor of the car.[6] From Frankfurt they quickly caught a train to Zurich, where they arrived on March 24, 1933, with "the clothes on our backs, one small suitcase and enough money to last a few weeks."[7] Erich and his wife would later join Eva and other ISK colleagues in exile in Paris.

Eva's younger brother Hans, a teacher, was also forced to leave Germany in 1933. He would flee first to Switzerland and then to France, where, after staying for a while with French teachers, he would also join Eva and Erich at the vegetarian restaurant in Paris. A few years later, Hans would return to teaching in Minna Specht's school, first in Denmark and then in England.

Eva would be separated from the rest of her family members for many years. After World War I, her brother Ernst had become an apprentice engineer and went to South Africa in the 1920s for his firm, a large railroad construction company in Berlin. Ernst would later help their mother Charlotte, Eva's younger brother Rudi, and her younger sister Ruth escape from Germany to South Africa.

With her escape from Germany, Eva was about to embark on her first experience as a refugee. "A new chapter starts; there is no longer a country that I can call home."

# 4. Early Years in Exile in Paris (1933–1935)

After Hitler took power in 1933, political parties opposing him were forced to work in exile or to conduct increasingly dangerous underground resistance work in Germany. The ISK members did both. Eva, her brother Erich, ISK leader Willi Eichler, and other ISK members would form the ISK's prewar headquarters in exile in Paris.[1]

One historical account of the formation of the ISK's Paris headquarters simply states: "In November 1933, [Willi] Eichler fled to Saarland and a month later from there further to Paris, where he built up ISK's exile center."[2] The formation of the ISK's headquarters in Paris, however, was far more complicated than that. Difficult groundwork had to be laid well before Eichler's arrival in Paris in November 1933.

Eva arrived in Paris in the early summer of 1933. The first task for her, as for all refugees, was "somehow to eke out an existence, to make a living no matter how modest."[3] Eva could speak French well and was able to find work quickly at the office of a German-language literary and political publisher, Éditions Nouvelles Internationales, that had been well known in Germany before Hitler. Not long after she arrived in Paris, she made contact with Erich and Herta, who were in Switzerland with their young son Theo, but could not remain there because Switzerland strictly prohibited the employment of aliens.

While living in Zurich, Erich made plans to go to Paris and open a vegetarian restaurant. Without permits to work legally in Switzerland, he and his wife were able to earn some money from friends who were willing to employ them secretly on a temporary basis. They sought to learn what they could about the operation of vegetarian restaurants, observing the kitchen at the vegetarian sanatorium of Dr. Maximilian

Bircher-Benner, where Eva had restored her health after her emotional breakdown at the Walkemühle, and kitchens at other local Swiss vegetarian restaurants. Erich decided to ask his friend, a lawyer in Zurich named Dr. Rosenbaum, to lend him money to start a restaurant in Paris. But before he could request the loan, Dr. Rosenbaum directed his secretary to give Erich a check for 10,000 Swiss francs as a gift without conditions. Erich regarded the gift as a loan to be repaid. Erich and Herta arrived in Paris in August 1933. Erich spoke a little French; Herta not a word.[4]

Erich and Herta then made a wrenching personal decision: recognizing the demands and dangers of their commitment to the ISK's anti-Nazi work in exile, they decided not to bring their seven-year-old son Theo with them to Paris. The ISK's school at the Walkemühle had been shut down and confiscated by the Nazis, and ISK educator Minna Specht had decided to start another school in Denmark for students and other refugee children. After spending time in a children's home in Switzerland, Theo was to attend this new school in Denmark as one of its first four students, from seven to nine years old. Theo later recalled that his mother came from Paris to Lille and joined him and the other three children on the train to his new school. He noted that she "accompanied us to Dunkirk, where she saw us off on the boat to Denmark the next day. My pleas to go back with her and to stay with them in Paris fell on deaf ears."[5] This decision would result in years of painful separation.

Erich's wife Herta recalled that they found a good location for the restaurant, "a new office block" that had just been completed on the Boulevard Poissonnière, and decided to rent about three-quarters of the first floor. Herta noted that they "went to Galleries Lafayette . . . and bought cutlery, crockery, pots and pans, tablecloths and everything else that we thought we would need." As they were setting up the restaurant, they got ideas for their menu from other restaurants by ordering different vegetables for each person: "When the meal was served, we all got beans, different kinds of beans of course. It was a good way to learn."

As they prepared for the opening in October 1933, Herta urged Eva to give up her other job so she could help with the restaurant. Eva agreed. Others also joined the effort, including Eva's brother Hans. As Herta recalled,

> By October we were ready. We invited everyone we knew for a free meal on our opening night. There were many refugees and

Le Restaurant Végétarien des Boulevards.

many French friends as well. An Italian artist we knew drew a big poster for us.

> "RESTAURANT VÉGÉTARIEN DES BOULEVARDS
> après Bircher-Benner
> 28 BOULEVARD POISSONNIÈRE"

We employed a Sandwich Man to walk up and down the Boulevard with it.[6]

Eva was amazed at how the restaurant was inundated with customers from the outset:

> Contrary to conservative estimations, our restaurant was immediately a success. People loved the food, the tasteful way in which it was served, the atmosphere of people gathering in some kind of warm relationship, French men and women as well as those now without nationality. And at the end of the first week, there were so many people wanting to get in and be seated that Erich had to rent more of the floor (it was a new building), had

the walls torn down, and continued to operate successfully for eight years, until war broke out.

> It was a tremendous amount of work. . . . We all were cooks, and shoppers at les Halles (the central Paris market) where, in the early morning hours, you got the most beautiful produce. And we were also waiters when that was needed, or hostesses, or cashiers, especially those of us whose French was good.[7]

Another friend in Switzerland loaned Erich an additional 10,000 Swiss francs for improvements to the expanded space, without question or demand for any security for the loan. The restaurant was so successful financially that by January 1934, the gift and loans from Erich's Swiss friends were repaid in full.[8]

In short, by the time ISK leader Willi Eichler arrived in Paris in November 1933, other ISK members, including Eva, Erich and Herta, had already laid the groundwork for the ISK's headquarters in exile in Paris. This had been accomplished at substantial economic risk and sacrifice, with profits from the restaurant available to support the ISK's work.[9]

Eva later reflected that the work in the restaurant had "something exhilarating" about it. "The restaurant was financially very successful, and the loans could be paid back within a few months. We each took only a very nominal salary for ourselves, and the surplus served to help the underground work in Germany." But it was also physically demanding:

> Due to overwork, Erich became very ill in the first year of our operation, and had to be hospitalized for many weeks with a severe case of pneumonia. Then I had to take over at the front desk. That is when and why I met Otto one night who had come to dinner with a group of young French students. I don't forget that evening. I had hit a real low of sadness and loneliness that night; yet somehow, a spark between us two strangers lit up that was to become a lifelong association and love.[10]

During her initial years in Paris before she met Otto, Eva devoted virtually all of her time and effort to the ISK's work against Nazism. On a personal and emotional level, these years were painful for her. In light of the unparalleled death and destruction that ultimately resulted from

Hitler's rise to power in 1933, it is easy to overlook the impact of life in exile on those who, like Eva, escaped Germany in 1933, continued to fight against Nazism, and survived. The rise of Nazism and Eva's commitment to fight against it irrevocably uprooted her from her homeland; foreclosed her from exploring and pursuing personal, artistic, and professional interests; and tore her from her family and her first serious love relationship.

While she was devoting herself fully to her work in Paris in 1933 and 1934, Eva agonized about the loss of her relationship with Rudi Lieske. She struggled to understand herself, revealing her deep desire to have a child, her need to be strong and fulfill her duty to her work, her love of nature, and her regrets about the personal losses suffered by her generation. She expressed these feelings in the diary she kept at that time with entries in the form of letters to Rudi, often marked "not sent."[11]

Eva later commented that before she met Otto, the years in Paris were perhaps the saddest of her life: "Rudi is far away; my love for him is still alive, but it gets no nourishment; the present is filled with hard work and little hope; the future is bleak. I start again questioning my life, where it has led me, and where it will take me. There are some friends with whom I spend many night hours in one of the Paris cafés, philosophizing, trying to help one another by listening and talking. But basically I am alone, and I write a lot."[12]

Eva sought relief from her sadness in music. In an entry in her Paris diary on April 13, 1934, she noted: "Now I am going to a concert—actually I am happy—music—from it the thoughts become free and soft." But she could not escape the feeling of loneliness. "I need to find someone to whom I can give warmth and love, perhaps a very young person, a child . . ."

Eva wrote several poems in her Paris diary. She later explained: "Somehow it seemed to help the loneliness and agony of these years to write, and I started to express feelings in what very loosely might be called poetry." One short poem, written on August 5, 1934, is titled "Blick durchs Fenster auf den Boulevard Poissonnière" (View through the Window to the Boulevard Poissonnière):

I look at the trees in the big loud street,
It is a hot summer day.
The leaves are still green, but dusty and brittle.

And when the wind brushes them, they fall,
Tired, helpless, as in autumn.

And I look at myself.
I am young. Why do I lack the strength?
More and more often I am brushed by
Sadness in my soul,
And tears fall, unable to be held back.[13]

Eva slowly grew to accept the end of her relationship with Rudi. In a diary entry dated August 16, 1934 (marked "not sent"), she wrote "Rudi, I watch with inner fear how we are coming apart." She observed that her fate was to go her own way and noted that "the time we were together was very beautiful. Perhaps it therefore could not last." She concluded:

I must go through everything alone. And the strangest: I am not at all so very sad about this development; it sits well that I come through alone. I am stronger and proud that I am now able to stand completely alone. Do you understand that? Can you do that too? You will experience it sooner or later. . . . And I wish you would go the same way in your development.

Eva at the restaurant window overlooking Boulevard Poissonnière.

In late August/early September 1934, Eva was able to take a brief vacation from her work in Paris. She traveled alone by train to Saint-Malo, a small port city in Brittany in northwestern France.[14] This vacation gave Eva more time to reflect on her separation from Rudi. It also gave her a rare opportunity to write, briefly relieved from the pressures and responsibilities of her work and stimulated by the peace and calm of nature. In her diary entry to Rudi on August 29, Eva began with a description of the setting:

> St. Malo is a small cure-town and also a fishing village. The rough rocks that appear in low tide interrupt the uniformity of the ocean. If one looks the other way inland, one sees a beautiful, soft meadowland with hills, many trees, all possible greens, streams, cow and sheep pastures, potato and vegetable fields. The houses lie like toy boxes scattered around; gray building stones, mostly with roofs of slate and sometimes straw. Not at all poor, but small and secluded. Other than green and gray and the blue of the sea that is sometimes fantastic, the landscape has no colors. But the effect is peaceful, almost cheerful.

In her diary entry on September 2, Eva expressed in a poem her desire to have a child and her belief that it would never happen:

> Oh you my child, you unborn,
> my heart constricts with pain,
> whenever I must think of this great stillness
> that you will continue to sleep in me forever
> and I can never embrace you with my love.
>
> It is not bad of me, my child,
> that I do not give you life.
> Sometimes I believe I could not endure it myself;
> for my entire being presses me to you, my child,
> in bitter unquenchable longing.

In her diary entry on September 6, 1934, Eva wrote a poem describing the landscape and the "gift" of her loneliness. Understanding how the calm of nature allowed her "to hear the quiet voices in me," she ended the poem with trepidation about returning to work in Paris. And on September 8 as her vacation came to an end, Eva took a bus along the coast from Saint-Malo to Granville.[15] In her diary entry on that day, she described that trip in a poem that ends:

The sky is like the clearest water,
the clouds dark red-violet;
at one place it is as if someone
dipped a fine paintbrush in a cloud
and drew the sky with a long, tired-swinging stroke.

The picture disappeared.
One drives further into the deepening evening.
It becomes even more still, peaceful and clear
and one becomes so engrossed in this expanse,
that there is only one wish:
never again to lose it.

Eva returned to Paris on September 9, 1934. In a diary entry to Rudi (marked "not sent") written that day, she reported that she was "now on the way back to work after a wonderful, very peaceful vacation alone by the ocean." The "calm and greatness of nature" made her happy:

> At high tide, the waves strike up around the house . . . nothing to see except a great, great gray surface. At ebb tide, broad beautiful beach; out of the sea, rocks emerge everywhere, often in the most remarkable shapes. Lighthouses, ships, far in the distance a cape, above that the sky, sometimes gray and heavy, then radiant blue with small white clouds—always new and beautiful.
>
> When it rained, and I walked for hours along the beach, climbed over rocks, saw no people, the feeling: I am in all this greatness completely alone—and feel gloriously free. When the sun shines and I swim and let myself be whipped and tossed by the waves, and see cheerful, healthy, tanned people, children—that is also beautiful. And when I don't want to see the people, then I only go a few steps further, up on the dune meadows, and see nothing but ocean and sky. And the long nights with clear stars—it was hard to leave that.

The happiness from this vacation was short-lived. In her diary entry written in Paris on September 29, 1934, Eva spoke again of numbing loneliness, of a "remarkable twilight existence. . . . No great sadness, no great joy, only great fatigue and the feeling, almost the wish: that everything would become completely still." On New Year's Eve, December 31, 1934, Eva asked in her diary what the future held for her—resigned to the fact that her work foreclosed the exploration of her interests:

Inclination to art, to writing—all very much in danger of being numbed. . . . It would be too bad if all of that were buried; for sometimes the conviction and wish are alive to be able to develop deep strengths that are dormant. Perhaps, if one would give me freedom, I would need to concede that these strengths are stunted dwarf plants not worthy of being matured. Perhaps. But why must I live in a time that does not allow me the possibility to give it a chance.

Eva expressed her desire: "Only once, to be alone in another city without assignment, without having to give direct account, responsible only for myself." Yet she knew this was impossible because she could not abandon her commitment to continue the anti-Nazi work:

The work, which I am convinced must be done, should it remain hanging on the others? Again the old point, about which there can be no debate. For the others do not leave the work. They can't. Just as I have not been able to do it to date. I believe that my life will remain stuck with this point, and I will, to be sure, not die as a fulfilled person at peace with herself. I will not create any positive works, but I will at least not have damaged my duty.

In her diary entry on January 1, 1935, Eva reflected further on the experiences of her generation: "A person needs calm to develop. My, our generation's misfortune is that it did not have time to mature. I have experienced a lot, and some deep and harsh."

In her diary entry on February 3, 1935, Eva revealed again her desire for a close relationship:

I have such a longing for a person who is there for me. This person does not come. Whether it will take a long time for me to wait for him, that I desperately look for him from time to time? One always says that one gets calmer and clearer over the years. Until now, my development has gone exactly in the opposite direction. For everything that earlier appeared obvious and settled forever, begins to waver and must be struggled with again. That is often terribly difficult.

Also to sit here—I am so tired. Human conversation rustles around me, all somehow connected. They look right through me as if I were air.

This was the inner world of that "strange, sad, shy girl" who was looking for the sign of a human being on the night she met Otto at the Restaurant Végétarien des Boulevards in 1935.

# Part II.

## Otto's Path to 28 Boulevard Poissonnière

*It was spring when I reached Paris, and spring in Paris is overwhelming.*

—Otto recalling his move to Paris in 1927

# 5. Childhood in Munich (1900–1920)

Otto was born in Munich, Germany, in 1900, "the first year in a brand-new century," as Otto put it.[1] His parents were Catholic. His father Jakob was a bricklayer and his mother Martina delivered newspapers to help with the family's meager income. Otto had an older sister Rosa and three younger sisters: Dora, Tina, and Lina.[2]

Jakob was twenty-three years old when he met and married Otto's mother. They started their young family in a poor suburb of Munich where Otto was born as their second child. The family then moved to a tiny flat in Schwabing, a borough in the northern part of Munich. Otto recalled,

> The earliest memory I have of my childhood is when we moved from Haidhausen to a new place in Schwabing. I was about three years old. My mother pushed me in one of those old-fashioned high-wheeled baby carriages along the cobblestone streets. It was a long walk, and it must have been tiresome for my sister Rosa who was only five, and who went with us alongside the carriage.
>
> The tiny flat at Schleissheimerstrasse 73 had only a kitchen, two bedrooms, a very small "Kammer" [room], and a toilet. This was to be the home that saw all of us five children grow up, and where our mother still lived alone at the time when her life came to an end. As a bricklayer, my father did not earn much, and it was hard to pay the rent; so, one of the bedrooms and the little "Kammer" had to be sublet. I still can hardly believe that at one

time, the five of us children and my father had to stay in one room. My mother slept on the kitchen sofa.

Otto recalled his father's humble background: "My father, Jakob Pfister, was born in 1875 in Gerolzhofen, a small town not far from Schweinfurth, in Lower Franconia. He was the oldest of the seven children of Kaspar Pfister, a day laborer (Tagelöhner), and his wife Margarete. The small house in which the family lived . . . leaned against an old, massive, round tower that was part of the town's medieval fortifications." Observing and experiencing hard physical work dominated Otto's memories of his early childhood—including his summer visits to his grandparents:

> Grandmother had a vegetable garden, and she kept, besides a few goats and chickens, half a dozen geese. It was one of my chores to drive them every morning to a stream running through nearby meadows, when I spent my summer vacations there. Another chore was to take lunch to grandfather who worked not far away at the railroad station, shoveling coal day in and day out from freight cars into horse drawn carts. It was a backbreaking job.

The life of Otto's mother had even more humble beginnings. In a brief account of her early life, she wrote, "Was born a poor Christ child on December 29, 1871, and half a war-child, and because of that born out of wedlock—so three times poor." She suffered hardships as a child, including injuries sustained when she became stuck in the snow while delivering bread during a severe winter storm. The injuries caused bone splinters and open sores that nearly resulted in the amputation of her legs. She recovered and later became a salesgirl at the Marienplatz in Munich, where she met Jakob Pfister; they married in 1898. This did not end her struggles: "Then the worries began again, until one had brought up five children while also having to go to work. And when I thought that finally better times would come now that the children were grown—the hardest thing hit me: the husband left me." Otto recalled his mother's burdens:

> Life was hardest for my mother. To add to her household money, she had taken on a job of delivering newspapers. At that time,

that was done by women. The paper had to be carried to the subscriber's door, often three or four flights up, twice a day, even on Sunday mornings. She left the house at 5:30 a.m., and came back only after we had already left for school. At night, she did not get home until after 5:00, when she hurried to get dinner ready. A grueling task that had to be done day in and day out. In winter, father sometimes helped her, carrying the pouch through heavy snow.

I also see her scrubbing the clothes on the kitchen table, after they had been boiled on the kitchen range. To dry the wash, she had to carry it two flights up to the attic. Once a week, she went down on her knees to wash and scrub our bare wood floors. In the evenings, she sat for hours darning our socks and stockings, and mending our clothes. We children did not always realize how hard she worked all the time.

Otto closely observed and admired his father's work and training as a bricklayer:

For a while, he was an apprentice with a cobbler, but he decided soon that this was not what he wanted to do with his life. At fifteen, he set out for Munich where he had a cousin who was a builder; and he became a bricklayer. At night, he went to trade school. I remember being very impressed as a boy when I discovered a big roll of drawings he had made at school, all executed meticulously in China ink. I also remember how proud I was when his cousin, Baumeister Michael Reinhard, who was my godfather, told me once that Jakob was a very hardheaded fellow, but surely he was the best bricklayer in town.

Otto's father was stern—a man of few words. Yet Otto was filled with pride on weekends as he walked to the flea markets by his tall father's side, without talking, through the streets of Munich. And during the week, Otto looked forward to his father's return home from work: "I see myself standing at the kitchen windowsill, eagerly waiting for my father to come home for lunch, pushing his bike across the backyard. We had window boxes with geraniums, and sturdy iron crossbars, to keep us from falling out the window—the flat was on the third floor."

Otto especially admired his father's ability to repair things. "On Sunday mornings, we kids had to go to early Mass. Often, when we came home, father was busy repairing our shoes. He had even learned how to fix half soles with wooden pegs. He taught me how to insert a hog bristle to the end of a pitched twine. In the afternoon, then, he sat sometimes for hours to clean and repair watches that he had bought at the flea market."

His father's interest in literature deeply influenced Otto. "Father liked to read. He also liked to memorize, and to recite, long ballads, such as Schiller's 'Die Glocke.' From auctions, he came home with hauls of books that he had bought for little money. Although he was not active politically, though he was a union man, he read liberal publications such as the *Simplicissimus* and *Die Jugend*." Otto inherited his father's love of reading and memorizing. Throughout his life, Otto would recite poems by Goethe, Schiller, and others that he had memorized as a child.

Otto had only eight years of formal education, from 1906 to 1914. He was anxious about attending school at first. "Shortly before school started, I was filled with great fear—as though a big dark wall was falling onto me, and I could not escape. By that time, I was six, and really was in great distress." But Otto did very well academically. "All that fear turned out to be groundless: I liked school! And I liked it all along, and always had excellent grades, through the eight years of *Volksschule* (elementary school). I loved geometry and drawing, and I liked to read. My playmates teasingly called me *der Leser* (the reader)."

Otto developed a craving for learning. He was fascinated by nature and history and by the achievements of human beings. As a child, he stood on the hills outside of Munich and watched young men attempting to fly in contraptions similar to those used by the Wright brothers in America. Otto loved to read about Greek and Roman history and about art and architecture. He would have loved to continue his schooling beyond his eight years at the *Volksschule*, but his family could not afford it. "One great disappointment came when I could not move to the *Realschule*, as did many of my friends. At that time, higher education was reserved for the well-to-do. We had no money, and I had no access to any of those rare token scholarships given to the poor. The only alternative was to learn a trade, which I started to do when I was fourteen."

It was Otto's father's decision that his son should learn the cabinet-making trade as an apprentice. Otto recalled, "Already as a little boy, I

Otto in Munich shortly before beginning his apprenticeship in 1914.

had loved to make doll furniture for my four sisters—out of cigar boxes. So it was easily decided that I should become a cabinetmaker." Otto was not happy with this decision. "I wanted so badly to be something 'better.' So I begged and begged my father to find a place for me with a friend of his, a wood carver. His friend was willing to take me on but advised strongly against it: with the modern trend in furniture styles, carving was out; there was no future. So, cabinetmaking it had to be."

Otto began his apprenticeship "that fateful August in 1914 when World War I broke out." Too young and frail to serve as a soldier in that war, Otto worked as an apprentice from 1914 to 1918—not learning to craft beautiful furniture but instead making ammunition boxes:

Those were hard years. Soon, the boss took in defense work. We toiled up to 60 hours a week, making ammunition boxes by the never-ending thousands. Working conditions were most unhealthy—no dust exhausts provided on the machines. I still marvel how I made it without getting tuberculosis.

Since we did not often get our hands on a piece of furniture, I did not learn too much of the trade. But dovetails [hand-crafted corner joints], which we used on the boxes, I could do almost blindfolded! Added to all the hardship was the scarcity of food through the war years. As a growing youngster, I seldom got my fill. Sundays, we went out to tramp from farm to farm to gather some eggs, some butter, some meat here and there. And I was always tired.

Despite his long hours of work, Otto still found time to read. He borrowed books from the library and read newspapers. What he learned began to test his views of the world:

At sixteen, a friend gave me Darwin's *The Evolution of the Species*. I had already felt a growing alienation from my Catholic upbringing. Although I could not fully follow Darwin's writings, to read him made me abandon the dogmatism of the Church. At random, I discovered writers like Hoffmannsthal, Chamisso, Kleist, among others, and even Poe, Maupassant, and Shakespeare. My early patriotism, nourished by our chauvinistic textbooks, petered out, and when I came across writings about the Socialist movement in Germany, I read them with strong interest.

When World War I ended in November 1918, the so-called November Revolution swept away the German monarchy. As Otto recalled,

A revolutionary regime was formed by the homecoming soldiers, the workers, and the peasants, all over Germany, and also in Munich, the capital of Bavaria. Civil war came to our homeland. Conservative officers of the old army had gathered enough disgruntled veterans and adventurers up north to march towards Bavaria, to wipe out the revolutionary government. After a few months of fighting, they prevailed. A regressive democratic government was formed as part of the Weimar Republic.

Otto was not involved in the fighting. As he explained, "My political outlook had not crystallized enough to drive me to active participation." But his future in Munich was bleak. He continued to work as a journeyman cabinetmaker in the old shop where he had apprenticed until he too joined the growing masses of the unemployed. Facing a shortage of food in Munich and economic collapse in the form of runaway inflation, Otto dreamed of immigrating to America and even began to study English on his own. Then came an opportunity that would change his life:

When, at the end of the war, a coworker had departed for Italy where his father had reopened an icebox factory, I begged him to look for a job for me. I had forgotten all about it when, in 1920, a letter came for me from Rome, inviting me to come to work for his father and also, to bring along another fellow.

Seldom had I felt so exhilarated in my life! To escape the short-age of food, to be able to work again, to see Italy, the traditional yearning of the German *Wandersmann* [wanderer]—it seemed a dream too good to be true. My father encouraged me; my mother was sad but did not try to hold me back. While I was waiting for my papers, I set out to learn Italian, with intense application. And come fall, I started out with a friend for the Eternal City.

# 6. "Education" in Italy and France (1920–1935)

Otto lived and worked in Rome from 1920 to 1926. After years of limited physical and mental nourishment, he devoured everything Rome offered:

> Quite a new life it proved to be, exciting in many aspects, broadening my horizon in different ways. I loved the Italian language, and learned it quickly and well, enjoying the progress I made every day. I liked the people and their songs, their lightheartedness, their love for beauty, and their familiarity with their history. And what a history it was! Rome is an open book of that history: a never-ending richness of monuments, of ruins, of churches and museums, of fountains and parks. Every weekend, our *Baedeker* [tourist guidebook] . . . directed us to new marvels.
>
> And there was food, inexpensive and wholesome food. With it went wine, fine wine that even the poorest working man could afford to have with each meal. After the many years of deprivation, this was a most satisfying experience.
>
> Other new vistas opened. For the first time in my life, I saw the ocean. It was only an hour's ride by bus to the beach of Ostia, the old Roman harbor. I spent many happy Sundays there.
>
> Then there was the theater. I had been deprived of it back home, since it had been out of reach—I had seen only one opera. Here, the little people could afford theater and the opera, and they took advantage of it. In time, I saw many operas, and

for a while, I was even an extra at the triumphant march in *Aida* at the Costanzi.

Even work was more fun. I had taken a new job in an old, established firm that built richly designed period furniture. Italy had, as I soon found out, a great tradition of the finest craftsmanship in woodwork (as of course also in other crafts and arts), and during the years I worked there, I acquired a great amount of new knowledge and skill.

And there was the beautiful climate of Rome. The abundance of sunshine most of the year made outdoor life easy and pleasant. We roamed the countryside, discovered many historic sites, of which Cerveteri with its vast excavations of the remains of the early Etruscan civilization is still vividly in my mind.

Otto (*center*) with friends in Rome in 1922.

In time, I visited Naples and Pompey, escalated the Vesuvio, and went to the beautiful Island of Capri. In later years, I traveled to Florence, Milano, and Venice. All of these were exciting places for me to see, since I always had a keen interest in history and in art.[1]

In 1922, Otto invited his sister Tina to join him. "She was then a lively eighteen-year-old girl, and she also wanted to break out of a frustrating life in inflation-ridden Munich." Otto was able to find her a job taking care of the little children of a wealthy Italian family, Count and Countess Lazzarini. But as Otto recalled, "She was exploited, and she soon found another place. Now, at least, her earnings were not wiped out overnight, as they had been back home, and she was eager, during

Otto with his sister Tina in Rome in 1922.

the little free time she had, to fill her hungry mind with all the beauty and knowledge life in Rome could offer."

Otto's time in Italy was cut short by political developments:

> Stormy clouds had developed over this country. A political movement that in time brought disaster over all of Europe and indeed the world had started when Mussolini, at the head of his Blackshirts, marched into Rome. I was a silent spectator in the crowd who acclaimed the new "Duce." After the Fascists had taken power, the people began to experience the true nature of the new regime. Soon freedom of speech and of the press was gone, the trade unions were taken over, and life for the working people became progressively harder. And in time, Mussolini engaged the country in a disastrous war in Africa.

"As a foreigner," Otto explained, "I lived on the margin of these portentous events. But, hating the new ideology, I began thinking of leaving Rome. Paris had always held a great attraction for me. So, in the fall of 1926, I left for France."

On his way to Paris, Otto was "taken in by the beauty of the Riviera" and decided to stay in the city of Nice on the southeast coast of France. "Since Nice is a bilingual city, it was possible to acquire some knowledge of French while using my Italian at the working place. A wonderful climate, picturesque surroundings, and lighthearted people, easy to live with, made that winter at the Riviera one of the happiest periods of my life."

One day in Nice while looking for a new place to eat, Otto discovered a modest restaurant at the Old Port. "It was a place organized on a cooperative basis by a group of vegetarians. At refectory tables sat long rows of young people, with heaping plates of beans, rice, and salads, engaged in lively discussions." Otto was intrigued not only by the vegetarian food but also by the people he met there:

> Most of them were Spaniards—Catalans and Basques—sturdy, hardworking laborers. Among the books, displayed near the exit, were works by Kropotkin, Bakhunin, Tolstoy, and Max Stirner—all new to me—and a number of French poetry selections. It was an unexpected atmosphere. I went back there often, and made friends with a small group of young people from Paris who, on weekends, went out to the countryside.

Through conversations with his new friends, Otto's French quickly improved. And when some of them decided to return home to Paris, Otto decided that it was also time for him to move on. So, after living in Nice for about a year, Otto packed his tools and moved to Paris.

Otto's life in Paris from 1927 until he met Eva in 1935 was another phase in his quest to experience and learn. Just as he had done in Rome, this young man who had been deprived of formal schooling after the age of fourteen now eagerly absorbed what he could about this great new city:

> It was spring when I reached Paris, and spring in Paris is overwhelming, or at least it was that way, fifty years ago. I roamed through the city in all directions, learned to love her incomparable charm, her boulevards, imposing avenues and squares, her museums, churches, and beautiful parks. Later, I learned also to love her people, and the language, although that took some time. Parisians do not mix as easily with foreigners as Romans do, and with the haunting memory of the war, many still looked at Germans as the despised "Boches."

It took Otto weeks to find a job in Paris. When he finally did, it was in the shop of a cabinetmaker from Holland who built fine period furniture and modern interiors. "Again I started to learn, and found out how little I knew about the intricate art of veneering."

Shortly after he began to work, Otto became ill with a severe inner-ear infection. Despite hospitalization with excruciating pain, this illness left some fond memories:

> During those lonely days at the hospital, I experienced warm human kindness. One of my friends from Nice, Paul, a young student in Paris, came to visit me, and brought me fruit and books. One book I vividly remember was a biography of Beethoven by Romain Rolland. This was the first book written in French that I was able to master; and Rolland's prose made me aware of the great beauty of the French language.
>
> Through Paul, I got to know and to love French poetry. When we went on walks, he endlessly recited Victor Hugo, Rimbaud, Verlaine, Baudelaire, and many others, in his beautiful diction, and I was an appreciative audience. From him, I also learned a lot about French history and literature.
>
> He loved plays and music, and we often went to the Comédie Française and to the opera. As I had been able to in Rome, I could easily afford to go; a seat at the "poulailler" (last balcony) cost less than an hour's wages.

Along with Paul, Otto participated with idealistic pacifist groups in Paris:

> Ever since Nice, I had kept my habit of not eating meat. We often had dinner in a newly opened vegetarian restaurant that belonged to a group of "return to nature" enthusiasts. They had also built a rustic camp in a lovely valley (La Vallée de Chevreuse), not far from Paris. Their philosophy encompassed the development of body, mind, and spirit. We joined this group, and I have fond memories of many marvelous weekends spent among these people who were earnestly searching for a new way of life. Each summer, the camp was the gathering place of young pacifists from all over Europe, and I made many new friends.

And Otto learned whatever he could from his new acquaintances. He recalled that one of them, a German professor of linguistics, explained to him the origin of his name: "There was a time when some Germans liked to Latinize their family names. One ambitious forebear of ours, not satisfied with the humble name of 'Bäcker' (baker), adopted the Latin word 'Pistator' for it. Erosion and contraction did their work: 'Pistator' became 'Pfister.' This transformation must have happened before 1461, because in that year, a book of fables had been printed by an Albrecht Pfister in Bamberg (a town not far from Gerolzhofen in Lower Franconia where my father was born)."

Otto also made furniture for his new friends in Paris. It was not lucrative work, but it contributed to what would become lifelong friendships with some:

> Now I had rented a corner in the shop of some chair makers, and I started to work for myself. . . . At that time, I met Theo Fried . . . and I made the furniture he designed for a friend's house.[2] Most of the work I did then was for "little" people, students, friends.
>
> I did not always get paid. In one instance, I had designed and made tables and benches for a new vegetarian eating place opened by a young "naturiste." Since he was an idealist, he wanted to forego profit, charged too little, and soon went into bankruptcy. He had not paid me yet and forewarned me that an auction was imminent. So I spent part of the night before to clear out the furniture on a pushcart. It took me a while to sell it piece by piece.

Although this time in Paris was filled with positive experiences and growth for Otto, not all was easy:

> In November 1933, I got a telegram saying that my mother had undergone surgery but was recovering well. A few days later came another cable with the news that she had died of complications. She was only 62, worn out too early by a life of toil, and the final grief that father had left her. I went to the funeral, although at that time that was not a wise thing to do: After Hitler had come to power early that year, I had received,

Otto working in Paris shop in 1927.

as had many other young expatriates, orders from the German Consulate in Paris to report in Munich for a period of military training. Since I had disregarded that request, I faced the danger of being held at the border upon my return trip. Luckily, I had my resourceful sister Rosa who found ways to get the right rubber stamps for my passport, and so I was able to leave Germany again without any problem.

Back in Paris, I soon got into trouble that could have caused my expulsion from France. In February 1934, civil war had broken out in Austria. In Vienna, the workers fought desperately against the fascist regime of Dollfuss. The working people of Paris took to the streets then, for a peaceful demonstration of solidarity with their Austrian brothers. I too went with my friends. At the spot where the throngs of people dispersed, detachments of police waited to arrest people at random. I too was caught. Since foreigners were forbidden to be active in politics, I ended up in city jail.

Otto in Paris in 1934.

A phone call to an influential French friend set me free. It had not been a pleasant night—with a dozen people stuffed into a small cell, there was standing room only. Every once in a while, some of the prison guards came in to provoke and rough some of us up. I wore a full, long beard at that time, and one of them, grabbing and pulling it, yelled: "Hey, Jesus-Christ, what are you doing here?" After that, of course, I stayed away from street demonstrations.

All of these years in Rome, Nice, and Paris provided a rich informal education for that "tall fellow" who encountered that "strange, sad, shy girl" in the vegetarian restaurant that night in 1935—the man with a look that was "open and great" who spoke to others in the restaurant about idealistic philosophers and who loved the poet Rainer Maria Rilke.

# Part III.

## Resistance and Love in Paris, 1935–1940

*Bertholet informed me of the arrival in less than a month of a friend, a certain Otto, who would deliver me the bombs.*

—Jef Rens, Belgian labor leader

*When I visit you the first time in your workshop, when you talk to me with love of the nature and life of wood. Then I clearly feel that you are all one, that you stand by who you are and what you do. At that moment, I think I loved you.*

—Eva to Otto in Paris

# 7. Anti-Nazi Work in Paris

There is no question that Eva and Otto were intrigued with each other on that night in 1935 when they first met at Le Restaurant Végétarien des Boulevards at 28 Boulevard Poissonnière. But how would they react to each other when they discovered the gaping differences in their backgrounds and personalities?

In her Paris diary, handwritten in the form of letters to Rudi Lieske, Eva included comments about the early development of her relationship with Otto. In a diary entry dated December 20, 1935 (marked "not sent"), Eva noted that it had been a fairly long time since she had written to Rudi. "I have the impression that it is becoming more and more quiet from me to you." She then reported how her relationship with Otto was developing in connection with her work:

> With Otto, things are going well on the whole. We see each other much less often than in summer and for very different, more work-related purposes. On the whole, the development of our relationship goes on clearly because a personal connection has become a working one, upon which basis a good comradeship probably will survive, as long as we do not live too far away from each other. Naturally, sometimes—completely apart from work connections—merely the presence of a person to whom one can give something of one's warmth and affection, does one good. . . . It is in such moments that my hands, that can be good, feel like beings outside of myself. *They* are really happy and thankful, while I, myself, remain at bottom cold and indifferent. Otto knows this.

In one of the last entries in this Paris diary, dated January 1, 1936, Eva summarized the uneasy early growth of her relationship with Otto:

> I remember back on the development of my relationship with him: first happy, to have found a person, who with his confidence in me helped put my self-confidence on its feet. Then nothing, put off by his lack of culture, lack of understanding and sense of tact. I stubbornly crawl into myself—the light cheerful springtime dream of being in love with its bitter effect, I withdraw from all people. Turnaround: Then Otto, who *demands* an explanation for my behavior, respect is born anew, forming the basis of a friendly working relationship. Weeks, months, the woman in me is dead. One evening at the lake, she awakens to the friend—there follows an unintended, beautiful pure night together. Other such hours are lived without regret, not as a substitute for something else, without any obligation, in complete freedom.

As Eva would explain in more detail to Otto several years later in another diary, it took time for her to accept him as a man whom she could respect and love. Otto persisted. He knew that he wanted this woman to share his life, and he would continue to strive to be worthy of her. In turn, Otto's positive attitude and admiration of Eva's capabilities nurtured her self-confidence and inspired her hope.

But this relationship was being forged in the context of Eva's commitment to the ISK's goals and in the fire of cataclysmic historical events. For Eva and her ISK colleagues in Paris at that time, everything personal in their lives was subordinated to their anti-Nazi work. Otto could not have gained favor with Eva if he had not recognized the priority of that work or had not been willing and able to participate effectively in it. Otto was to prove his commitment by actions that put his life at risk.

Before examining Eva's and Otto's anti-Nazi work in Paris, it is helpful to take a closer look at the background of the ISK and its commitment to resist Hitler after he assumed power in 1933.

The ISK's anti-Nazi work in Germany faced a formidable foe. On February 17, 1933, the Nazis prohibited the further distribution of the ISK's primary publication, *Der Funke* (The Spark), after 325 issues had appeared since January 1, 1932.[1] In 1933, the Nazis boycotted Jewish businesses on April 1, banned trade unions on May 1, and burned books on May 10. A system of terror and violence was established in Germany to crush any group or individual opposition to Hitler.

Even before Hitler took power, it became increasingly evident to ISK members that they would need to be prepared to conduct illegal activity in their resistance against Nazism. They discarded membership books and badges, produced false papers, and agreed on pseudonyms (*Decknamen*) and code words. They simulated police interrogations and trial proceedings, and they learned their "stories" if questioned, including false explanations of how they knew each other if interrogated about other ISK members. They became accustomed to the need for absolute confidentiality, timeliness, and dependability in their resistance work.[2] The unusual nature of ISK's philosophy and practices became the organization's special strength as a resistance fighter. Because of the harsh personal demands for ISK membership (rigorous ethical education and training, full devotion to goals of the organization above any personal relationship, and no marriage, religion, meat, smoking, or alcohol), the total number of ISK members remained very small and unusually committed.

The number of ISK members is estimated to have been no more than 300, and an estimated 1,000 dedicated friends of ISK members were sympathizers supporting the ISK's work.[3] Because of their extreme level of voluntary self-sacrifice and their relative anonymity, ISK members were able to trust and rely on each other to an extent that members of most political groups could not. They were therefore uniquely suited to engage in effective clandestine resistance work against the Nazis.

Under Willi Eichler's leadership, a group of ISK members met secretly on Easter Sunday, April 16, 1933, and decided immediately to form an illegal group in Germany to focus on anti-Nazi work under these dramatically altered circumstances.[4] In July 1933 in an illegal meeting in Saarbrücken, ISK members discussed the new organizational structure of the illegal ISK group in Germany. The ISK members remaining in Germany (of both Jewish and non-Jewish heritage) would be divided into resistance groups of five. For secrecy/security reasons, only one member of each group was to know a member of another group at any given time. Twenty-six local ISK groups were established in six districts: Berlin, Hamburg, Hannover, Cologne, Frankfurt, and Munich. Five vegetarian restaurants and a bread wholesaler were available to ISK members in Germany for secret meetings, and many ISK members worked in these restaurants.[5]

The ISK's resistance work was designed to demonstrate to the German people that active resistance against Hitler was still possible and to encourage Germans to rise up against the Nazi regime. The primary focus of these efforts was the distribution of the extensive anti-Nazi publications, pamphlets, and recordings produced by ISK members in exile in Paris and smuggled into Germany. But the ISK's resistance work in Germany also included other illegal acts of considerable ingenuity that, until the late 1930s, allowed ISK members to avoid detection and arrest. In this respect, the ISK distinguished itself from both the German Communist Party (KPD) and the German Social Democratic Party (SPD), whose resistance efforts after Hitler assumed power were readily identified and crushed by early and massive arrests by the Nazis.[6]

An example of the ISK's unusual resistance efforts was the action taken by ISK members in Frankfurt on May 19, 1935. On that Sunday, Hitler had planned to preside over a ceremony celebrating the opening of a new stretch of autobahn (highway) between Darmstadt and Frankfurt. The night before the ceremony, ISK resisters painted "Nieder mit Hitler!" (Down with Hitler!) and "Hitler = Krieg" (Hitler = War) on bridges and pavements where the celebration would be filmed. The resisters used ink at night that was initially invisible, and the anti-Nazi messages would appear only when exposed to light, allowing the resisters to remove themselves from the scene long before the messages appeared. When the words were exposed prior to the ceremony, the Nazis covered the messages on the bridges with swastika flags and placed sand over the words on the pavement. However, rain and vehicle traffic swept away the sand, and the words were revealed to those in attendance. The Nazis had to make substantial edits in their propaganda film of the celebration.[7]

Similarly, ISK resisters brought large suitcases to train stations and left them on the platforms to be loaded by porters. The suitcases contained compartments at the bottom with ink that was released through stencils onto the platform. The suitcases were effectively turned into large stamps, leaving imprints of anti-Nazi messages in large letters on the platforms, also not immediately detectible, for all to see after the resisters had long since departed. ISK resisters even used special fertilizers to enhance the growth of grass along the countryside adjacent to train tracks so that anti-Nazi messages would emerge after weeks in the speeded growth and deeper green of the words.[8] Other examples of the ISK's novel resistance activities in Germany included leaving pictures in trains inside toilet paper rolls that depicted the swastika hanging from gallows, and placing anti-Nazi messages in bottles that were set afloat by ISK resisters in small boats in lakes in Berlin to be read long after the ISK resisters had deposited them and left the scene.[9]

The commitment by ISK members to undertake illegal anti-Nazi work obviously involved tensions and apparent inconsistencies. ISK followers of Leonard Nelson who had been taught to make ethical decisions through the rigorous use of reason were now being asked if they were willing to use lies and deception in their fight against Nazism. The majority concluded that the ethical imperative of defeating Hitler justified such behavior.[10]

## The ISK's anti-Nazi work in Paris

Apart from operating the restaurant in order to finance its resistance operations, the ISK's work in Paris before the war involved publishing anti-Nazi literature and smuggling it into Germany. The primary political objective was to give support to the ISK members in Germany who were trying to convince the people in Germany, particularly members of the trade unions that had been taken over by the Nazis, to rise up and overthrow Hitler. Another objective of the ISK's publishing work in Paris was to convince the French and others in Europe and the world that Hitler was a monster who was preparing for war and needed to be stopped.

The ISK's commitment to publishing was founded on its belief in the power of education to improve the human condition. It is therefore not surprising that despite its small number of members, the ISK group in Paris was the most active producer of anti-Nazi publications among all groups forced into exile by Hitler.[11] One of these publications was the *Sozialistische Warte, Blätter für kritisch-aktiven Sozialismus* (Socialist Viewpoint, Pages for Critically Active Socialism), which became one of the most important journals of political groups in exile in Europe at that time.

After Willi Eichler arrived in Paris in November 1933, the first issue of the *Warte* was published in May 1934. It began as a monthly publication and later was published every two weeks and then weekly.[12] Issues of the *Warte* were printed on especially lightweight paper to make it easier to smuggle them into Germany for distribution. The *Warte* published articles by a number of prominent intellectuals, including Thomas Mann, Ernst Fraenkel, and Leon Trotsky. The ISK also published numerous articles in the *Warte* using pseudonyms.[13]

The ISK group in Paris also regularly published anti-Nazi information in pamphlets known as the *Reinhart Briefe* (Reinhart Letters) for use and distribution by their ISK colleagues who were continuing to do illegal resistance work in Germany.[14] Also printed in Paris on thin "Bible paper," the *Reinhart Briefe* was published once or twice a month and included reports about methods being used by the Gestapo against the working class and about the resistance movement against the Nazis. It also included news about political events that was not available in Germany.[15]

The ISK's ability to smuggle its anti-Nazi publications from Paris into Germany was significantly enhanced by the cooperation between ISK members in exile and leaders of the International Transport Workers Federation (ITF). This relationship grew out of Willi Eichler's friendship with Edo Fimmen, the Dutch secretary-general of the ITF.[16] Eichler was introduced to Fimmen in August 1933 by a mutual friend, René Bertholet, a remarkable resistance fighter with the ISK who would later work closely with Eva and Otto. Fimmen's commitment to resistance work was not based on Leonard Nelson's philosophy, but he agreed completely with the need for a "United Front" against Nazi Germany. He and the ITF joined with the ISK in the fight "without reservations."[17] In trial proceedings against German resistance fighters in 1938, a Nazi prosecutor stated that "the Dutchman Edo Fimmen is Germany's greatest enemy."[18]

The support of Fimmen and his anti-Nazi union workers on trains running into Germany and on ships within Germany allowed the ISK to distribute large numbers of publications in Germany. Up to 1,000 copies of the *Reinhart Briefe* could be transported over the border. Of these, approximately 700–800 copies would then be distributed through the ISK membership network in Germany, and 150–200 would be distributed by Fimmen and the ITF network.[19]

This cooperation between the ISK and the ITF would continue with even more dangerous resistance activities during the war, and Otto would become directly involved in those activities.

## Eva's participation in anti-Nazi work in Paris

Eva's first job in Paris had been as an editor with Éditions Nouvelles Internationales, the publisher of a weekly literary political magazine with works of exiled German authors. After she left that position to assist with work at the vegetarian restaurant, she focused on the ISK's anti-Nazi publications and other resistance activities:

> The efforts to help our friends in Germany carry on their underground work were varied. We helped write and produce materials that were somehow gotten into their hands, on rice paper that could easily by swallowed if one was caught; or camouflaged by headlines that sounded as though they were Nazi propaganda, or harmless advertisements.
>
> We made little records spoken with a voice that could be taken for Hitler's, and that, after a harmless introduction, brought important factual information to help in the fight against Hitler's Germany.
>
> We were in touch with our [ISK] friends in Germany, and when their lives became endangered, we made every effort to get them out into freedom and safety. These efforts were not always successful—a good many of our friends spent time in jail; a few died. But some were helped and, once outside of Germany, could continue the work. In this task, Labor friends in France, England, Holland, Luxembourg, Switzerland gave much help.[20]

Although Eva's brother Erich was an attorney, his biographer acknowledged that "from a political point of view, Eva Lewinski had a more important role to play in the Parisian ISK colony than her brother Erich, whose entire time and efforts were needed to manage the restaurant."[21] Apart from Eva's work at the restaurant and on the ISK's publications, there was time for little else. Her only personal outlets were a few short trips into the country to regain strength from the peace and beauty of nature and from her writing.

The importance of Eva's role in Paris increased substantially in April 1938 when ISK leader Willi Eichler was expelled from France. Eichler was not given any official reason for his expulsion, and German historian Heiner Lindner concluded that the grounds could never be explained.[22]

Another historian noted that Eichler "left Paris in April 1938, having probably been denounced by local communists."[23] Whatever the reason, it is clear that Eichler left Paris against his will. With the help of Edo Fimmen, Eichler found asylum in Luxembourg. After failing to have his expulsion order rescinded, Eichler eventually obtained permission to go to England. In January 1939 he arrived in London, where he began to build a new ISK center to lead the organization in exile.

With Eichler gone, the leadership of the ISK's Paris office fell on the shoulders of two women: Eva and Hanna Fortmüller. Although Eichler's absence was a serious loss to the ISK's Paris office, virtually all of the resistance activities of that office continued under the leadership of Eva and Hanna, including the publishing and distribution of anti-Nazi materials and efforts to rescue endangered colleagues in Germany.

As a political group at that time, the ISK was notable for the number of women who assumed important leadership responsibilities.[24] No one questioned the enormous capabilities of these two women in leading the Paris office. But gender discrimination was still an issue. Historian Antje Dertinger observed that "Eichler's absence from Paris was a severe loss. It is perhaps surprising, therefore, that so many of the ISK's activities, especially their publications, continued as before." Dertinger explained:

> This was due above all to the two women who took over the leadership after Eichler's expulsion from France. They were Eva Lewinski and Hanna Fortmüller, who later married René Bertholet. These two women had been close colleagues of Willi Eichler's in the past. They were among the most able personalities of the ISK's activists in exile, but as women, they found themselves in a difficult position. In December 1938 [ISK member] Werner Hansen wrote to Willi Eichler: "It is regrettable that the ISK in Paris is now only represented by women, however able they might be. . . . It is an unfortunate fact that even within the Socialist movement, especially in the Trade Unions, women are not yet fully accepted."[25]

A document in the ISK files in the archives of the Friedrich-Ebert-Stiftung in Bonn, Germany, compiled by Karl Heinz Klär in his extensive research work about the ISK, is titled "Decknamen" (pseudonyms). The document contains a list of the many pseudonyms used by ISK members in their resistance work and helps researchers identify references to ISK members in correspondence. One entry on the list reflects the recognition of Eva's importance to the ISK's work in Paris at that time. The pseudonym used by the ISK for "Paris" was "Evastadt" (Eva City).

Hitler's aggression in Austria and Czechoslovakia in 1938 and 1939 resulted in a flood of new political refugees into Paris. On March 12, 1938, German troops marched into Austria as Hitler announced the Anschluss (annexation) of Austria by Germany. Facing the Nazis' ruthless policy of persecuting all political dissidents, Austrian opponents of Hitler, including prominent leaders of the Austrian Socialist Party, fled to Paris. The relationships that Eva developed with these Austrian refugees in Paris would become critically important in her future. For example, Josef Luitpold Stern, an exiled Austrian social democrat, educator, and poet, became a close friend of Eva and Otto during this time in Paris. Stern would play a special supportive role for Eva, primarily through his regular correspondence with her during the war years. Eva also became acquainted with Joseph Buttinger (aka Gustav Richter), an exiled Austrian socialist leader who later would became a key advocate in America for Eva in her attempt to obtain an emergency visa for her escape to America after the Nazi invasion of France.

Similarly, members of the SPD, who had set up headquarters in exile in Prague after Hitler's takeover in 1933, also flooded into Paris in 1938 after the Munich Pact of September 30, 1938, attempted to appease Hitler by allowing him to take over the Sudetenland (followed by the Nazi invasion of Prague on March 15, 1939). Paris had become the last center of refuge for all German-speaking anti-Nazi political parties in exile. With over six years of resistance work in Paris, the ISK leaders participated in meetings and discussions among the leaders of all of these groups. Eva participated actively in those discussions and came to be known and respected by leaders of the SPD as well. These connections would also help her later in her efforts in America to rescue others endangered by the Nazis.

Some refugees from these German-speaking political groups had already immigrated to America to work in exile. They included leaders of the SPD such as F. William Sollmann, who came to America in 1937. Sollmann had served as secretary of the interior and as a member of the Reichstag before being driven out of Germany by the Nazis. The refugees also included Karl Boromäus Frank (aka Paul Hagen), a representative of the socialist splinter group *Neu Beginnen* (New Beginning), who became active in America rallying financial and other support for the rescue of other endangered political refugees.[26] The positive impression that Eva made on members of these groups in Paris would help her develop relationships with other members of these groups in the émigré community she was later to encounter in New York.

## Otto's participation in anti-Nazi work in Paris

While working with ISK members in Paris, Otto became involved in the distribution of the ISK's anti-Nazi literature to the network of ITF members directed by Edo Fimmen in Belgium and Luxembourg for delivery and distribution in Germany. Otto also helped prepare and deliver false papers to endangered colleagues in Germany to aid in their escape. Otto's identity as a working man and his comfort in relating to trade union workers helped him forge strong relationships with representatives of the ITF. After the war began in September 1939, he would make far more dangerous deliveries to ITF members.

Otto was also directly involved in producing and distributing the small *Gramophonplatten* (phonograph records) containing anti-Nazi information. One such record was prepared by the ISK to encourage people in Germany to believe in the continuing strength of the resistance and to have the courage to vote "no" in the March 29, 1936, "Abstimmung," the election and referendum in which the German public was asked to approve the military occupation of the Rhineland.[27] Historian Ursula Langkau-Alex noted that ISK leader "Eichler had Otto Pfister—who had long been living in Paris, was unknown in Germany, and whose Bavarian accent resembled Hitler's pronunciation—make a small recording under the pseudonym of Dr. Franz Forster."[28]

In March 1936, Eichler wanted "several hundred" of these records to be distributed in Germany by Rhine shipmen who were affiliated with the ITF. The records found their way to opponents of the regime, including former youth and sports organizations of the SPD and other splinter anti-Hitler groups. But the recordings also fell into the hands of Nazi organizations and even relatives of SS officers. The Gestapo intercepted many of the records in post offices in Wuppertal, Eisenach, and the Weimar district, among other locations. The Nazis were thereafter on the lookout for the unknown disseminators of the recordings, whom the Nazis considered guilty of "high treason."[29]

The following is the substance of the message on the recording in Otto's voice (translated from German by Langkau-Alex):

> On 29 March [1936] you are to say whether you approve Hitler's foreign policy [the military occupation of the Rhineland]. The position foreign countries will take against Germany depends on whether you agree with this policy of aggression, because it is, in fact, a policy of aggression. No one has the intention to attack Germany, neither France nor the Soviet Union. The Franco-Soviet Pact only came into being after the wild rearmament of Germany, after the crazy threats of attack against the Soviet Union, after Hitler's refusal to participate in the Eastern Peace Pact—of East Locarno. The assertion that the Franco-Russian Pact conflicts with the Locarno Pact is wrong. But even if it were correct, a peace-loving Germany would have called for a Hague arbitration. No one can trust a deal breaker.
>
> The result of the constant unrest in the world from Hitler's provocations can only be war. Exactly like William II, Hitler will rattle his saber so long that he will unleash a world conflagration. The consequences will be even more terrible, for each country and for Germany in particular. Because this must be reckoned with: If Germany wants carelessly to provoke a war, it will most likely cease to exist. The responsible circles in Germany know that very well. They have plunged into this adventure to distract attention from domestic economic and social problems. For the same reason, the postponement of the referendum elections.
>
> Only an honest, peace-serving foreign policy and a domestic policy serving the welfare of *all* can help bring Germany out of its desperate position. The saber rattling of the government and the repressive measures of the Gestapo will only plunge Germany into misfortune. Therefore, on March 29, say "NO" to Hitler's foreign policy![30]

On the front side of the record was written "You are receiving a record—spoken by Dr. Franz Forster." On the back was written "Please

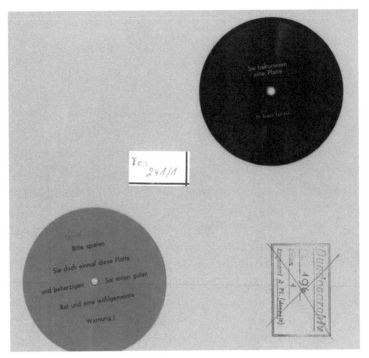

Record using Otto's voice urging Germans to oppose the Nazis' military occupation of the Rhineland in 1936. Courtesy of Bundesarchiv, B 198 Bild-2018-0114-001/Photographer: o.Ang.

play this record once and heed the good advice and a well-intentioned warning!"

The fact that this March 1936 recording was considered an act of "high treason" added to the danger that Otto would face four years later when he was captured by the Nazis. But by then he had done much more that would have earned Hitler's displeasure.

## The Nazi crackdown on ISK members in Germany

The Nazis ultimately crushed the ISK's resistance within Germany, but to the credit of the group's discipline, it took over five years. German historian Heiner Lindner summarized the series of arrests:

> In 1935, came the first arrests of 12 ISK members. Because of their good preparation for the illegal work in the Third Reich

and their outstanding disguise, the Gestapo still did not recognize that those arrested belonged to a nationwide network of resistance groups. It was not until the summer of 1937 that a specially prepared department of the Gestapo arrested 100 people out of the ISK network. As the southern German groups also were destroyed in the summer of 1938, this was—after "at least five years of continuous work"—essentially the end of the ISK's resistance capability in Germany.[31]

Lindner noted that Eichler counted almost ninety specifically named cases in which ISK members had to suffer punishment in prison or concentration camps. He also observed that some ISK members made costly mistakes:

> So, a courier lost a pack of *Reinhart Briefe*, on which the addresses of ISK members had been carelessly written. Based on that, the Gestapo arrested numerous members and with the help of brutal interrogation methods extorted the identification of still further names and addresses.[32]

Lindner concluded that the ISK's resistance organization in Germany did not recover from this "wave of arrests" that occurred into 1939 and that the ISK's resistance work was all in exile from that point on.[33]

## The Philippson case

The danger of the ISK's work in Germany is illustrated by the case of Julius Philippson, who was caught by the Nazis in 1937, tortured to reveal information about the ISK, and convicted in a Nazi show trial for his involvement in the ISK's resistance activities. In 1938, he was sentenced to life imprisonment for high treason. In the court judgment condemning Philippson, Otto was referred to as a key participant in Philippson's illegal anti-Nazi activities.

The Bundesarchiv (German Government Archive) in Berlin contains records from the trial of Julius Philippson. The *Abschrift Urteil* (judgment) against Philippson is a detailed and sobering account of how the Nazis tried and convicted a man—and in the process the entire

ISK political group—who dared to oppose Hitler's policies. One of the profoundly disturbing aspects of the Nazi regime is the careful documentation that purports to explain and justify its brutal actions as lawful. It is chilling precisely because it demonstrates how a society that purports to be civilized can use the legal process to crush dissent and then to commit the most hateful crimes against humanity. And it is an example of how deeply the "legal analysis" of the Nazis' case against Philippson and the ISK was infected by anti-Semitism.

The court first summarized Philippson's background, including his academic performance and his remarkable military record fighting for Germany during World War I. It noted that Philippson interrupted his university studies to enlist voluntarily in the German Army, was wounded twice in the Russian theater, and was a prisoner of war in Russia for four years until April 1920. The court further noted that Philippson, a staff sergeant and officer candidate, had earned the Iron Cross I and II and the Austrian Medal of Bravery. After describing how Philippson resumed his studies at the University of Göttingen in 1920, passed the state examination for higher teaching service in 1922, and assumed various teaching positions from 1923 to 1933, the court recounted, with cold detachment, how this Jewish German war hero and highly educated teacher was removed from his teaching and his civil service position in 1933 because he was "a full Jew."[34]

Among the "highly treasonous activity of the Accused," the court referred to Philippson's involvement in distributing the ISK publications that were smuggled into Germany from France:

> Apart from the material he himself produced, the Accused [Philippson] in 1935 and the beginning of 1936 also distributed the *Reinhart Briefe* . . . and the *Sozialistische Warte*, which arrived in packages in Berlin.[35]

As we know, the source of the *Reinhart Briefe* and the *Sozialistische Warte* was the ISK group in Paris, including Eva. And Otto was heavily involved in the process of smuggling these publications into Germany with the assistance of the International Transport Workers Federation.

The court also specifically referred to Philippson's communications with ISK leader Willi Eichler through a "Mr. Pfister" in Paris:

From the end of 1936 until his arrest, the Accused sent to the addresses "Mr. Pfister, Paris XI, 1937 rue du Faubourg St. Antoine" and "Herta Walter" in Paris for Eichler certain political and economic news items in addition to newspapers such as *Der SSA-Mann, Schwarzes Korps, Arbeitertum* and other specialized leaflets of the German Labor Front (DAF).[36]

And the court referred to Philippson's participation in the distribution of "records from Paris, in which listeners were exhorted to vote 'No' during the elections in March 1936."[37] The court did not know that the voice on these records was Otto's.

The court acknowledged that Philippson might have acted out of "idealism" rather than a "lowly motive," but it observed that as a "disciple" of ISK leader Leonard Nelson, Philippson "endeavored far more than other disciples and followers of Nelson to disseminate Nelson's thoughts through action." Returning to the core of its anti-Semitic "legal reasoning," the court concluded that this was "based on the Jewish mentality which the two have in common."[38]

Regarding the penalty that should be imposed on Philippson, the court first quoted from the prior decision of the People's Court against another ISK member, Hans Prawitt, which concluded that the danger of the ISK could not be underestimated despite the "relatively low number of their followers." Adding to this danger, according to the court in the Philippson case, "is also the world political situation, in which the more time passes, the clearer is the intransigent battle of world Jewry against the National Socialist [Nazi] state." The court found that the ISK "qualified as a forward post of world Jewry in this fight, and at the head of this forward post stood the Accused, who is a member of world Jewry."[39]

The court concluded that Philippson deserved the death penalty but instead imposed life imprisonment. After spending years in different prisons, Philippson was sent to Auschwitz in 1943, where he was killed in 1943 or 1944.

At bottom, Philippson was sentenced to life in prison and ultimately murdered by the Nazis primarily because he exercised what human beings should never take for granted: the right to assemble and to express opposition to oppressive government policies. Opposition to Hitler's policies, however, was a criminal act. For the Germans of Jewish and non-Jewish origin to engage in resistance to the Reich required a willingness to risk imprisonment or death.[40]

At some point in the late phases of the crackdown against ISK members in Germany, it became clear to the ISK group in Paris that their colleagues in Germany faced certain decimation at the hands of the Nazis. One of the surviving ISK members in Germany criticized Willi Eichler for his refusal to recognize the vulnerability of his ISK colleagues in Germany earlier.[41] But when the crackdown occurred, the ISK members in Paris did whatever they could to help rescue those in Germany who had not yet been captured. With his steady and artistic hand, Otto prepared false papers to assist ISK members in escaping from Germany and helped smuggle those lifesaving papers into Germany.

Although the Nazis' succeeded in crushing the ISK's underground organization in Germany, the anti-Nazi publishing efforts of ISK members in exile in Paris continued until the very eve of the Nazi blitzkrieg to the west. The last publication of the *Warte* by the ISK in Paris is dated May 2, 1940, one week before the German invasion on May 9, 1940. That issue included an article by Alfred Wolfenstein titled *"Die Gefährlichkeit des Buches"* (The Danger of Books) that commented on the upcoming anniversary of the book burnings in Nazi Germany on May 10, 1933. The article (translated here into English) concluded:

It is vital to preserve the noble, and for that reason striking, power of the book, the book of the poet and the fighter, especially in the face of the most vulgar power. It is vital to strengthen its reputation against the failed desecration. The danger of the book form, apart from the danger of its contents, must do its part for the benefit of civilization. The poets will keep this wonderful form of human voice alive in her fire. We shout out when those people call for the burning of free and good writings: The book is dead? Long live the book!

The resistance efforts of ISK members including Eva and Otto, their *Pflichtgefühl* (sense of duty), their devotion to the ethical obligation to commit their lives to resisting Nazism, were extraordinary. This is true of all ISK members, Jewish and non-Jewish. Their story has hardly

Excerpts from the *Warte*, published on May 2, 1940, including article on upcoming anniversary of book burnings in Germany on May 10, 1933.

been told in the English language, much less recognized, studied, and honored. Perhaps some ISK members who survived were reluctant to tell their stories because of a persisting commitment to confidentiality. Perhaps they were reluctant because some of their colleagues perished or because all of their efforts ultimately failed in stopping the horrors of the Holocaust. In any event, when reflecting on the extraordinary commitment and sacrifice of ISK members in their fight against Hitler, it is fitting here to quote the following words that Julius Philippson wrote to his parents during his earlier imprisonment in the Zuchthaus Brandenburg (Brandenburg prison):

> What drove me, I cannot better express than with a verse from Tagore, that a friend once wrote me for my birthday: "I dreamed that life would be joy. I awakened and saw: Life was service. I acted and now I see: Service was joy."[42]

As the judgment in the Philippson case confirmed, the Gestapo now knew of a "Mr. Pfister" in Paris who was participating with the ISK in activities that the Nazis determined to be "acts of high treason." And as the severe punishment of Philippson confirmed, when the Nazis invaded France at the beginning of May 1940, any German in Paris determined to be a member of the ISK would be in imminent danger of capture, imprisonment, and death.

## 8. War Begins: Internment, Sabotage, and Love

On August 23, 1939, Hitler entered into a nonaggression pact with Russia, the Molotov-Ribbentrop Pact. The pact provided that Germany and Russia would not attack each other for the next ten years. From Hitler's perspective, this meant that if Germany attacked Poland, causing Britain and France to declare war against Germany, Russia would not enter the war and open an Eastern Front against Germany. On September 1, 1939, one week after signing the pact with Russia, Nazi troops invaded Poland. France and England declared war on Germany on September 3, 1939, marking the beginning of World War II.

Very little overt military action took place on Germany's Western Front during the first six months of the war, the period referred to as the Drôle de Guerre (Phony War). But the declaration of war had an immediate impact on Otto and Eva. Eva recalled:

> Within France, things changed rapidly, especially for the refugees. At first, it hit only the men: all were put into internment camps, as potentially dangerous "enemy aliens." Without any screening as to their loyalty, all had to report, including all our friends, and of course also Erich and Otto.[1]

Otto was interned by the French first in St. Jean de la Ruelle near Orléans, about ninety miles southwest of Paris, and then in Camp Cepoy, about a hundred miles southeast of Paris, until he was released at the beginning of February 1940 to assist France in the war against Germany. Otto's internment began what would become a pattern compelled by wartime events that separated him and Eva: exchanging letters to convey their thoughts, love, and support. Eva retained some of the letters she wrote to Otto during this period. They were written in French and in German, sometimes using both languages in the same letter. Otto also wrote to Eva, but his letters from this period were not preserved.

On September 10 shortly after Otto was interned, Eva wrote to him in French, assuring him: "Be calm, I will too, I will not lose courage; little by little I get used to the new way of life, the nerves adapt as well." She noted that late one evening she "even had enough strength to arrange our vacation photos. . . . How beautiful it was, the purity of the Bréda Valley! Almost unimaginable that it was scarcely three weeks ago that we stayed down there!" She informed Otto that his other letters had not yet arrived and that she was trying to get permission to send him a package: "Your pullover, I still haven't been able to get permission to send it. . . . I will send you another in its place that, while not very beautiful, will be useful for you."

On December 23, 1939, while Otto was still interned at St. Jean de la Ruelle, Eva wrote to him in French with two paragraphs in German. She attached a small fern leaf at the beginning of the letter that remains attached to the fragile paper over three-quarters of a century later. Eva erased some of the names from the original, apparently to protect the identities of their colleagues. After thanking Otto for his "beautiful, beautiful letter and card of the 20th," she noted that "there wasn't much Christmas spirit during this last year; but nevertheless tomorrow evening we will have our friends with us; [name erased] who is here. . . . He will

Vacation photos of Eva and Otto in the Bréda Valley near Grenoble in 1939 shortly before Otto was interned by the French as an "enemy alien."

tell us some of his impressions; he is otherwise in good form and of good morale although personally he really has had bad luck: About a week ago, his friend was taken to a concentration camp—no one knows why." She ended the letter with

> Voilá, my dear young man, I must go. Don't be sad tomorrow [Christmas Eve]; all of you know that we think of you with warm hearts and great sympathy, and are bound to all of you. All of you there, we here—the space divides us, but our way of seeing and shaping life binds us. No one can take that away from us. I hug you, from within and firmly, in great, great love.

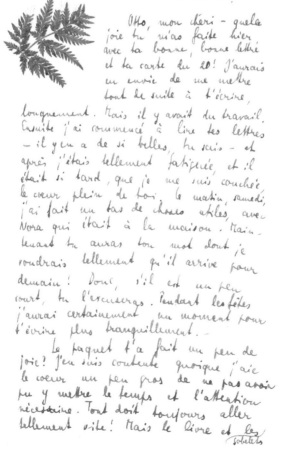

First page of Eva's letter to Otto on December 23, 1939, while Otto was interned by the French.

The next day, December 24, Eva wrote another letter to Otto before she was to join her ISK colleagues for Christmas Eve:

> My dear, dearest Otto—How happy I am that all of you received the gift. How thankful for your good words and the beautiful wooden page! Now you are all probably sitting with each other and celebrating for a few hours, in which one is happy to be close to friends and wants to be good to them. We are doing the same. Tonight friends are coming to us. . . . We will read, make music, talk; each for ourselves will think *very* much about all of you, and all of us together will feel very close to all of you. . . . In the afternoon, a greeting came from [name erased, likely Stern] that was quiet, beautiful, deep: a letter and a small notebook full of new poems, full of melancholy and confidence. Good Otto, how I look forward to a quiet evening in which we could read in it together! Perhaps I will at some time send you one poem or another, but I just don't have the right peace and quiet to do it today.[2]
>
> On the whole, I would much rather talk the entire evening just with you—I feel so close to you. But that would be egotistical; and I am also, at bottom, happy again to be together with the others, because I feel so rich, basically, to get to live in this world despite great sadness at times, that I happily give in. For my riches, for the fact that I am at bottom deeply calm and happy, you my dear man are the decisive cause. Do you know that?
>
> Now the others are just coming. Is your tree already beautifully lit? Many people think the same things in these hours, are moved by the same concerns, the same hopes; work at the same work. That gives courage. And that, in addition to this larger bond, we two still have each other, you me, I you, is so much that I am almost ashamed. Do you remember the evening in the Tuileries years ago where I said I was becoming religious? That is true, perhaps deeper and stronger, tonight.
>
> Give best wishes to all, all friends; tell them that I and we all are close to all of you. You, my dear man, I hug in great, thankful love.

The end of one year and the beginning of a new one were special to Eva throughout her life. It was a time for her to reflect on the past and to look for hope in the future. In Eva's letter to Otto dated December 30, 1939, while he was interned at Camp Cepoy, she again attached a few leaves, now dry and brittle, as fragile and faded as the ink and paper:

Otto, my dear man—Now it has again become so late, and my letter will not be more than a warm greeting. After a loud, turbulent day, quiet now gradually returns to us. I think about you, about the sky, snow and stars, and about the great love that binds me to you. Both of your greeting cards were like your warm, good hand that gently, tenderly strokes over my heart, when it is sad and hurts. Now it is happy and open, again capable of embracing much with love. . . .

You know, my Otto, what I wish for you and us for the New Year. You also know how I thank you for last year and for past years that, along with much heavy difficulty, brought back to me the most beautiful thing: the certainty that I am at home with you and you with me. Do you recognize these leaves? They bring to me the memories of beautiful deep hours coming back to life with you!

My two small gifts (socks and trousers) will make you happy. Something very nice will come soon! And now, my love, let me close my eyes for a moment and go with you in my thoughts to that mountain forest path through the high deep-green pines, through which the sun throws such a magical light that I would think I have never seen you so beautiful.

During this period of separation from Otto, Eva felt compelled to start a new diary to describe the development of her relationship with him. She wrote the first entry on January 15, 1940:

I really am not sure why I want to write about "our story" right now. I barely have time to write you the way I would want to. . . .

And yet there is the need to write this. Perhaps for fear that all the beautiful and hard things that happened to us may get blurred because of all the events that rush in on us, that they may drown in the whirlwind of the new happenings? Or perhaps the desire to be close to you, to have alive before me the development of our relationship, the development of our love, your and my development, to get joy and strength from it.

There are two photos of you in front of me. In back of me is the drawing that someone made in camp. On the one, you are rowing forcefully, you look at me (I think it was me?) with love and tenderness. A picture of sunny serenity; when I look at it, I nod at you and tell you: "Yes, my dearest, I love you." On the other one, you look with a frown, and with concentration, at something in front of you: a bug, a rock? . . . There I am quite excluded from your thinking, your whole attention is focused on the object in front of you. But there also you are close to me, and I feel the same love as to the tender, cheerful man. And in back, in the drawing, there is much, and much is missing.

There is above all the desire, the yearning, not to become small in front of hard things, to master the events, and, even with you away from me, still to remain close and keep serene. The same effort carries me along, far from you. Separated by wide spaces, we still move in the same direction. Perhaps our ships will have to continue their voyage for a while separately. Yet nothing can really part them.

In this diary entry, Eva recalled the depth of her loneliness at the time she met Otto: "I was suffering under the inner split in me: to be a woman, but not only a woman, a political human being, but not only that. I was afraid to continue my life in this half-way situation. Fear, discouragement, hopelessness—they defined me at that time."

Eva's writing in this diary about her early relationship with Otto paused at the end of January 1940

Drawing of Otto in the French internment camp in September 1939.

when he was released from his internment and returned to live with her in Paris. She would resume this writing a few months later when Otto was again away from Paris on anti-Nazi missions to Belgium and Luxembourg that had become more dangerous now that France was at war with Germany.

## Otto's sabotage work against the Nazis

At the beginning of February 1940, the French released Otto from his internment because they understood that he could be of assistance in the war against Germany. Eva later explained that Otto and some of his colleagues were released "because of their willingness to continue to work against the Nazis—now that war was there, this had become a matter of first priority. So, Otto got out, and undertook travels to neighboring countries to take materials and information to be forwarded to friends in Germany."[3] Eva provided no further details about the nature of Otto's "travels to neighboring countries."

Another document describes Otto's release from the French internment camp from a very different perspective. Two years later and long after the Nazis had occupied Paris, Otto's oldest sister Rosa wrote from her home in Munich to German officials in an attempt to find out what had happened to her brother.[4] Rosa and her sisters had heard nothing from Otto since before the war began. She received a one-page notice from the Deutsche Botschaft, Paris (German embassy in Paris) dated July 16, 1942:

> Your brother Otto Pfister, born on April 8, 1900 in Munich, was interned at the beginning of the war in the camp "Cepoy." He was committed on February 1, 1940 to entry in the French army and was thereupon released from his internment. About his current residence, a determination from here could not be found.

During this period of the Drôle de Guerre, the German Army was moving military supplies in preparation for its invasion, and the French Army was covertly engaged in defensive actions. Neither Otto nor Eva ever spoke or wrote about the specific nature of Otto's underground work for the French Army during this period. In our research for this

**Deutsche Botschaft, Paris**

Konsulatsabteilung

Section Consulaire de l'Ambassade d'Allemagne à Paris

Fernsprecher: Littre 30-90       Besuchszeit: 9 - 12 . Außer Mittwoch und Sonnabend
Absender/Expéditeur: Paris (6e), 2, rue Huysmans

Frau
Rosa  W a l d m a n n

München 5
Frauenstr. 10

Ihr Zeichen:       Ihr Schreiben vom       Aktenzeichen:       Tag:
Votre référence:       Votre lettre du       Notre référence:       Date:

K 15410/Kult 6 Nr/42    16.7.42

Auf Veranlassung eines hier im Hess-Ver-
lag tätigen Herrn Amschel teile ich Ihnen mit,
dass Ihr am 8,4,00 in München geborener Bruder
Otto  P f i s t e r  zu Beginn des Krieges
interniert wurde. Im Lager " Cepoy " hat er
sich am 1.2.40 zum Eintritt in die französische
Armee verpflichtet und ist daraufhin aus der
Internierung entlassen worden. Über seinen
jetzigen Aufenthalt konnten Feststellung von
hier aus nicht getroffen werden.

Im Auftrag

Notice sent to Otto's sister by the German embassy in Nazi-occupied Paris in 1942 about Otto's release from French internment and entry into the French Army on February 1, 1940.

book, we were shocked to learn that Otto's work included his delivery of bombs to sabotage German trains and inland ships carrying war materials for the coming Nazi invasion.[5]

In these missions Otto worked closely with ISK member René Bertholet, a Swiss-born anti-Nazi resistance worker; Jef Rens, a Belgian labor leader; and Johannes (Hans) Jahn, a leader of the International Transport Workers Federation. Rens later wrote a book about his experiences during the war, originally published in Dutch and later translated into French.[6] One chapter in the book is titled "René Bertholet et Otto Pfister." The chapter describes encounters by Rens with Otto and Bertholet—encounters that Rens referred to as "among the most unique that I had in my life."[7] Rens described a visit from Bertholet in which Bertholet explained the ISK's involvement in arranging the collaboration with the French Army:

After a brief moment of hesitation and after making me promise to keep this secret, he [Bertholet] began to speak: "The majority of the members of the 'Internationaler Sozialistischer Kampfbund' have remained in Germany, but a certain number of others have immigrated to England and France. All of this has been decided by mutual agreement. The members who remained in Germany continued their propaganda and covert action against the regime." "I," said Bertholet, "I settled in Paris, as did Willi Eichler and other members of the organization."

"Shortly after the entry into the war of France and England, we weighed the alternative courses of action to adopt in the new situation. Unanimously, we decided to offer our services to the French Authorities. After having studied various possibilities, we came to reach an agreement of collaboration with the Fifth Bureau of the French army."

"In exchange for French passports created with aliases for some of us and paraphernalia for bombs, we committed to form small groups of determined and committed anti-Nazi activists in all the so-called neutral countries located around Germany. Some of these groups are already in action in Denmark, Holland, Luxembourg, Switzerland and Yugoslavia. Only in Belgium have we not yet succeeded in creating one." "I wonder," Bertholet then said, "if you're not the man we need to take the responsibility of such a group."

"The activities of these small groups must, of course, remain secret, as they are incompatible with the laws and democratic rules in force in these neutral countries. The groups of our network, of whom some are active in the railway and as port workers, and if possible in customs, are responsible for planting timed bombs in the trains and inland ships that transport equipment for use in German war production."[8]

Rens described his first encounter with Otto:

Bertholet informed me of the arrival in less than a month, of a friend, a certain Otto, who would deliver me the bombs. . . . After the departure of Bertholet, weeks passed without receiving news from the "Internationaler Sozialisticher Kampfbund." I was ending up believing that this whole affair would come to an abrupt end when one beautiful morning, our secretary Mariette announced that "the citizen Otto" was in the waiting room. I let him in immediately. A true giant! I would barely come up to his shoulders. At the end of his arms . . . two large suitcases . . . visibly very heavy.

Otto began by listening attentively to the story I told him of my conversation with René Bertholet; then, without much movement, he opened one of his suitcases. It was full of the announced bombs, arranged with care next to each other, each composed of three distinct parts and . . . sparkling new. Without waiting, Otto explained to me how to assemble the elements of these infernal devices, and then how to operate the timing mechanism. He was careful to add that we had nothing to fear as long as the clock and the explosive charge remained separate. I was reassured!

For my guidance, I then asked him what was the destructive power of the contents of the two suitcases. With that, Otto gave a glance out the window and replied coolly: "There's enough to blow into the air this entire neighborhood, including the Maison du Peuple and the church of la Chapelle." A shudder ran through my spine. But without further ado, Otto took his leave and left me with "my" bombs. The drawers in my office were full. From then on, it is on a true small arsenal that I conduct my trade union business affairs![9]

The previously secret files of the British intelligence agency during the war, the Special Operations Executive (SOE), contain a file titled "Operations of Johannes Jahn (1936–1940)." That file includes more information about this short-lived and largely unsuccessful effort to interrupt Hitler's early war preparation through sabotage.[10] A *Bericht* (report) written in German on November 22, 1940, noted that the success of these efforts had been limited because the "time to play it out was too short."[11] The report (translated here from German) stated:

From February until May [19]40, 27 railroad carloads from Belgium and Luxembourg were bombed. In March and April 1940, Rhine ships in Strassburg, Hohenfels, Rhenania 2,

Oberrhein and Duisburg were bombed. . . . The cargo was largely destroyed. The ships partially damaged. No ship was sunk.[12]

The report further described in detail where the explosives were placed on the vehicles for maximum effect:

The explosives were attached directly behind the axle casing of a railroad car on the *Stossenende* [pushing end] of the axle and then set with the timing device. The left half of the axle was always taken, so that the expected derailing to the left would follow and thereby achieve an obstruction of the entire body of the track.[13]

The SOE's Jahn file also contains a brief memo dated May 8, 1940:

The following is an extract from a letter, intercepted in Censorship, dated 15.4.40. from the I.T.F. representative in Luxembourg to I.T.F. headquarters:
"During the past week a goods train between Aachen and Köln—120 axles—was completely blown into the air. What a good shot!"[14]

## Eva's reflections on her relationship with Otto

On March 15, 1940, Eva returned to her diary to reflect on the growth of her love for Otto. She had not written anything in this diary for two months. But with Otto again away from Paris—this time on extended anti-Nazi missions involving serious risk to his life—she felt the need to look back in time and continue her written account of the early development of their relationship.

Two months have gone by. Good, that that could be, because the greatest part of it, you were with me; we lived together, and I did not have the urge to write about the past. Now I am alone again, the long evening hours and the night when it is hard to turn off the light, to sleep; there are the moments of the day, filled with longing, that cannot be forced into the work program of the day. In the past, I could then write you a note, a letter. Today I can only be with you in my thoughts, lovingly. And when calm finally comes, perhaps after some music, I am writing.

It is in this diary entry on March 15, 1940, that Eva described for Otto her vivid recollection of their initial encounter five years earlier at the Restaurant Végétarien des Boulevards that is quoted in the prologue of this book—how she first noticed Otto while she was sitting at the cash register and how they immediately saw something special in each other.

Eva then described a miscommunication not long after their initial meeting—on her birthday in April 1936—that had nearly ended their relationship. She had opened up to Otto about her personal past in a vulnerable moment, and Otto misread that as an invitation to a more intimate emotional relationship than she was ready to accept:

You then came back very often; we talked a lot, discovered many things that we had in common, also things that separated us. One Sunday afternoon we went to St. Cloud. That was beautiful. Lovely was the return in the subway that was very crowded; I was sitting, you were standing next to me, your warm, trusting look rested on my face. I was grateful—perhaps my expression showed that to you?

My birthday came, a sad, heavy day. No letter from Rudi, not in the morning, not in the afternoon. At noon I see you. "What plans do you have for tonight?" "I would gladly go and have a cup of coffee with you after work." In the evening, there is a letter from Rudi, but so empty that it makes me even sadder. My heart was so full on that evening, full of bitterness and loneliness, that I would have talked to a wall, to a piece of paper. You were there, and it talked out of me, towards you. You listened, calmly, and full of goodness; but I barely saw you. What did I tell you? I spoke of Nancy, I believe, of this first deep experience of my life, of my desire to have a child then, of my running away from the man, from me.

When I stopped talking, it seemed to me as though I came from another world. I felt not only me, and what I had lived through then; but I also felt your presence, you, the stranger to whom I had just opened myself up. You had no idea of these complications; you did not know that in front of you sat a human being whose inner life threatened to overflow from having been held back so long. You did not interpret my talking to you as such an overflow, but rather as the gift of my trust in you. This trust, you felt you could best respond to by using the familiar form "Du" when you spoke to me.[15]

A thrust of cold water could not have made me come back to myself more. An inner panic was seizing me, and there was only one thought present: to never again have to see this person to whom I had shown myself, without shame, just never again. I begged you not to use the "Du" again, to let me go home, quickly, right away. You did not understand anything. I still see the sad look with which you said goodbye in the subway. Then I am finally alone, with a horrible sadness that I had destroyed the beginning of this friendship, that I had humiliated myself.

In her next diary entry on March 17, 1940, Eva described how Otto had insisted on an explanation:

To this day, I do not understand what made you stay with me. I had been so ugly, so unfair and cruel toward you—anyone else would have left me alone. When I think of all my evasions, of the unsparing way with which I derided your efforts to get close to me again, I am deeply ashamed. Your answer to these humiliations? One evening after work I hear steps behind me, long steps, a hand is put onto my shoulder, and you confront me with such a straightforward seriousness that demanded openness, that for the first time I listen again, I respect you, and I am ashamed.

You demand an explanation for my behavior. And I tell you what it looks like inside me, explain the explosion of my "confidences" the other night; talk of my love for Rudi, that I don't want anything else, that, contrary to what you must have assumed, there is no love that ties me to you, perhaps a growing friendship, but that I was afraid that feelings of possessiveness would result from that, that you expect feelings from me that I cannot give. I feel that especially with this last statement I am hurting you badly—how much, I understood only much later. But you seem to understand some of what is going on inside me. Because, after everything has been said, you don't leave; you keep walking alongside me. I am happy that you are there.

For a long time we walk silently in the streets, the Boulevards, to the Rondpoint des Champs Élysées. We sit under the trees in the Champs-Élysées. Silence is broken; we talk of the magazine,[16] of ideas, and of people. Great, deep calm. You accompany me in the subway to the Porte St. Cloud. The warm handshake, the open regard when we say goodbye give courage and hope: now we can begin to build our friendship.

Eva's March 17, 1940, diary entry went on to describe how her "dead" feelings became "more alive" when she first visited Otto's workshop and when she went with him to Chevreuse, a village in a nature park south of Paris:

Friendship is all I want, but not more. And yet I cannot give very much; my feelings are dead; always the fear to do something which I cannot totally accept. You are infinitely good during that time, and I am grateful for your presence that does not ask for anything. In certain moments, more becomes alive in me: when I visit you the first time in your workshop, when you talk to me with love of the nature and life of wood. There I clearly feel that you are all one, that you stand by who you are and what you do. At that moment, I think I loved you. Or on our long evening walks, where we talked of our work, where you express without hesitation your respect for my work, where slowly, uncertainly, yet clearly, confidence floods into me, in my strength, in myself. Then also I loved you.

Yet, these were passing light points in me, not more. Then, two weeks later, our two-day excursion to Chevreuse. It was more that I let myself be persuaded than that I followed a desire of my own. Again the fear: In these two long days, in that night, will he ask more of me than I am willing to give? In the dormitory, together with many other people, our beds stand next to each other. I'd just as soon go home. There, while I am still debating, you already have your swim trunks on, are at the door, call to me to meet you at the pool, the path is right along the house. Relieved, infinitely grateful, I changed clothes. Then into the water, we eat, we walk along a path up the hill into the green starlit night—the great freedom, purity and stillness penetrate me solemnly. We don't talk much. Down in the dorm, it is dark, everything is asleep; quickly, unseen by anyone, I get into bed. And as I am there, happy, for the first time the pressure falls away from me. And across the space that separates our two beds, I hold out my hand to you: "Good night!" In me is deep joy that you feel when you give yourself away.

Eva ended her March 17, 1940, diary entry with her recollection of another harsh outburst she had directed at Otto in Juvisy, a village located about eleven miles southeast of Paris, followed by a night they spent together there when they missed the last train back to Paris:

Now I loved you, not always admittedly, yet I did. But your "Frau" I had not yet become. Often we went to Juvisy, bathed our bodies in light, air and water. Once again, I was horrible. Perhaps you wanted to be good to me, perhaps you wanted to kiss me. I burst out, asking whether you really had not known that I would never really be able to love you, that it would always be Rudi. Quietly you walked away. Realizing what I was in the process of destroying, I asked you to please come back: "Couldn't we quietly talk about it?" You came, sat down next to me.

We talked. It was a beautiful, warm summer night. The sun was about to set, tall green bushes, no other human beings anywhere. We talked, and warmer and broader it came to me. We did not talk any more, or you said gentle words, in Italian, and your good hands, and your mouth, said more than words could do. We had forgotten the time. Then there was no longer a train—we had to spend the night there.

Again fear, unjustified distrust perhaps, and then a deep, pure night, next to one another, not yet united in body, but a unity in spirit. Another six months, and we took the last step. That was less decisive, tied me to you less deeply, than the handshake in the night in Chevreuse, than the night hours we were awake together in Juvisy.

On April 23, 1940, while Otto was again away from Paris on a mission just weeks before the Nazis launched their blitzkrieg toward Paris, Eva wrote a diary entry expressing her longing that they could be together in peaceful times:

> A greeting only today; I am not relaxed enough to write. These last few weeks with all their upsetting events kept me so busy that there was no room and strength for quiet thought. Often in these warm, clear nights I wished you were near me; I would have wanted to sit with you, hand in hand, and look at the trees, sky, moon, and stars. But for that there would have to be peace. And you would have to be here. How far from reality are these two things!
>
> On the table next to me, there is a single rose in a glass. It has tender forms, and a sweet aroma. I am thinking of you.

## Parting at the train station in Paris on May 9, 1940

On May 9, 1940, Eva went with Otto to the train station in Paris as he departed to Luxembourg on a dangerous anti-Nazi mission involving Jef Rens. Eva recalled:

> In the morning of May 9, 1940, I accompanied him to the railroad station, and he left for Luxembourg where he was to meet some important friends. During that night, the night of May 9/10, the war against the West became a reality: the German troops invaded the Netherlands, Luxembourg, and France.

It was an unforgettable moment, the morning of May 9, 1940, at the train station in Paris. Eva and Otto said goodbye. They expected to see each other again in Paris when Otto was to return in a few days. Instead, they would not see each other again for a full year.

# PART IV.

## GERMAN INVASION ON MAY 9, 1940: EVA AND OTTO FORCED ON SEPARATE PATHS

*And all of a sudden we know where we are going, we see a stone on the road: Gurs!*

—EVA, MAY 1940

*The Germans are here. So that is the end, I thought, and I felt like a trapped animal.*

—OTTO, MAY 1940

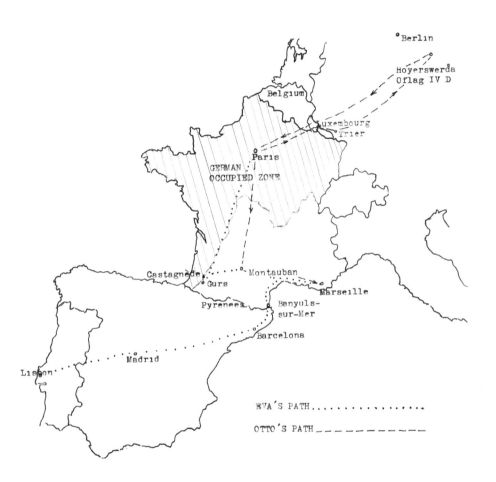

Paths taken by Eva and Otto from May 9 to October 3, 1940.

# 9. Eva's Internment at Vélodrome d'Hiver and Camp de Gurs

On May 10, 1940, Hitler's armies invaded Belgium, Luxembourg, and the Netherlands on their way to France. Eva's life was torn apart like the lives of millions of others. The impact on Eva, thirty years old at the time, was immediate.

On May 12, the French government decreed that men and women of German origin living in Paris must leave their homes and report to different locations for internment. As foreign citizens of an enemy power, these German exiles were suddenly regarded by the French as potential "enemy aliens" despite the fact that many of them, including Eva and other ISK members, had dedicated their lives to anti-Nazi resistance work in Paris for many years.

The order signed on May 12 by the military governor of Paris, General Pierre Hering, was posted on boards throughout Paris and published in the May 14 edition of the newspaper *Populaire*. The order required "German nationals . . . and foreigners of indeterminate nationality, but of German origin, residing in the department of Seine" to report to designated assembly points. Men between the ages of seventeen and fifty-five were ordered to report to the Stadium Buffalo on May 14, 1940. Single women and married women without children were ordered to report on May 15, 1940, to the Vélodrome d'Hiver (Vel' d'Hiv), a sports and cycle racing stadium in Paris on rue Nélaton near the Eiffel Tower.[1]

The order further stated:

Those who violate this order will be arrested. Foreigners referred to above may, at their own expense, take the train or any other

95

means of public transportation to arrive at the assigned assembly point. They should bring provisions for two days and the necessary utensils for food: forks, spoons, bottles, etc. Including provisions, they must not have more than 30 kilos of baggage.[2]

Eva began a new diary while she was interned in the Vel' d'Hiv, with entries directed to Otto. The first three entries are written in French and the remaining in German.[3] In her first entry on May 18, 1940, Eva described the hours in Paris before being separated from home and friends:

As I cannot write to you, I write for myself, with the still-alive hope that someday it will be for us. This life here is a completely new experience for me. The final hours before leaving were hard, very hard. The idea of never seeing you again, of never being able to live with you again, of not knowing anything about your fate, weighed on me terribly.

Then, there built in me the need to forget myself, or instead to find myself in music. A half hour before leaving, Stern was there, Hanna also, Nora. And I played. First the Mozart that you love so much. Strength, tenderness, beauty, all came alive in me; I saw you seated in the armchair, raising your head, looking at me with loving eyes, when I begin the last movement in great serenity. Then, Beethoven, and finally, the *Largo* from Handel. Tears fell, my heart hurt, hurt deeply. Afterward, saying farewell to Mousy, to Hanna, that feeling of separating from those with whom you are connected in so many ways, and where, after all, it is not really a separation of the things that tie you together.[4]

Eva in Paris in 1940 shortly before her internment by the French.

When she wrote this diary entry, Eva did not know that Otto had been captured and taken prisoner by Nazi soldiers as they swept through Luxembourg.

Eva was imprisoned in the Vel' d'Hiv along with several thousand other women for approximately a week.[5] The huge stadium was covered by a dome of glass and metal. Crowds of women arrived with their suitcases, waited in long lines, and were searched on entry. They slept on straw mats without pillows or covers. There was no privacy; one could not cry or cough without fear of disturbing others. Toilets were blocked without hope of repair. Planes circled overhead, and all felt vulnerable to attack by the advancing Nazis, knowing that any hit would result in a shower of metal and glass shards.[6]

The Vel' d'Hiv would later gain infamy when on July 16 and 17, 1942, the Vichy government collaborated with the Nazis to "round up" Jews in Paris (more than 13,000, including large numbers of women and children), hold them in deplorable conditions in the Vel' d'Hiv, and then deport them first to Drancy and other transit camps and thereafter by train to Auschwitz. The July 1942 roundup is now sometimes referred to as "the big roundup at the Vel' d'Hiv."[7]

The first roundup of German exiles, including Eva, at the Vel' d'Hiv on May 15, 1940, should never be mistaken for the 1942 roundup. But it should also not be forgotten. Those like Eva who had been actively resisting the Nazis were suddenly separated from their homes and loved ones, removed from their fight against Hitler, and deprived of their liberty as suspected Nazi collaborators.[8]

In her diary entry on May 18, Eva described her initial reaction to the mass internment and her fear about Otto's fate:

And thereafter in the enormous crowd of people, forming a line. The individual melts into the crowd—I have never before felt that with such intensity. Personal concerns recede to the bottom of your being, and you are completely filled with concerns of the world, of humanity. There remains something unreal in my reaction, a muffled noise in the ears, as if they were filled with cotton.

And it is at night that my own life once again begins to come back, like at other moments of the day, when a woman receives a letter from her husband. Then I would like to be completely alone, to allow myself to walk with myself, with you.

That moment passes, because the daily tasks press too much around me.

Where are you in this moment? All of this would be so much easier if I knew something about what has happened to you!

On the same day, Eva wrote a letter to Josef Luitpold Stern, the Austrian poet and émigré with whom Eva and Otto had become close friends in Paris.[9] Eva's relationship with Stern, who was twenty-four years older than Eva, was complex. They shared a love for poetry and nature and often exchanged poems they had written. Eva's friendship with Stern sustained her during difficult times, and they wrote letters to each other when they were apart. It is likely that Stern was in love with Eva; but as meaningful as the relationship was to her, it was without romantic feelings on her part, and Stern respected her commitment to Otto.

Stern was one of the group of friends with whom Eva spent the last half hour before she had to leave for the Vel' d'Hiv. As in her diary entry on that day, she wrote about the Vel' d'Hiv and the music she had played on the piano on her last evening at home in Paris:

> Centre de Rassemblement,
> Groupe 4, Vélodrome
> D'Hiv, Paris
> May 18, 1940, to Paris
>
> At this moment, I am sitting high up on the bleachers, next to me Nora, in front of us, down below, an ocean of sad colors; of noise, of movement. I am thinking of you. Nora told me that you had accompanied her to the Vel' d'Hiv, that you liked the music before I had to leave. To play those few pieces was a deep need for me. I know I played poorly; but I did it with all I had in me.

In a later diary entry written on May 31, 1940, Eva looked back on the previous three weeks, describing for Otto her feelings and experiences in the Vel' d'Hiv:

> Already three weeks of this life have passed since you have been far away. As each week passes, that distance becomes more difficult to endure. The only thing that soothes me is that my

companions don't seem to realize the great effort I must make to appear calm and stable.

Three, four stages in these three weeks. The first, your departure, the day after, the dreadful news of the invasion, and all the following week filled with anguish about your fate, about the fate of mankind. It is still filled with the warm feeling of standing together, of shared concerns, openly shared by all. Good not to be alone, to feel the concern and warmth of friends.

Then our departure, collapsing in the new community of the Vel' d'Hiv. The noise is so loud, human voices so numerous, that everything is lost in it—myself included—almost as if in an immense ocean. Sometimes, closing my eyes, I can imagine myself at the seaside, far, far from my surroundings.

Here, we are not allowed to take part in what is happening outside our community: we are denied access to newspapers. We still manage to find some, and, frightened, we share pieces of news that keep getting worse. Will we remain here in this trap when the worst comes? What are our options to act on our own in order to escape the mouse's fate as it is struck by the cat's paw? These are the questions we are trying to answer as best we can.

At least we are not without news from our friends in Paris: packages, letters arrive, people coming from outside telling us what is happening—we do not feel cut off from the rest of the world. Also, people are courteous with us; we make do with whatever little we have at our disposal. We have new experiences with people; for the most part they are nice enough, and do not lose their composure. There are others, naturally, and one has the impression that many could change quickly and become a kind of beast if it came to a dwindling supply of meat. But in the end, all is endurable, except the atmosphere of great political tension, and the sense of being powerlessly turned over to the enemy.

Suddenly, after a week, we are delivered the news of our departure to the south of France. Relief, accompanied by great amazement: the large majority did not realize the gravity of the situation and have an abrupt awakening. We are happy to leave.

The trip is beautiful, the night is tiring; but in the early morning, the country outside so calm, so peaceful—an old

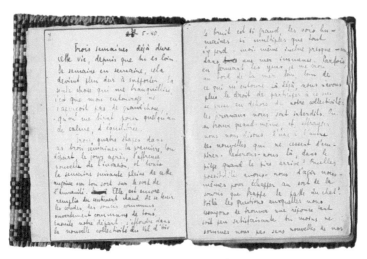

Pages in French from Eva's diary, May 31, 1940.

farmer who works the earth, children, trees, the fruit is growing—one can scarcely believe the reality of the war, in the fact
that we are prisoners.

No one knows where the train is taking us.

Eva soon learned that they were heading to Oloron, a small town near
Pau in the southwest of France at the foot of the Pyrenees. In her diary
entry on June 1, 1940, Eva continued her description of her trip south
on May 19 and her bitter discovery of their destination:

On the map that we were happy we took with us, we followed
the road, and little by little the sense became increasingly clear
that we were being sent to some part of the Pyrenees. Beautiful,
the first appearance of the high mountains—I could not prevent
the sadness from surging in me; the memory of our beautiful
and pure vacation is too alive.

Finally, after 19 hours of travel, a stop at the Oloron station. The large trucks await us. Standing, we leave, still to an
unknown destination. The village people are gathered: on the
street side they watch this procession of eternal wanderers. They
do not look at us with benevolence. Do they know the situation
causing their suffering does not emanate from our wrongdoing?
Do they have any idea of the tragic fate of the majority of those
they scorn?

And all of a sudden we know where we were going; we see on a stone on the road: Gurs! A bit further an immense row of barracks takes shape, behind the barbed wire, behind the soldiers with bayonets on their guns, and we feel we are going to join those who have already given their blood for liberty. You imagine, you whom I love so much, what sad bitterness fills me. We have never held back on our efforts. Our life was not easy. We have accepted everything, even the greatest risks. For this work, you are, I don't know where, you may not even be alive. And despite all of this we are prisoners.

Eva had been relieved at first to get out of the Vel' d'Hiv and away from the Germans—despite the uncertainty about where they were headed. But the atmosphere changed when they arrived in Oloron: "We were herded into trucks that were used to transport cattle, and there we were, all standing, pushed together. The people, the villagers, must have known we were Germans . . . they shook their fists, they were angry. They thought we were Nazis. . . . We knew about Gurs because of the Spanish internment. And then we felt fear, because this was where we were headed."[10]

Camp de Gurs, one of the largest internment camps in France, was built by the French government in April 1939 in the region of the Aquitaine in the Department of Pyrénées-Atlantiques. The original purpose of the camp was to intern political refugees and members of the International Brigade who fled Spain after the Spanish Civil War. In May 1940, the camp was used to intern these German women who had previously been held in the Vel' d'Hiv. Close to 10,000 women were interned in the camp at various points between May 1940 and October 1940.[11]

This camp would later gain its infamy in the period after October 1940 when the Nazis began sending Jews from the Baden region of Germany to the camp and continued to imprison Jews there until 1942, when the majority of them had either died from malnutrition or disease or were sent to concentration camps in occupied Poland, primarily Auschwitz.[12]

Camp de Gurs was a desolate and frightening sight. Covering sixty-nine acres, it was surrounded by a double barbed-wire fence inside of which stood 380 wooden barracks. A long narrow road ran through the center of the camp that was divided into thirteen *ilots* (islands), each one designated by one of the first thirteen letters of the alphabet. Each

View of Camp de Gurs from the camp water tower, 1940–1941. U.S. Holocaust Memorial Museum (03100). Courtesy of Hanna Meyer-Moses.

*ilot* held approximately 30 barracks and was separated from the other *ilots* by a wire fence.[13]

The barracks, measuring one hundred feet long by twenty feet wide, were crude. The walls and roofs were constructed of thin wooden planks that were lightly covered with tar paper, offering little protection from cold, rain, and wind. Each barrack held sixty women. Thin straw sacks were the only bedding, and the women slept parallel to one another in two rows of thirty, with the head of their sacks against the outside wall and a narrow aisle in the center of the barracks. Slanted roofs on the long sides made it difficult to stand except in this middle aisle. There was no furniture and barely enough room between each sack to put a small suitcase.[14]

The barbed wire surrounding the camp was not electrified, and there were no lookout towers. However, conditions in the camp were abysmal: no electricity, little sanitation or running water, and no plumbing. The toilets, consisting of small holes on an outside wooden platform six feet above the ground, were reached by climbing a crude ladder. Older women were at times unable to manage the steps. Food was minimal, mainly a few chickpeas in liquid and a small piece of bread each day. This time of year often brought relentless rain, creating mud that made it hard to walk and causing water to pound on the roof and seep into the barracks at night.[15]

Reconstructed barrack at Camp de Gurs Memorial.

## Daily life at Camp de Gurs

In Eva's diary entry on June 2, 1940, she wrote about her life at the camp and her sadness and worry about Otto:

> Sunday today. Clean dress, clean scarf. Much sun, clear, light blue sky, gentle, cool wind. New trucks with internees arrived this morning, with women and children. We ran to the barbed wire fence to wish them a warm welcome. Old women, with bundles, and black, heavy blankets; many children; then also women and girls of my generation, in city clothes. When we asked them where they came from, the answer: from Luxembourg! Otto! If so many were still able to get out, were you among them? My heart is heavy; the barbed wire separates me from these people who could perhaps have given me some clues about your fate.
>
> In the afternoon, I started to write, sitting on a tree stump next to a barrack. It has turned cooler. The excitement upon the arrival of the people from Luxembourg has subsided. Today the barracks don't look quite as gray as usual. The many colorful women and girls who sit around, or are lying down, or walking

by—all somewhat relaxed today—the sad ones stayed inside the barracks—these people almost give the impression of being carefree. But only to the one who does not look closely. Behind the laughter of even the very young girls is worry. And as far as the older ones are concerned—they cannot laugh any more.

And yet today is bearable. People don't burden themselves. The eye is happy about much and is consoled about the ugly barracks and the nasty toilets. . . . What a contrast to this gray, cold week that lies behind us. Never in my life, not in any night, did I experience rain as I did here on my hard straw sack. With cruel relentlessness, the raindrops hammer on the roof of the barrack, sometimes a brief calming, the raindrops softer; then it continues more strongly, unceasingly, the entire night. Sometimes I feel they hammer directly on my brain. For hours, the desire to be wiped out by this rain, to be washed away, forever. How is life going to continue? Without the possibility to participate in the shaping of events, without meaningful work. And without you. For the first time in my life, I am at a point where I no longer see a path ahead of me.

Before we knew each other, there was work. Even when I did it at that time without joy, the awareness of its necessity and the conviction of its possible success or partial success, were still there. Then you came, and my love for you came, and through you came my love for and joy in my work. When I imagined back then, and especially these last years and months, that you would have to disappear from my life, I had the comfort of finding in my work a place that was, to be sure, confining and a space for sadness, but still, in a certain way, a home.

I could also very well imagine a life with you alone, at some point in time, without the work. That would have been so nice. Now, both have been cut off. Can you understand that in dark hours I do not know how I should continue living? If we had a child—much would be easier. Of course, the responsibility of bringing a child into this world is enormous. Our child would have had to be raised by me *and* you. I cannot give it what strength lies in you.

It's getting cool now. I still want to read something, then in the evening walk through the avenue of barracks and try to see the mountains past the barbed wire and rejoice at their sight. I wonder if there is a letter for me in the mail tonight? Otto, my Otto, I am with you, one way or another.

During some of their time in Paris, and after Eva was interned in the Vel' d'Hiv and Camp de Gurs, she and Stern had developed a routine of writing to each other every Sunday. On May 26 approximately a week after she arrived at the Camp, Eva wrote to Stern:[16]

> Gurs, Basses Pyrénées, Ilot K
> Barrack 19, May 26, 1940
>
> The second Sunday in Camp. It is afternoon; after a mild, cool morning, the sun finally comes out, and shines indiscriminately on ugliness and beauty around me. I found a little place alongside our barrack, where I sit relatively peacefully, off and on touched by a light breeze, and where I can write to you—my Sunday joy. I often think of you. Mild is the sun . . . mild is the shade, beautiful the grass, soothing the chirping of the crickets in the meadow on the other side of the camp which we enjoy on a tiny plot of grass surrounded on three sides by barbed wire. Once in a while, I can even stretch out. Then I see the sky through the barbed wire. I also see mountains, very high mountains, covered with snow. Until your eyes reach the mountains, they have to pass over a never-ending row of barracks, their lines off and on broken by rails, on which tanned Spaniards transport lorries with buckets of refuse.
>
> I am only really happy about the mountains in the evenings when the grayness of our immediate surroundings disappears in the brilliant white and red of the mountaintops touched by the setting sun. In those moments the belief becomes more alive and stronger, belief in freedom that perhaps some day will emerge out of the shadow of barbarism and oppression.
>
> There are many good people here—much will have to be told about that later. In our barrack, there is a seventeen-year-old girl with her mother. She has become very attached to us; with warm eyes that want to learn and to know, she looks into the world. With a few friends to whom she also belongs, I discuss history every day, *History of the Third Republic*. And in the

course of this discussion a number of interesting problems are being touched upon. It is beautiful to see these alive, trusting, forward looking young people. The friendship of this young girl that is being offered without words or complications, makes me happy. Then I am reading Epictet [Epictetus] and Marc Aurel [Marcus Aurelius]—a small French edition. How we will be getting through this time in a physical sense, I don't know. Inside us, though, it will not be able to destroy anything.

In a diary entry on June 5, Eva expressed her increasing anxiety about the lack of communication from or about Otto:

My nerves now sometimes let me down. Also, much came during these days, one thing after another. Finally news from Paris; good, sympathetic words. They cause more sadness to burst out of me than to be left alone. Nothing about you. The mind begins to resign itself that you were not able to get out and clings to the small hope of hearing something from you before the war ends, and of seeing you again after the end of the war. Unfortunately, the mind is too alert to let this consoling hope grow, and too obtuse, of course, to let me wait yet again for the redemptive sign of life. And so the turmoil continues inside of me, finds no release or hardly any fulfilling work, and no true solitude. Hans [Jahn] is out, wife and child fell into the hands of the Nazis. So you weren't with him. Terrible, painful fate!

The evenings here are comforting. One can often get solitude, be left alone. The day before yesterday—I sat on the long side of the barrack, head all the way back and was alone with the sky and the stars, with a clear sky not fissured by the silhouettes of barracks or toilettes or barbed wire. One star is my companion through these clear evenings. It is bigger, shinier than the others, probably also longer there. Do our glances, our wishes cross each other upon this star? To look at it again and again calms me. It is soothing like your good hand that holds mine.

By June 5, 1940, the German armored divisions had advanced to the outskirts of Paris. Eva noted in her diary entry on that day that she had heard from Stern that he was also leaving Paris:

Yesterday evening a greeting from Stern. A few warm, deep words, expressive despite the poor French. He is also getting out of Paris, out of the silent attic room. One more stone towards loneliness.

Last night I was very sad, and did not feel well. Lying on the straw sack, heart pounding, tears. Suddenly, something like the fragrance of a meadow near me. There is Hannelore, the cheerful, bright, trusting young girl, holding in her hand a few sprigs of grass that she had picked from the tiny piece of lawn between the barbed wires. "Has the letter come that you had been waiting for? I wish so much it would come soon!" She puts her head on my chest, for one instant, then she is off, leaving the bouquet. Thank you, dear little Hannelore!

This human openness is the only thing that makes life here bearable. It is there in the letters, cards from Paris; from Gaby, Mousy, Hanna. . . .[17] They too sense it in our greetings. The new arrivals feel it when they see us alongside the barbed wire waving kindly to them. I will never forget the shine in Hilde's eyes as our glances met; the slight movement of the hand, the head. Just as we were moved by the silent greeting of the Spaniards when we arrived. Words are cheap compared to proof of common bond.

My Otto, I want to stay strong for you.

On June 9, 1940, Eva wrote a diary entry in which she again spoke intimately to Otto. Thoughts about Otto and Stern came to her mind as she was reading Rilke:

Last of all I come to you, you my dearest one; but on this entire quiet afternoon you were here. Every night you are in my dreams; early today when I was reading Rilke my thoughts were with you and Stern; yesterday after Hanna's nice, long letter, a sober report about what is known about you, I felt love and concern, I thought about you, somehow somewhat calmed; today after the account the woman from Luxembourg gave of her flight, a spark of hope glimmered. So you are always with me, even when I am externally and internally occupied with other things and people. . . .

Terrible is the feeling of being cut off from news, not to know what is happening on the outside. And yet, there were hours today where I could forget. Once a beautiful picture: the train of lorries rolls by on which the tanned Spaniards take away the refuse cans from the outhouses, loaded with innumerable children who are hanging on like ripe grapes on a vine, their faces radiant with happiness. How great to see these children who seem able to get joy out of the most pitiful circumstances, carefree, without any idea of what is ahead of them.

The mail just arrived, a touching card from Herta V. To feel friendship warms me. But there are constant alerts in Paris. Such is the unrest in which friends have to live, while in contrast we live in this artificially created seclusion, which only increases the inner unrest.

On the same day as this diary entry on June 9, Eva also wrote a letter to Stern, who by then had left Paris and was in Montauban in the south of France:

> Gurs, June 9, 1940
> To Montauban
>
> This morning, I have been reading in Rilke's Letters. A solemn hour. I was most moved by this passage: "Works of art are of an infinite loneliness and can be reached least of all with criticism. Only love can comprehend them and hold them and be just unto them."
>
> We live in painful isolation from everything that is going on around us; every newspaper, even if it is three days old, is something to cherish; every letter, every word out of Paris is confirmation that we have not yet been totally torn off from our friends.

For Eva, however, no letter from Otto arrived.

In her diary entry the following day, Eva described her feelings upon learning that Paris was being evacuated. She referred to the new moon that gave her comfort as it did throughout her life:

> The calm of last night quickly came to an end. Yesterday evening: Soup. Roll call. The beautiful red ball of the setting sun.

Rounds to the different barbed-wire fences. And news. Someone who got a paper reported that Paris had to be evacuated by Tuesday of all who were not officially detained there. What perspective this one piece of news brings out! And even more, the not knowing, the not knowing about your fate and about the fate of Europe bears down. With a heavy heart, I go to my straw sack. The sky with the finely etched lines of the new moon, and the stars so far away, had been peaceful and beautiful. I would much rather have stayed outside—sleep does not come easily these nights. And the narrow barrack with those many people whose pain speaks more clearly through their subconscious moans during their sleep than it does openly during the day—all this is like a nightmare.

Eva expressed her love for Otto in the face of this awful uncertainty:

What awaits us in the near future? The worst? Am I already at the end? If I am honest to myself: no. Certainly this vegetating without any meaningful work is not worthwhile. Your being far away and not knowing about your fate are so unbearable that I no longer want to live. I see no sense in it. But directly out of the *uncertainty* over your and our fate, I draw the strength again and again to continue to endure this life. If I *knew* that I would have to live for a long time in relatively good physical conditions without the possibility of a change, I would put an end to it.

But I don't know that. You might be living in Luxembourg, in Belgium, in France. If you are alive, you have it very hard. My belief is not yet shaken that I might ease your difficult life somewhat if I faithfully follow you everywhere in my thoughts with unwavering love. My thoughts don't find you in space. That is the difference from earlier difficult times. But often when I intensely think about you in the night, the certainty in me grows that you are still there, that you feel touched by me, soft and faithful just like earlier when your eyes hurt and I laid my hand on them.

I also don't know for certain that I will never be able to do meaningful work again. That is why despite everything I still want to live. And live in such a way that you, my Otto, you will find in me the woman and companion you lost. My faith in you, in your goodwill, in internally pulling through this difficult time without harm and getting the most out of it, and my faith in your willingness, yes even cheerfulness, to commit everything is infinite. Your faith in my ability to be able to bear the necessary consequences shall not be disappointed. On top of all your difficulties, worrying about me, about my inner limits need not be added.

My Otto, let me hold your hand, your strong, good hand that I love like you. I am very calmly beside you and my love flows in you like your strength does in me.

On June 14, Eva wrote to Stern from the camp:

> Gurs, June 14, 1940
> To Montauban
> This afternoon—it was a gray, rainy day, after heavy downpours at night—we invited a young girl who was passing by with her harmonica, to come into our barrack. She played passages from "Eine Kleine Nachtmusik," from the "Apassionata," she played songs by Brahms and Schubert. It was a giving of thanks, a greeting to all those to whom I feel close.

In a diary entry on June 16, Eva described her feelings as the Germans occupied Paris, knowing that as they moved south the women in the camp, especially those who had been active in anti-Nazi efforts, would be at extreme risk:

> That we continue to live in spite of everything that is coming down on us! The seizure of Paris is a matter of hours; trains with refugees are being bombed; the German troops are near Troyes, southeast of Paris; a final appeal to America. The heart ought to stop beating; for fractions of a second, all blood rushes to one's head—and then one continues to live, eat bread and pea soup. It's impossible to imagine what's happening at this moment; it can't be conceived intellectually, or felt physically. That I am sitting here in the sun, my body tanned and slim; that I see barbed wire, and green woods and mountains; that I study French history, learn English vocabulary; that I sleep, that I eat—it is incongruous that this is my life now. . . .

In this moment of impending frightful destruction, we have been tossed overboard, so much superfluous ballast. Is this going to be the end? We are still fighting, are making efforts to get out of this trap; but the atmosphere of psychological lack of oxygen in which we are forced to live becomes more and more suffocating, almost unbearable.

Eva now feared that she would never see Otto again:

Since Hanna, Mousy and Gaby are now out of Paris—and if they got out, how far?—one hardly dares to think about it—every hope to receive a message from you through them is now gone. And even if you now would try, could try, to establish contact—it would remain unanswered, because your letters would not have reached us. My Otto, I must hold my heart very tight when I try to imagine all the consequences of this.

When the others receive news from their husbands, often after several weeks of silence, it becomes difficult at times for me to be happy for them without reservations. I know that is bad, is petty, and I do not want to be bad and petty. But it is so very hard for me always to know nothing that sometimes without being able to help myself, a revulsion against other people's happiness joins my pain. I am ashamed of this, and know so well that you do not want me this way. How far distant I am from that greatness that in Stern's Psalms 10 so deeply moved me!

Eva described her complex relationship with Stern and reassured Otto of her faithfulness to him:

Stern—one of the few great friends in this time, this frenzy, his letters, the memory of our friendship. There everything, in every detail, is so beautiful and so without fault, even though it often brings sorrow to you, to him and to me. I am thankful for this friendship that is like a great gift and happy fortune. It could not have been allowed to develop differently between us, at that time, when he and you returned from the camp.[18] Guilt would have weighed down everything and suffocated the beauty. If I imagine today that during this horrible time you must also live with the feeling that I would not be there for you, I would

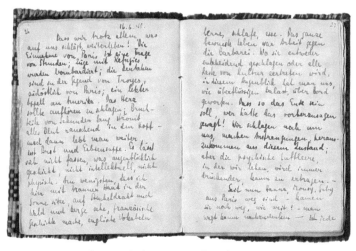

Pages in German from Eva's diary, June 16, 1940.

go crazy. And so, my Otto, you know that I am and remain faithfully by you. That in these boundaries of our exchange of letters and thoughts with Stern, I get such joy, will not, I am sure, upset you.

This was Eva's last diary entry while she was in Camp de Gurs. As France fell and the German troops moved south toward the area of the camp, Eva and her ISK colleagues had no choice but to take action:

> A number of us whose French was good, asked to be seen by the French Commander of the Camp. We explained to him that we had been active in the fight against the Nazis, and that, if we would be kept here for the German troops to pick us up, our lives would be in imminent danger. We convinced him, and a makeshift committee was set up to screen the internees, and to release those whose loyalty could be vouched for, and give them a slip of paper to that effect, with the precious stamp of the French authorities.[19]

Eva was given a Certificat de Liberation dated June 19, 1940, and was released from the camp.

The camp commander, Commandant Davergne, decided to burn the camp's records on June 24, five days after Eva and her group were

Eva's Certificat de Libération from Camp de Gurs, June 19, 1940.

liberated and before the Germans arrived and the camp was turned over to the complicit Vichy government.[20] The destruction of these records was likely intended to protect those women, like Eva and her group, who were in danger of being identified by the Nazis as having actively opposed Hitler. Unfortunately, the loss of these records eliminated the possibility of creating a detailed historical account of their internment. There are few contemporaneous documents from this period in the history of Camp de Gurs (apart from Eva's diary), and only a handful of accounts have been published.[21]

The French have labeled this internment of German women in Camp de Gurs the "Période des 'indésirables' (été 1940)" (Period of the "Undesirables" [Summer 1940]).[22] Lilo Peterson, who was interned in the camp during this period, commented on the painful irony of using the label "undesirables" to describe these German women in exile who had fought for years against the Nazis:

> "Undesirables?" Why is this term for that period given to us? Is this the final remembrance of us as refugees in the country of human rights—that we are undesirable?
>
> Among the internees at Gurs was a large number of women of the German Resistance. . . . One talks little about the German Resistance. . . . These women, refugees in France, were imprisoned at Gurs by the same country that had given them refuge

cards, and fought against France's real enemy. Some escaped the Gestapo by the burning of Camp records and were liberated from Gurs during the summer. Others confronted, as their fellow prisoners, hunger, vermin, sickness. Some died and rest in the clay.

They do not exist in the memory of the camp. Not as refugees, nor as resisters. Among all the women victims of the arbitrariness of the war, these are the most forgotten still, these are the ones who took measure of the Nazi danger and resisted, actively challenged Hitler as refugees since 1933, against an opposition active and dangerous, with their lives in peril. They published and distributed into Germany newspapers and other anti-Nazi material; organized and led demonstrations; infiltrated Germany, returning documents and sabotaging German propaganda; brought assistance to those in their networks and collaborated in developing political platforms. They put in place channels of escape and meeting, helping to hide those in danger; creating false documents. . . . Finally, they also tried to educate foreign public opinion . . . in particular about the ever-growing persecution of the Jews.[23]

Eva and her small group had gained freedom from internment in Camp de Gurs and were spared the immediate danger of being turned over to the German troops approaching the camp. But they now feared that they would not find shelter in time. Many villages in southern France had opened their doors to French refugees from Paris and other cities in the north who were escaping the German occupation. But would local French villagers believe that these *German* women were in grave danger because they had actively resisted the Nazis, and would the villagers provide refuge for these women?

# 10. Eva's Refuge in Castagnède, Montauban, and Marseille

Liberated from Camp de Gurs, Eva and her small group found themselves standing together on the country road just outside the barbed wire "before any thinking and planning could take place." They were nineteen women and three children, friends and colleagues through their anti-Nazi activities. They shared an urgent objective:

> We pooled what little money we still had, and started walking. Where to? How, by what means of transportation? We had no idea, just knew that we had to get away from the approaching German troops, had to get shelter somewhere with French people.[1]

The women walked to Oloron, the town where six weeks earlier they had arrived with other women from the Vel' d'Hiv and had been transferred from trains to trucks destined for Camp de Gurs. No public transportation was operating at that time. But, Eva later noted, "Good fortune was with us."

> [W]e found a bus driver who had a bus with some gasoline, and he was willing to take us inland a little ways. So he took us, and drove us from village to village, only to be told that all the shelter facilities were filled with French refugees from northern France, since Paris and the north had been evacuated.
>
> His gasoline gauge was getting low; he had to keep enough gas to get back. So, he decided to leave the main road and get into more isolated country where our chances might be better.

And there it was: a peaceful little hamlet, and the mayor running towards the bus and greeting "his" refugees for whom they
had prepared, and who had come from Paris.

Eva and her small group were relieved to find this village that appeared eager to accept them. But they faced another critical hurdle: the
mayor did not know that his refugees were of German origin:

We thanked our driver with all our hearts, and followed the
mayor to the hall that had been made ready with clean straw
sacks, and some other facilities. It was late in the afternoon, the
sun was about to set; we were very tired, and so glad and grateful. Then—I will never forget this—a loud roar of war planes
overhead, and our mayor, with flying coat tails, running for
shelter, crying out: "Oh, les Boches, les Boches!" [derogatory
name for Germans]. The planes flew on, we were alone, went to
our straw sacks, did not say much, but wondered what would
happen tomorrow morning when we would have to register,
and when the mayor would realize that we too were, at least
technically, "Boches."

Again, our good French helped: one other girl, Marianne,
a social worker, and I went to see the mayor in the morning
and explained our situation. He was totally taken aback—he
had prepared for, and expected, French refugees from Paris;
and instead, we had come. Finally, he decided to trust us, and
after a little while, shaking his head over this strange group of
women—teacher, social worker, lawyer, writer, a grandmother
with a broken leg, three children—he accepted us, and told
us that he would be pleased and proud to have us stay as "his"
refugees. We registered, and were safe.

For Eva and the other women who had experienced the confinement
and squalor of Camp de Gurs, the following days in the village were a
"brief period of unreal peacefulness, and even a feeling of belonging."

The people in the village were very poor; we helped in the fields,
we talked, we liked each other. At the Memorial Service for the

war victims, after the Armistice Treaty was signed, we could participate in the sad ceremony; we were with them; they and we felt that we had lost as much or more than they had.

But Eva continued to have a sense of foreboding about what lay ahead. On June 23, 1940, several days after her arrival in the village, she wrote to Stern who was then in Montauban:

> We found a very friendly acceptance in a small beautiful village, where we stay in a kind of hostel, and do our own cooking. What will happen later on, is completely shrouded in fog. If you and your friends consider solutions for the future, please think of us also.[2]

And in a diary entry, written in the village the next day, Eva lamented: "A new leg of the journey—how close before the last? The events press upon each other so that one can hardly comprehend them. This is not how I imagined freedom—connected to a universally hopeless situation."

The peaceful refuge in the village did not last. After about a week, the mayor awakened the women with bad news:

> Our mayor was in the habit of listening to the British radio, and he told us the war news. One morning, very early—we were all still asleep—he tapped at our window; two of us went out, and he told us that they had just announced the definitive lines of demarcation for the German occupied zone; his little village fell within this zone, and this day, at noon, the German occupation troops would come in, and he felt he had to tell us that from that moment on, he could no longer protect us.

The armistice between France and Germany had just been signed on June 22, 1940, establishing an "occupied zone" in northern and western France (including all ports on the English Channel and the Atlantic Ocean), to be occupied and governed by the Nazis, and an "unoccupied zone" in southern France that was to be governed by the French under the Vichy government. Among the provisions of the armistice was the notorious Article 19 that required the French government to "surrender on demand" to the Nazis any persons of German origin on French territory. This was a direct and immediate threat to the lives of Eva, Otto, and other ISK members of German origin who had been working against the Nazis in France. They were now vulnerable not only to the Nazis but also to any French citizen who might choose to collaborate with the Nazis and turn them in. Once again, Eva and her small group faced imminent danger. But their spirits were lifted by the farewell they received from the villagers:

> So we packed up again and left. Someone had given us an old baby carriage for our grandmother with the broken leg—this time, we knew we would have to walk until we reached shelter in the zone to be unoccupied—and the village people were standing in front of their homes, wiping tears with their aprons or skirts, one or the other coming forward with a few eggs, half a bottle of milk—a silent, moving offering and sharing.

The experience of being sheltered in this village with such acceptance and kindness had a powerful and lasting impact on Eva and others in her group. These highly endangered women, whose years of demanding anti-Nazi work had failed, gained renewed hope from the humble and generous human spirit they encountered in this small village. Eva later reflected:

> If I have any regrets about things not done in my lifetime, it is that I was never able to find that little village again, and give thanks to the people, or to their children or grandchildren, who had been so unbelievably good to us. I wrote a good deal in my diary during those times, but, probably for a good reason (perhaps not to endanger them) I never mentioned the name of the village, and it has completely slipped my mind.

This feeling of regret by Eva led us—her children and the authors of this book—to take a journey in 2011 in which we were able to identify this village as Castagnède and convey Eva's gratitude to one of its inhabitants, an elderly woman who had witnessed and recalled these events in 1940 when she was seven years old.[3]

## Temporary stay in Escou

Again this group of women urgently needed to find shelter. They found someone with a small truck who was willing to take them to Escou, a small village in the unoccupied zone about thirty-five miles southeast of the village that had first given them refuge. As Eva recalled, Escou was "crowded with refugees. It was not friendly, but we were safe. We could not do much—often we sat by the river, washing our clothes." On June 27, Eva wrote to Stern in Montauban:

> We had to move on, because yesterday morning we were told in our village that it would from now on be part of the occupied zone. So we landed here, as a very temporary stopover. Today I sent you a telegram to ask if there would be room for us where you are.
>
> A stay for any length of time here is impossible. It has gotten totally dark now—in the abandoned house where we found shelter; there is no lighting, and I can't see anything any more. This letter should leave tonight.[4]

While in Escou on June 30, Eva wrote an entry in her diary, again directing her thoughts and feelings to Otto:

> For the first time in weeks I walked alone yesterday for two hours through the fields. After a sad, restless day I walked through the green fields, framed on one side by the rugged mountains against the setting sun. Deep peace over the land, and beauty. Thoughts unravel, present themselves one after the other without understanding. Dark is the future in every respect, and especially when I add that enormous difficulties stand in the way of your return. Will life be bearable? In the long term, I don't know, I also cannot imagine. But in the immediate future, I believe that even against the worst possibilities, which I absolutely must consider, I am prepared.
>
> Now we sit here and wait with many good people, in an empty house, on straw, in the beautiful countryside. The days are very hot, very long; the evenings peaceful and nice. But

the waiting is agonizing, waiting for the paper, for the mail, for news. And even when news comes that we can move on to M [Montauban], perhaps, what then! Life has become joyless.

As Eva waited in Escou for an answer from Stern, she and the other women in her group spent time walking outside the village, hoping to come across other refugees who might have information that could be useful to them. On July 1, five days after writing to Stern to ask about room for her group in Montauban, Eva received an affirmative response from him by telegram. She immediately wrote back: "How great was our joy when we got your telegram this morning, in answer to ours. We will try to come as soon as possible. Do you know that we are 19 adults (women) and 3 children?"[5]

Eva began to work with the others on plans to get to Montauban. Public transportation had still not been reinstated, and Montauban was over 150 miles northeast of Escou. The group walked from Escou to Oloron (approximately 4 miles), hoping there would soon be a train to Montauban. They were able to take the first train out of Oloron to Montauban. In a telegram to Stern from Oloron on July 7, Eva wrote "We are leaving for Montauban by train today at 17 o'clock."[6]

## Two months of refuge and work in Montauban

Eva and her small group were among thousands who found refuge in Montauban, a small city north of Toulouse. The socialist mayor of Montauban at the time, Marcel Guerret, opened the doors of his city to refugees from many areas of Europe. Montauban already had a long history of offering refuge to politically oppressed populations, and it holds an important place in the history of the resistance in World War II.[7]

Eva's brother Erich had also arrived in Montauban in June 1940 after being interned by the French government as a German "enemy alien" in a men's camp in Orléans. When the German armies neared his internment camp, Erich and some of the other anti-Nazis of German origin were released by the French. He was able, with great hardship, to get to Montauban.[8] Erich later described how "after long weeks of separate wandering, men and women exiles find themselves reunited in the beautiful small town of Montauban in the south of France."[9]

He recalled that "parts of this wonderful old Huguenot settlement date back to the eleventh century" and added that "normally some twenty to thirty thousand people live in the lovely old houses of this town. Suddenly the population swells to eighty thousand with the arrival of refugees from northern France, Belgium and Holland, as well as political activists from all manner of countries. Spaniards, Austrians, Poles, Italians, Russian socialists who had to leave their homes after the 1917 revolution, and Germans."

With gratitude and admiration, Erich described how the people in Montauban made room for this flood of refugees: "They offer accommodation and household goods. Hardly a soul grumbles about the refugees. Those foreigners who have crowded into their living space and who are now competing for the rapidly shrinking supplies of food. What an example." He noted that "never during our weeks in Montauban did we hear nationalistic or chauvinistic sentiments expressed. There was no hate. . . . Dire need, distress and human misery increased as millions of people were forcibly uprooted by the events of war. . . . [T]here arose a spirit of helpfulness and solidarity."[10]

Eva and her group of women arrived in Montauban on July 7, 1940. It was the first time since their internment in the Vel' d'Hiv two months earlier that they were able to reunite with their other ISK colleagues in a place that gave them at least a temporary sense of freedom from fear of capture by the Nazis. Eva later recalled the warm greeting they received from Stern at the train station in Montauban:

> Stern met the train with a beautiful peach, as an offering of thanks, and he just marveled at how we looked after all this ordeal we'd been through. . . . We all lost weight. . . . We got tanned because of the sun . . . and we were slim. I remember how Stern said how beautiful I looked when we arrived in Montauban.[11]

In a letter Eva wrote several months later to Willi Eichler, the leader of her ISK group, she described this reunion with her ISK colleagues in Montauban:[12]

> There, in Montauban, gradually all met, or gave word of their whereabouts. The men had had very strenuous flights behind

them; for instance, my brother and others walked on foot for 200 kilometers across France, the Germans behind them; at times there were bombs, at times they crossed the German lines, carrying the little baggage they had on their back (towards the end they were so exhausted that they had to throw away part of those belongings). But all were in good spirits, somewhat emaciated, but upright and in a good frame of mind.

Then Jeanne [Johanna Bertholet], Gaby [Cordier], Mousy [Hélène Perret] and a French friend arrived there, after having fled Paris and occupied France on their bikes. They also were very courageous and beautiful.

Eva later described their crowded lodgings in Montauban: "They had given us a small apartment. There were a lot of us there. I think we got some ration cards, which we had to share among many of us. I remember it was always noisy, all these people—and at night, we didn't have lights, and I wrote until my eyes could hardly see anything."[13] Eva's sister-in-law, Herta, recalled that their apartment was in "an old abandoned house, which was said to have once been a brothel. . . . Twenty people in two small rooms, sleeping on the floor, one next to the other."[14]

Eva remained in Montauban for approximately two months. On July 23, 1940, she returned to her diary for the first time since the June 30 entry she had written in Escou. She reflected on her parting with Otto in Paris in early May and the German invasion the following day:

On the first quiet evening here after a month, I just read through these lines again, alone. Years seem to have gone by since that last afternoon when we sat in the Tuileries, boarded the metro at night in the dark city, went into our quiet parlor, packed your things. The next morning, I brought you to the station. As we parted, nothing in me said that it would be for *this* parting. Then as I lay awake in bed the next morning, the horrible news came, something like a numbness spread throughout me like a cold, wet towel was laid heavily on me. Basically, this inner state has, still today, not subsided. What has happened in the meantime has not resolved anything.

Eva then expressed her despair over the apparent futility of their years of anti-Nazi political work in light of recent events, noting that the stresses of her life "make it hard to carry any joy." She confirmed that she knew the struggle was necessary but confessed to Otto, "I don't believe in its success and I hardly believe in its significance, when measured against what I actually want in life." She explained that for a long time, she could express the significance of her work "only in a negative sense"—that its success was not "impossible or precluded by natural law." She lamented that her pessimistic view had been "terribly confirmed through recent events." But she felt the need to continue the struggle even in such dire circumstances: "I still deem it to be right. But it offers no courage."

Eva described the painful contrast between the beauty of Montauban and the oppressive responsibilities of her work:

> I cannot warm up to the city here. Beautiful were the first few days finding again many believed to be lost; beautiful were the wide-open views of river, bridge and fields. But too painfully present is the contradiction between this peaceful tranquility and the reality of the world in which we live. Internally my gaze turns away from the tranquil fields—their sight pains me.
>
> Today I yearn for them again, because from morning until late into the night people and their concerns surround me, and because my life is filled to bursting with work, the usefulness of which I question, but which I do because I feel obligated to do. The work is a burden, for I cannot always do it accompanied by the warm trust of friends.
>
> Obstructions, differences of opinion, and hard, not always fair, decisions make life more difficult—as does the awareness of great responsibility, of the horrendous consequences of avoidable mistakes, and of the clear recognition of one's own inadequacy.

At the end of this diary entry, Eva described an experience that took her away momentarily from the stresses of her work in Montauban. Ultimately, her thoughts turned to a memory of a time with Otto that provided a sliver of hope:

Our bike tour on Sunday was nice after these noisy days. Joy about overcoming fear; about the wind that is powerfully drawn into the lungs; about the peaceful fields. . . . My fear sometimes constricts my throat. But for fear, too, I often don't have time and that is good.

In the quiet hours, however, you are with me. I think about the note that you scribbled before you went to the internment camp about a year ago now: "I so much still want to live with you, my E." Me too. If nothing remains for me of you, no letter, no picture other than the two small images that stood before me when you were away, that memory will stay with me. And a tiny hope for the future.

Eva's work with the ISK in Montauban focused on the urgent need to procure visas for ISK members who were in grave danger if they were not able to escape from Europe. This danger was real. What they had left behind in their apartments in Paris would now be fatal evidence to the Nazi occupiers. As Eva later explained in a letter to ISK leader Willi Eichler,

Discussions and conferences about the future brought agreement about the need to prepare emigration speedily. There was alarming news from the camps: German Commissions also in the unoccupied territory who had accurate knowledge of the personal files (from the Paris police), and also anticipation of general new internment. There was no possibility of contact with Paris, so that we did not know what had happened with the apartments; apartments had been prepared to prove to the French our loyalty in the fight against Hitler, and now it was not the French but Himmler who ruled in Paris.

So we sent lists to our friends in America, in order of priority, where we did not only consider the degree in which they were endangered, but also the question who would be especially competent for work to come. We renewed contact, insofar as they did not already exist, with friendly refugee groups (for instance the official leadership of the German Social Democratic Party). And we also decided that our Swiss friends [Bertholets] should return, in order to help more actively with the preparation for emigration from there.

In France we were more and more handicapped. Even the shortest trip was forbidden, and travel permits were issued only in exceptional cases and with help of protection. So one either had to stay put and could not go and see anyone, or one had to accept the risk of unauthorized travel (danger of new internment). Also, there was very sharp censorship within France; and all overseas mail is gathered in Bordeaux, that means it goes through German controls—at least one has to expect that.[15]


## A postcard from "Paul Bois": Otto is alive

During this period of intense work in Montauban, Eva received her first sign that Otto was still alive. During their time together in Paris when Otto was doing his dangerous resistance and sabotage work, Eva, Otto, and their group of ISK colleagues had made a plan to be used if Otto fell into the hands of the Nazis. Otto would write to a mutual friend, Yvonne Oullion, if he wanted to reach Eva but could not write directly to her.

On August 3, 1940, Eva received a postcard via Yvonne, who by then was living in Castres near Montauban. The sender was Otto using the pseudonym "Paul Bois." The card was stamped "Oflag IV D [abbreviation of "Offizierslager" (Officer's Camp) IV D]." Handwritten on the postcard were the following words (translated from French):

May 26, 1940
My dear Yvonne—
    As you see, I am a prisoner. Don't worry, I am in good health and confident despite everything.
    I still don't know for certain where I will be taken, you can write to me when I am able to give you an address.
    My best wishes to Paulette, Pierre and the other friends.
Affectionately,
Paul

Postcard sent by Otto to ISK colleague in Paris from Nazi prisoner-of-war camp, using the false identity "Paul Bois."

Eva immediately recognized Otto's handwriting. That night, she wrote in her diary:

> Perhaps all was not in vain. You live. I hold the postcard with your writing in my hand, read it, again and again, and am deeply grateful. Your handwriting has not changed; it is calm and sure. I would like to have a small spot for myself now, where I am not surrounded by constant worries, noise of others. I would also like to look further into your, our fate. I am very tired. But you are there. And tonight, my thoughts can come to you.

In her next diary entry on August 10, Eva yearned to write to Otto but was unable to find the necessary quiet time:

That a part of this precious, silent evening—completely alone in the house, after a long swim in the river—must be spent with yearning is a shame. I had wanted to write to you, here, and by mail; there is much to tell. But already the door is opened, the room is full, there is talk of matches, salad, tomatoes, bread—interruption. Now everyone has gone to rest and I, myself, very tired, would like so much to be with you. But the contact is gone. Outside a clock strikes eleven. Many loud people move through the streets, the narrow streets, where their steps and voices echo urgently. This town is never quiet; never have I experienced it quiet.

## The painful decision for Eva to marry Stern in order to obtain a U.S. visa

While Eva was in Montauban, a decision was made by her ISK colleagues that she should seek an early visa to escape to the United States. Because of Eva's language ability and the competence she had shown with her work in Paris, she was considered the person most capable of working effectively in America to obtain emergency U.S. visas for them and other endangered refugees. Eva's *Pflichtgefühl* (sense of duty) compelled her to agree.

Eva and her ISK colleagues also decided that she would need to marry Stern in order to obtain a U.S. visa. Stern had already obtained a U.S. visa; and if Eva were married to him, she would be eligible for a visa as his wife. In Eva's diary entry on August 11, she described the impact of this decision. She planned to leave this diary with her brother before she departed, and she hoped that Otto would someday read her explanation.

I have a very heavy heart and I wish you were with me—here in this fresh, green silence surrounded by high, old trees. Below, water trickles. Occasionally distant, soft human voices from the sun-cast silhouettes that walk over the narrow wooden bridge in the garden. I've known for a week already that you are alive; and yet I have hardly been able to allow this feeling to calmly, thankfully spread through me. This uncertainty, which goes back two and a half months, is too heavy; I am so inhibited when I have to write you a strange card with a pseudonym. And too uncertain of what might happen here if you come back and I am no longer here.

The decision to go away with St. [Stern] is hard for me in another unexplainable way. If you were in some area close enough for me to reach you, I could talk through with you calmly the whole complicated situation. I am convinced that my worries would resolve themselves. A consensus is impossible: I must decide alone for the both of us, for the three of us, for work. So at least allow me calmly to explain to you in these pages, which you will read before you see me again, how it appears to me.

Several things are getting mixed up: the formal and the substantive aspects of the matter. Formally: I should certainly get away from here soon for many reasons, including, which should not be omitted, making the departure of those staying behind easier. Judging by the state of things today, that is better to accomplish from there [America] than from here. If this final reason didn't exist I could relatively calmly and safely stay here in a quiet place with friends and wait for you. But simply living and waiting is not enough for our life—about that we have been in agreement for a long time. Thus the need to get away.

The opportunity to leave, perhaps very soon, offered itself through my connection with St. [Stern]. Without it, my chances don't look good. It appears I am obligated not to turn down the offer. That means: that I will not wait here for you; that you will come to see me with joy in your heart and you will hear that I am gone, and gone with St. [Stern]—This also means that a number of people, whose opinions I value, will completely misunderstand me, us. Ultimately this means that the possibility for the two of us to live together somewhere peacefully and openly will become enormously complicated.

Eva then expressed her concern that Otto might not fully understand the reasons for her decision to marry Stern:

Must we accept all this? As of yet, I don't know. Moreover, what I have just enumerated is not quite everything. Connected with it is also the fact that I am not going away with just anyone, but rather with St. [Stern]. Is it conceivable that this fact, provided I take up the offer, would appear to you in another light? I don't know. I only know that it will very much depend on what you went through during the months of our separation.

I can only wish, fervently wish, that your faith in me will remain unshaken, that you will not have forgotten our conversation from back then before you went away. If something serious were to befall you, you had said that you would be comforted for me since I would, I should, go to St. [Stern]. And I responded to you precisely then, I would stay by you even more firmly, bound with you; you should never forget that you are at home with me, that if things are going poorly for you, my concentration on you constitutes for me an inner necessity, because it is the only possibility for me to participate in your story.

You sensed, Otto, that I was serious with what I said to you. Do you still feel today that nothing has changed? If I were certain about that, if I could give you this certainty, then I would go down the hard road much more easily.

In a brief diary entry on August 12, 1940, Eva described her writing to Otto in her diary the preceding day as a "conversation." She seemed comforted by it:

Tonight I thought long about our conversation, then slept peacefully. The silent afternoon had already resolved much. The night hours then on the bridge after the difficult conversation left me cheerful and relaxed. I believe we will succeed, within these constraints, in remaining so close to one another. I am very grateful.

## Eva's receipt of her own U.S. visa

Against all odds, Eva was able to obtain her own U.S. visa on September 16, 1940. This was made possible only because of an extraordinary process that had been initiated in the United States by the Jewish Labor Committee and the American Federation of Labor. That process allowed for the expedited issuance of emergency temporary visas to lists of political refugees whose lives were imminently threatened by Hitler following the German invasion of France in May 1940. Eva's name was one of the last to be added to these lists.[16]

In terms of Eva's immediate personal future, this precious visa meant that she did not need to marry Stern. But she still felt the need to say more to Otto about the fact that she had been willing to marry Stern. In a diary entry on September 1, Eva wrote:

> The difficult explanation—hard for you, hard for me—about why I had decided to go away with Stern is now without any particular purpose. I will certainly have to go, but alone and with friends, and not in the close, formally binding, combination with him. That is a good thing, good for us three. It surely would have gone well after the difficult shock from this decision and after clarification and calmness had entered the picture. Certainly not without burden. But also with much good. It is better so. The closeness is preserved. But its borders are discernable in every breath of air, and account for the beauty of our relationship.
>
> St. [Stern] is very close to me, you know it. Spiritually, I feel ever more strongly a deep connection. When I read his words, it is as if finally I had expressed what I feel, as it corresponds to the contents of my feelings. Beautiful were many hours spent together here: Once in the meadow under the peach trees; often in the evenings on the bank of the softly murmuring spring; later on the arched bridge, when at night we looked at stars and the rising moon and the city that had become still. Beautiful was the short path through the night on the day that the first message came from you.
>
> You will later read letters about the in-between station, Montauban; between not yet concluded past, to which one is connected by all fibers, and future, still so hazy that it is hardly possible to grasp it as negative. And you will retroactively experience with us the melancholic beauty of these hours and days.

In this same diary entry on September 1, Eva wanted Otto to understand her feelings about Gaby Cordier, who had worked with Eva and Otto in Paris and, more recently, with Eva in Montauban. Apparently, Gaby and Otto had experienced a relationship in Paris that had strained Eva's relationship with Gaby:

> My relationship with Gaby makes me happy at times in and of itself, and because I know how deeply you will be pleased about our friendship. There is nothing, no trace of bitterness left behind; I enjoy her way of mastering things. I take part in her life; she takes part in mine too. If you came back today—there would be an open, comfortable relationship between the three of us without tension. Where she is so close to me now, how well I understand what she brought close to you at that time! Perhaps I have just become more advanced and mature during these difficult months.

In the last part of this diary entry, Eva referred to cards she had sent to Otto—cards that she had to send under Yvonne's name rather than her own:

> The cards for you, they weigh on me. I cannot write freely, because I do not know whether anything reaches you or how it reaches you. Here in these pages I am so much more connected to you because I speak to you as if you were with me; in reality it would be much more important that you felt the authenticity of my being connected to you in the little that might reach you today. But until at least one answer arrives from you, I believe that I cannot write any differently. Perhaps you sense my closeness from my handwriting, from the fact that I am there. And my sadness, which I can prove to you no other way.

On September 3, 1940, two days after this entry and shortly before she was to leave for Marseille, Eva received dismaying news. A Red Cross package she had mailed to Otto—addressed to him as "Paul Bois" with Yvonne as sender—was sent back to Yvonne with a small handwritten note in French and German: "Return to Sender."

In a diary entry on September 3, 1940, Eva wrote:

> A mountain of sadness presses on my heart. Nothing has reached you, and you are today in greater uncertainly about my fate than

I am about yours. And if I try to speculate what all the reasons for the "addressee not found" note could be, I become dizzy. Do I really have to leave here, in this uncertainty that tears me apart? I do not know, cannot say anything else to you, only that I am terribly, hopelessly sad.

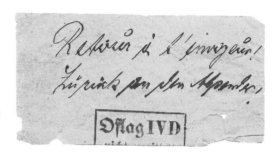

Note on Red Cross package returned from Nazi prison camp.

Eva now had to leave Europe and Otto—to move across an ocean to a strange new continent. It is difficult to imagine how she could survive this emotionally. After four months of separation from Otto, the uncertainty about his fate, and the hope she felt when she first received his postcard, she would need to carry the bitter uncertainty of "addressee not found." And she would bear the burden of helping to rescue her ISK colleagues who were left behind. Her decision was based on her ISK-driven commitment to the needs of others; it was a decision made with the knowledge that she would likely never again see the man she loved. Of all the choices that Eva had been forced to make between her personal desires and the duty to others, this was the most painful.

Eva left Montauban by train for Marseille on the night of September 11, 1940, and arrived the next morning. She was picked up at the station by her brother Erich, who was then working in Marseille with Varian Fry and the Emergency Rescue Committee.[17] After several attempts over the weekend to get her visa at the office of the American consulate, Eva obtained it on Monday, September 16, 1940. In her diary entry on September 15, she described her feelings about her visits to the American consulate in Marseille:

The green branch from the garden of the American consulate—It is beautiful. But everything else is oppressive, difficult. I cannot get used to the thought of going away, cannot get rid

of the feeling that I can do valuable work here and if I do not
do it, then I leave you and our friends in the lurch. If it were
only about me, I would not go away, certainly not.

The drive along the sea today was wonderfully beautiful;
the wide, open view, the single seagull, gray against the gray sky.

In a diary entry on September 28, she looked back and sketched briefly
her experience in Marseille:

Sunday [September 15]: in the morning a walk through the
harbor area, a marvelous ride in the streetcar along the ocean, a
swim in the ocean, a film at night (much too long), interesting,
but not moving. . . . Monday, the 16th, I get my visa, Tuesday
the Portuguese travel visa. . . . Decide to leave Thursday night,
the 19th. A very painful farewell.

In a letter to ISK leader Willi Eichler, Eva later reported in more
detail on the perils of escaping from France. She also described the difficulties faced by the two other ISK colleagues who had been granted
U.S. visas, Willi Rieloff and Hans Jahn, and the menacing uncertainties
faced by those seeking to escape from southern France:

Willi [Rieloff] was still in [French internment] camp, and had
to be helped to get out. Kramer [Hans Jahn] and I went immediately to Marseille after a temporary halt of the issuance of
visas, and picked up our papers.

That did not work without difficulties. Before one could
obtain the visa, one had to furnish proof of being well known
(proof of being "famous" or a "Labor Leader"). The Spanish
transit visa could be obtained only with great difficulties; one
had to get in line at one o'clock in the morning, and yet often
one did not get in at 9 a.m.

We were in Marseille without a permit since we had trav-
elled there without permission; often there were razzias [raids]
at street corners where simply everyone caught of German background was arrested and put into a camp. . . .

Then there was no Exit Visa; that meant one had to climb
across the Pyrenees, and the most recent news of this entry

into Spain, after many had done it successfully, was that Jacob [Wachter] and three other friends had sent telegrams from a prison in Spain, and asked for help.[18]

The ports in Marseille were now under German control. Even though Eva had her U.S. visa and Spanish and Portuguese travel visas, she needed to find a way to escape from France without an exit visa. In a biography of Eva's brother Erich, Antje Dertinger described the dangers facing Eva:

> Like many other exiles, she [Eva] had not attempted to apply for the compulsory exit visa from France. Due to the collaboration between the French authorities and the Germans, even in the unoccupied zone, such an application could easily have led to arrest, internment, or even deportation to Germany. The illegal route over the mountains offered no guarantee of safety either. It remained risky because Franco's Spain was sympathetic to Hitler, and German agents were on the constant look-out for political refugees at the border. There were Gestapo lists of wanted people at every Spanish border post. Since the Portuguese transit visa was only valid in combination with a Spanish "Entrada" stamp, it was essential for all refugees to pass through a Spanish border post to obtain this important stamp on their papers.[19]

Eva added a brief diary entry on September 19, 1940. It was the last entry in the diary she had started on May 18, 1940, at the Vel d'Hiv in Paris—the diary written for Otto from whom she had now been separated for over four months. It was the day before she left France on her escape over the Pyrenees. She still did not know if Otto was alive:

> Farewell to these pages—and to much more. These pages should tell you, my dearest one, that despite all the external commotion, I have spent these months with you, and they should give you certainty that it will continue to be so. The farewell is dreadfully hard for me because it does not leave me with the certainty that we will see each other again. And yet it must be. Farewell, my Otto!

Last page of the diary Eva left for Otto in Marseille.

Eva made this final entry in her diary before using all of the pages in the little book. Twelve blank pages remained. When Eva said "farewell to these pages," she meant that literally. She did not take this diary with her when she departed from Marseille. She left it behind for Otto, entrusting it to her brother Erich with instructions to send it to Otto if and when his location could be ascertained. Along with the diary, Eva also left a small photograph of herself for Otto. On the back of the photo Eva wrote the words "pour toi" (for you).

# 11. Otto's Capture and Imprisonment by the Nazis

When we last left Otto, he was at the train station in Paris saying good-bye to Eva as he departed for Luxembourg on May 9, 1940. Otto was expecting to see Johannes (Hans) Jahn, a leader of the International Transport Workers Federation, in Luxembourg and then to make connections with Jef Rens, the Belgian labor leader to whom Otto had been delivering bombs to sabotage trains carrying Nazi military supplies during the Drôle de Guerre. Rens later described the tense atmosphere in Belgium during those days and his unsuccessful attempt to connect with Otto:

> On the 5th and 6th of May 1940, the rue de la Loi [road in Brussels with key government buildings often used as a name for the Belgian government] was suffering under feverish agitation. The news, especially from the Hague, reported an imminent German invasion. On the 7th, Foreign Affairs believed that the warnings had not been well founded. It is in this climate of uncertainty that I decided to embark the next day, that is, Thursday, May 9, to Saint-Vith via Liège.
>
> We set up a telephone appointment with Otto. . . . But Otto advised Clajot that he had not finished in Luxembourg. . . . In Saint-Vith, we were expected by comrade Simon, a railroad worker who was also alderman of this community. He disconnected several cars carrying large tires that clearly were intended for armored vehicles. We set our explosive charges; then, after having reconnected the cars as professionally as possible, we went to drink a glass in a café near the border.

We took the opportunity to ask our friend Simon how he saw the situation on the other side of the border. His comments confirmed what I had heard in Brussels. "A few days ago," said Simon, "I thought that the German attack was imminent. The roar of the engines did not stop for three days and three nights. Then Tuesday, the calm returned." However, Simon did not trust the apparent calm much, because his bike carrying a travel bag with his toiletries was always ready for departure. He had reached an arrangement with the customs office that he be called at the slightest threat. . . .

We know what happened in the following days of May and June: the recollection of these events is engraved forever in the memory of men and women of my generation.[1]

Otto recalled, "I arrived in Luxembourg, went to Hans J., unloaded my anti-Hitler material, and spent the evening with him and his family."[2] In light of what we learned about the nature of Otto's work during the Drôle de Guerre with Jahn, Rens and Bertholet, we now understand his cryptic reference to his meeting with "Hans J" where he "unloaded" his "anti-Hitler material."[3] Otto briefly described his evening with Jahn on May 9:

> He told me a number of things that he had organized with the railway worker trade unionists in Luxembourg, and he also told me how often Nazi planes had been flying over Luxembourg, insolently, and how the Luxembourg government could not do anything about it. It got very late. We parted and we agreed to see each other the next morning at 10 a.m.

It was so late when Otto left Jahn that the streetcars were no longer running, and it took him thirty minutes to walk to his hotel. He was exhausted and immediately went to sleep. "During the night, I was awakened occasionally by the roaring of motors. But after what J. [Jahn] had told me the night before, I did not let the noise bother me." The next morning, Otto heard the alarming news:

> In the morning I went down to breakfast. Nobody was around; only the owner of the hotel stood behind the counter with tears

in her eyes. I told her I would not be back that night, and she answered "Oh, that's probably because of the events!" I said, surprised, "What events?" And she replied, "Well don't you know? The Germans are here."

So that is the end, I thought, and I felt like a trapped animal.

Otto knew that Nazi officials, including the Gestapo, were aware of his anti-Nazi activities. If captured and identified as the "Pfister" who had been a primary contact in Paris of ISK member Julius Philippson, Otto faced death or life in prison. He immediately locked himself in the bathroom and made plans.

> I was sharply aware of the hopelessness of the situation and knew that I could only try to save whatever I could. First order of priority: under no circumstances must they find my French passport (made out in my real name). So I returned to my room, took some of the money that I had with me, and went to the bathroom. Locked in there, I felt safe to make plans for different contingencies, and if worse came to worse, I could flush the passport down the toilet.
>
> I had an entrance visa for Belgium, and although I had no idea whether or not it would still be possible to get into Belgium, I thought I had better not destroy the passport just yet. I looked around for a place where I could hide it. I was lucky: there was a hole in the floor left after an unfinished repair, into which I could reach with my hand. So I put most of my money into the passport and pushed the whole thing into the hole so that it would not fall through and I could reach it again when I needed to. Then I went back to my room.
>
> I knew that a good many of the things that I had with me would give me and my real identity away. So, I carefully examined every single object, tore laundry marks off my underwear, destroyed papers, and put only those things that were completely uncompromising back into my suitcase. Then I went to the phone and tried to reach the French embassy. No answer. I tried the Belgian embassy. The disturbed voice of a young girl answered. She said she did not know what was going to happen; they were completely cut off from their country. That meant that the Nazis had not yet occupied the Belgian embassy.

Then suddenly it came to my mind that in similar cases, neutral countries had protected members of countries at war, and I called the American embassy. A secretary answered. I told him that I was a Frenchman, and since my efforts to contact the French embassy had not succeeded, I took the liberty to ask if in this unusual situation, the American embassy could protect me. He asked where I was, said he had to confer with the consul. A few moments later, he came back and told me that the "Consul himself would pick me up within ten minutes."

This was more than I had ever dared to hope. When a short while later a tall, elegant gentleman entered, I greeted him with joy, introduced myself, and was about to thank him for his help when he interrupted me and asked again who I was. I repeated my name, and he said, "Vous dites vous êtes du Consulat Français?" (You say that you belong to the French consulate?). When I said that I did not, he became very irritated, and said, "Il doit y avoir erreur. Je ne peux rien faire pour vous" (There must be a mistake. I can't do anything for you). And he left. Obviously, the secretary had misunderstood me.

That was a cold shower after the great relief I had felt only a few minutes ago. I knew that there was no point staying at the hotel any longer. Perhaps German troops were already stationed in front of the hotel. But I felt instinctively that I ran a smaller risk getting arrested outside, among the throngs of people, and that perhaps I could gain time to think and to look for a way out.

Otto left the hotel and wandered the streets of Luxembourg to see what he could learn. The streets were initially empty but soon filled with Nazi soldiers:

I went out—nobody bothered me. The street was fairly empty; only, from time to time, German gray military trucks drove by. I saw a bakery and thought that perhaps I might learn more about the events of the night. But nothing. I bought half a dozen bars of chocolate, and the man acted as though nothing had happened.

On I went to the nearest main street. Quite a few people had gathered there. When I was about to join them, I noticed the avant-guard of a German infantry regiment that was approaching. As I learned later, these troops had crossed the Luxembourg border at 2 a.m., and now, singing, they were marching through the city. They were powerful young men; most were over 6 feet tall. There was little comment on the part of the spectators, and I had the impression that these people were not aware of what was happening now in their country.

I watched for quite a while, and felt at times rather unreal—like an onlooker who had nothing to do with the things that were happening. And then there were moments where I was sure every one of the marching soldiers could read my face and know who I was.

Otto finally decided to leave Luxembourg and asked for directions to the streetcar going to Belgium:

At the terminal, a very friendly conductor told me that these cars were not running any more, and he suggested that if I absolutely wanted to get into Belgium, I had best get a bike. He went with me to a store that sold used bikes. I found one that I was about to get, but after talking some more with the conductor, who was extremely skeptical about the chances of getting through because, he said, the Germans were everywhere, I finally left without the bike.

Again Otto walked through the streets of Luxembourg uncertain about what to do. Suddenly he saw an empty cab and asked the driver if he could take him to the Belgian border. The cab driver "had just come from there and said that although he could not get there all the way, he could at least take me close enough so that I could cross the frontier [border] on foot." It was a memorable cab ride:

One thing was absolutely clear to me: Under no circumstances must I give the impression of a traveling tourist, and therefore, I must not have any luggage. So I asked the driver to first take me to the hotel; with great effort, I got my passport and my money out of the hole in the bathroom, told the landlady that for the time being I would leave my bags there, and quickly went back into the cab.

Of course, I knew that in all probability we would be stopped and checked by German personnel at any moment. Although I would need my passport at the border, I absolutely could not let it be found on my person while riding in the cab. So I hid it under the floor covering of the car.

In the meantime, we were back on the main road along which Germans were marching without interruption. The cab drove down the street, alongside the regiments that were heading west. It was a bizarre situation, scary, and at the same time like a farce.

Finally, we turned north, left the town behind, and drove now through sunny, hilly country towards the Belgian frontier. When we came to a small bridge, a sudden command: "Halt." German soldiers opened the door. I tried very hard to look as innocent and unconcerned as possible, leaned comfortably back in my seat, and when they asked "Any weapons?" I smiled and shook my head. The soldiers talked some more with the driver and then let us go. Again, what luck!

After a while, we came to a little village that later on turned out to be Kehlen. The driver stopped and said that this was as far as he could go; the cab was not his, and he had to make sure that he could bring it back. He showed me in which direction I had to walk in order to get to some forest; after crossing the woods, I would be at the Belgian frontier. He thought that I could make it in about two hours. I paid, gave him a most generous tip, pulled out my passport from under the carpet, and got on my way.

## A forced change in plans: the fabrication of a story that would save Otto's life

After leaving the cab, Otto walked briskly for about ten minutes. "Suddenly, I saw a German convoy on the road parallel to mine, going in the direction of the Belgian border. Shortly after that, a German military vehicle with four men drove by me. 'So it is too late,' I thought."

There was absolutely no point now to keep on walking. What I needed urgently was to gain time and make plans, and so I hid in the thick underbrush next to the road.

Again and again I thought whether in spite of everything, it would not be better to try to make the Belgian border. Continually, German convoys sped by on both roads, and it became certain that the border would be occupied by their troops, so that there would be no chance to cross it. But what else could I do? Go back to Luxembourg? And hide there? But where? To wait for a change in the military situation, where the French troops that had been taken by surprise, would chase the Nazis out of this small country? I really did not believe that that was likely. But when one is caught in a trap, one can't help harboring ridiculous hopes and believing in miracles. While I was debating in my mind all the pros and cons, I hear heavy squadrons of military planes above, and the thunder of fighting at the French border hit my ears.

Finally, I came to a decision: I will return, try to get back into Luxembourg, and hide there. Whether and for how long this might be possible was more than questionable. Therefore, I had to be prepared for the event of getting caught.

First order of priority was once again to get rid of my passport, and I hid it under a big rock in the field, wrapping it carefully in the aluminum foil in which my chocolate bars had come. And then I went about the job of constructing a story. With hard certainty I knew that if that story did not hold up, it would be curtains. "Si elle ne tient pas debout, ça te coûtera la peau."

This was the story: I was to be a Frenchman; I got a simple first name, Paul, and a one-syllable family name, Bois, easy to pronounce, easy to remember [*bois* is French for "wood"]. I had an Italian mother, a French father, and was born in Nice. I spent most of my childhood and adolescence in Italy—that explained the slight Italian accent. For years now, I worked as *metreur* (construction work surveyor) in Paris, with a fictitious address in one of the faubourgs. Parents dead, no other relatives. No military service because of health reasons. I had come to Luxembourg during the Whitsuntide holidays in order to visit my lady friend whom I had met in Paris. In the morning when I heard the incoming German troops, I quickly ran into the street, where it became suddenly clear to me that I had to flee, and I ran away. I had left everything behind, even my passport, which had been in my wallet, on the night table. That's why I was now without any identification. Unfortunately, I would not be able to give my friend's address or to return there, because the lady is married.

After thinking it over for a long time, I also decided that I neither understood nor spoke German.

## Otto's capture by German soldiers

It was already late in the day when Otto finally left his hiding place by the roadside:

I returned to the village, found a little inn, ate dinner, and asked for a room. There was no vacancy. I asked around in the village: nothing available, at least not for a Frenchman. Back to the inn where I asked the owner if she would let me sleep at a table. Putting my head on my folded arms, I tried to sleep, and really dozed off for a little while.

Awakened by the noise of heavy steps and loud voices, I saw a troop of German soldiers in the room. I pretended to be asleep. The soldiers bought chocolate and tobacco, paid without any trouble, and asked for the Social Hall where they wanted some straw to be put. Suddenly seeing me, one of them asked the innkeeper, "Who is that fellow?" She answered, "A Frenchman who had dinner here, and could not find a room."

The officer came towards me, tapped me on the shoulder, and asked, "What are you doing here?" I looked up, as though coming out of deep sleep, and asked him to repeat his question, saying, "Je suis Français." "What are you doing here?" "Je ne vous comprends pas" (I don't understand you). "Vous êtes Français? Que faites-vous ici?" (You are French? What are you doing here?). "Je viens de Luxembourg. J'ai visité une amie, et j'ai essayé de rentrer en France via la Belgique" (I come from

Luxembourg. I visited a girlfriend, and I tried to return to France via Belgium). "Passport!" (Your Passport!). "Je ne l'ai pas sur moi" (I don't have it with me). "Aha! Do you speak German?" "Je ne vous comprends pas" (I don't understand). "Parlez-vous allemand?" (Do you speak German?). "Non, mais vous parlez bien le français" (No; but you speak French very well). I thought a little flattery could not hurt. "Yes, I have been to Paris to study. Do you have weapons?" The officer ordered a man to search me. And then he asked me how much money I had. Shortly before being arrested, I had folded a 1,000-francs bill many times so I could hide it in an inner pocket, and I showed him what was left: 300 francs. He asked me to put the money in an envelope and to write my name, address, and profession on it. Then he said, "Vous êtes mon premier prisonnier de guerre!" (You are my first prisoner of war!), and he asked a soldier to take me to headquarters.

The man took me to different places where the officers did not know what to do with me, and on we went. I became aware of the fact that they would no doubt find the concealed l,000-francs bill when they searched me thoroughly, and that would make my situation worse. It was not easy to get rid of the bill without being noticed, but I finally managed to throw it over a fence.

At the next stop, an officer wanted to know more precisely what a *metreur* was (that was the profession that I had indicated as mine). I explained that it had to do with taking measurements of works on construction sites.

Later, they took me to a field telephone office. There I overheard the conversation to the effect that they had here a French civilian prisoner who said he was a geometer (surveyor)—suspicion of him being a spy. It was very hard for me not to react and say "You are in error; I am not a geometer, I am a *metreur*," and for the first time it became sharply clear to me how hard it would be to maintain the fiction that I did not understand any German.

Soon the military police took me by car to a farm in the vicinity of Luxembourg. A brief interrogation at which the farmer served as interpreter: My statements were taken down.

My questioners made every effort to learn the address of the "woman" from me. I refused, saying that the lady was married. I had nothing to fear, they replied, if my statements proved to be true, and I had to realize how much I worsened my situation by my refusal. They would be extremely tactful checking up on the address; I could be sure that the husband would not know anything about it. The old peasant took my side; he seemed to understand the situation, and he tried to make my interrogators see that a man, and above all a Frenchman, could not compromise a lady. Finally, I had to sign my statements as they had been taken down.

From there, I was taken to a school where German soldiers were stationed and where they also kept a few dozen freshly captured French prisoners. I had to go to the bathroom, and as I crossed the courtyard, I heard some of the German soldiers speak in Bavarian dialect. Immediately I realized what an additional danger that was. If by some fluke one of these soldiers was a former acquaintance or schoolmate of mine from Munich, all would be lost. From now on, I did not leave the room whenever I could avoid it. I also realized that I had to do whatever I could to change my appearance.

## Transport to prison in Trier

The following morning, Otto and the other prisoners were lined up to be loaded in a truck. As they later found out, the truck was headed to Trier, a German city on the Moselle River near the Luxembourg border. While waiting in line, Otto hoped to avoid any attention. "When we had to wait for a while, I cursed my height for the first time in my life; a German soldier was taking pictures of our group, and it was impossible for me to hide." Otto recalled his good fortune on the way to the prison in Trier:

The trip to Trier was beautiful. It was a great, sunny day, and the country in that area is lovely. When we arrived in Trier, the truck stopped in front of local headquarters. I was taken inside, but apparently there was nobody who wanted to have anything to do with me. Next stop was a high building with the inscription "Geheime Staatspolizei" (Gestapo, Secret State Police).

Now, I thought, I will have the thorough Gestapo interrogation. Repeated ringing, however, brought nobody to the door. It was high noon, Whitsuntide Sunday, and that might again have been the lucky break I needed.

Otto was initially incarcerated in the city prison in Trier. "My belongings were taken from me, and I was put in a solitary cell. In this cell, I waited for almost three weeks for the dreaded interrogation. Again, I experienced how hard it was to pretend not to understand German. For example, when the warden unexpectedly opened the door and yelled 'Wasser!' I had to make an effort to hold back and not to reach instinctively for the water can."

Despite the danger he faced, Otto—the optimistic, self-educated lover of history—recalled the positive moments along with the challenges of several weeks in this prison:

The food was very simple, yet nourishing. I certainly did not suffer from hunger. Under the cell's ceiling was a window. Pulling myself up on the iron bars, I could see the sky and a panorama of the city, with the impressive "Porta Nigra"—a 2,000-year-old monument erected by the Romans.

After a few days in prison, I found out that one could put a sign through the door that indicated that one wanted to report for physical exercises. Of course, that was a relief. We did our exercises in the courtyard for half an hour, together with two or three dozen other prisoners. Some were criminals. The man next to me during the exercises, for instance, had been arrested under suspicion of murder.

Every day, I waited for the interrogation, tried to prepare myself for it, to check over and over again the statements that I had already made and those that I was to add, to keep everything sharply in my mind.

In the meantime, I had not shaved for a few days and planned to grow a beard. However, I had not counted on the prison rules, and finally I had to accept a shave from the prison aide. I tried to make him understand that I would rather not get shaved, because once before I had gotten a skin infection (that was not true); he became very angry and said that such a thing could not happen in a clean German prison, and so I had to get shaved.

After about two weeks—a lot of time to reflect and to speculate—I was taken downstairs and had to wait in front of a closed door for about twenty minutes. I thought "Now, it is coming." I tried everything to remain calm and concentrated and managed to do it at least outwardly. But inside, I experienced for the first time certain physical manifestations of raw fear, and in spite of all efforts, concentration, and willpower, I could not check them. In the end, it appeared that this was not an interrogation but only once more a check on the valuables that had been taken from me.

After another week in this prison, Otto was moved to another location: "modern barracks on the Petrusberg . . . on top of a hill overlooking the City of Trier." He quickly learned that it would not be easy for him to maintain his false identity with French-speaking prisoners:

Now I was no longer the only civilian: a mining engineer from Luxembourg who also had been taken prisoner somewhere was with me. On the way to the barracks with me, the following happened: On this trip, the German soldiers who accompanied us talked about reports from the front, and they mentioned Abbeville and other French cities which the Germans had already conquered. I talked about that with the engineer, saying, "I just heard the name Abbeville. Do you think they are already there?" Immediately he asked me "Are you a naturalized Frenchman?" I said, "No, I am Italo-French." Obviously, I had not pronounced the name of the city in the proper French way. From then on, I was very careful not to mention names of French cities with which I was not thoroughly familiar. And I became even more aware of the fact that it would be extremely difficult to maintain my position as Frenchman with French-speaking people.

While he was in these barracks on May 26, 1940, Otto decided to take the risk of writing the postcard to Yvonne Oullion, using his false name "Paul Bois" so he could let Eva and his other ISK colleagues know that he was still alive:

During the next days, thousands and thousands of French officers arrived in the barracks on the hill and also a few American civilians who had done voluntary service with the evacuation. We learned now that it was permitted to write a postcard to one's relatives. I had to think this over very carefully: Should I or should I not write to Yvonne? The fact that during the whole time in prison I had not been interrogated thoroughly made me wonder if they had not missed out on my file, if they had perhaps forgotten my existence. If I write this card now, I thought, and if the censor would see it, I might perhaps, through my own fault, direct their attention to me, all the more so as all the officers would put as sender "capitaine" or "lieutenant," while I could only put down my assumed civilian name. This one fact alone could lead to a special screening of my card.

Finally, I decided in favor of writing the card so that my people in France would at least know that I was still alive. I wrote the card to Yvonne, with the special request to write only after I would have given her a definite address. I did not want any mail; I wanted to decide myself when it would be safe to write to me.[4]

## Transport to officers' prison camp (Oflag) in Hoyerswerda, Silesia

Otto was then transported by train from Trier to a prisoner-of-war camp (Offizierslage or "Oflag") for French officers at Hoyerswerda in Silesia. Hoyerswerda is about 440 miles east of Trier and 40 miles east of Dresden. Otto continued to fear that Gestapo interrogators and even fellow prisoners would expose his true identity:

Soon, the quota of the transport to a PW [prisoner-of-war] camp was filled. About 5,000 French officers were packed in a long train. We civilians also boarded it.

The destination of the convoy was an Oflag at the eastern border of Germany. We civilians, as it transpired, were directed to Gestapo headquarters in Hannover. However, by some lucky circumstances, we were not taken off the train in Hannover but continued the trip with everybody to Hoyerswerda in Silesia, the site of the camp. The receiving authorities were greatly astonished and disoriented by our presence but admitted us temporarily.

I expected—and of course dreaded—to be taken back to Hannover soon. Yet, this did not happen. And now started a dreary camp life. We were assigned to rough three-tiered bunkers, slept for a few nights miserably on the bare planks, until they issued sacks filled with excelsior (packing material made of wood). Food was edible, but the rations were so small that for the first time in my life I experienced real gnawing hunger.

To anyone who has never felt raw hunger, it is very hard to convey what it is all about. Thinking becomes almost entirely concentrated on food. Hardly finished a meal, one is longing for the next one. Many coveted the empty marmalade pots to clean out the meager remains. I went around to gather from potato peels whatever less meticulous fellows had left on them. Hunger erodes pride! Since we got very little greenery and hardly any fruit and I feared a deterioration of my physical and mental capacities, especially in view of the dreaded interrogation by the Gestapo (which indeed finally occurred), I went out every evening to gather *Sauerampfer* (sorrel), which grew in the cracks of the dirt in the camp.

Besides hunger, other things worried me. Puzzled by the presence of two civilians among them, some of the French officers whispered among themselves, wondering if we had been planted by the Germans. As anticipated, someone asked about my slight accent. I told my story of my Italo-French background. Fortunately, I was able to corroborate it by talking Italian to a lieutenant from Corsica (they are bilingual). It sounded plausible. But since I was not to know any German, I feared that I might talk in my sleep in that language. So I managed to get an upper berth. Being painfully aware of the fact that all the clothing I had was what I wore, I was concerned about wearing it out. Since I did not smoke, I had saved the cigarette rations we were issued, and I was able to barter them against a pair of French uniform pants. This had the added advantage to help me blend better into my surroundings.

Finally, the event occurred that Otto had feared most since his arrest: an extensive interrogation by the Gestapo:

> Continually, I recapitulated what I had told my captors back in Luxembourg. This proved to be highly useful when I was called to an hour-long interrogation by a Gestapo agent. He took my deposition and remained stone-faced. Perhaps he was not satisfied, because a few weeks later came another call to the Camp Office. A Gestapo man had come from Goerlitz—a town some distance from Hoyerswerda—to take me through another grilling. All this, of course, was in French. This time again, I got through the grueling hour without giving myself away.

## The "University of Hoyerswerda" and a hand-carved chess set

Not all was grim at the camp. Otto used his skill with woodwork to craft stools out of discarded wood for the prisoners, and he received food in return. He also carved a complete chess set with a small pocketknife. Remarkably, he was able to save this set and ultimately brought it with him to America:

> In the meantime, food parcels had started to arrive for the officers from their families in France. None for me, of course. In order to direct some of that food my way, I made little stools from sticks I had salvaged from the excelsior crates, and I traded them for whatever foodstuff I could get. The only tool I owned was a pocketknife I had smuggled in. Nails I found in the dirt around the barracks, dropped there by the construction workers. The stools were well liked to sit on and listen to lectures under the sky at what was proudly called the "University of Hoyerswerda." This had been arranged by teachers and other professionals among the officers. I myself followed many of these courses—they were a welcome diversion from the monotony of camp life.
>
> Another diversion was to play chess. I had whittled a set of chessmen, a task of many days. Some of my partners played

Chess pieces carved by
Otto with a pocketknife
in Nazi prison camp.

a better game, but I remember with satisfaction that I beat a
colonel a few times. Strategic skills did not help him to win.

## Release

Several weeks after the signing of the armistice between France and
Germany on June 22, 1940, Otto was able to obtain his release from
the camp. But at the very moment he was advised that the decision had
been made to release him, he slipped and made a mistake that could
have cost him his life:

> By now, the Armistice had been signed between France and
> Germany. The other civilian, the engineer from Luxembourg,
> started to make written requests to be released. One day, the
> German officer who occasionally dealt with us (he spoke French)
> came to talk to me. He was wondering what kept me from mak-
> ing the same request as the other fellow had done. I was to write
> the story of my capture and request my release.
>     Now that was precisely what I shrank away from doing.
> Although I wrote French fluently, I was aware that I had never
> acquired the characteristic French handwriting. Possibly, my
> writing would be scrutinized by somebody who knew the dif-
> ference. I also was not sure anymore of all the details of my ear-
> lier depositions. All I wanted was to lie low. But since I risked
> arousing suspicion by refusing to follow the suggestion, I finally
> decided to write my request.
>     Some weeks later, the officer who always spoke French to
> me came to me and said in German: "Sie werden morgen ent-
> lassen!" (You will be released tomorrow!). Overwhelmed by this

news, I forgot for a moment that he had spoken in German (which I was not supposed to understand), and I answered with a short sentence in German. Immediately I was aware of my lapse, and cold fear ran down my spine. I continued to talk, now in French. So did he. I still can't explain by what miracle he had not realized my mistake.

# 12. Otto's Return to Paris and Flight to Montauban

The day after Otto was released from the Nazi prison camp, he boarded a slow train to France with a dozen French prisoners of war from a nearby camp who were being sent to work at the railroads in Paris. But he managed to transfer to another train:

> I had found out that our travel orders allowed us civilians to use faster trains. So, at a stopover in Hannover, we convinced the German non-commissioned man in charge to let us continue alone. This was very fortunate, since I was to report to the German authorities at the railway station in Paris and wanted to avoid that at all cost.
>
> We traveled on without a guard, and at another stopover in Luxembourg, I picked up the suitcase that I had left at the hotel and then took the train to Paris. The problem now was to get off the train before it reached the Gare de l'Est in Paris. Fortunately, the train stopped at Le Bourget (one of the Paris airports), at the outskirts of Paris.[1]

Belgian labor leader Jef Rens, to whom Otto had delivered bombs during the Drôle de Guerre, provided additional details of Otto's train trip back to Paris, as Otto later described it to him:

> Before leaving the camp, Otto had to go to the commander to get his train ticket and *Passierschein* [safe conduct pass]. The commander almost apologized for his arrest and gave him five

hundred marks, saying "A gift from the Führer to compensate you for your unjustified arrest!"

In Hanover, his two guards told Otto that they had a 24-hour leave, and they would go visit their wives and children. They assumed that Otto himself had the desire to see his wife in Paris quickly, so they let him continue the journey alone, with his promise never to veer from the route. And so it was that Otto, activist German anti-Nazi, traveled alone by train between Hannover and Paris in the middle of the war, furnished with a safe conduct pass in perfect order, a free ticket, and five hundred marks in cash as a gift from Hitler.[2]

Otto got off the train at Le Bourget and checked his bags at the train station. After about an hour's walk, he arrived at the house of a friend in Pantin, a town about nine miles from the center of Paris:

Nobody was home. I spent the night on the landing. Nobody came the next morning. Early then, I went to the house of a young French couple for whom I had made some furniture. They were my friends. But would they still be friends now, with the Nazis in Paris? It turned out that my fear was groundless: they heard my story, accepted me warmly, and helped me in every way, with money, food stamps, and shelter.

Otto then went to the Paris apartment of Eva's brother Erich. The Gestapo had already entered and sealed the apartment, but the concierge knew Otto and gave him the keys. Otto was also able to get into Eva's nearby apartment. "The next day, I loaded a two-wheel cart with whatever was worth salvaging from the two places, and I sold it later."

A few weeks after his arrival in Paris, Otto learned from their colleague and friend, Gaby Cordier, about what had happened to others since the invasion on May 9. Gaby had been to the unoccupied zone and had returned to Paris. She told Otto that many of their colleagues, including Eva, Erich, and Herta, had managed to escape to Montauban in the unoccupied zone after getting out of internment camps.

Despite her friendship with Eva, Gaby also loved and admired Otto. Gaby's interest in Otto had created some tension in the past when they were all working together in Paris, but it had been resolved. After his return to Paris from the prison camp, however, Otto had a brief intimate relationship with Gaby despite his love for Eva. He would later express his deep regret about this to Eva, and her reaction would say much about Eva and her feelings about Otto and Gaby.

Gaby and Otto soon left Paris and headed south to join the others in Montauban. Gaby led the way to a crossing point she knew in the demarcation line. A farmer helped show them the way through a forest at night. As Otto recalled,

> Dawn found us walking along a country road. Suddenly, out of the mist appeared two German soldiers. There was no way to escape. They questioned us. I kept mum, and Gaby did some fast talking. Incredibly, they let us go.

Once in the unoccupied zone, they took a train to Montauban. They were relieved to find their colleagues there, but Otto was crushed to hear that Eva had recently departed for the United States. He later observed that "at least, both of us now knew that the other one was alive!"

Even in the unoccupied zone, Otto's life was in serious danger. Because the French government had agreed in the June 22, 1940, armistice to "surrender on demand" all Germans named by the German government in France, anyone who had been actively involved in anti-Nazi work was in imminent danger. If Otto were identified and turned over to the Nazis, he would be killed. And the woman he loved was now on a different continent with an ocean between them.

Otto in Montauban after his release from the Nazi prison camp.

Several weeks later while Otto was in southern France and Eva was in New York, they were able to exchange letters. Writing to Eva from Marseille on November 8, 1940, Otto summarized his capture and release by the Nazis and his return to Paris in more detail:

My dearest, did you get my first letter from Montauban? And now I am here, and found with great joy your brother and his wife. How good it was to talk about so many things! I got right away your answer to his cable, and now we wait for your promised letter.

There are so many things to tell you that I really don't know where to start and how far to go. You know: down there (at the Prisoner of War Camp) I never received anything from you, no letter, no package. I believe that at the first center where I was held, they probably did not know where I would be sent, and now I believe that was probably all to the good. So many times afterwards I had to force myself not to write you again; but reason spoke against it, and even now I believe it was better that I did not do it.

I had slept well that famous night [May 9, 1940, in Luxembourg] until 9 a.m., and barely heard the noise of the planes above. You imagine what I felt when the brutal fact of the invasion hit me. Once in the street, what a spectacle! I tried nevertheless to return [to Paris]; but it was too late, and quickly I was apprehended. From that moment on, I had to pull myself together and mobilize my resources. I knew that there was barely a chance that I could get out of the spot I was in. But I was unbelievably lucky, and that fact, supplemented by daily efforts which were guided by reason as well as by instinct, finally brought me to the point where one morning I was liberated. My return trip took me in the end to Paris, all alone.

You imagine my joy to see Paris again. I went right away to Jeanne—nobody home. But letters that I found there told me a number of things that had happened to you, and at least there was hope that you and the others were alive. From there, I went to #5 [the apartment they shared in Issy de Moulineaux, a Paris suburb], where the concierge was very nice. I was surprised that nothing had been touched, and that nobody had been there—that took care of a great deal of worries.

I did immediately the things that were most urgent, and there was so much to do that I missed by ten minutes the date with Josy [a mutual friend] I had set over the phone earlier. I nevertheless go to her place—nobody there. It is late. I sleep in the staircase because it is forbidden to be outside at night—cur-few. At dawn, near les Halles, I look for J's truck—nothing. Then I remember that Henriette and Victor [a young couple, trade unionists] lived close by. They welcomed me in friendship, gave me lodging with Henriette's mother, and invited me to eat with them until I would find a better solution.

My good luck continues. Victor [an ISK colleague] lends me some money; both of them help me to move the things from #5, from where, despite the difficulties, I was able to take almost everything. Later, the brother of Bravi [Maurice Abravanel, a well-known orchestra conductor and friend] also removed his piano. Our friend from St. Denis was great also; with his help, seven bags of books and other things were moved.[3]

Otto then expressed his anguish about learning of Eva's departure and his gratitude for the "little booklet"—the diary Eva had written "to him" following their separation on May 9, 1940, and left for him with her brother in Marseille:

Paulette [mutual friend] arrives. She has to leave right away, but brings news of a letter from you from Lisbon. I had accepted that; my reason had accepted this solution. But it took some time to overcome the sadness and bitterness in me against the irony of the fate that had permitted me to escape successfully, only a month or six weeks too late to still see you before you left.

Finally, we find a way, rather expensive, to pass across the line of demarcation; it was not without danger, but all went well again, and we arrived, all in one piece, in Montauban. It felt good to find all our friends in good shape. And you, my dear-est, did not seem too far away; you lived with me in your little booklet that I read and reread—how you must have suffered![4]

# 13. Eva's Escape over the Pyrenees and Unexpected Delay in Lisbon

Eva had traveled by train from Marseille to Banyuls sur Mer with three colleagues on September 19, 1940. Banyuls is a small fishing village at the foot of the Pyrenees on the border between France and Spain. Eva was with Stern, Hans Jahn (who had engaged in anti-Nazi work with Otto and lived in Luxembourg), and a woman named Irma (last name unknown).

Having left her diary in Marseille, with its entries covering the period beginning with her internment in the Vel' d'Hiv and Gurs until her departure from Marseille, Eva started another diary in Lisbon. In her first entry on September 28, she sketched her recollection of her arrival in Banyuls: "Friday morning [September 20], Banyuls, visit with the mayor who shows us the path we will have to take in the morning. The ocean, the beautiful, poor little fishing village. Great desire not to have to leave."

The mayor of Banyuls, Victor Azema, like the mayor of Montauban, was committed to helping political refugees. Eva later recalled the guidance she received from him and the dangers of the crossing:

[He] said to carry nothing, just maybe a little satchel with a sandwich and a piece of fruit so it looked, if anybody stopped us, as though we'd just be on a hike. He told us to follow the vineyard workers. They would know that we would be following them, but we would not communicate with them.

We constantly received news about people who had done it, and the regulations changed from day to day. It was very dangerous to travel through Spain in our condition, and often they would just hand people over to Germany. . . . We wanted to just get this over with as soon as we possibly could . . . so we didn't stay there [in Banyuls]. I would have loved to stay because it was so peaceful, and I thought if I should ever have a chance to see Otto again I'd have a better chance there than all the way across the ocean. But that was not to be.[1]

In a letter Eva later wrote to Otto on March 24, 1941, when she was in New York and he was still in Europe, Eva described the night before she left to cross the Pyrenees:

I have to think again and again of the night before we had to take off early in the morning. We were staying in a small hotel, with a view of the ocean, Irma and I in one room, Stern and Jahn in the room next to us. For a long time I was standing on the balcony that night, looked at the ocean and the serene sky, this beautiful country, and remembered all the good people that we had seen during the day; and I just did not want to leave, because my heart was waiting for you in this country, because part of my heart remained in you and in this country. How sad I was that night, how alone in spite of the three people near me.

Eva and the three others left Banyuls on foot on September 21, 1940. In her Lisbon diary entry on September 28, 1940, she described the crossing:

Very early the next morning, before dawn, we leave, following the silent French workers who are out to pick grapes, follow them on a six hour long hike, climb, through vineyards and rocks and mountains, and fog. On top of the mountain a quiet handshake, thanks, and farewell. Now the fog rolls in for real, we are on our own, and are totally lost, don't know in which direction is Spain or France. Then, after a long while, we hear the whistle of a train. And suddenly we are oriented, know where the coastline is, and where we are headed. Then we see an old woman with a donkey coming our way. She understands our Spanish "Buenos días"—and we are safe.

Eva later described this disorientation in the fog as a "strange feeling of blindness, of helplessness, nobody to turn to." She added: "The rest was relatively easy—the Spanish border officer gave us our entrance stamp without consulting any Nazi lists (something they had done in other cases)."[2]

Eva's safe crossing into Spain on September 21, 1940, was hardly ensured. The illegal escape over the Pyrenees by foot was challenging physically and psychologically. Moreover, Spain's willingness to grant entry was changing day by day. Eva later reported to ISK leader Willi Eichler that Willi Rieloff was unsuccessful in his attempt to cross the border three days after her crossing because "a few days earlier new rules had been issued saying that people without a regular national passport could no longer cross Spain; up to then, the American visa itself had been recognized in lieu of a passport, and transit visa had been affixed to it." She further reported that Rieloff was again in Marseille waiting for some intervention and noted that the danger of new internment was "menacing" because Marseille was now under German control.[3]

Less than a week after Eva's escape, German philosopher Walter Benjamin was arrested at the Spanish border after crossing the Pyrenees. He committed suicide on September 27, 1940, rather than be turned over to the Nazis.[4]

Other political refugees who had been granted U.S. visas at around the same time as Eva, such as Rudolf Breitscheid and Rudolf Hilferding, leading members of the German Social Democratic Party during the Weimar Republic, delayed attempting their illegal escapes from France with the hope that they would obtain legal exit visas—until it was too late. They were arrested by the Vichy government and turned over to the Nazis. Hilferding committed suicide while imprisoned by the Nazis in La Santé prison in Paris. Breitscheid perished while a prisoner in Buchenwald shortly before the end of the war.[5]

Eva and the three others arrived in Port Bou, the Spanish border town at the foot of the Pyrenees, at the end of a long and strenuous day. In her diary entry on September 28, Eva briefly sketched her impressions of Port Bou and their train trips to Barcelona and Madrid.

> We are in Port-Bou—custom formalities, the police. No problems. Shocking impression of the ruins that had not been cleaned

up, that the Civil War had left behind; burnt out houses; on the other side the ocean, mountains, and sky. Falangist youth in uniform;[6] beautiful colors, blue and red, march, accompanied by military music, to the church from where one sees ruins and the ocean. At the same time, at the ocean, two young fellows take off their clothes, stand there with their slim brown bodies, dive into the water. When we ask them whether they don't all have to march to church, one answers: "Only those who sign up for it!" Port-Bou—Europe, September 1940.

Sunday, 21st, off to Barcelona. Misfortune and bad luck and tension among us because of the baggage left behind. Gratitude for the natural help of Enoch (friend of Erich's). Walk through the streets at night, sadness, tension . . . attempt to clear up misunderstandings, all in a well-lit, wealthy street. Suddenly, on the sidewalk, an emaciated pregnant woman, with two children holding on to her skirt. Pale, starved—Europe 1940.

The next two days all sorts of errands because of lost baggage, unpleasant days and hours.[7] Finally, Tuesday night, with baggage on train to Madrid. An ugly voyage, with beautiful people. A priest from a Mission, a young worker who makes one think of the Loyalist survivors of the war in Montauban. Resting in Madrid, a nice room, with beautiful view of city.

Eva later recalled, "In Madrid, we didn't even go to the Prado, we saw nothing, we just stayed in a hotel."

The girl and I stayed in a room, and then the two men in another. Then we walked the streets, and I remember the horrible discrepancy between great wealth and absolutely awful poverty. The women with hanging breasts, standing there and begging with their children—just awful. We wanted to get out of there. So we did.[8]

In her diary entry on September 28, Eva briefly described the journey from Madrid to Lisbon: "A long trip, arrive at Portuguese border Thursday morning. Beautiful, simple people, a donkey, a Don Quixote, desert of rocks and of olive trees—finally peace."

## Lisbon: reuniting with friends, impressions of the city

Eva's four-month journey between her internment at the Vel' d'Hiv in early May 1940 and her arrival in Lisbon in late September had been filled with sadness, danger, strenuous work, and loneliness after being separated from the man she loved. Throughout it all, however, her diaries reflect some hope for the future.

That hope was challenged when she reached Lisbon and faced the ocean she was to cross to another continent—to a strange place where she feared she would never be reunited with Otto. In the final segment of her diary entry on September 28, Eva wrote:

> It is great to see many friends, Lene, Marianne,[9] Oskar [Austrian socialist]. Great sadness with increasing exhaustion. Departure for the States in perhaps four days. Today, Saturday night, for the first time again a half hour alone with Stern; then one hour quite alone. . . . I really would like to be alone more often; I have to practice that. Life will be hard in this great loneliness; but I am going to try.

In an entry written on October 7 while aboard the *Nea Hellas*, the ship that was taking her to the United States, Eva further reflected on her time in Lisbon:

> The days in Lisbon were so strangely unreal. Suddenly, without any transition, to be able to move freely, without legal documents and yet without concern, pass by policemen, sit in cafés; to talk without fear in the language that just comes to mind. Brilliantly lit streets deep into the night; rich displays in store windows; newspapers in all languages, of any orientation; and books, books—
>
> When one is standing at the harbor, at the large, strange square in the middle of which the statue of some king is riding on his horse towards the water; when one is sitting in the Botanical Garden, under these gigantic trees that don't seem to have any human dimensions—what does this giant

willow have in common with the gentle trees along the river at Compiegne—those immense palms . . . those tall, wild succulents—then one realizes that one stands at the edge of Europe, that in reality one has already left it behind.

Then, not far from the main streets, the Alfama (an area in Lisbon), barely ten minutes away, with its indescribable misery, dirt, and horror. That children are being born there . . . bodies covered with eczema, little legs like brittle sticks, without any flesh on them, dressed in some poor rags which barely give protection against heat or cold; that people are living there and get old, in dark hovels into which never a ray of light enters, with open wounds and protruding bellies, and covered with dirt—that all this can exist today—one must never forget it.

In the face of this misery, Eva described in this diary entry what she saw as the inner beauty of these people. She related a romantic fantasy about how she and Otto might take some of these people into the home she was still able to imagine might be theirs in the future:

And yet, how many beautiful human beings with a light in their eyes, with a barely conscious, and yet clearly noticeable yearning for a different world! The little fellow, like a cut out of a Murillo painting, with a large water jug, much too heavy, balanced on his head. I look at him, he smiles back, he replies to human warmth with warmth and serenity, and confidence.

I would like to take him with me, to the two of us. First put him in the tub, then give him some decent clothes; then sit him down at a clean dinner table. And then, when he would have eaten enough and would no longer be hungry, he would go with you into the workshop, where there would be many children, and he would learn to handle hammer and plane, and he would become a human being like you, secure in his work, and constantly finding new confirmation for what he is.

Or the woman, no longer young, who explains which way we will have to go, who firmly and friendly keeps on repeating the name of the street until we pronounce it accurately, people like her also would belong in our home. But above all you.

At the end of this entry, Eva returned to reality:

> Well, let's leave this fantasizing alone. First, I'll have to have you
> again, first we have to have each other, before we can begin to
> plan our life. Also, all this is just piecemeal talk. The quarter
> about which I just wrote [the Alfama] is the only part of Lisbon
> that was not destroyed during the big earthquake.[10] Without a
> social earthquake, such quarters will never disappear.

## Unexpected obstacles to departure

In Eva's diary entry written on Tuesday, October 8, 1940, while on board
the *Nea Hellas*, she explained to Otto how she was nearly precluded from
boarding the ship because arrangements had not been made to pay for
her trip. Having arrived in Lisbon on September 27, the day before the
*Nea Hellas* was scheduled to depart, Eva was told that the departure date
had been delayed and that the boat would now leave around October
3. The next morning, the refugee organizations in Lisbon checked her
documents and advised her that "the Hicem would have to cable to
America to make sure that my passage was paid for, but it probably was
only a formality. We were told that we ourselves did not have anything
to do with this . . . the representatives would take care of it for us all."[11]

HICEM was a Jewish organization formed through a merger in
1934 of three Jewish migration associations: HIAS (Hebrew Immigrant
Aid Society), based in New York; ICA (Jewish Colonization Association),
based in Paris; and Emigdirect, based in Berlin.[12] After the German invasion in May 1940, HICEM's European headquarters moved from Paris
to Lisbon because Portugal was a neutral country with a neutral port in
Lisbon, where refugees could be assisted in escaping from Europe. Eva
confided to Otto that it was a relief for her to be told that the HICEM
representatives would take care of making whatever contacts were necessary to ensure payment for her trip:

> I feel free, really relieved that I do not have to do any of these
> errands. You know me: I am always reluctant and afraid to get
> in touch with people I don't know, to find my way in new, un-
> familiar situations (the same way that each time I am afraid to

jump into the water, especially when you are not there. Once I have done it, I don't do too badly in the water, and with new people). So I did some sightseeing in Lisbon, wrote some letters, did not go to any organization, with the pleasant feeling that one has when duty, and desires, coincide for once.

But the day before the ship's planned departure, Eva received stunning news: "Suddenly, Tuesday night, when the others get their tickets, I am told that I am definitely canceled, because there had been no reply from America. Only at this moment it becomes clear to me that I had been in error thinking that Hicem would pay for my fare; in reality, I had to pay myself, and Hicem would only advance the necessary amount." Eva noted with dismay, "Had I known this from the beginning, I would have taken the necessary steps with our American friends. Now, one day before embarking, it is too late for any effort beyond the perimeter of Lisbon. So I don't expect any more that things will work out, yet don't want to give up entirely."

The "American friends" referred to by Eva were Anna Stein and Klara Deppe, ISK members who had immigrated to America in September 1938. There was no time left to contact them about trying to arrange payment for her trip. Eva had no choice but to do whatever she could to find a quick solution in Lisbon:

> And so I decide to go to Hicem myself the next morning, to explain the situation, to guarantee the repayment of the fare, and to ask Oscar (one of the leading Social Democrats from Austria) to give a formal voucher for me from his group if that should be necessary. Oscar is very friendly and helpful, goes with me to Hicem. There I discover that the main secretary on whom much of the decision depends had been at our house in Paris. . . . What a pity that I find this out only now! Three days earlier, a short talk with this girl, and she surely would have helped me arrange things. Now, however, everything is too late. The lists are definitely closed, our names are canceled because there had been no reply from America.

Eva began to accept that she would not be able to leave on this boat. "Now all is finished. I begin to plan for the new situation, to cable to

America for money, to give up the furnished room, to reduce my living expenses, to move in with someone's sister, to give requests and wishes to St.[Stern] for the friends in America, so that at least now everything stops because I can't get there yet." As she explained to Otto in her diary entry,

> Strange: although it is so very difficult for me to leave Europe because that would make it so much harder to see you again. I don't want to stay in Lisbon, am absolutely at odds with the way things have developed. In the afternoon, once more a meeting with the Austrian friends, at 4:30, in a café. All are honestly indignant about the fact I have to stay behind.
>
> At 4:45 Oscar arrives saying that he urgently had to talk with me. He had once more tried everything humanly possible at Hicem, and against all his expectations, he obtained this result: if by 5 p.m. I can put the necessary sum for the fare—$175—on the table, then the cashier would go with me to the Greek Line and try his best for me. But where can I get $175 within ten minutes? "Perhaps someone could lend it to you," says Oscar. "Can you send a cable tonight that the borrowed money would be sent by cable here?" "Yes." "Well, good, wait a moment." He talks to Katia (Friedrich Adler's wife), he leaves; in less than five minutes he is back with $200 in his hand from Friedrich Adler, whom he meets by chance in the street.

This fortuitous help from Friedrich Adler, a well-known Austrian scholar and trade union leader who was also seeking to escape to America, kept the door open for Eva.[13] Another coincidental encounter provided a bit more hope but resulted in disappointment:

> I go by taxi to Hicem, to the cashier who is willing to come along to the Greek Line, although not very friendly about it. Somehow, I think I know him, for a moment it seems to me that he could be Erich G (one of my former co-students from college); but no, that cannot be, this one is smaller, younger, different. But his hairline, his voice, the shape of his head—amazing. While we wait for a cab in the street, I ask him, without believing in it, if he is perhaps a brother of Erich's. And in fact

that is who he is, and now he is much more interested in my case, as he realizes that I really know his brother well.

He now pleads with the Director of the Greek Line, as though it were his own case. Ten minutes intense waiting while he talks with the Director. Then he comes back, and we only hear the last words: "But you cannot demand the impossible from me." I realize that now everything is really over, because it is too late. During the last 24 hours, nothing had been neglected; from the part of many people everything had been done, much more than I had a right to expect. Now it definitely is all over.

Eva dreaded having to wait four weeks for passage on the next ship:

The next morning, I spend a few hours in the Botanical Garden; a quick farewell to St. [Stern], then a walk to the boat, see many friends, say a very sad farewell. I walk back a short way with Marianne whom I like more and more. Then I leave to where I am going to stay now. I feel totally empty, exhausted, start to read something, begin a letter to Erich. When the lady at whose house I stay now comes home, we eat, listen to the radio. I am so tired that I can't do anything anymore, and just go to bed very early. The four weeks in Lisbon are looming ahead of me, like an insurmountable mountain. I sleep, heavily.

Eva's exhausted resignation did not last:

The next morning, I make my plans for the day: write, go again to the boat, to Hicem, study English. I begin to write. The telephone rings—I am wanted. A hope that I did not want to admit to myself flares up when I hear the ringing of the phone—now it becomes somewhat stronger. On the other end of the line is Marianne: "Eva, you better sit down: You can go! Be at the Hicem at 11 a.m. with your luggage." And now begins a strange back and forth which ends with my really boarding the ship at 8 p.m.

The explanation: in the morning, the awaited cable had arrived, but without my name. Since the secretary now knew who I was, and since Oscar also vouched for me, the Hicem included me in their efforts: the fact was that another month's stay in Lisbon would be very costly for Hicem, and they would not be reimbursed for this, while the fare for the trip was without any financial risk.

But now the officers of the Greek Line did not want us anymore. Thereupon, the Hicem, through one of their high-ranking people, got in touch with the Portuguese police who informed the Greek Line that the police would have to refuse me permission to stay in Portugal, and for that action, the Greek Line, also foreigners, would be held responsible, because there was no factual reason why I could not get on the boat. This "ultima ratio" made the Greek Line give in, and so, for the first time in my life, upon leaving Europe, the police intervened in my favor!

Eva's close call was reflected in a list attached to a letter dated October 11, 1940, from Isaiah Minkoff, executive secretary of the Jewish Labor Committee, to Joseph Savoretti, the acting district director of the U.S. Immigration and Naturalization Service at Ellis Island. Minkoff informed Savoretti that he was enclosing "the corrected list of our friends who are expected to arrive on the Nea Hellas Sunday, October 13." He added: "This list includes a couple of additional names." Eva's name had been written in by hand at the bottom of the typewritten list.[14]

Eva departed for America on October 3, 1940.

# 14. Eva's Voyage from Lisbon to New York

For Eva, the ten-day voyage on the *Nea Hellas* from Lisbon to New York offered a time for reflection. She felt the weight of the responsibility she was given to secure visas for her colleagues who had been left behind. And she knew that she would be alone in a foreign city in which she did not yet have command of the language. On October 7, 1940, Eva wrote in her diary—again with her words directed to Otto:

> I don't seem to leave behind me the strangeness of life. Am resting here on a long chaise, gray sky above me, through which the sun tries to break; in front of me water, all around me water, worldwide, never ending, gray, hardly moving, plain. I am sitting at the rear of the steamer, looking back at a wide expanse beyond which I can sense what I left behind, where I left you. Unconscious symbolism; not yet is my look directed forward, only backward. I know what I am leaving behind, and am totally unsure what is awaiting me, what—apart from very vague plans—I will have to make with this new life.

On the following day, Eva wrote:

> It begins to be very windy. The waves are not yet very high, but they have small foamy crowns, and last night they hit heavily against the small windows of our cabin. The sky is cloudy again; but every so often the sun breaks through, more than yesterday; the eastern horizon is quite clear; only small, transparent clouds. There is for a moment a broad, shining bridge

that reaches from me to the sky, so brilliant that it hurts the eye. The stripe along the horizon has become very small—there are only a few isolated spots of light. But the sky above us is getting lighter—soon there will be the bridge again. I look forward to it. When the wind blows strongly—at the front of the ship it always does—memory comes back of our last vacation, at the moment when we were standing high up in the mountains, near Grenoble, and were looking all around us.

Eva then described an encounter on board the *Nea Hellas* with Jef Rens, the Belgian labor leader who had worked with Otto prior to Otto's fateful trip to Luxembourg on May 9, 1940:

The first person I get to know here, on this ship, on this transition from the old to a new life, is a man I recognize, one who is in close contact with you and the work that caused you and me to be separated: Jef R.! It was the first day of the trip. In front of me, on the upper deck, is a group of people whom I notice because they are speaking French. Soon I am aware that they are Belgians. And immediately the thought: if one of them is perhaps Jef R., if I could ask one of them about him.

I ask myself: why this wish? If he [Rens] were there, he certainly could not tell me anything about you; he could also not help you, and the wish to obtain contacts through him that might be important for our work was way in the background. The decisive thing was probably simply the need to establish, through the relationship with this man, my contact with you. When, after a while, R. joins the group, I was immediately reasonably certain that according to his type, he was the only one who could be him. I hardly needed confirmation when we were introduced. At first distrust, then hesitant recognition that what I told him was true; slowly growing confidence, and not negligible mutual liking which went, I think, a little beyond the motivation that initially made me want to establish this contact.

Eva was not alone in recalling this encounter. It also had a special significance to Rens, who later described it in some detail:

These Belgians would regularly get together on the bridge after
meals and gather . . . to comment, in great discussions, on the
events of the war whose echo arrived to us by the radio. I often
attended these improvised debates, which were always passionate.

On this occasion, I had noticed a pretty young woman
who often came to sit among us and seemed to take great interest in our exchanges. It seemed to me that these glances were
particularly directed to me, which, given her beauty, did not
displease me!

After a few days, this lady got up, walked towards me and,
in impeccable French, asked me if we were Belgian. I confirmed her intuition at once and asked her how she had guessed.
Somewhat embarrassed, she mentioned our accent, then, looking me straight in the eye, said, "Are not you Jef Rens?" I was
amazed because I was certain I had never met this woman before
this trip.

Naturally, I hastened to know how she knew my name. To
which she responded that she was Otto's close friend! Her name
was Eva. . . .

It took me a few moments before I recovered from my surprise. Then I remembered my missed appointment with Otto
[on May 9, 1940]. Did she know where Otto was? She then
showed me a postcard . . . sent from an "Oflag" (prison camp
for officers) in Silesia. . . .

Eva knew nothing of the appointment I had with Otto on
May 9 in Liège and that it had been canceled at the last minute.
Thus, she learned that Otto had stayed in Luxembourg on May
9 and probably a few following days. How, after that, he had
ended up in Silesia remained a mystery for me and for her. All
our hypotheses did not carry us far. But the conversation allowed me to discover in Eva an intelligent woman, a trustworthy
friend who had the absolute conviction that Otto would escape
from his difficulties. The situation in which Otto found himself
remained for us a mystery that preoccupied us, and we did not
stop talking about it during the rest of the trip.[1]

One of the painful feelings Eva had described while interned at the
Vel' d'Hiv and Camp de Gurs was the powerlessness of forced isolation

from events threatening the world. She and others had been abruptly removed from the fight against fascism that had dominated their lives for a decade. On board the *Nea Hellas*, Eva began to feel the strength of returning to the fight. In an entry on October 9, she wrote:

> I am thinking now a lot about the future. Yesterday, I was read-ing British and Swiss newspapers, and I feel more in touch with what is going on in the world than I was before, don't feel quite so hopeless about the possibilities of development. . . .
>
> A play is being written and now produced in London whose topic is the first strike of English women workers which cul-minates in the call to organize in trade unions in order to fight for better living and working conditions. Surely, that can only be maneuvers with the intent to make the working class accept this war as their war. But even such an admission would be tre-mendously important, or at least it could become so, if only we understand how to get the best for the cause from this situation in which we and our positive support are needed.
>
> And alive and more urgent becomes the wish in me to par-ticipate in this work actively, and not only by saving others. The question what I should do, somehow presents itself under a viewpoint that is not quite as resigned as it was before. In this connection, I thought yesterday especially intensively about you, about our life in those months before the catastrophe, filled with steady tense worries, but also with intensive living. After the last six months of enforced passivity, my will begins to be revived to unite my strength with that of others: it becomes alert and strong. Talks with Jef R. . . . help to get me out of the passive, waiting attitude.

She then turned her thoughts to Otto:

> I wonder what you may think about the possibilities today to participate again? I don't believe that you, in spite of the 100% failure of your, our, efforts, regret that we made them.
>
> Of course, one does not want to waste one's strength for senseless acts. Up until a very little while ago, I thought that the situation and its perspectives were desperately hopeless. But

built on awareness of my growing feeling that efforts still do
make some sense, I will be able to pick up the work and wait
for the time until you return, with greater inner reserves.

Eva's next diary entry, written on October 10, reflected a very different mood. She moved from her new hope about the possibilities for
meaningful political activity to anxiety about what she now faced, alone:

Like a stream of ice water the knowledge comes over me that I
am without friends, also for the new tasks. The situation of 1933
is repeating itself, only with the difference that then I could correspond with R. [Rudi Lieske], and yet was convinced that our
relationship would eventually break off painfully. Now I know
that you and I will remain together even though no word from
you can reach me. Of course, I also am older now, have a firmer
hold on life, have gotten through a number of crises, and am so
happy thinking of you, even now.

But in spite of that, to be quite alone, without real friends
who had lived with me through these years, with whom one
could go through thick and thin, from whom one does not
have to hide when things don't go well, and one does not think
one can move on—this causes deep anxiety. It is true that St.
[Stern] will be there. He is a friend, a good one. But probably
only for quiet, contemplative hours. Not in the conflict with
ugly circumstances, surrounded by people some of whom are
not real friends.

Eva then considered the passengers on the ship and the different paths
they would likely take:

Strange, and not encouraging, this ship, or rather the "saved
ones." If an outsider would observe us here, he neither would
get the impression that the people here barely escaped a catastrophe, nor that they plan to commit their lives at least partially to
the fight against the evil, for the construction of a new world.
Some of course are not what they appear; we did have some
serious talks with each other, and there are many I don't know
who hide their concerns and plans behind facade. But there are

many who will fall off, and withdraw as much as possible into a private life. Perhaps that will result in a healthful selection; yet, this process is sad.

Eva found herself defending her political views in a discussion with other passengers:

> I don't think I handled myself too badly. It is not easy to defend our convictions, because they violate one's comfort, and yet most people defend their comfort with dogmatic phrases. Probably we made a lot of mistakes in the past while defending our opinions, did not always clearly enough separate single problems from the whole. Because of that, so many misunderstandings. But during this discussion also, I was alone.

The final entry in the diary that Eva began in Lisbon was on October 12, 1940, the day before arriving on the shores of what would become her new home. It was a difficult and lonely moment. Yet she found the place inside her that allowed her to see the beauty in nature that had always sustained her:

> The last day on the ocean. We exchange addresses, shake hands; the new life approaches, for none of us hopeful, yet probably for no one as hard as for me, because most of them are not alone.
>
> All day long, I have been reading, without seeing or listening to anything around me. Only once, I looked up: In second class, above us, a steward had caught a seagull, put a string around its legs, and pulled the tortured bird gasping for air and trying to obtain freedom, all to the pleasure of a hoard of people. A gruesome spectacle—fortunately, a good many people turned away from it, in dismay.
>
> Hellmut interrupted my escape into my book; the lovely little boy who wanted me to read him a story. Finally, I was finished with my book, and reality took over again. . . .
>
> I have a cold fear of being alone. The only thing that holds me up is the thought of your hard life, and that I want to remain for you the way I was in our good times. But I am very sad. And yet, in beautiful clarity and transparency of water and sky, the sun is setting.

PART V.

## NEW YORK, 1940–1941: URGENT EFFORTS TO RESCUE ISK COLLEAGUES, INCLUDING OTTO

*I am glad to vouch for the fine character of Eva
Lewinski and to declare my belief that the statements
she makes about Otto Pfister are true.*
— LETTER FROM DOROTHY HILL TO THE PRESIDENT'S
ADVISORY COMMITTEE ON POLITICAL REFUGEES
ON OCTOBER 28, 1940

*I have been to Washington. . . . I have tried to present
your case with the full strength of my convictions, and
not without some success I would think. You see, Otto,
that I am being diligent. And I also have hope.*
— EVA'S LETTER TO OTTO ON NEW YEAR'S EVE, 1940

# 15. Eva's Daunting Task of Obtaining U.S. Visas

When Eva arrived in America on board the *Nea Hellas* on October 13, 1940, she was surprised to see trees. She was convinced that there would be few trees in New York City. She later recalled that "Ellis Island was not a pleasant place," and when asked if the Statue of Liberty was a dramatic sight, she said "no, not at all . . . I wasn't happy to be there. I didn't want to be there. I didn't come out of my own free will."[1] Eva further reflected on her escape to America: "It meant going to a completely uncertain new life, one that I really did not want. I went only because of *Pflichtgefühl* . . . only out of a feeling of duty, to help people. . . . I wanted to stay in Europe. Europe was my home."[2]

The two ISK members who had immigrated to the United States before the war began, Dr. Anna Stein and Klara Deppe, had been Eva's former teachers at the Walkemühle. Stein lived in Buffalo, New York, and Deppe lived in Cleveland, Ohio. Neither was able to come to New York City to meet Eva when she arrived.

Eva's initial apartment at 52 W. 68th Street in New York was dramatically different than the lodgings she had shared with other refugees since her departure from Paris. "It was a little brownstone house where they rented furnished rooms; and from where I came—Vélodrome d'Hiver and the Camp de Gurs and Montauban cramped together—I had a room all for myself! That sounded like a paradise, but it was a junky room, and at night when I came home, the cockroaches were running up and down the wall. I had a tiny little sink with running water and a little two-burner stove. A chair."[3]

Shortly after her arrival in New York, Eva contacted Maurice Abravanel, a well-known Jewish conductor of classical music. Eva and

Typewriter given to Eva
by Maurice Abravanel.

her brother Erich had become friends with Abravanel in Paris before
Abravanel moved to America in 1936 to accept a post at New York's
Metropolitan Opera.[4] When Eva told Abravanel about her task to seek
visas for Erich and others who were still trapped in southern France,
Abravanel gave Eva a small typewriter to help her with that task. Eva
later described this special gift:

> [Maurice Abravanel] was in New York; I had his address, and I
> called him. I knew him from Paris. He was a very close friend
> of Erich's and he liked me too. He was very emotional. And he
> was a conductor. . . . He did all the Gershwin pieces. He was an
> important man and rich. . . . He had me come over and meet
> with him. And when he heard what I was going to do, he said,
> "Well, you need a typewriter. Here, take this typewriter." He
> had a little Hermes Featherweight. My first typewriter.[5]

On this typewriter, Eva would soon begin her urgent work of corresponding with all those involved in supporting applications for emergency visas. She would use this typewriter all her life.

Eva sent a brief letter, written in English, to ISK leader Willi Eichler
on October 20. Eichler was then living and working in exile in Welwyn
Garden City in Hertfordshire, about twenty-five miles north of London.
Eva wrote, "Only a few words today to tell you that I arrived here . . .
for the moment I am very busy to get visas for my friends who are still
in F. [France]." She advised him that the task will be "terribly difficult,"
and she did not know if she would be able to succeed: "We are very,

very late; but I try my best, and as I know a lot of people here I think it is not hopeless." Eva also informed Eichler of the distressing news she had received in Montauban about Otto:

> Did you get my letter from Lisbon? I hope so. So you will know that on the contrary of what you supposed in one of your letters, O. *is* in the hands of the Nazis; he is prisoner of war. I had no other news from him than just the fact of his prisonership.

Eva wasted no time in turning to her task. The first step was a trip to Buffalo to meet with Anna Stein—a week after her arrival in America—to make initial contacts with American citizens and organizations that might assist in rescuing their endangered colleagues. When she returned from that trip, Eva received the first news about Otto since she had learned in Montauban that he was in a Nazi prisoner-of-war camp:

> As I came home tonight, exhausted, there on the table is a telegram, some notes, mail. I open the cable: You are in Paris! Oh, I don't know what to do with my heart. Should really everything turn out well, should we be able to get together again, to live with each other?[6]

Eva would wait many months for answers.

## Eva's unlikely visa: a special "visa list" process

In order to understand the challenges that Eva faced in seeking U.S. visas for her ISK colleagues, one must first look back and examine another important question that Eva sought to answer shortly after her arrival in New York: How had *she*, a relatively unknown political refugee, managed to obtain *her* U.S. visa when she was in Montauban in the fall of 1940? Eva was virtually unknown to any Americans. She knew then—and throughout her life—that she had been extraordinarily lucky to receive a U.S. visa. She later became intimately and painfully aware of the multitude of Jews and political opponents of Hitler who were denied refuge in America and lost their lives in the Holocaust. Who were the individuals and groups responsible for allowing her entry into the United States, where she could survive and help rescue others, including Otto?

Congress had established restrictive immigration quotas in the 1920s because of fears about the adverse impact of immigration on American society and the U.S. economy. The Great Depression and the outbreak of World War II, accompanied by widespread anti-Semitism and rumors of foreign spies, fanned the flames of popular anti-immigration sentiment and contributed to official resistance to the granting of U.S. visas. American consulates found ways to restrict immigration, so the quota limitations were not even approached.[7]

With the outbreak of war in Europe in September 1939, it had become apparent to some individuals and organizations in America that extraordinary measures would be necessary to rescue political opponents of Hitler who were in exile in Europe. The two American organizations with the most crucial roles in initiating a special visa list process that ultimately resulted in the issuance of an emergency visa to Eva were the Jewish Labor Committee (JLC) and the American Federation of Labor (AFL).[8]

On February 28, 1940, the president of the AFL, William Green, and the secretary-treasurer of the AFL, George Meany, wrote to officers of national and international labor unions. They explained that the old German labor movement had been "attacked and wiped out when Dictator Hitler gained control of the German Government." Green and Meany urged American unions to support their endangered labor colleagues in Europe.[9]

Following the German invasion of France in May 1940, the European socialist and labor leaders who were now trapped in the unoccupied area of southern France were in imminent danger of capture by the Nazis. On July 2, 1940, a delegation of American labor leaders, headed by Green, and the JLC, headed by its executive secretary, Isaiah Minkoff, met with Assistant Secretary of State Breckinridge Long and hand-delivered to Long a letter addressed to Secretary of State Cordell Hull. The letter urged Hull to make it possible for a group of "men and women prominent in the democratic and labor movements in Europe" to find "immediate temporary haven" in the United States. The delegation met with Hull shortly after the meeting with Long.[10]

Hull was convinced by this delegation that a limited number of prominent refugees in the labor movement in Europe, on lists that were recommended by the AFL and the JLC, should be permitted to enter the United States on visitors' visas. It appears that Hull then consulted with President Franklin Roosevelt after meeting with the delegation and that Roosevelt signaled his approval of AFL president Green's request to help these endangered European labor leaders.[11]

Even Breckinridge Long supported this unique rescue effort. Much has been written about Long's resistance to the immigration of Jews and political refugees at this crucial time in history. Among other things, Long had initially praised the Italian fascist regime when he was U.S. ambassador to Italy, his diary suggests that he was prejudiced against East European Jews, and his record at the State Department confirms that he was more concerned about preventing "undesirables" from entering the United States than trying to save innocent political refugees and Jews who were threatened by Hitler.[12] However, Long agreed with this request by the JLC and the AFL to adopt this special rescue process for members of the European labor movement.

On July 3, 1940, Green wrote a letter to Long thanking him for the opportunity to present to him "the tragic plight of our refugee friends in Europe." Green confirmed that the JLC would present a list of names "of those who we earnestly request be accorded governmental visas in order that they might come to the United States as visitors. Such action will, no doubt, result in saving the lives of many, if not all of them." Green assured Long that the individuals on the list had been carefully vetted: "We have prepared this list with scrupulous care and are prepared to vouch for each one whose name appears on this list."[13] On the same day, Long confirmed that he had received the list from the JLC and assured Green that the State Department "has been glad to telegraph to the appropriate consular officers regarding the persons included in the list and has requested the consuls to give every consideration to their applications for visas."[14]

In preparing these lifesaving lists, the JLC and AFL representatives in New York relied heavily on information provided by political refugees who had moved to New York during the 1930s. Leaders of several German-speaking socialist groups were well represented in New York City in this process, and each advocated for inclusion of endangered refugees from their own group.[15] Many of the individuals initially selected by the JLC to be placed on these lists were not German-speaking political refugees. The JLC's focus was on exiled Jewish members of the labor movement, some of whom were Russians (Mensheviks), Poles, and Lithuanians who were endangered by the Soviet regime. However, the JLC did include a significant number of endangered Germans and Austrians.[16] The first list of refugees from German-speaking countries, completed in Washington on the day that Hull agreed to provide visas, contained a total of eighty-eight names; the second German list, composed of Austrians, contained twenty-four names.[17] These first two German lists included the names of prominent members of the German Social Democrat Party in exile.[18] No ISK members were on these initial lists.

Based on cables from Europe, the JLC and the AFL determined that other participants in the anti-Nazi labor movement who were not on the initial lists were in extreme danger in unoccupied France. Fortunately for Eva, supplementary lists were made.[19]

By telegram to the American consul in Marseille dated September 7, 1940, the State Department transmitted the third and last of the German lists. Eva's name appears on the third page near the end of the telegram.[20]

The U.S. consulate in Marseille issued the visa to Eva on September 16. A document with that date titled "Alien's Registration Record" briefly outlined Eva's background, noting that she had been a "journalist for different immigrant papers at Paris, and engaged in social welfare work" from 1935 to 1940, had never been arrested, and had been "interned in France during period 15th May–20th June, 1940, owing to German birth." This document was signed by Eva and Hiram Bingham Jr.

Bingham served as vice consul at the U.S. consulate in Marseille from 1939 to 1941. He has been properly but belatedly recognized for his efforts in assisting endangered refugees to obtain visas to escape from southern France in 1940 and early 1941.[21] Bingham's superiors in the State Department, opposed to his efforts to facilitate the granting of such visas, later transferred him from Marseille to Lisbon and then to Buenos Aires. Shortly before his transfer from Marseille, Bingham would also play a role in the granting of a visa to Otto in February 1941.

When Eva arrived in America, she was only vaguely aware of this special visa list process. She desperately needed to understand the procedures that would be available for her to seek emergency visas for her ISK colleagues. She first tried to piece together what she had learned about the visa process while she was in Montauban back in the late summer

Last page of September 7, 1940, telegram from the U.S. State Department to the American consul in Marseille, with Eva among the "additional names" on this visa list.

of 1940 with information she was able to obtain from other political refugees shortly after her arrival in New York City.

On November 2, 1940, two weeks after her arrival in New York, Eva sent a detailed letter to ISK leader Willi Eichler reporting on what she had learned. Because of concerns about confidentiality, Eva often used pseudonyms, abbreviations, or code words in this letter to identify individuals and groups.[22] Eva reported to Eichler that while she and other ISK members had taken refuge in Montauban, they had sent lists to Anna Stein and Klara Deppe of the names of colleagues who were in

**7575687**
ALIEN'S REGISTRATION RECORD.

September 16, 1940.

1. Name : Eva LEWINSKI.

2. Proposed address in the United States : C/- Mr. M. d'Abravanel, 41 Central Park West, New York City.

3. Born April 2, 1910, at Goldap, Germany.

4. No nationality -- German refugie.

5. Female sex, single, white race.

6. Weight : approx. 157 lbs.        Color of hair : dark brown
                                    Color of eyes : brown

7. First visit to the United States.

8. (Length of expected Stay in United States) -- 6 months.

9. Usual and previous occupation : Journalist.

   (B) no occupation.

10. Proposed activities in United States : wishes to continue as writer.

    (B) During the years 1935-40, have been wholly occupied as journalist for different immigrant papers at Paris, and engaged in social welfare work.

11. Military service : none.

12. Have never applied for first citizenship papers.

13. No relations in the United States.

14. Judicial record : never arrested.   Interned in France during period 15th May--20th June, 1940, owing to German birth.

15. Foreign political activities in United States: none.

Signature of Registrant: *Eva Lewinski.*
                         EVA LEWINSKI

Subscribed and sworn to before me this 16th day of September, 1940.

                         Hiram Bingham Jr.
                         Vice Consul for United States of America.

Admitted at
on  10/13 1940
graph   Section 3
Act of 1924, for  6 m o o.

Alien Registration Record for Eva dated September 16, 1940, signed by Eva and Hiram Bingham Jr. in Marseille.

great danger and needed visas. Eva explained that the lists were in order of priority, considering not only the degree to which they were in danger but also their ability to do the necessary rescue work in America.[23]

Eva described the disappointing news they had initially received while they were in Montauban that no ISK members were on the initial visa lists. She explained to Eichler that the ISK group in Montauban had written again to Stein and Deppe, asking them to contact Joseph Buttinger, the leader of the Austrian socialists, and Karl Frank (aka Paul Hagen), head of the German socialist splinter group Neu Beginnen (New Beginning), who were then in New York City.[24] Eva explained that the "decisive reason" why the ISK did not receive any visas on the initial lists was that the ISK did not have representatives in New York City who were familiar with the visa list process, noting that Anna Stein lived in Buffalo and Klara Deppe lived in Cleveland.[25]

Eva also informed Eichler that Joseph Buttinger, whom Eva had come to know in Paris, had been a key advocate for the addition of her name to the supplemental visa list. She reported, "Buttinger spoke up for me when my name was cabled from France; it was true that of our people in France he knew me best, and the others only barely."

Buttinger had risen from a working-class background to become the leader of the Austrian socialists and of the anti-Nazi movement in Austria. Following the Anschluss (the annexation of Austria into Nazi Germany in March 1938) he fled to Paris, where he was chairman of the exiled Austrian socialists. When the Nazis invaded Poland and war was declared in Europe in September 1939, Buttinger and his wife and daughter had moved to the United States. It was in Paris, between the summer of 1938 and the autumn of 1939, when Buttinger came to know Eva through their participation in the group discussions among exiles from different anti-Nazi groups.[26]

## The role of the Emergency Rescue Committee

Joseph Buttinger and his wife Muriel were also among the group of political refugees who helped establish the Emergency Rescue Committee (ERC) in New York shortly after Hitler's invasion of France and the announcement of the terms of the armistice between Germany and France on June 22, 1940. That armistice included the notorious Article

19 requiring the French government to "surrender upon demand" the German opponents of Hitler in France. A few days later on June 25, the American Friends of German Freedom (which had been set up in 1936 by the eminent American theologian Dr. Reinhold Niebuhr) held a large fund-raising luncheon at the Hotel Commodore in New York.[27] The ERC was formed at that time.[28]

In addition to the lists of political refugees being prepared and submitted to the State Department by the JLC and the AFL, including the list with Eva's name, the ERC created additional lists of endangered refugees. The ERC's lists focused primarily on prominent European artists and writers whose lives were threatened by Hitler. These lists were prepared with input from such people as Thomas Mann, the renowned German author who had already immigrated to America, and Alfred H. Barr Jr., an art historian and the first director of the Museum of Modern Art in New York.[29] The ERC also decided that it needed to send a representative to Europe to assist with rescue efforts there. In mid-July 1940, Varian Fry was selected. The ERC arranged for him to travel to Lisbon via Dixie Clipper and then to go by train to Marseille.

Varian Fry has been recognized for his vital work with the ERC through the offices of the Centre Américain de Secours in Marseille. He was posthumously honored and named "Righteous Among Nations" by Israel's Holocaust memorial Yad Vashem in 1996 for his work in 1940–1941 in assisting with the rescue of approximately 2,000 of Europe's artists, writers, and political refugees threatened by Hitler.[30]

Fry's involvement in Eva's escape from southern France, however, was very limited. The most critical hurdle that Eva had to overcome in escaping from southern France was obtaining her U.S. visa, and Fry was not involved in that extraordinary process. In addition, shortly before Fry arrived in Marseille in August 1940, an American journalist, Dr. Frank Bohn, had been sent to Marseille by the German Labor Delegation. His mission, supported with funds raised by the JLC, was to assist those political refugees who were on the emergency visa lists approved by the JLC and the AFL with the logistics of their escape to America—including help with their living and traveling expenses.[31]

Fry's assignment to assist those on the ERC's visa lists included coordinating with Bohn on the similar work that Bohn had been assigned to do for those on the JLC/AFL lists of political refugees.[32] While in Marseille, Bohn claimed to be working on behalf of the AFL rather than the JLC, presumably because he believed that this would enhance his authority.[33] Eva's brother Erich and other European anti-Nazi political leaders were also in Marseille in August 1940 when Fry arrived. They worked with Bohn, Fry, and others at the Centre Américain de Secours to assist with the escapes of these political refugees.[34]

In his book *Surrender on Demand*, Fry acknowledged his limited role with the early escapes of these political refugees:

> Fortunately for me, the first of the refugees to come to the [Hotel] Splendide in response to my summons were Paul Hagen's German socialist friends and some of the younger Austrian socialists. They were all young and vigorous and not at all lacking in courage. Most of them had already received American visas. All they needed, they said, was money. With enough money in their pockets for the trip to Lisbon, they would take their chances with the French and Spanish police and the Gestapo in Spain. They would get Portuguese and Spanish transit visas

Eva's brother Erich Lewinski (*second from left*) working with the ERC in Marseille in 1940–41. Others include (*clockwise from Erich's left*) Fritz Heine, Jaques Weisslitz, Daniel Bénédite, Heinz Ernst Oppenheimer, Hans Sahl, Marcel Chaminade, and Maurice Verzeanu. COURTESY OF THE VARIAN FRY INSTITUTE, CHAMBON FOUNDATION.

and go down to the frontier and cross over on foot. I gave them money and they went. All of them got to Lisbon. It was as simple as that.[35]

Eva fit into this category: the young, courageous political refugees with U.S. visas (issued on the basis of the JLC/AFL lists) who escaped over the Pyrenees shortly after Fry arrived in Marseille.

## A return to tightly restrictive U.S. immigration policies

It is a tragedy that the expedited emergency visa list process to rescue politically active anti-Nazi refugees was so short-lived and that the term "political refugees" would not be more broadly defined to include Jews whose lives were threatened by Hitler solely because of their Jewish heritage. The record of decisions made by President Roosevelt and his administration about the rescue of refugees during World War II has been exhaustively examined, evaluated, reexamined, and reevaluated.[36] In considering Roosevelt's support of this early effort by the JLC and the AFL to rescue endangered members of the European labor movement, one must recognize a crucial fact: Roosevelt faced reelection on November 5, 1940, and he relied heavily on the continuing support of organized labor. He likely felt strong political pressure at that time to respond positively to the AFL and the JLC. Whatever the ultimate historical judgment, Roosevelt's decision to support this visa list process for endangered political refugees was a bright spot in the tragic history of America's response to the refugee crisis in Europe at the time. That process resulted in saving hundreds of lives, including Eva's and those she would help rescue.

In her November 2, 1940, letter to Willi Eichler, Eva explained that when she and her group of ISK members were still in Montauban in the late summer of 1940, they had received word from exiled European socialists already in America that "the visa list action" was likely finished and would be replaced by careful scrutiny of individual applicants. She noted that visas "might be granted if for each individual case one could provide affidavits, political guaranties signed by Americans, and if one could bring proof of the endangerment of the individual in question."

This reversion to the "normal" restrictive U.S. immigration policies and procedures is reflected in the diary entry of Assistant Secretary of State Breckinridge Long in September 1940. Long explained that the

United States had been "very generous in offering hospitality" to groups including "a category of leaders in the labor movement in Europe who were recommended by . . . the American Federation of Labor." However, he confirmed that these exceptional procedures needed to end.[37]

Even before the State Department had adopted the special visa list process that had benefited Eva, it had begun to tighten U.S. visa restrictions in telegrams to consuls in June 1940. Applicants were required to show not only a good reason for needing to leave Europe but also a legitimate purpose for entering the United States.[38] And because of growing fears of German spies and communist radicals, State Department circulars to American consuls in Europe in June 1940 included directives to withhold visas unless the consuls had "no doubt whatsoever concerning the alien."[39]

In seeking emergency visas for her ISK colleagues, Eva would also need the endorsement of each individual candidate by the President's Advisory Committee on Political Refugees. The President's Advisory Committee had been formed in 1938 following a conference in the White House on April 13, 1938, among interfaith leaders and President Roosevelt to discuss the current and potential plight of refugees in Europe.[40] Following the Nazi invasion of France, the committee assumed the role of vetting applicants for emergency visas.[41] However, U.S. officials took actions to constrain the committee's rescue efforts.

In a now notorious secret memorandum sent on June 26, 1940, to State Department officials, James Dunn, and Adolf Berle Jr., Assistant Secretary of State Breckinridge Long suggested that the State Department could "simply advis[e] our consuls" to engage in bureaucratic delay tactics to obstruct the granting of visas:

> We can delay and effectively stop for a temporary period of indefinite length the number of immigrants into the United States. We could do this by simply advising our consuls to put every obstacle in the way and to require additional evidence and to resort to various administrative advices which would postpone and postpone and postpone the granting of the visas.[42]

On October 9, less than a week before Eva's arrival in America, James McDonald, chairman of the President's Advisory Committee, arranged a meeting (through Eleanor Roosevelt) with President Roosevelt to challenge Long's restrictive views about the rescue of refugees. Before the meeting, however, Long had asked Roosevelt to read a lengthy cable from the U.S. ambassador to the Soviet Union, Lawrence Steinhardt, that criticized the President's Advisory Committee as undermining American security and urged a firmer State Department position against organizations that sponsored such emergency visas.[43] Influenced by Steinhardt's cable, the president expressed his approval of Long's position that suspicious aliens should be excluded "no matter how prestigious their sponsors."[44]

Despite these security concerns, there was still *some* chance for refugees to obtain emergency visas. On October 18, five days after Eva's arrival, an agreement was reached among top officials of the State Department and the Justice Department that the President's Advisory Committee would continue to have the semiofficial status of recommending the issuance of emergency visas to intellectual and political refugees and persons who were in imminent danger. These discussions in October 1940 did not address the important question whether "political refugees" included Jews who were threatened by the Nazis simply because of their Jewish heritage. Not surprisingly, Long would seek to implement a narrow interpretation of "political refugees" as prominent individuals whose achievements or activities had antagonized the Nazis.[45]

This was the U.S. immigration policy that Eva now confronted in her rescue efforts. Affidavits had to be submitted by individuals with personal knowledge of the applicant. Such affidavits would have to confirm that the applicant was in imminent danger of capture by the Nazis because of anti-Nazi activities, was not a communist or a member of any other revolutionary organization, and was sponsored by an American citizen who would guarantee that the applicant would not become a financial burden on the United States—backed up with sufficient proof of the sponsor's financial resources. Precious few would be able to meet these vetting requirements.

Eva had been among the very last to be admitted to America through the door that had been opened by the JLC and the AFL for the expedited issuance of emergency visas to lists of endangered political refugees. That door had slammed shut even before Eva's arrival in New York on the *Nea*

*Hellas.* It would be Eva's challenge to gather the affidavits and American sponsors necessary to convince the President's Advisory Committee to recommend the issuance of an emergency visa to each ISK colleague. Ultimately, the State Department would have to approve the visas, the U.S. consulate in Marseille would have to issue them, and each refugee would have to find a way to get to America—over the Pyrenees, through Spain and Lisbon as Eva had done, or by some other route.

This was a formidable challenge. Eva was a young woman, burdened by all that she had endured in her life, still learning English, separated by the Atlantic from the person she loved, virtually alone. Fortunately, Anna Stein had developed a relationship in Buffalo with a wonderful American woman, Dorothy Hill, who knew Eleanor Roosevelt. The first lady would be of vital help to Eva and those she needed to rescue.

# 16. Help from Eleanor Roosevelt and Other Americans

On her first trip to Buffalo, Eva was grateful to learn that Anna Stein and Klara Deppe "had become part of the community of liberal Americans there." They introduced Eva to their American friends, who embraced Eva. "They saw me, a young woman who didn't know if her fiancé was still alive, who lived through a French internment camp. They wanted to hear. They were very interested in that. And so they organized luncheons and meetings of the League of Women Voters and some church groups." Eva later reflected: "I had never seen any nationality in my life that was so nice and welcoming to people who had trouble expressing themselves. They were wonderful."[1]

"My English was very poor at that time," Eva recalled, "just elementary school learning—and I was terribly self-conscious about that fact. But soon I learned how generous my new American friends were about that, and I became more at ease, and gradually more fluent."[2] Eva had taken three or four years of English in school in Germany. She had also learned some English from two British students in her group at the Walkemühle who did not know any German and taught her English songs. While on board the *Nea Hellas* to America, she had also tried to read Dickens's *Christmas Carol*: "I had a pocket dictionary and remember how painfully I had to look up every third word."[3]

Eva had no illusions about her task: "In this situation, it did not do to be shy and reserved. Since each potential receiver of an emergency visa needed an American sponsor who would vouch for him financially, I had to make it my business to find such people, and then to convince them of the justice of my requests."[4]

Eva's first and most important American friend was Dorothy Hill. "Apart from my two teachers [Anna Stein and Klara Deppe], and several organizations in New York, such as the Jewish Labor Committee, the Emergency Rescue Committee, and the President's Advisory Committee, the one person who helped more than anyone could have expected, and who quickly became my, and later our, best friend, was Dorothy Hill." Eva later fondly described Hill:

> A friend of Anna Stein, a graduate of Wellesley College, the director of the Wellesley Summer Institute of Social Progress, she was a lady—a lady in the true sense of the word—who knew all the right people, who was respected by all and loved by most, and she took us into her heart. Her letters of recommendation carried weight; her phone calls opened doors that otherwise would have remained closed to me. . . . Dorothy, in her warmth and generosity, helped me do things that normally would have been impossible.[5]

Dorothy Parmelee Hill was born in Buffalo, New York, on July 1, 1893. After graduating from the Buffalo Seminary, she received her degree from Wellesley College in 1915, where she was a "Wellesley scholar." Hill began her career as cofounder of the Hill Publicity Bureau in Buffalo in 1916, where her first clients included poet Edna St. Vincent Millay and writer Margo Asquith. Hill then worked with the Buffalo branch of the Consumer's League and was appointed to the New York State Joint Legislative Committee headed by social reformer and feminist Mary Dreier. Through that committee's efforts, legislation was passed in New York state establishing the minimum wage and the eight-hour workday for women factory workers during the administration of Governor Alfred E. Smith.[6]

In the 1930s while Hill was the only woman serving on the mayor of Buffalo's Committee on Unemployment in New York state, she became acquainted with Eleanor Roosevelt. Hill assisted Mrs. Roosevelt with the investigation of cases of needy families in the Buffalo area who had made personal appeals to the White House. In 1933, Hill was appointed by the president of Wellesley College to a committee of eight alumnae to find good use for the campus in summertime. She founded

and was the director of the Summer Institute
for Social Progress, an annual two-week conference that continued for twenty-five years.
Hill also helped establish the Buffalo Branch
of the ERC.[7] She was working with the ERC
when she met Eva in the fall of 1940.

Dorothy Hill found something deeply
compelling in the story of the young refugee, Eva Lewinski. And Eva was drawn to the
values of her new American friend and the
loving help she so generously offered.[8]

Because Eva was attesting to the good
character of her ISK colleagues in seeking visas for them, including Otto, it was critical
to have a respected American vouch for *her* to

Dorothy Hill.

the U.S. officials. On October 28, 1940, two
weeks after Eva's arrival in America, Dorothy Hill provided a reference
letter for Eva. "I am glad to vouch for the fine character of Eva Lewinski
and to declare my belief that the statements she makes about Otto are
true," Hill wrote. "I find her to be a young woman of unusual honesty,
courage and spirituality." Hill further reported that "Ms. Lewinski is engaged to be married to Otto Pfister for whom she writes the biographical
sketches attached. She is suffering terrible anxiety for his safety." This
was partially inaccurate. Eva and Otto had not yet decided to marry, but
Eva did not correct this—for reasons she would later need to explain to
ISK leader Willi Eichler.

Hill also commented that Eva belonged to a group that taught "doctrines contrary to the Hitler regime" and that the group maintained the
publishing house Éditions Nouvelles Internationales in Paris. Hill added
that this publishing house had "published Irmgard Litten's recent book
so favorably reviewed by Mrs. Franklin D. Roosevelt which gives further
evidences of the sacrifices for democracy made by the whole group of
which Otto Pfister is a prominent member." Hill concluded:

> My confidence in Miss Lewinski is strengthened by the fact
> that she is an intimate friend of Dr. Anna Stein who in turn is a
> close friend of mine living at 447 Potomac Ave. in Buffalo. Since
> her arrival in September 1938, Dr. Stein and I have worked

closely together on a local refugee committee and have become strong personal friends. Dr. Stein cannot say enough about the fine personality of Eva Lewinski and of Otto Pfister. I am convinced that they both are people of integrity who have been very active in anti-Hitler work and that Miss Lewinski has given a really restrained picture of Otto Pfister's fine work and his present danger.[9]

Dorothy Hill's comment about Eva's work with Éditions Nouvelles Internationales and its publication of Irmgard Litten's book would provide an important connection between Eva, the unknown refugee, and First Lady Eleanor Roosevelt. Litten's book *Beyond Tears* was about her son Hans, who had been imprisoned and tortured by the Nazis until he committed suicide in the Dachau concentration camp. In her newspaper column "My Day," published on September 17, 1940, less than a month before Eva arrived in America, Mrs. Roosevelt had reviewed *Beyond Tears*, noting that the archbishop of New York had written a short foreword to the book in which he stated "I hope this book may be widely read as a moving human record which illustrates the spirit of the Nazi tyranny."[10] Roosevelt concluded her column:

> I hope with the Archbishop, that many people who are not yet awake to the menace of power which knows no restraints except the measure of its own physical force, will read this book. But I shall not blame them if they put it down occasionally with a feeling that they cannot bear the human suffering it depicts.[11]

With a letter dated October 31, 1940, just over two weeks after her arrival in America, Eva submitted reference letters in support of a number of her ISK colleagues to George Warren, the head of the President's Advisory Committee on Political Refugees, along with the reference letter that Dorothy Hill wrote about her. Regarding her own background, Eva also referred Warren to additional reference letters submitted by "Mr. S.L. Levitas" and "Mr. Wilhelm Sollmann."[12]

Sol Levitas, who became executive editor of the *New Leader*, wrote: "Political refugees who are now stranded in France . . . will, no doubt land in concentration camps if not rescued in time." He advised the committee that he had known Eva personally for many years and praised her "intellectual and political integrity." He concluded: "I know that she is very much interested in the fate of her friends whose names she has supplied to your committee, and I can vouch for the facts which she has presented to your committee in connection with these cases."[13]

F. Wilhelm Sollmann had been a member of the Social Democratic Party in Germany during the Weimar Republic and had served as secretary of the interior in Germany and a member of the Reichstag for eight terms before being driven out of Germany by the Nazis. In 1937 he had immigrated to the United States, where he became a staff member of Pendle Hill, Quaker Graduate Center for Religious and Social Studies, in Wallingford, Pennsylvania. Noting that he had known Eva since 1932, Sollmann wrote: "Although I do not belong to her political group, I am glad to testify that Miss Lewinski has a splendid record in the struggle against Hitlerism and Communism in Germany as well as in France where she has lived as an exile for several years." He concluded:

> The friends of Eva Lewinski were very active in the underground movement inside Germany and in the work of German refugees in Western Europe. Many of them have sacrificed freedom, health and even their lives. There is no doubt that each member of that group would have to risk imprisonment for many years or execution if the present German government would get hold of them.[14]

We have previously referred to portions of the detailed letter written by Eva to ISK leader Willi Eichler on November 2, 1940, less than a month after her arrival in New York. Now we have reached the date on which she wrote that letter and can more fully appreciate the context. Having worked night and day since her arrival in America on October 13 to obtain U.S. visas for her colleagues trapped in southern France, she finally found a moment to report to Eichler about these efforts.

Eva's November 2 letter provides not only specific information of historical interest but also a glimpse into the complex relationship between her and Eichler. The letter was written in the dry objective style of a dutiful and dedicated business subordinate presenting a factual memorandum to a ranking superior. It presented in chronological order the actions taken by their small Paris ISK group since the German invasion in 1940. As previously noted, Eva often referred to others by their initials or pseudonyms, and at one point she referred to herself in the third person by a pseudonym, "Helene."

We know from Eva's diaries and letters to Otto about the emotional pain she had endured during the period she now reported with such dry objectivity to her ISK leader. In a brief note introducing her translation of this letter, Eva later commented about the nature of her relationship with Eichler:

> If my letter sounds like an account of what I had been doing since leaving Europe, and if it is factual rather than personal, that is exactly what our relationship was. We were friends, close friends; but Willi was in charge of the group, and even if it often ran counter to our emotions, we discussed decisions, and abided by them.[15]

Eva began by apologizing to Eichler for her delay in writing to him. She explained, "I had to run around so unbelievably much in order to make progress in the matter of the visas, I simply did not get around to writing sooner. There was just enough time to do all the necessary typing late in the night which had to be done in connection with the efforts to get visas. Now some of this work is under way, and today is the first day since I came here, where I was able to stay at home from morning to evening, and where I can write with a little more calm." Eva then addressed another preliminary matter that she did not want to leave to the end of the letter "because the news is so good":

> Last night I got a cable from my brother in Marseille in which he tells me that Otto arrived in Montauban, and that they expect him in Marseille. You can imagine, Willi, how happy I am, although, obviously, he is by no means out of danger. But whatever I have heard about the way he got out of the prison camp (I don't know any details, just that he was discharged, and that Gaby [Cordier] met up with him in Paris, from where he wrote to our friends in Montauban on September 26, the day I had arrived in Lisbon, and from where he now, apparently with Gaby's help, has arrived at our friends) gives me confidence that things will continue to go well.

Eva noted that obtaining a visa for Otto "will probably be made easier through the fact that Jef Rens happens to be here [in New York] who has great confidence in Otto and in [René Bertholet] because of the work they did together, and who has important relations here which he is willing to put into action on Otto's behalf. I assume you agree with me that Otto should try to get away from there as fast as possible?"

Eva provided a brief summary for Eichler of what happened to their colleagues in France since the German offensive in May 1940. She reported about the detention, flight, and entrapment in southern France that she and the others in the Paris ISK group had experienced. Unwilling to focus on the difficulties she endured, Eva wrote only one sentence in this long letter to Eichler about her own escape through the Pyrenees, not even mentioning the trauma of being torn away from Europe and the man she loved: "I will not write any details about the crossing of the border, the trip through Spain and Portugal etc., although some interesting experiences were connected with it. More important now is the situation here."

Eva then turned to the challenges she now faced in seeking visas. She explained to Eichler how the procedures had changed and how she had to "search for well-known personalities who knew our friends personally, and who could confirm that in all concreteness and why these people were in danger." As if breathing a sigh of relief, Eva reported that "as of today" the cases for her ISK colleagues had been submitted with all completed documents. In view of the presidential election the following day, she cautioned, "It is possible that all will go well now. But it is also possible that the doors may be closed entirely tomorrow (perhaps after unfavorable election results)."

One of Eva's tasks in submitting these applications for emergency visas to the President's Advisory Committee was to prepare biographical sketches of her colleagues stranded in southern France, explaining their work against the Nazis and the danger they faced. In a typed summary, Eva provided brief descriptions of the backgrounds of Otto Pfister, Erich Lewinski (Eva's brother) and his wife Herta, Hans Kakies, Erna Blencke, Eugen Albrecht, Nora Block and her sister Herta Walter, Gisela Peiper, Frieda Timmermann, Irmgard Amelung, and René Bertholet and his wife Johanna.[16] This summary, set forth in full in Appendix A, includes the following succinct description of Otto's background:

*Pfister, Otto,* born on April 8, 1900, at Munich. Cabinet-maker and interior decorator. Has done on close relation with French, Belgium and Luxembourg trade-unionists underground work from different borders into Germany, especially during the war. Has been captured by German military authorities at Luxembourg's invasion, was prisoner in Germany for several months. Germans did not realize his identity. So he succeeded in coming back to France. He is now in the unoccupied part of France and must soon leave so the Gestapo may not put its hands on him.

Anna Stein submitted a memorandum accompanying these biographical summaries. She explained: "All of the persons named here worked predominantly in the anti-Nazi movement. Some of them managed to work for five years in the underground-movement in Germany, some had to flee from Germany, as soon as the Nazis came into power." She described the danger they faced: "During the last years they chose to stay in the former democracies around the German border, because they considered it their duty to fight Hitler directly and carry out underground relations with the illegal movement in the Nazi ruled countries as long as possible. Their names are well known to the Gestapo. In case they fall into Nazi hands, they will face death or lifelong imprisonment."

Stein also provided a brief summary of the background of the ISK, including descriptions of the ISK's philosophical foundation, its school (the Walkemühle), and its publishing activities. Stein concluded: "Members of the group are therefore in a great danger and in urgent need of obtaining speedy help. Their devotion to the ideals of justice and liberty recommends them as desirable citizens in America."[17]

## Eva's first contacts with Eleanor Roosevelt seeking support for visa applications

Dorothy Hill arranged a meeting for Eva with Eleanor Roosevelt in late November 1940, less than two months after Eva's arrival in America. Hill and Malvina Thompson, secretary to Mrs. Roosevelt, also attended. In this meeting, Eva presented the story of her friends trapped in southern

France, and Roosevelt agreed to write a letter to the State Department on their behalf.

Roosevelt was diligent in following up on her commitment to Eva. In a brief letter to Miss Thompson dated December 9, Undersecretary of State Sumner Welles wrote: "I refer to your letter of December 2, 1940 enclosing a communication from Dr. Anna Stein . . . regarding the cases of ten refugees which have been presented to the President's Advisory Committee on Political Refugees. I am having these cases looked up and will write to you again shortly regarding their present status."[18]

It is not surprising that Eleanor Roosevelt directed this matter to Sumner Welles. Welles had a long and close personal relationship with Mrs. Roosevelt; and in the face of bitter resistance from his colleagues, he was one of the few officials in the State Department in Washington with sympathy for the plight of political refugees and Jews threatened by Hitler in Europe. His successes in contributing to the rescue of those trapped in Europe were tragically limited by many factors, including the political infighting at the State Department and a personal scandal that led to his resignation. But there is no question that he helped with the rescue of Eva's colleagues.[19]

On December 11, Mrs. Roosevelt wrote a note to Welles inquiring about the delay in the State Department's handling of visa cases submitted by the President's Advisory Committee. Not knowing of Roosevelt's follow-up communications with Welles, Eva sent a letter dated December 12 to Miss Thompson at the White House. Eva politely reminded Thompson of their visit:

> I do not know if you remember my name: Miss Dorothy Hill from Buffalo and I were at your house two weeks ago to see Mrs. Roosevelt. After having listened to the story of our difficulties, Mrs. Roosevelt was kind enough to promise to write the State Department a letter about our friends, several refugees now trapped in France, in order to hasten the issuance of an emergency visa on their behalf. But up to today, Mr. Warren's office [the President's Advisory Committee] has not received any answer from Washington concerning these cases. May I therefore ask you if you or Mrs. Roosevelt did get a reply? I am extremely sorry to trouble you again, but I think constantly of our friends

and the lives they are obliged to lead. So I can't help but to do all I can to get them over more quickly.

I do not need to repeat how deeply thankful I feel for all the help Mrs. Roosevelt has granted us.[20]

Meanwhile, Welles responded to Mrs. Roosevelt's December 11 inquiry about the status of these cases by letter dated December 13, 1940. Welles described the further vetting by the State Department of recommendations submitted by the President's Advisory Committee. He assured Mrs. Roosevelt that he had made "carefully inquiry" and that there was "no unnecessary delay."[21]

Even with the persistent support of First Lady Eleanor Roosevelt, obtaining these visas on an individual basis was an onerous and time-consuming process. Otto's visa application would be the most challenging.

## 17. Three Crucial Meetings on December 27, 1940

Despite Eva's efforts, Otto's application for an emergency visa was initially rejected. "It was desperately urgent for him to get out. I did what I had done for all the others: affidavits, letters of recommendations, biographical sketch in which I included as much of his capture and release as I then knew. The fact that he was my fiancé seemed to be an additional factor in his favor. To my dismay, my request for an emergency visa for him was turned down. . . . Dorothy [Hill] was shocked, but determined that we win the case."[1] Eva later explained why Otto's case "went totally sour":

> I got a sponsor very quickly and I got these people like Jef Rens who wrote letters vouching for him, and I had what I thought was a pretty good dossier put together, and they turned it down because it was too unbelievable a story: he was not a Jew; he had been captured by the Nazis; he had gotten out, how? Was he a Nazi? Or maybe a Communist? Either one of them . . . in any event, it was a story that was just . . . they couldn't buy it and so they refused.[2]

In a letter dated December 20, 1940, to Eliot Coulter, the acting chief of the Visa Division in the State Department, Hill urged prompt action on Otto's behalf. Referring to her telephone conversation with Coulter about Otto that morning, Hill wrote "I send you hereby some supplementary information concerning the activities of Mr. Otto Pfister. Mr. Pfister has been for many years active in the German trade unionist movement. He has always championed democratic ideals and protested

202

against totalitarian methods of whatever kind."[3] Using information provided by Eva, Hill outlined Otto's background. She explained how Otto had left Germany when he was about twenty years old, lived in Italy for about five years, and then for more than twelve years lived in Paris, where he had participated in anti-Nazi work. She noted: "In an important court proceeding against several of his friends in Germany in which the leader, Dr. Julius Philippson, was sentenced to life-long imprisonment, Pfister was named as one of the important contacts of the accused in France."

Hill also explained that Otto had been interned by the French at the outbreak of the war along with all other men of German and Austrian origin, and that he "was released in January 1940 on the special request of the French authorities so he could go on with his activities against National Socialism, activities which had become, of course, much more dangerous." She then provided the limited information she had about Otto's capture by the Nazis:

> It happened in this way that he went to Luxembourg on May 9, 1940, the day before the German invasion, and could not return to France. For three months there was no news of him, so that his friends considered him lost; then came a postcard from a French prisoner-of-war camp in Germany: by hiding his identity—the only way he could possibly save his life—he had been arrested on May 10th, as an ordinary civil internee by the German military and put into a prisoner-of-war camp.
>
> Owing to his ability, his courage and his perfect knowledge of the French language, neither his identity nor his activities became known to the German authorities while he was in the German camp. They released him, like other civil internees, at the end of September, and at the end of October he arrived in the unoccupied part of France, where he is living now.

Hill concluded with her urgent request:

> It seems quite certain that not only his liberty, but his life as well would be in danger if the Gestapo got hold of him. I know the ideals of Mr. Pfister are in complete accord with the ideals in this country, and for these reasons it is of mutual desirability

that he be allowed to come to this country at the earliest possible moment.

I hope to get a favorable answer soon, and will greatly appreciate your help on behalf of Mr. Pfister for whose fate I feel really anxious.

This letter resulted in a series of three meetings in Washington, D.C., that all occurred on December 27, 1940. Whatever one may conclude about the U.S. response to the refugee crisis at this moment in history, it is remarkable that all three of these meetings took place two days after Christmas. Dorothy Hill was the key in arranging two of these meetings. With the help of Paul Benjamin, a member of the Emergency Rescue Committee of Buffalo and a prominent member of the Welfare Department in Buffalo, Hill was able to arrange a meeting for Eva with Eleanor Roosevelt.[4] And Hill managed to arrange an appointment for Eva on the same day with the acting chief of the State Department's Visa Division, Eliot Coulter, with the help of one of Hill's former Wellesley classmates who was married to Coulter.

## Eva's December 27 meeting with Eleanor Roosevelt

Eva and Paul Benjamin met with Eleanor Roosevelt in the White House. A few weeks later on January 13, 1941, Eva sent a letter to Benjamin enclosing her detailed memorandum of their meeting with Mrs. Roosevelt.[5] Eva's memorandum provides a fascinating glimpse into the nature and depth of the first lady's concerns about the plight of refugees stranded in Europe. Eva began:

> Mrs. Roosevelt received Mr. Paul Benjamin from the Emergency Rescue Committee of Buffalo and myself very kindly and simply. She knew all the details we came to explain to her of the difficulties which the refugees seeking to come to this country are meeting. She agreed with us that the speed by which the different administrations are dealing with the emergency visa cases is by far insufficient. She did not think that the articles in the New York papers give a real picture of the situation, nor did she agree with Mr. George Warren [head of the President's

Advisory Committee] who, after a conversation with the officials of different administrations, and also with Mr. Cordell Hull [secretary of state] himself, seemed to be reassured and to think that things would go on better now. In her opinion things are going on too slowly even after the examination of each case. Those who are obstructing a more liberal refugee policy still hold their places in the State Department. She herself makes many interventions, but not always with success.

Eva then described Mrs. Roosevelt's strong interest in the case of the second son of Mrs. Irmgard Litten who was still trying to escape from Europe:

[Mrs. Roosevelt] simply could not bear that this mother should lose another son. She has written almost every third or fourth day to the Department of Justice, but the visa has not yet been granted. She felt very sorry for all these facts. She is of the opinion that America is losing very high moral and intellectual values by not admitting these refugees to this country. "We can expect much more from them than they can from us," she said. "It is very sad."

Eva further noted that "in Mrs. Roosevelt's opinion, those in the State Department who are obstructing the liberal application of the refugee dispositions are almost the same people as the 'appeasement-politicians,' a group small in number, but very influential." She added that Mrs. Roosevelt's mail is always very significant to her:

Every time, when Lindbergh has made a speech, she gets a lot of postcards, with this content: "We do not want to send our sons into the war. Your and your husband's policy are driving us into the war. We do not want to aid England, because that aid drives us into the war, into the war for England. We do want to get to an understanding with Hitler." "Well," Mrs. Roosevelt says: "I really cannot understand how one can still hope for an understanding with Hitler, even after the French experience, which should have opened the eyes to the last of us. But they do not seem to understand; and they do not see either that

England is making the war for us for those ideals for which we stand in this country."

Eva summarized the advice that Mrs. Roosevelt gave to her and Mr. Benjamin in their efforts to rescue others:

"If you want to get an improvement of the dealing with refugee problems, you have to fight at the same time against this appeasement policy. You have to push the public opinion all over the country, to make them understand that we do not object to investigation of these people who seek entrance to the United States, but that we have to go on quickly. And that these people for whom applications for visas are made, are for the most part not Communists or fifth columnists, they are known for their fight for the democratic ideals of this country. You have to go to your Congressmen, make them understand that if they are opening a reactionary campaign inside the Congress concerning the refugee problem, that would possibly influence the elections against them. That argument makes an impression on Congressmen and the attitude of Congress is very important since it influences the attitude of all the little officials in the administrations and Consulates, who do not want to take any risk.

Go to your local papers, organize mass meetings, as you did in Buffalo. The situation today is so that the utmost left wing is joining the utmost right wing. You have to show the just way to a real peace, and not appeasement policy and one part of such a policy is a liberal refugee policy."

Finally, Eva noted Mrs. Roosevelt's doubts about getting help for refugees from the French ambassador, Gaston Henry-Haye: "As to the situation concerning French exit-visa and Spanish transit-visa, Mrs. Roosevelt is rather skeptical. 'We have to understand finally that Mr. Haye (French ambassador) is a fascist.'" Eva concluded her memorandum with her more hopeful understanding that Mrs. Roosevelt was committed to continuing to help with the rescue of those on the list that Eva had submitted: "She promised to intervene again, and to send the list we submitted to the Department of Justice."

Eva noted at the end of the memorandum that the conversation took about thirty minutes. It had a profound and lasting impact on her. She later reflected:

> A few words about my visit with Mrs. Roosevelt. That I, an unknown refugee, should be able to enter the White House; that the wife of the President would receive me, shake my hand with great warmth, listen to what I had to say, ask questions, and then promise to try to help—that was perhaps one of the most profound experiences that I ever had.[6]

## Eva's December 27 meeting with Eliot Coulter

On that same day, Eva and Paul Benjamin met with Eliot Coulter to present Otto's case. Dorothy Hill described this meeting in a letter to Mrs. Roosevelt dated December 30, 1940, that was transmitted with a cover letter to Malvina Thompson. In the cover letter, Hill stated simply and urgently: "Were I not so worried I would not think of troubling you and Mrs. Roosevelt again about a refugee, and want you at the same time to know how grateful I am for what you have already accomplished. Reading the enclosed letter to Mrs. Roosevelt will explain my anxiety and I beg you to act in Otto Pfister's case now."[7] In the enclosed December 30 letter to Roosevelt, Hill wrote:

> My dear Mrs. Roosevelt:
>
> In behalf of Otto Pfister, Eva Lewinski's fiancé, Paul Benjamin and Eva Lewinski called on Eliot Coulter, Acting Chief of the Visa Division of the State Department, the same day you were good enough to see them. Otto Pfister's case has been held up so long in the State Department that we all have become seriously worried.
>
> Mr. Coulter talked forty minutes with them and they were able to answer all his questions satisfactorily. Finally he said he was now personally satisfied with Otto's fine character and devotion to democracy as opposed to fascism. But when asked if he would not now cable the visum he said he would prefer

to have the Consul in Marseilles first look up Otto's references there to corroborate all that they had told him and that I also had told him over the long distance phone.

Since we know how busy the Consul in Marseilles must be and have heard that in other instances he has been cold and hard and appears prejudiced against political refugees, we are much worried for fear the delay incident to putting responsibility in his hands may cost Otto his life.

Eva Lewinski has been so scrupulously fair in working impartially for her whole group in order of the danger she feels each is in, that we beg you now to act in her beloved Otto's case before it may be too late. We are convinced that Otto is of the same high caliber that she is.

If you should call Mr. Coulter and ask it I feel sure he would now cable Otto his visum without all this further investigation which we all feel is absolutely unnecessary. Believe me, Mrs. Roosevelt, that we do appreciate all you have already done and that we feel the others of our friends would never have been given their chance to escape without [your] personal help![8]

Dorothy Hill's December 30 letter not only confirmed her high regard for Eva but also evidenced Eva's unwillingness, as an ethical matter, to favor Otto among those she was seeking to rescue. In fact, one subject conspicuously missing from Eva's memorandum about her December 27 meeting with Eleanor Roosevelt was the need to expedite the process of seeking a visa for Otto. The only individual case referred to by Mrs. Roosevelt in that meeting was that of Irmgard Litten's son, and most of the discussion involved broader policy issues.

Given the principles of the ISK, including the prohibition against allowing personal relationships to interfere with the greater good, that was her ethical duty. Indeed, Eva's later decision to marry Otto when he arrived in New York would be considered by Willi Eichler and some other ISK members to be a betrayal of ISK principles and would drive a painful wedge between Eva and the organization for which she had worked so effectively and had sacrificed so much. Eichler would harshly criticize Eva for even disclosing the existence of her personal relationship with Otto to the Americans involved in the visa process (much less that

Otto was her fiancé)—and Eva would explain and vigorously defend her decision to marry Otto in a letter to Eichler in 1941.

## December 27, 1940, meeting of the Inter-Departmental Committee on Political Refugees about Otto's case

On the same day, the Inter-Departmental Committee on Political Refugees held a crucial meeting in which Otto's visa case was one of the cases considered. This committee was composed of representatives of five different U.S. agencies: the Military Intelligence Division of the War Department, the Office of Naval Intelligence of the Navy Department, the FBI, the Immigration Section of the Department of Justice and the State Department. The committee acted in an advisory capacity, presenting recommendations and providing assistance to the consuls in considering visa applications.[9]

Minutes dated December 28, 1940, titled "Political Refugees" summarized the cases considered by the committee and noted that "the action indicated was agreed to by all the persons attending the meeting."[10] The following paragraph referred to Otto's case:

> Otto Pfister (892), Marseille. It was agreed that the case should be referred to the Consul at Marseille for careful examination, in view of the questions raised regarding possible tie-up with the Nazis because of the statement that Mr. Pfister was released from the internment camp by pretending to be a French soldier. As soldiers usually carry some identifying documents and as it is difficult to believe that the Nazis would be unable to identify a German, the case calls for careful examination. However, as Mr. Pfister is said by his fiancée to have resided in France for twelve years, he may be able to show that the apparent discrepancy does not exist. It is believed that he should be given an opportunity to take his case up with the Consul. It was agreed that the Consul should be requested to report to the Department after conducting an investigation and suspend action pending the Department's further instructions after the case shall have been considered by the Committee.[11]

The committee erroneously stated that Otto obtained his release from
the Nazi internment camp by pretending to be a French *soldier* (as opposed to a French *civilian*). But the essence of the committee's concern
cannot be faulted. The story of Otto's background and his capture and
escape appeared on its face to be incredible. Given his German (and
non-Jewish) origin, the committee needed to assess the risk that he
might be a potential German spy or Nazi sympathizer. The committee
determined that further investigation by the U.S. consul in Marseille
was warranted before reaching a decision.

An FBI memorandum summarizing this same meeting, written
by the FBI's representative on the Inter-Departmental Committee on
Political Refugees, Edward A. Tamm, to FBI director J. Edgar Hoover,
raised an entirely different concern about Otto. Tamm wrote that "a man
named O. Pfister had been reported by the American Chargé d'Affaires
of the Hague to the Secretary of State about 1923 as being a revolutionary propagandist." He further stated: "I pointed out that if this were
the same individual, I did not think, without considerable additional
information, the Committee should recommend his admission."[12]

We have seen no other reference to this report about Otto's activities
in 1923, but it does not appear to have any factual basis. In 1923, Otto
was a struggling twenty-three-year-old cabinetmaker who had recently
moved to Rome. It is highly unlikely that he was the "O. Pfister" who
allegedly was reported to the American chargé d'affaires of the Hague
as a revolutionary propagandist in 1923. The interrogation of Otto by
the Consul in Marseille was likely intended to cover this issue as well.
With Otto's background as a German who was not Jewish, he had to
establish to the satisfaction of American authorities that he was neither
a Nazi sympathizer nor a revolutionary communist.

Tamm also discussed in this memorandum the question of how
the United States should consider the applications of refugees who had
close relatives in Germany or in Axis-occupied countries. Tamm advised
FBI director Hoover of his "very strong position" that persons entering the United States with such close relatives "constituted a probable
hazard because of the pressure which could be exerted upon [them]
to take action against the United States in order to prevent personal
harm to their relatives in the occupied countries." Tamm also reported
a strong contrary view: Henry Hart, representing the Immigration and
Naturalization Service at the meeting, was "very vehement" in his view

that "if the Committee took an affirmative stand upon this proposition it would eliminate a bulk of the refugees." Tamm commented that the discussion of this subject "became rather heated."[13]

This was a debate with enormous consequences. Obviously, most refugees would likely have some close relatives remaining in Germany or German-occupied countries. In fact, a strict adoption of Tamm's position would have precluded the issuance of a visa to Otto because a number of his close relatives still lived in Munich. No resolution of this debate was reflected in these minutes. In six months, this debate would be resolved by the State Department in favor of Tamm's view.[14]

So, December 27, 1940, was indeed an important day for Eva and Otto. Eva met with Eleanor Roosevelt in the White House and also met with Eliot Coulter in the State Department. And Coulter attended the Inter-Departmental Committee meeting on behalf of the State Department that further vetted Otto's case. Eva had effectively advocated Otto's case at the highest levels of the U.S. government, but the process was not over.

On December 30, Sumner Welles wrote to Malvina Thompson advising her that "the names of Erich Lewinski, Hans Kakies, Erna Blencke, Eugen Albrecht, Gisela Peiper, and Frieda Timmermann were forwarded by the Department of Justice, with the recommendation of the President's Advisory Committee, and have already been telegraphed to the appropriate consular officers for special consideration." He further reported: "The names of Otto Pfister and Nora Block have been received in the Department and are receiving consideration. Action in these cases will be expedited. The names of Herta Walter, Irmgard Amelung, and René and Johanna Bertholet do not appear to have been received as yet. As soon as they shall have reached the Department, action in these cases will be expedited. I shall write to you again regarding the action taken in the cases not already forwarded to the consuls."[15]

In less than two and a half months after her arrival in America, Eva had achieved the nearly impossible: obtaining approvals of visas for seven of her ISK colleagues, including her brother Erich and his wife Herta. However, as 1940 was finally coming to a close, other cases, especially Otto's, were not moving so quickly. Eva would have no time to rest.

## 18. 1940 Correspondence

Once Eva learned that Otto was alive in Montauban, they began an exchange of letters.[1] After six months without communication, Eva could finally hear directly from Otto, who was with their ISK colleagues in southern France, and Otto could hear directly from Eva about her efforts to rescue him and the others. Otto wrote at greater length and more often than Eva during this period. As she would explain to him, this was a time of overwhelming work for her, including her efforts to obtain a visa for him. Significant delays in delivery of some of the letters often created confusion and anxiety. Eva also sent periodic letters to ISK leader Willi Eichler, then in exile in London, reporting on her progress in seeking to rescue their ISK colleagues.

In their letters, Eva and Otto made several references to a "little book" or "little blue book" that Eva had left for Otto. They were referring to the diary Eva wrote during the period from May 18, 1940, until her escape from France in September 1940. This is the diary that Eva left with her brother Erich before she departed from Marseille so Erich could give it to Otto if Otto survived his capture by the Nazis.[2]

Apart from the postcard from "Paul Bois" to Yvonne Oullion that Otto had written from the Nazi prisoner-of-war camp, the first letter from Otto to Eva after his departure from the Paris train station on May 9, 1940, is dated October 28, 1940. Writing from Montauban in the unoccupied zone, Otto informed Eva, "I just reread your little book, your last letter. At one point you say: 'My belief has not yet been shattered that I somehow can ease your hard life if I follow you in my thoughts everywhere, in unshaken love.'" He shared his agreement with her belief: "I was so unbelievably fortunate to get out of a number of difficult, seemingly hopeless situations and finally landed here, that I cannot and do not want to refuse the feeling that the strength of your love really was a factor in what happened, what still is unbelievable to me."

Otto then promised Eva, "I will try to write you as much as possible about what happened to me. Right now, I neither have the time for it nor am I relaxed enough to do it. And although you got the cable in the meantime which Erich sent you immediately, I do want for you to get at least a few lines from me." He assured her:

> My dearest, do, do know that I am the same in every respect. What I lived through, and even the shattering of our work, the hopelessness on the horizon, has not destroyed my confidence in our good cause. My readiness has not suffered. And my love for you has not lost anything of its depth, and my thanks for what you are and feel for me, burn stronger than ever in my heart.

Otto noted that he had just heard from Eva's brother Erich and his wife Herta. They had advised him that the chances of their trip to America were not favorable at the moment. Because their departure was not imminent, he told Eva that he might still see them. He closed by asking "When will I have the first lines from you? Want you to know that everything from Issy (les Moulineaux) [Eva's apartment in Paris] was saved. Also letters and books are well taken care of."

In her first letter to Otto from New York on October 31, Eva wrote: "I can express only poorly or not at all what is happening within me. The days pass in strenuous work; the nights are filled with thoughts of you, of us. Sometimes it is quiet and solemn in me, with thanks that everything after all seemed to work out. Often great sadness. Oh, you understand without my saying any more." She assured Otto, "Now, I do everything possible so that you too can come here. Jef [Rens] helps me, he proves to be a good friend." Eva ended the letter by asking: "Could you read the letters that I wrote you during these months [diary entries in the "blue book"]? And did they tell you what they wanted to say?"

In his next letter, written in French from Marseille on November 8, Otto described briefly his capture and release by the Nazis, his return to Paris, and his bitter sadness upon learning that Eva had already left for America. He informed Eva that he was in Marseille "for a few days to be brought up to date about the situation by your brother." He told her of the plan that if Erich and his wife could escape soon, Otto would replace Erich "as best as I can" in the work Erich was doing in Marseille (with Varian Fry and others) and would then return to Montauban.

Otto confided to Eva, "I would so much like to be near you, at least for a little while. Is this going to be possible? My reason tells me to be skeptical—what I have heard of the possibility of leaving does not permit much hope. And there are so many others of our friends who are also waiting." He added, "However, I don't want to abandon hope now when so many difficulties have already found their solution." Otto ended the letter:

> Now, let's go for a little walk, you and I. I take your hand, and we walk through the streets of Marseille which have seen your eyes—sad like on the photo that you left for me, but in-finitely good.

In a brief letter on November 25, Eva told Otto: "My dear-est—Yesterday I finally had in my hand your card, this one greeting that came to me in the long hard months. It came as there was almost no hope in me. I looked at the few lines, at what was in them and what was between them. And I was not completely alone. Great is my longing to see your handwriting again, at least to have that in a moment when I don't know when I will have you again." She added:

> The photo of you is in front of me, serious, concentrating, the one that I like so much, and that always was with me when you were away. Sometimes you appear very sad. Then I would like to talk to you, softly, for a long time, from within. You should not be sad because I am there, I will stay there. Despite all the vast distance.
>
> Write, write to me, my dear man. In you is my life.

Otto wrote a long letter in German to Eva from Montauban on November 28, and he completed it in French from Toulouse on November 30. It must have been a difficult letter for him to write. After telling Eva that he had "a long, long wait" for her letter, he confessed about "straying from my path" with Gaby:

Today [your letter] came. I am so glad! And sad at the same time. Because I am telling you only now what Gaby had written you while I was in Marseille. I read your letter to her, and hope strongly that things are still the way you said when you wrote to her.

I would give a lot if I could only be with you now. Then it would not need any words; then everything in me would tell you how much I love you, and that the past weeks have not diminished my deep relationship to you. And if once in a while I am overcome by anxiety, it is because of the thought that in addition to all that has been burdening you for so long, and still now, bitterness might be added about my straying from my path. It is therefore doubly hard for me that I did not find you here any more, that I did not get here in time.

Otto added, "Now all I can do is wait, and I can't do a thing to come to you. That's why I will go to Toulouse tomorrow morning." He reported that their artist friend, Theo Fried, was in Toulouse and believed that Otto could work there. He informed Eva, "Finally, finally our luggage arrived—a case for everyone. My toolbox arrived also. That will make it easier to find work."

Otto closed the first part of this letter by giving Eva a brief picture of his current life in Montauban:

I would be happy to again have some regular work, at least for a while. Here it is not easy to fill the days well, although there are only five who live here, and nine for meals. There is only one room that can be heated (and we are privileged to have that—so many are miserably cold). I sleep in the corner, in your sleeping bag. Am getting along well with the friends, although we are very crowded. But should I hesitate to admit that I wish to be alone with you? It is much easier for me to be generous and warm to others when you are with me.

Please write me how you live. Can you be alone? I am so happy that Jef [Rens] is helping you, and that nothing happened to him; tell him that, also my thanks, and best greetings. How is Stern? Do you see him often? Also to him very warm greetings.

Continuing the letter on November 30, Otto wrote, "I could not finish yesterday. Now I just arrived in Toulouse. . . . I'll see Theo—am very happy to meet up with him again." He told Eva that he "just had a letter from Paulette (Yvonne's sister) who is back from Amiens, in Castres.[3] She told me of all the things that you have done for me, and she said it warmly as Yvonne did also when I had seen her in Paris. Yvonne was great, offered me some money, and when I was ready to leave, she lent me 3,500 ffrs [French francs] for your furniture, and said she would try to find a buyer for it."

Otto again explained that he had been able to move almost everything from their Paris apartment. He then told Eva that without letters from her, "I read nothing but the little blue book, and you know that over there (at the camp) I received no sign of life, nor inquiry from you. This little blue book . . . If you could know how precious it is to me!" Otto then turned back to Gaby:

> Now, my dearest, I am waiting impatiently for a word from you that tells me that you don't worry about Gaby and me, that you don't think that anything has changed between us. I am waiting anxiously to be near you again, to live and work again with you. Is that going to be possible? But don't you see, I have seen so many things that seem impossible during these past months that in spite of a certain skepticism I don't want to give up hope that the day will come when we'll be together again. I love you.

On December 6, 1940, Eva wrote to Otto: "My dearest, please don't mind that this is being typed. It is faster, and I am in quite a rush, and don't want to miss the opportunity of this Clipper [overseas mail carrier] without telling you how deeply happy I was about your letter, the first after so many awful weeks and months." She reassured him:

> Yes, I am sure you have remained the same, and so have I. My love for you has gotten even stronger, if that is possible, since we had to separate, stronger and perhaps a little less selfish. I wish so much that your and my hope to be able to build our life together again would materialize. I read and reread your letter

again and looked at that little photo of you. How close I feel to
you! The thought that you can read in the little book that I left
behind, that you have already read it, spans a strong bridge over
the months of our separation.

Eva's comment in this letter about "that little photo of you" refers to
the photo of Otto that is on the cover of this book. On the back of that
photo, Otto wrote "Pour toi! Il n'a pas changé."

In his letter of December 7, Otto gave Eva an update on their colleagues in France. He had not yet received Eva's assurances and was eager
to hear her reaction to his November 30 letter about Gaby:

Did you get my letter from Toulouse? I hope it did not take as
long as yours of Oct. 31, the first and only one that I got so far.
And when will I get an answer? I hope very much that it will
be before Christmas—I am not at ease until I know that there
is no shadow between us.

Otto reported, "I was in Toulouse for only a few days. I don't think it
would be too hard to find work; for the moment, I have looked the
situation over, and I am waiting for Roger [René Bertholet] now who is
supposed to get here next week, and who might be able to help."[4] Otto
also told Eva that he had started to take English lessons that day. "Gaby
takes them also, but she is more advanced than I am; so I have to make
a special effort. Too bad that among our friends, there is no one who
speaks it well." He then asked:

And you, my dearest, how are things for you? It must be terribly cold . . . Is that true? How can you take that? How is your
health? I am very worried when I think about your life; and
when you are alone, I fear that you don't do much to take care
of yourself!

Every morning, I am waiting for a letter from you, a sign
of life. Don't keep me waiting too long! Oh, I know I don't
have the right to tell you that. But I love you, and the fact that
we are so far from one another is very hard for me to accept. I
miss you so.

Otto started another letter to Eva from Montauban on December 20, continued it on December 21, and finished it on December 23. He began: "Yesterday they woke me up at 5 a.m., and there was Roger [Bertholet]! Now I have seen almost everyone." Otto then lamented, "I feel homesick for you, in a dark and heavy way. During the day this feeling somehow disappears, is drowned out in noise, tension, efforts to master the problems of the day. And then it comes back. If only I could start walking, find a road that would lead to you. I would walk for months, every day. And every day would be a blessing, and I would be happier every day." He told Eva:

> If I only knew that you are not sad, if I could see you, see your big good eyes. And if I could see some joy in them, quiet joy of which we should not be deprived in spite of these heavy, dark times.
>
> Soon it's going to be Christmas. Perhaps I will still get a letter from you before the holidays, perhaps a letter that tells me that you got mine, that you are without bitterness. If only my letters did not get lost! This is my fourth. Tomorrow I'll send a cable; perhaps that can be done without difficulty.

The next day, December 22, Otto added "Could not continue yesterday, had to move to Nora's to make more room for the others. It is not far from here." He then exclaimed, "And this morning, a telegram from Erich: seven visas! So there is progress. How much effort that must have cost you!"

Regarding his own visa status, Otto observed, "I will have problems with the exit visa if I am not able to have my carte d'identité [identity card] extended. Now I am waiting for Roger [Bertholet]; he may be able to do something about it." Otto then described some special gifts he received from Bertholet and plans for New Year's Eve:

> By the way, he brought us a lot of things: clothes, chocolate, coffee, and, above all, soap. Great! Also a beautiful book: *Grapes of Wrath*. That is supposed to be the most recent American best seller. Do you know it? On the 31st, we will have an evening together, and I am supposed to read from it. Roger [Bertholet] will perhaps bring the beautiful album that Fried has; he told

me that you liked it so much. Erich was able to send a cable for Theo's visa. It is still very difficult to live in this town (Toulouse).

Otto was not able to finish the letter until the following day, explaining "Again interrupted. Please forgive me; here, the plans for the day are often changed, and quiet minutes are rare." He noted that "today it is again very cold" and concluded: "How is it where you are? I would like so much to know whether there are good people around you, whether you are not too lonely. Your last letter—wasn't it a little sad? I have to end now. I take your face into my hands."

As we know, the year-end holidays and the beginning of a new year were always times of reflection and introspection for Eva—likely stemming from the traumatic loss of her father at Christmas when she was eight years old. One can hardly imagine a more tumultuous year in her life than 1940: her internment in the Vel' d'Hiv and Gurs, her flight to Montauban, the wrenching decision to leave Europe and the man she loved, her escape over the Pyrenees, and the last two and a half months of 1940 in this strange new country filled with endless work and continuing uncertainty.

Eva began a letter to Otto on Christmas Eve. She recalled their exchange of New Year's greetings a year earlier when Otto was still interned by the French shortly before he was released:

Otto, my most loved, my good man—it has now become completely still in my quiet room. The work is done; it is 10 o'clock at night; in one hour I will go to the train station to travel to Buffalo and Washington to try to bring your case forward. It is quiet, completely quiet. A candle burns, the clock ticks. . . .

How hard was this year! And despite that, how much happiness has it brought! Today, almost at the end of this year, I hold the greetings in my hand that you first sent; tomorrow you should have my greetings. That we are able to overcome such distances of space and time is for me like a symbol that nothing can separate us. I love you so much, with the entire strength of my heart. Next to the love for you, there is no place for small feelings, also no more fear and uncertainty that I will lose you. Give my best wishes to Gaby. My thoughts are also with her tonight. That she made your return to life warm and heartfelt, makes me quietly grateful and does not hurt any more.

Eva ended this part of the letter by expressing her gratitude for those who had helped her in America, and for Otto's love:

> I have so much to tell you, my Otto. About many good people whom I have met here and who like me, me the stranger; often thoughtful, caring people. About my being alone, that is something I chose myself, it is so and cannot be otherwise; about Stern and his great selfless friendship. About my work, my efforts to help. But it is hard for me to write, just now, when these efforts were successful for many, but not yet for you. As long as I have not made more progress, my heart and mind are completely full of afterthoughts about what still can be done. Every other step is in the background.
>
> Your letters—what a joy they were and are (two arrived so far)! Now I can go along with you at least in part.
>
> I have to go now. Let me close my eyes for a moment. You are with me, your good hands touch me—oh Otto, I want that we can live together again. Thank you for your love. You help me not to become small. I hug you, within, completely.

Continuing this letter on New Year's Eve, Eva expressed her hope for the future as symbolized for her by the new moon. Having met with Eleanor Roosevelt and Eliot Coulter just a few days before, on December 27, Eva briefly noted her advocacy on his visa case with cautious optimism:

> Now the last evening of this year has come. I spend the evening quietly at home and my thoughts and love are with you. As I walked along the street tonight, I was greeted after a hard day with a clear, still starry sky. The small delicate crescent of the waxing moon—*the* sign of hope for me since I was a child—the two stars, the large shining one next to the smaller one, that never leave each other, that since Gurs have never left me—they were there. And since I didn't hold your hand and couldn't squeeze it, I nodded to them as if they were understanding beings, and thanked them for their comfort.

I have been to Washington. . . . I have tried to present your case with the full strength of my convictions, and not without some success I would think. You see, Otto, that I am being diligent. And I also have hope.

Dear, dear Otto, now the letter must finally end. Be certain with your thoughts about me, as I am about you. An inner, quiet kiss.

Otto sent a year-end letter to Eva on January 3, 1941, before he received Eva's year-end letter. Like Eva, he commented on both the pain and the hope that 1940 had brought to them: "My dearest, a year has gone by, a year that brought us so much hardship, so much pain, so much disappointment. And yet, it also brought good things. Good the hope reinforced through your last cable that the possibility to get together again comes a little closer, a little more real. How I am looking forward to that!" He thanked Eva for her response to Gaby: "Your letter of December 6, your unbelievably beautiful letter to Gaby, were like gifts. You are so great in them, so much that my heart hurts, and that I ask myself if I am worthy of it."

Otto also thanked Eva for the diary and photo she had left for him:

Again and again I take out your little book—it warms my soul. . . . Do you know there are twelve empty pages? They seem to wait for you to write about our being together again, of a happiness such as we did not know before.[5] I would like to read in it every evening, would like to look at your picture. But I can't do it when other eyes are there. . . . And in order to write to you, I try to hide someplace. Because when I write, I feel so close to you, loving and tender. I am sure those feelings show in my face. Am I ashamed about it?

Otto then provided some news about himself and others waiting in southern France. He told Eva that "the last few days it has been very quiet here" and that he again lived on the Rue de la Comédie in Montauban. He further reported that some of their ISK colleagues were in Marseille, and others including Bertholet were away traveling: "Imagine, for one night I was almost alone!" He noted Eva's progress with visas and commented hopefully, "I am preparing myself also—I don't accept any work now."

Knowing that Eva had lived in Montauban during the summer, Otto described the same city he was now experiencing in the winter: "It is very cold outside, sleet and snow. On the good old bridge there blows an icy wind. White and different the profile of the river's bank. Many people are very cold." He explained with gratitude that "we have one warm room. That is a lot." And he noted that he was getting along with others sharing his room "as a whole, pretty well. I have to watch myself not to be petty at times. . . . Sometimes, we are aware of the fact that too much is being talked about food, and we are ashamed. But things are not easy now; yet, we are not actually hungry. Sometimes, lately, we get together and talk about the situation, about problems and questions. . . . I also try to study English—you will be far ahead of me with that!"

Otto then told Eva that he was happy to hear that she had a better room now and a radio. He asked, "Do you see some good films? Here there are some from time to time, yet one would have to take along a heavy blanket in order not to freeze hopelessly." Noting that "Stern's letter was beautiful and warm," Otto asked, "How is he at his new place? How are his eyes? Who takes care of them? I am concerned that he does not do it properly. Tell him when you write him that I do not forget him." Otto ended this letter with a description of the corner of his room in Montauban:

I also made a picture of my corner to send to you. It's not very elegant, and looks better on the picture than in reality. My tools are in the large box, then the large suitcase that you know, then a cheese box that became a cupboard. On top of that a chessboard on which Hermann [Platiel] wins most games. There are ice flowers on the windows now that make the room unusually bright. Despite the cold, I sleep well in my corner.

And you, dear, do you sleep well? How is your health, how the heart? Do you eat properly? There is so much I want to know, and I look forward to a long letter.

In a brief year-end letter to Otto dated January 1, 1941, Gaby wrote:

I have a few moments, Otto, and I must say hello to you. I have been close to you in my thoughts today; because it is the beginning of the year, but also because of the good talks we had. . . .

Normally, I don't like to send special New Year's wishes. But this time it is different. You know well what I wish for you, and for Eva, and today I wish this more strongly than ever.

My trip is being extended. I will have to organize all that so that there is less loss of time and less fatigue.

A warm, strong handshake, Gaby

Eva also provided a year-end report to ISK leader Willi Eichler who was still living and working near London. In a letter dated January 1, 1941, she began, "I hope so much that the last fearful bombings have not caused too much harm, and I wait with great impatience for news from you." She reported, "I was also able to cable you that we finally received some visas. Now it all depends on whether those who received the visas can still get out in time, and whether the visas for the others will arrive in time."

Eva explained, "I consider the situation in France to be anything but stable." She observed that as much as she would like to see the French resistance "crystallize" against the German rule in France, "that would most probably mean in the short term the German occupation of the rest of France. That [occupation] would have incalculable consequences for our friends who would then still be in France."

Eva urged Eichler to provide additional support for Otto's visa application (referring to Otto by his pseudonym "Tom"). Specifically, Eva asked Eichler to expedite the delivery to U.S. officials of a reference letter for Otto from Edo Fimmen, secretary of the International Transport Workers Federation, with whom Otto had worked closely on anti-Nazi activities in Europe:

I will try here now as before to achieve for our friends as much and as quickly as possible. Unfortunately, Tom's [Otto's] case just now creates problems, the sources of which I cannot write in detail now, and which hopefully in the meantime will be removed at least in part, but which have resulted in very uncomfortable delays in the processing of his case. In any case, very good references for him are an extraordinary help. If Edo's would arrive soon, that would be very good. It is a matter of confirming that Tom [Otto] is a faultless, upstanding character, whose anti-Nazi convictions can stand no doubt, and that one can confirm this on the basis of personal knowledge. One should also comfortably write something about his personal conviction.

Eva explained to Eichler that because Otto's case "appeared to be difficult, I went, myself, to the Department of State in Washington with one of our American friends from Buffalo, and I spoke with the leading official of the Visa Division. I think the discussion eliminated some doubt and hesitation." She added, "That Tom [Otto] also is my boyfriend, or much more my fiancé according to the documents here, adds something to my personal testimony." Eva told Eichler that "more references can only help." She urged him to see if Jef Rens, who could be reached in the Belgian embassy, "could also send a cable to Eliot Coulter, Acting Chief of the Visa Division, . . . in which he vouches for Tom's [Otto's] integrity."

Eva updated Eichler on the status of visas for the others. She concluded: "If we have still a little time without a big reversal occurring, we will still get, I hope, most of them over here."

# 19. Eva's Other Activities before the End of 1940

During her first ten weeks in America, Eva had focused on her primary task of seeking visas for her ISK colleagues while finding time to correspond with Otto and Willi Eichler. In her remaining waking hours during that period, she also sought sponsors and gathered support for the rescue of other endangered refugees stranded in Europe. In addition, she made speeches in meetings arranged by Paul Benjamin and others to seek broader political and financial support for these refugees. And she found moments to write to her mother, who had previously sought refuge from Nazism by immigrating to South Africa.

## Assistance from Albert Einstein

In a letter to Albert Einstein at Princeton University dated November 18, 1940, Eva requested Einstein's help in preparing a biography for Wilhelm Herzog, a German historian, writer, and publisher.[1] It is one example of her many efforts to help endangered refugees in Europe other than her ISK colleagues. Eva informed Einstein that she had arrived in America five weeks earlier from France. She briefly explained her involvement with the ISK's publication in Paris of a book by Herzog, and that she had received a letter from him before she left Marseille urging her assistance in obtaining a U.S. visa as soon as possible. She noted that Herzog had just sent a telegram a few days earlier in which he specifically requested that Eva get together with Einstein to expedite his visa application.

Eva further advised Einstein: "A particular difficulty arises from the fact that no one here knows Wilhelm Herzog's biography exactly, and the required biography must contain fairly precise details about his activity. I will try to locate some facts from the library, but would be thankful for any help in this area." She concluded:

Perhaps you would be able to write and sign his biography? I believe, and there can be no doubt, that Herzog is in extraordinary danger in today's France; and although I hardly know him personally, I feel obligated, as one of the "rescued," to help with his rescue.

I would be thankful to you, if you would let me know soon whether and in which way your help might be possible, and I greet you with the greatest respect.

Einstein replied to Eva in a letter dated November 27, 1940: "I know Wilhelm Herzog very well personally, but know nothing about his biographical data. It is certain that he belongs to the deserving political fighters for whom the action of the President should be called upon. I enclose a letter in which I speak on his behalf." Einstein concluded by expressing his "hope for quick success in your praiseworthy efforts."

The effectiveness of Eva's work in preparing and gathering the papers necessary to support applications for emergency rescue visas was quickly recognized by Americans working in the Emergency Rescue Committee (ERC) in New York. Eva would soon be hired by the ERC as a case worker and would continue her rescue and relief work for the ERC in New York until the end of the war.


## Speeches in support of endangered refugees

On November 28, 1940, Eva gave a speech to German American immigrants who were representatives of other exiled political groups.[2] This speech is an example of the messages she conveyed to various audiences about the plight of refugees in Europe and the need for a unified and urgent effort to help those in danger:

It is difficult for me to speak to you this evening in the name of my colleagues. For these colleagues are not here. They still den 27.November 1940

Frl.Eva Lewinski
52 West 68 Str.
New York City

Sehr geehrtes Frl.Lewinski:

Ich kenne Wilhelm Herzog sehr gut per-
soenlich, weiss aber nichts ueber seine biographische
Daten. Es ist sicher,dass er zu den verdienten politi-
schen Kaempfern gehoert, fuer welche die Aktion des
Praesidenten ins Leben gerufen wurde. Ich lege Ihnen
einen Brief bei, in welchem ich mich fuer ihn einsetze.
In der Hoffnung auf einen schnellen Erfolg
Ihrer lobenswerten Bemuehung,bin ich

mit freundlichen Gruessen

Ihr

*A. Einstein*

Albert Einstein's November 27, 1940, letter to Eva.

sit in France; some in the tiny sector of freedom that is left for them in today's France; others in captivity, behind barbed wire, on straw; in St. Cyprien, in Les Milles, in Rieucroz [French internment camps], in Ceret, in Africa, yes in Spain, captured on the way to this country. They should all be here with us tonight. For none of them has ever hesitated, in the interest of their own lives and liberty, to make the issues of freedom and justice their own.

So, when tonight I thank you, our American colleagues, for the great assistance efforts that brought so many of us to a country in which one can breathe freely, and can live and work for freedom, allow me to add to this obvious thanks, an equally obvious addendum: We can only accept your help without shame when we convert that help to assistance for those left behind, if we pull together all of our strength and apply it to work toward a common goal. Only because they expect such a commitment from us, did those we left behind let us go without bitterness. To disappoint them would mean to disappoint you, and would mean to fail to continue the work of humanity we have begun.

Humanity! How can one speak of humanity in a time in which inhumanity appears to triumph, in which the lead fighters for humanity sit in prison camps behind barbed wire, in which cities are leveled to the ground, countries invaded, human dignity stomped under foot. And still: We all, all of us who came out of France, have we not, despite much degradation, repeatedly felt humanity?

We have felt humanity as we, thousands of women, were brought to the prison camp in the Pyrenees, standing pressed against each other in a large truck, our hearts filled with sadness and shame. We have felt it as suddenly behind the barbed wire, between the gray barracks, the hands of Spanish fighters reached out to greet us. Those who arrived later felt humanity when we passed on the same greetings that the Spaniards had offered us, waving our welcome from behind the barbed wire. All of us in the Summer of 1940, torn away from every meaningful life activity, separated from those closest to us, not knowing when we would ever see them again, when we would ever again, with our will, be able to engage in normal life. We all felt humanity in those hard weeks and months in the Gurs prison camp, when people who, until then strangers but also sufferers, accepted us with warmth and compassion.

The wine grower in the south of France, who left his vineyard and led us on our walk through the Pyrenees, until we could no longer lose our way, who declined our modest offer of money; the women farmers in Spain with their donkeys, who did not understand our language, and yet spoke the liberating words "There lies Port Bou and that is the Spanish border"; rescued friends at all connecting stations, who went to meet all trains coming from France and Spain in order to give help to the newly arriving strangers—the same help that had been given to them yesterday by others; the stranger in Madrid who drove us through the city, to the police, brought us to a room, not because of the small amount of money we could give him, but because he knows: here are comrades. Because he himself is a French metalworker, who himself escaped from France over the Pyrenees—they are all proof of the living humanity, that no fascism can extinguish, that no bombs can completely destroy.

This humanity lives in the hearts of countless oppressed. It gives courage and it is also a reminder. It gives courage: because never is everything lost, as long as human beings live in whom the consciousness of lost values, of lost freedom burns. And a reminder: because good people have not been able to avoid that inhumanity can triumph, and that it seeks to eradicate everything that is humane. Humanity, it is there, but it now stands in the ranks of the conquered. To help them triumph is not merely an assistance effort, but a far-reaching challenge. It is our challenge. It is the challenge of people who have grasped something about the worth of humanity. It is a political challenge.

One can imagine the effect of this speech—coming from this serious young woman who had just survived the German invasion of France, internments. and escape.

## Correspondence with Eva's mother

During these first few months in America, Eva also reconnected with her mother Charlotte, referred to as "Mutti" by the family. Eva's brother Ernst had moved to Johannesburg with his business firm before Hitler came to power. Ernst later arranged to have their mother, their brother Rudi, and their younger sister Ruth escape Hitler's Germany and move to Johannesburg. Eva's youngest brother Hans had moved to Paris and then to England. Eva's mother was able to visit Eva once in Paris on her way to South Africa. Otto met Eva's mother at that time, and they liked each other very much.

The first letter to Eva in New York from her mother was dated November 16, 1940. It was handwritten in English, the language of her new home in Johannesburg:

> My dear, dear Ev,
>
> Can you imagine how happy I was when I got your cable from New York? I was nearly crazy for joy and I couldn't stop crying. My sweet darling, I do hope you will always be in health and you will find some work. And I know you are so clever and so good and you will try everything to help all the other children. I can hardly await your announced letter from New York. I got your letter from Lisbon last week and it was more than 3 months on the way. Dreadful things must have happened to you, my poor, dear Ev. Thank you so much for your letter and for the foto. You look so sad my dear, dear Ev, but nevertheless I enjoy it. And I am so glad you wear the necklace I gave you. . . . I am so sorry about Otto. I share your uneasiness about Otto my Darling. I do hope and wish so very much you can be together with him very soon. How terrible hard for you my dear Ev!!! . . .
>
> My Eva-Darling, excuse my broken English; it is not so easy to learn another language in my age. Christmas is not far and all the sadness from 1917 [the death of her husband and Eva's father] becomes alive.
>
> Ev, my Dear, my Darling, I love you so much and with all my senses I am with you. My best wishes for your future. And be always healthy, my lovely daughter.
>
> I embrace you with 1000 kisses.

Eva's mother's letters confirmed her receipt of some cables and letters from Eva, but it is apparent that Eva did not respond to all of her mother's letters during the first few months she was in New York. Given the intensity and urgency of Eva's work to obtain visas, that is understandable. There were also major delays in the delivery of letters between New York and Johannesburg. In a letter to Eva dated November 30, 1940, her mother wrote:

My dear, dear Evchen,

I was so glad when I got your letter that you are in health
and safe. And I am sorry too, because your life is so hard on the
other hand. And I feel it is a shame that I can't help you, especially with some money. But what can I do? I haven't got money
at all. Perhaps I can send you a few shillings in January. . . .

Where may be Otto? It is so dreadful you don't know anything about him. I can imagine how sad you are and I tell you,
I feel with you with all my heart, my Dear.

In a letter dated December 12, 1940, Eva's mother expressed some
frustration about not receiving more letters from Eva: "I must have
patience till I get another letter from you. How may you feel, my Dear?
Have you had success to bring the other children to America? With all
my mind and with all my love I am with all of you and especially in
these days."

And in a letter dated January 6, 1941, Eva's mother wrote:

I am so glad to hear from you that Otto is with Erich together
[in southern France]. I didn't know it before. Oh my Ev, if you
could manage that, to help Otto, Erich, Herta, Gaby and the
other ones to go to New York!!! It would be such a relief to know
they are safe!!! With all my thoughts, I have been with Erich
on his birthday. I am so longing for him and for all of you my
dear children!!! It is only naturally that I worry about all of you.
Could I be together with all of you again!

Eva's mother Charlotte was a warm and loving person. Unlike Eva,
whose early life was consumed by her commitment to political action to
help others in need, her mother appeared to treasure, above all else, her
children and music. Her great wish was for the war to end so she could
finally have a reunion with all of her children.

But the war was far from ending. Eva's attention and energy remained focused on saving others, including Otto. His visa case would
continue to be her most challenging.

# 20. Further Pleas to Help Otto and Other Refugees

At the end of 1940, even those endangered refugees in southern France who had received U.S. visas faced further delays and risks in escaping to America. At the same time, others who desperately needed visas, including Otto, waited anxiously. Eleanor Roosevelt pressed for answers from the State Department about these delays.

In a letter to Undersecretary of State Sumner Welles dated December 30, 1940, Mrs. Roosevelt focused her inquiry on the delays facing those who already had their visas. Welles responded by letter dated January 2, 1941: "The answer to your question presents quite a difficulty. Some of these people are in unoccupied France and some are in Switzerland. I assume that all, with the possible exception of one [Otto], have received visas and I assume that that one will receive his in due course." He explained: "The difficulty is not with the visas but with traveling through hostile territory in which the Gestapo is active; in getting permits to cross frontiers; and in getting over borders and through lines which are controlled by the military authorities." Welles added: "These people cannot reach a port from which they could embark to the United States unless they travel through Spain into Portugal."[1]

For Otto, all of these future difficulties were secondary. He still faced the more urgent and immediate hurdle—obtaining a U.S. visa. A Visa Division memorandum to Breckinridge Long dated January 3, 194[1], stated that "the names in the letter submitted by Mrs. Roosevelt have been checked with the [State] Department's records as indicated in the attached sheet."[2] The attached sheet included the following entry for

"Pfister, Otto": "Recommended by the President's Advisory Committee on Political Refugees and is now under consideration. Before taking final action in the case, however, certain additional information is being obtained from the Consul General at Marseille."[3] Despite the support of Eleanor Roosevelt, the recommendation of the President's Advisory Committee, and the clear and immediate danger that Otto was in, this process of obtaining "additional information" from Otto in Marseille appeared to be delayed.

Eva did not pause in her advocacy for Otto. She asked her close friend Josef Luitpold Stern to write an additional reference letter on behalf of Otto. After arriving in America on the same ship as Eva, Stern had moved to Haverford, Pennsylvania, where he worked at the Cooperative College Workshop of the American Friends Service Committee, and continued to correspond with Eva.[4] In a letter to Eliot Coulter dated January 3, 1941, Stern wrote:

> Among the applications for visas now awaiting the decision of the Department of State is that of Otto Pfister. I have known this excellent and earnest worker since the spring of 1939, and I feel impelled to write in his behalf, to express my appreciation of his ability and to testify to his exceptional character.
>
> It would be a great grief to see this man lost in the gap between the clutching hand of European Fascism and the saving hand of American democracy. Like myself, he was interned on French soil late in 1939. . . . Freed early in 1940, he at once took up the fight against Hitler Germany, at risk of his life. In the spring of 1940 he fell into German hands. During the summer he succeeded in escaping. Now, in Marseille, the dark cloud hangs over him again, unless he too can be rescued by America, by you.
>
> Otto Pfister is the very pattern of a German democrat, an unknown worker for the cause of freedom. A skilled cabinet-maker, he is a man of culture and independent judgment, upright and straightforward. I am glad to answer for Otto Pfister. I recommend him most heartily to your favorable consideration.[5]

## Seeking public support for endangered refugees

In the December 27, 1940, meeting with Eleanor Roosevelt at the White House, Mrs. Roosevelt had urged Eva and Paul Benjamin to continue to publicize the plight of these endangered refugees. They followed Mrs. Roosevelt's advice.

An article in the *Buffalo Courier-Express* dated January 6, 1941, described an invitation by the Buffalo branch of the Emergency Rescue Committee to local congressmen "to enlist their interest in speeding issuance of visas for political refugees in Lisbon, Portugal, and southern France." The article quoted Benjamin's observations following the meeting with Mrs. Roosevelt:

> "[T]here needs to be a tremendous upsurge of concern in this country for the democratic way of life and a swinging back of the old doctrine that the United States is and should remain a haven for the oppressed. Mrs. Roosevelt expressed the greatest concern for these people, who are in such danger, and I feel that it is up to us to arouse public opinion against racial and religious prejudices that might arise out of the attempt to give refugees a place in the United States."

The article then turned to the presentation made by "Miss Eva Lewinski of New York, herself a political refugee from Germany and France." The article quoted Eva's descriptions about the conditions facing refugees in southern France, conditions that were deplorable when Eva was there in the summer and were far worse now in the winter:

> "We were in wooden barracks, with no means of being heated, with roofs that leaked and with only a straw sack to sleep on. The food problem was very bad as the refugees had increased the population of the area by one-third, and the sanitary situation was deplorable.
>
> "However, it was warm when we were there, and we had some hope of escape. The people who are still stranded in southern France must have almost reached the point of collapse, and that is why I feel it is our duty to make every effort that is humanly possible to rescue them now."

Another newspaper article appeared in the January 10, 1941, issue of the *Cleveland Press*. This article focused on Eva, noting that she was visiting Cleveland to encourage support for endangered refugees in Europe:

> MISS EVA LEWINSKI is 31, a tall and darkly handsome German refugee from the oppressions of Adolf Hitler. In her brown eyes and low voice you catch a hint of the scars of suffering left by weeks of uncertainty a step ahead of the Gestapo, of the nights on a filthy straw sack that was her bed in a French internment camp, of the suspense of escape across the mountains into Spain.
>
> Back of her slow and pleasant smile you catch the hint of anxiety for a brother and fiancé in France towards whom the Gestapo comes a step closer with each day, for her two brothers now fighting for Britain, for a score of her friends trapped in disease-breeding camps on starvation rations.
>
> Eva Lewinski's family history is a case document of shattered lives and wanderings in search of peace and freedom.

After describing Eva's anti-Nazi work, internment in Camp de Gurs, and escape from Europe, the article concluded: "Eva Lewinski is here today to further Clevelanders' efforts to rescue hundreds more like her—from disease, from mental and physical sufferings, from the ever-closer Gestapo."

## Concern about delays in Otto's case

In Eva's letter to Paul Benjamin dated January 13, 1941, transmitting her memorandum of their December 27, 1940, meeting with Eleanor Roosevelt, she informed Benjamin about recent developments in the pending case of Mrs. Litten's son which had been of special interest to Mrs. Roosevelt. Eva also expressed her concerns about delays in Otto's case:

> Some days ago, Miss Hill received a letter from Mr. Coulter informing her that he had required some additional information from the Consul General at Marseille, concerning the visa

application of Otto Pfister. So, unfortunately, this case has not yet been decided. I am afraid that during the next week or so we cannot do anything else but wait the answer of the Consul. If only the decision would not come too late![6]

Pressed by Dorothy Hill's further inquiry to Eleanor Roosevelt's secretary, Malvina Thompson, about Otto's visa case, Sumner Welles provided a clearer description of the rigorous vetting process in a letter dated January 22, 1941:

Mr. Pfister's name was recommended by the President's Advisory Committee on Political Refugees, under serial no. 892, for special consideration in the issuance of a visa. Under an arrangement agreed upon with the Department of Justice, the names of the refugees submitted by the Committee to the Department of Justice and to the Department of State, are considered by an Inter-Departmental Committee composed of representatives of the Military Intelligence Division of the War Department, the office of Naval Intelligence of the Navy Department, the Federal Bureau of Investigation, the Immigration Section of the Department of Justice, and the State Department. The Committee acting in an advisory capacity, offers recommendations regarding the action to be taken in the cases, for the assistance of the consuls in considering the visa applications of the persons concerned.

The case of Mr. Pfister was considered by the Committee and the conclusion was reached that as certain aspects of the case required clarification through a consular examination, the Consul at Marseille should be requested to obtain the desired information and to report his findings to the Department. A cablegram was sent to the Consul on January 3, 1941 and he was requested to expedite his report to be submitted to the Department by telegraph. As soon as the report shall have been received it will be presented to the Inter-Departmental Committee for consideration.

I shall inform you regarding the final conclusion reached in the case.[7]

Because the Inter-Departmental Committee had determined that Otto's case still "required clarification," his fate remained to be determined after another examination of him by the U.S. consul in Marseille. Welles's letter to Thompson confirms that the Marseille consul had been requested by cablegram on January 3 "to *expedite*" the report of the examination and to submit it to the State Department by telegraph so it could be presented to the Inter-Departmental Committee for further consideration *as soon as it was received*. But as confirmed by the date of Welles's letter to Thompson—January 22—this process had already been postponed for unknown reasons.

# 21. Otto's Wait for a Visa in Southern France

During this time of uncertainty about Otto's visa application, the correspondence between Eva and Otto provides an intimate and revealing account of events. Their letters reflect their love and hope that Otto still might be granted the precious visa that would allow them finally to reunite. They also shed more light on the delays of the consulate in Marseille in arranging the additional interview of Otto and submitting a report on that interview to the State Department in Washington. During this period, Eva also sent letters to ISK leader Willi Eichler with periodic reports on her efforts to rescue her ISK colleagues.

Waiting for word about his visa in Montauban, Otto wrote to Eva on January 9, 1941:

> My dearest, do you know that I feel that you are closer to me now than ever? I cherish your face when I fall asleep, and again, when I wake up. You don't always have the same expression; at times you look serious, grave. Your deep eyes look at me with infinite goodness, mixed with signs of past sadness, of desperate efforts, of tiredness perhaps, but where hope is not absent. Your mouth is closed, tired to have wanted so much to convince, but without bitterness, ready for a good smile, for tenderness.
>
> And your look, sweet and penetrating, seems to want to commit me, I know to what: to do my best. I feel that I am not going to disappoint your look.
>
> But there are other moments where another face comes to me. Your eyes then are full of joy, your forehead has forgotten your worries. . . .

I would like so much a photo of you, a recent one that shows me that you have not forgotten to smile. Will you send me one, please? Did you get mine?

Turning to his visa case, Otto informed Eva that he had learned in a letter from Johanna Bertholet about a cable Eva had written and what it said about his chances. Based on that information, he said, "I may perhaps hope soon to be called to the Consulate."

Resuming this letter the following day, Otto explained: "Last night, I could not finish. Yet, it had been one of those rare quiet evenings. . . . And this morning, there is a lot of news. Gisa [Gisela Peiper] came back, with an immigration visa. Great, isn't it? . . . And then, Gisa brought me your cable of December 25 that made me very happy, also to hear that you had gotten mine for Christmas." And he assured Eva that "Gaby has been traveling for almost two weeks. She seems to be in good shape, and content with her work. . . . All is clear and good now; I am happy." Otto also shared with Eva some of his recent reading:

Last night I was reading in a little booklet that comes from you: It's French poems by Rilke. I found it in Mousy's [Hélène Perret's] room, and it had been a present from you for her, I believe. I kept it like a little treasure. . . . And now I don't feel that I want to return it to Mousy. In all the poems in this little book there is one that you will like especially.

Just finished the book about which I already wrote you: *The Grapes of Wrath*. That is a book that is extraordinary and beautiful from many viewpoints. I would like for you to read it also. What a marvelous figure the mother is! There are so many passages that I would like to read again, with you.

In a letter from Marseille on January 13, Otto reported that shortly after his arrival there, he had a lengthy interview with the U.S. consul in Marseille. "He questioned me for a long time, but I believe that in the end, he had a good impression. He told me that he would still have to cable to Washington, and he gave me an appointment for Jan. 23. So I return to Montauban and come back here on Jan. 22." Otto was hopeful. "I am glad that I can add this very recent news. I believe, and so does Erich, that we are not too optimistic to think that I will soon have my visa." Otto added to this letter a French poem by Rilke (later translated by Eva):

> Let's stay at the lamp, and let's not talk too much.
> Whatever one can say does not equal the vows
> Of a lived silence—it's like the hollow of a divine hand.
> It's true, the hand, this hand is empty.
> But a hand does not ever open in vain;
> And that is what joins us.
> It's not ours; we precipitate the things that are slow.
> It's already an action when a hand opens.
> Let's look at the life that pulsates in it.
> The one who moves is not the strongest.
> One has to admire the tacit agreement
> Before the strength disappears.

In a letter on January 16, Eva thanked Otto for his recent letters. She told him that she was looking at photos on her table that she had received from him and others. She described them:

> On the one, you are playing with a beetle, move it from one hand to the other. On the other one, you are sitting proudly on a wagon, next to an old white-haired Swiss farmer, and look into the world, totally carefree, in this unburdened serenity that I love so. But again and again I look back to one of the three that you sent me. You look so full of love, of deep, consoling tenderness. I wonder if you were thinking of me when that photo was taken. I can't look at it often enough—it is almost as if you were talking to me, encouraging me.

Eva then confessed, "Sometimes I do need encouragement. I am longing for you deeply, and have no answer to the question what my life would be like if one day there would no longer be any hope to see you again, to live with you. As of now, there is still hope. And believe me, my dearest, I don't give up the struggle. But it is awfully hard that you are not here yet, that your application is not yet progressing as well as many others." She added:

How much your letters move me; how they make me richer and better; how I walk with you wherever you go; how happy I am that your eyes (the dear ones—how I would like to touch them gently) are seeing the same streets, corners, old houses, trees, rivers that mine have seen—I will have to tell you much about that. Do you understand that I can't do it now? Altogether too present are the many concerns and tasks, the big responsibility.

I believe I have never been as alone as I am here. And that has to be learned. It's true, I have met many good friends—feel close to some of them. But nobody is there for me entirely. . . . When my thoughts are free, they are gravitating around your life, about how I could help more. And when they want to rest, I come "home" to you, to us, to our love, to your letters, to my diary notes, to your photos. That is my real world.

Eva then informed Otto about her recent contacts with other friends. "I had two beautiful, warm letters from Gaby. Be assured, everything is well, can no longer be damaged by either of us. And you: be good to her." Responding to Otto's inquiry about Stern, she wrote: "I can't really say. We don't hear much of each other. His letter was intended for you. I'll have to write more about him later—he is very lonely, and very generous, and not at all happy. It's very hard."

Eva then asked Otto, "Did I tell you that I also am reading the *Grapes of Wrath*—my first American book? Such coincidences somehow make me happy. You too?" She ended the letter by telling him, "I would like to write much more; but the Clipper leaves tomorrow morning, and I still have a lot to write tonight. Let me imagine for a moment that you are here, with me—I love you as much as one can love someone."

In an extensive report to ISK leader Willi Eichler on January 16, Eva first provided an update on the pending "difficult cases" for their ISK colleagues who were still seeking emergency visas, noting the perplexing delays in the processing of Otto's case.[1] Eva advised Eichler that Otto's case was still not complete because the State Department found it necessary to have the consul in Marseille make special inquiries before deciding. "I cannot say at all whether a favorable or unfavorable outcome is probable, because to date we have not been able to figure out what exactly is snagging this. But I still have not given up hope that it will work out. It would be too miserable if just this case would not succeed."

Eva then shared with Eichler the disturbing recent information she had received in letters from colleagues in France about the horrid conditions suffered by thousands still interned in the French camps, including Camp de Gurs, in the cold of winter:

> I have received in the last few days a great deal of mail from France of pretty recent dates. The conditions in the camps, apparently especially in Gurs, where we were in the summer, and where since then 8000 Jews from southern Germany and many men from other camps were transported, are so horrible, that it sends chills down the spine. Women, elderly, children, nothing to eat; unheated, leaky barracks; newborn children wrapped in newspapers because there are no rags or cloth; old men fall down, simply broken by cold and hunger; several die daily, human beings who can no longer hold on physically, others who no longer have the courage to wait out the slow dying. It is dreadful; the worst of it is the hopelessness for these many thousands.

Eva ended this letter to Eichler warmly by asking, "Is your new apartment somewhat peaceful? Write, if you can, often and much: human contact and factual information, at least in letters, is the only thing that makes life tolerable in these times, when it comes from real friends."

On January 18, Eva sent Otto a postcard with a print of *Chestnut Trees at Jas de Bouffan* by Paul Cézanne from the Frick Collection in New York—an image of barren trees in the winter. Otto tucked the postcard in the cover flap of Eva's "blue book" diary, where it would remain. Eva wrote:

> And you, my loving, good man, I take this opportunity to give you an inner greeting and many warm thoughts. Do you like this card? I saw it here in the museum. And despite the unbelievably sad bleakness of the trees, they appear hopeful—in a few months, they will gratefully carry buds, leaves, blossoms and fruit. Perhaps also a symbol for our two lives? Let us believe! I hug you in great, great love!

Postcard from Frick Collection, New York, with Eva's January 18, 1941, note to Otto.

In his letter of January 24 from Marseille, Otto began by noting, "No word from you since your last letter of December 6. Wonder if something got lost. Sure, we have news through your cable—and what good news it is! But I would like very much to see the long letter which you had promised." Otto had not yet received Eva's New Year's Eve letter that included her assurance that the incident with Gaby had not diminished her love for him. The delivery of mail from Eva to Otto was apparently even slower than from him to her.

Otto then described disturbing delays by the U.S. consul in Marseille in handling his case:

Since yesterday, I am again here with Erich, had a meeting at the Consul's. When I had been there on the 13th, he told me that he still had to report to Washington before he could issue the visa. Now yesterday, I got the same answer from the second Consul who is now in charge of my case. Apparently, the cable had not been sent. I have to come back within ten days—things don't seem to go too smoothly. . . . Hope that there are no serious difficulties. Perhaps you have been successful again—we have such confidence in you, in what you do—you have already obtained so much. I don't want to be impatient, and am happy that things went well for the other friends. But I am so looking forward to being again with you—why should that not be granted to us after all the hard times?

Why had the report not been cabled to Washington, D.C., in the ten days after Otto's lengthy interrogation by the Marseille consul on January 13? Why was Otto asked again on January 23 to come back ten days later? Given the extreme danger that Otto faced and the directions sent to the Marseille consul on January 3 to *expedite* the report and telegraph it to the State Department in Washington, what could have caused these delays? Because individual visa files from this period were apparently destroyed by the State Department and telegrams about Otto's case between Marseille and Washington were also apparently destroyed, we may never know the answers to these questions.[2]

In a brief letter to Otto on January 28, 1941, Eva wrote:

Yesterday, they brought me a letter from you; I was so happy that I ran upstairs. And only when I read it, did I realize that it was an old one, of Dec. 7, superseded by the ones of Dec. 30 and Jan. 3 which I got two weeks ago, and already answered. Yet, it was good to read it and to feel that you are with me with your thoughts and your heart.

I am with you also. And that's why it is so awfully hard that again I can't tell you that your case has progressed at least as much as that of the others. Even after that, there are still great difficulties to overcome. But if only the first step would finally be taken! No, I don't want to complain, don't want to be faint-hearted. But I am so longing for you, and sometimes I am afraid.

Please don't be sad that this is only a short greeting. . . . On the table is your picture—I look at it, and know that we are as close to one another as one can be.

Eva sent Eichler an updated report on January 28, noting her growing concerns about the delays in Otto's case: "Otto's matter is still not decided. The Consul had the intention to send a favorable report to Washington; however, [he] forgot to do so for more than a week so that again precious time was lost. By now the report should have been sent, and Washington will hopefully soon come to a decision. The whole thing concerns me deeply, as you can imagine."

She also expressed her disappointment that "Fimmen's letter does not appear to have arrived. What a shame! It perhaps could have been of use for Otto." She asked Eichler, "Have you seen Rens yet? If you have not already done so, ask him to send a cable to Mr. Coulter, Acting Chief of the Visa Division, Department of State, Washington D.C., in support of Otto's case. He would be the right man, emphatic and impressive (if he would also mention his current position) to vouch for Otto's integrity. Give him my greetings!"

Eva reported on disturbing information she had received about others still suffering in the French internment camps. "Rosa's [Erna Blencke's] friend has unfortunately been put again into a camp, and, in fact, in one of the worst camps in Argelès, where about 10,000 people are staying, some on the bare, damp sand without sufficient straw and blankets. They seem to hope to get him out when his visas are complete. It is appalling!"

Eva then told Eichler that she had given "a few talks about the situation facing the political refugees in France, in Buffalo and Cleveland." She added, "The effect appeared to be very good. Although I gave nothing more than a report of the facts, indeed with a certain point of view that seemed to me important, but without exaggeration, the people were very shaken and stirred up, and probably ready to help more, and with greater understanding, than before."

## Good news about Otto's visa

In a letter to Eva in French on February 1, Otto exclaimed:

> What a great day this is! I have an appointment with the Consul for Febr. 14, and then I'll get my visa. I wrote you in my previous letter that they had forgotten to cable, and also that I was concerned that something was wrong. Now, this is all of the past, and the rest is not going to be too difficult.

Otto informed Eva that he helped Herta fill a suitcase with Eva's things that he had recovered from her apartment in Paris, and they would be sent to her via American Express. "It felt good to hold in my hands the clothes that you liked . . . and your mountain boots. What memories, what hope! I can't help dreaming that we will again be together, even in the mountains, with sun, trees, and strange rocks. . . . I could read happiness on your face." He added, "I was very glad that Dyno [Lowenstein] brought me from Paris a photo from Port-Giraud. You know, the one from the cis-

Photo of Eva at the cistern referred to in Otto's February 1, 1941, letter to Eva.

tern. How I love that photo, how happy you are in it!"

Otto confessed that he was sad sometimes. "I don't know how you are living, who is with you, if you can relax from time to time." He praised Eva's efforts. "The work that you are doing must demand a lot of strength. But you can really be pleased about all you have accomplished so far." He assured her that "as far as food goes, things are not too bad. It is a little difficult, but we don't have to go hungry." He closed by saying, "I believe these last two weeks will be the hardest to take. How I wait for some word from you!" He added: "P.S. I am enclosing a photo of the chess pieces that I carved while I was in the camp. The photo is not very good, but it might give you some pleasure to have it. P.P.S. What do you think about my bringing my tools with me?"

Eva wrote a letter to Otto in French on February 4 in which she marveled about learning that they were both reading *The Grapes of Wrath*:

> What has been moving me the most for quite a while is the parallelism in your inner life and in mine. You are reading, one of the first books after your return, the *Grapes of Wrath*. The first novel that falls into my hands here is the *Grapes of Wrath*. The

day after having gotten your good letter, I finished this book, and I was overcome by the last scene: the never-stopping rain; the hunger; the man who is going to die because he had wanted to save his child; the girl whose child could not live, and who despite that became a mother, with a heart as great as that of her mother. And that mother—the incarnation of love that never tires—how I would like to become like her!

She asked Otto, "Can you imagine what your letter (of Jan. 9 and 13, with the poem by Rilke) gave me? I cried, and that does not happen to me too often anymore. I would so much want to be with you. And yet, I don't have the certitude that you will be able to come. Sometimes I feel tired, tired to wait, tired not to be able to do anything. . . . But I know that is not gracious. And I pick up my life again." She told Otto that when he mentioned his plan to go to Castres to visit a friend, it reminded her of her departure from France:

It brings back to my mind the evening when I took the bus in Toulouse to go to Castres to say goodbye to Yvonne and to Paulette. It was one of those marvelous clear summer evenings. This beautiful country, with its hills and fields, passed by my eyes. I would so much have wanted to stay there, to live with you, to return. But I had to continue on my way, my heart full of anxiety about your fate, and so sad that I might perhaps never see this country again.

Eva assured Otto that she loved the Rilke poem he sent. "I always think of your hand when I read it again, and of the good quiet times we lived with each other. Do you remember our 'dome' high in the mountains, in the forest? I love you. I love every bit of memory that ties us, the memory of happy and profound moments, and also those that made us suffer. Thanks also for having sent me Gaby's letter. Tell her that I think of her with confident friendship, and with love."

Eva wrote again to Willi Eichler on February 11, 1941. She had not yet received Otto's letter of February 1 with his news that he would be receiving his visa on February 14. She told Eichler, "For Otto, still no decision," and she then detailed the status of other pending visa cases. Eva concluded, "You see from this brief exposition how unpredictable the entire situation is." Eva advised Eichler that the letter from Edo Fimmen in support of Otto's case had never arrived. Persisting, she asked, "It would perhaps be appropriate if he sent a new cable, in which he vouches for our friends who until now have received no visas. Do you think he will do that?"

Eva then addressed a disturbing suggestion made by Eichler that Otto should seek a British visa so he could do work with the ISK in England. Eva objected to this and explained her reasons, attempting to separate her personal interest from her rational assessment of the best "fit" for Otto's abilities in continuing his work with the ISK. Eva explained that the "more serious" option of having Otto remain in France to work in the underground with Bertholet was simply too dangerous: "Due to his work and experiences, he is in disproportionately greater danger in the event of a total occupation of France by the Nazis, than are most of our other friends, particularly our French friends."

The best option, Eva concluded, was for Otto to work in America, where "he can help with calm, steady work to expand the diverse opportunities offered us here." She explained: "That a large part of our immediate work here, and probably also our future work, is dependent upon our people being not only trustworthy, but also visibly of a character borne of strong conviction, who reflect the good of our cause by who they are, and who convince strangers to follow, I believe—and you will probably confirm this—that Otto would be very well situated here." Separate from her personal feelings, Eva shared with Eichler her positive assessment of the development of Otto's character in his work with the ISK: "its naturalness; calm, independent and focused." Eva urged,

> In a favorable "climate" that he could use so well after this difficult year, I know that he will make the best of it. In the interest of his development, in the interest of the significance of that development for our work, I would very much like that he be given this climate, when other important interests will not be harmed by it.

Eva concluded her plea that it was right for Otto to come to America: "Willi, I hope that you do not misunderstand me? I have the need to tell you where I stand on this matter, and to know whether we're in agreement and also whether there is a problem."

Eva ended the letter with a response to Eichler's concerns about how she was holding up under the pressures of these times:

> It is not easy, "not to see these times as too depressing," as you suggested I try, and I still for the most part have not succeeded. But it does not help anything, and I am doing okay. Last Sunday afternoon I was at the museum and saw a wonderful exhibit of French artists, from David, to the Impressionists, to contemporary artists. Despite the large crowd, it was indescribably beautiful, and my homesickness for France became very, very intense. You also would have loved the exhibit: there are very beautiful Daumiers, previously unknown to me, very warm and socially sensitive; unknown Van Gogh's, Manets, Corots, very expressive Dégas, Cézannes.
>
> Farewell, dear Willi. I hope good news about you and all friends will soon arrive. Warm, heartfelt greetings!

Otto began a letter to Eva in Marseille on February 11 and continued it on February 12. He first reported that he finally received Eva's Christmas Eve letter and eagerly awaited his visa:

> My dearest, how beautiful, how good is your letter written on Christmas Eve. How you make a gift for me of that evening! And you were successful again—in a few days, on the 14th, I'll hold this success [the visa] in my hands. Then there will be only a few weeks for the transit visas. Now it is even possible to cable for the Spanish visa as soon as one has the receipt for the Portuguese one. I think that I will be able to apply for the Spanish visa by the middle of next week. And then one only has to have a little more patience, and a little good luck.

Otto also reported that Eva's brother Erich and his wife Herta expected their Spanish transit visas soon and would perhaps be able to depart within a few days. He added, "I spent many good days with them, and we will miss them. But I am very happy that you will see them again. They'll bring you part of me, and you won't be that alone any more; you will have, above all, Herta who is such a great person. And Erich is going to bubble over—he thinks more of you, more than ever."

Continuing this letter on the following day in a hotel across from the train station in Marseille, Otto expressed his longing to see Eva again:

> I am sitting in my hotel room, opposite the station. A nice, clean room, nice people. There are some mimosas on my night table; will put a sprig of them into this letter. The greens from your last letter lie between the pages of your diary which always gives me great pleasure. And then I am thinking of the daisies that we picked high up in the mountains, of the butterfly, of the mushrooms and berries, on our struggling through the rocky mountain, of the Cathedral, of the happiness that shone in your eyes. How I am looking forward to go hiking again side by side with you. And how happy I am at the thought that before long you will again open the door for me. . . . And how I look forward to the day when, near you, I can work again, create something.

Otto ended the letter by quoting another of the rare poems that Rilke wrote in French:

> Along the dusty path
> The green becomes almost gray.
> But this gray, only slightly,
> Has in it shades of silver and blue.
>
> Higher up, on the other mountain,
> A willow shows the clear
> Reverse side of its foliage to the wind
> In front of a black that is almost green.
>
> Next to it, a green that is quite abstract
> A pale green of vision,
> Enfolds with deep abandon
> The turn that the century defeats.[3]

The following day, in a letter dated February 13, 1941, Edo Fimmen informed Eichler that he had just sent a telegram in support of Otto to George Warren, head of the President's Advisory Committee. Interestingly, Fimmen also advised Eichler that he was unaware that his previous letter in support of Otto had not reached America. "In any case the telegram has now been sent, and hopefully has its desired success." Fimmen's telegram to Warren, dated February 12, 1941, advised: "Further to previous correspondence urge grant of permit to Otto Pfister. Is trustworthy fighter against Nazism and in constant danger in France."

On February 14, the day Otto went to the U.S. consulate in Marseille to get his visa, he began a letter to Eva with joy and gratitude:

> What a rich, happy day this is! Early in the morning came your beautiful, loving letter. I took it along to the Consulate, as a good omen. All went well. I now also have such a thing [the visa] that looks at you with your own eyes, makes another person out of you, perhaps makes you again the person you are. . . . And at noon, Erich arrives, full of joy, with my Portuguese visa! He had handled that very cleverly, was able to cable for it before I had my American visa. You see, sometimes there is good luck. Now I can apply for the Spanish visa right away. I never thought that things would work so smoothly, from this end. What it had cost you to accomplish this success, I can only guess. It really is getting closer now that we'll see each other again, and yet it is somehow like a beautiful dream.

Otto continued this letter on February 17, telling Eva, "Three days have passed since I interrupted this letter. This morning I got my Portuguese visa, and had Erich's and Herta's extended. Tomorrow I can get the Spanish visa, and then all one can do is wait." Otto then commented on the postcard he received from Eva with the print of Cézanne's *Chestnut Trees at Jas de Bouffan*: "You are right, dearest, let's hope that our life also, as those trees, the trees around us, will bear leaves and fruit." He described a hike he took the day before in Marseille:

> Here, we occasionally have beautiful, warm, sunny days. Once in a while, there is a heavy mist, like yesterday when Herta and I with Mrs. Kaegi, who sends warm greetings, climbed up to Notre Dame de la Garde.[4] Did you also see that marvelous view of the city and the ocean? There was wind and sun—white foamy powerful waves were beating high up on the Chateau d'If.[5] We were happy and full of confidence.

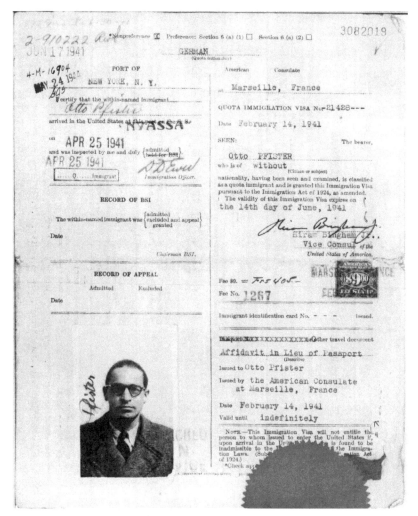

Otto's U.S. visa issued on February 14, 1941.

In Otto's continuation of this letter on February 19 and 20, he described the progress of those with U.S. visas in Marseille who were still confronting the additional challenges of escaping to America, including obtaining Spanish and Portuguese transit visas for the trip to Lisbon. After explaining how others were overcoming serious challenges in planning their escapes, he bursts with optimism and confidence: "And now I have here your letter of Jan. 28. This is really a rich week. Am waiting now eagerly for your next one. By then you would have known that my visa had been approved. How I look forward to that letter, to read of your joy." Otto then reflected on how he would write to Luitpold Stern:

And then, there is Stern's letter. It is so noble, so full of rare, human dignity that it almost hurts me to read it. What can I tell him? I am almost afraid to write him. How can words, my awkward words, help him in his suffering? How can I console him, I who am holding that trembling happiness in my shy hands that is not granted to him? How should I try to give advice to someone who is as knowing as he is? But I am going to write him, as soon as I have a quiet hour and am relaxed.

Otto ended his letter:

This morning I picked up Frieda [Timmermann] from the station, and now the Spanish visas for Herta, Erich, and Eugen [Albrecht] arrived. This means they will leave within a few days, perhaps even together. Erich would be happy about that. How great that soon you are not going to be alone anymore! There will be so much to talk about. And I, I will remain confident, and they will bring you something of the love I have and hold until we see each other again.

In a letter dated February 17 to Eliot Coulter, acting chief of the State Department's Visa Division, Eva expressed her gratitude about Otto's visa. "I wish to inform you that I got a cable from Marseille with the good news that my fiancé, Mr. Otto Pfister, has finally received his visa on February 14th. I am so very glad about this outcome, and I thank you sincerely for the interest you have taken in that case. I am convinced Mr. Pfister will never disappoint the hospitality of this country, nor will I."

Stern wrote a short note to Eva on February 17 conveying his joy upon receiving her telegram about Otto's visa:

No one other than you could have worked so diligently and so tenaciously for Otto's rescue.

Otto has received his American visa on Valentines Day. That is the day here that one celebrates love.

It is again a step taken toward the reunion. Stay completely confident. Your days will become brighter, dear friend.

I stay with my dream: That the two of you will celebrate your birthdays together.

## 22. Otto's Escape to America

As with other political refugees in southern France, Otto's success in obtaining a U.S. visa was the crucial first step in his escape to America. After obtaining the necessary transit visas for Spain and Portugal, he had to escape into Spain by foot over the Pyrenees, as Eva had done. He then had to travel through Spain to Portugal and wait in Lisbon for a spot on a ship to America. In the two months between his receipt of his visa on February 14, 1941, and his departure from Lisbon to New York on April 15, 1941, Otto and Eva continued their correspondence. Eva also continued to report to ISK leader Willi Eichler on the status of her rescue efforts.

In a letter to Otto on February 18, Eva wrote, "Can you imagine how happy I am since Saturday when I got your cable telling me that you finally got your visa? Now, without being too optimistic, there is hope that we will see each other again. And then—I don't want to think any further, but you are always with me. I almost hope that this letter may not reach you any more, that you are already on your way." She added: "Saturday night, your cable came. Then there was Sunday, as calm and fulfilled as none had been for a long time. The whole afternoon felt like a holiday; I listened to music, and thought of you." Eva reflected on her happiness with a twinge of guilt:

> Is it bad that I am so happy about the news of your visa, happy despite all the other concerns and sad news? I don't believe that I am selfish; but the burden of these times worrying that your application would not work out right, has been so great that now, quite naturally, I feel relaxed. Had I a little more money,

I would have bought some flowers for you and me. That could
not be. But in the Sunday paper, I found a beautiful photo that
I am enclosing, and that should replace the flowers. By the way,
I am not the only one who is happy about your news. You have
many good friends here—however, some of them know you
only through me.

In a brief letter to Eva on February 21, Otto reported that "tonight,
there is a great farewell. Herta, Erich, and Frieda [Timmermann] are
leaving. It's going to be empty here without them—we will realize that
fully only later. Erich really did a great job here." He added: "How happy
I am that you now will have Herta with you, that Erich can help you. I
would very much have liked to send you something with them, but time
went by so fast, I could not get anything for you." Otto noted, "Gaby
asked me to tell you that she thinks of you lovingly" and concluded, "Let
me be with you, my dearest, now in this rare moment of happiness."

In a letter to Otto on February 25, Eva lamented that the last
weeks were "sad and empty" because no letter had come from him,
and she hoped that he had at least received some mail from her. She
hastened to add:

Let me not be unfair: the beautiful telegram with the news of
your visa shined brightly in the still of these weeks. But human
nature, mine at least, is complicated: before you had your visa, I
had the feeling that everything depended upon on your receipt
of it, and my happiness with the news matched that feeling. But
that happiness did not last. Now I see so clearly all the other
difficulties facing you that the fact you have your visa appears
meaningless compared to them.

In a letter to Eichler on the same day, Eva reported the news that Otto
had finally received his U.S. visa and his Portuguese transit visa. She
also reported on the progress of other ISK colleagues who had their visas
but were working to overcome other difficult barriers to their escape
from southern France. She added, "I nevertheless still hope one day to
see them arrive here, although the situation naturally worsens day by
day. In any case, the tickets have been paid for all those who thus far
have visas."

In a letter from Marseille on March 3, Otto told Eva that things were progressing well for his escape to Lisbon: "I already have my Spanish visa, and now it's just a question of days. Yesterday we cabled to you and to Erich who is already in Lisbon. If all goes well and quickly for me, it's not impossible that I will still see all the friends in Lisbon. . . . What a success! You can be proud and pleased my dearest." Otto explained, "In half an hour, I have to go to the Committee in order to find out details about the trip. If nothing unforeseen happens, it's possible that I can leave within two or three days." He added, "Every day I look in the mail for a letter from you that tells me that you know about my visa." And he reported on his decision to ship his luggage and his toolbox the next day via American Express: "I had wanted to hear what you thought about it, but now I thought I'd better send it anyway. I am not sure if it makes sense as far as the tools are concerned; but if worse comes to worse, it's a loss of 500 [francs]." In closing, Otto wrote:

> It's going to be true that we will soon be able to live together again. I can hardly believe it. It's hard for me now not to be impatient, and yet, there is no reason for it, because everything went so much faster than I had a right to expect. Now these last few weeks will go by quickly, and when I'll see you again, it will seem to me that fate has given me such an extraordinary happiness that it will be hard for me to merit it.
>
> Now it will be true that I am coming home to you.

In a hasty letter to Otto on March 11 Eva wrote, "I now dare to challenge fate and write this to you in Lisbon, though I still have great concerns about whether you have arrived there safely." Eva told Otto that she had received a cable the day before from Gaby that Otto "had left France for Spain on March 5." Eva noted, "Today is the 11th but still no news that you arrived. . . . Oh dearest, how very hard it is to learn patience! . . . How good it would be if it were true that this letter will actually reach you in Lisbon!"

Writing to Eva for the first time from Lisbon on March 12, Otto described his departure from Marseille, including Gaby's reaction to their parting:

> My dearest, I cannot yet quite realize that I am here now, already so close to you. And that I still found our friends, and especially

Erich and Herta here! And then—you can certainly feel with me what that means: I can again be myself. How that lets one breathe more deeply!

It's true, I'll have to wait again, one more time. But I, we, must not be impatient now, after this long wait, and after these months of unbelievable pressures. And that waiting is taking place in this friendly city, among these good people, under this bright sky! No, we don't want to be tense now, want to use these days well to prepare for the hours when we'll see each other again. Now I can have your letters with me, and the little blue book, can put it on my night table, can read in it when and where I want.

There is much to tell you. These last days were so full of varying events that I don't know where to begin.

Sooner than we had hoped, the Spanish visa arrived, and the next morning, I left. Gaby came along until Narbonne [city between Marseille and Banyuls sur Mer]. It was not easy for her when we had to part; but she was courageous, and I was grateful for that. What she is writing to you in the enclosed letter, is really in her. What she says of me almost makes me feel ashamed—am afraid she sees me in too generous a light. Do write to her; she feels close to you and is happy to hear from you.

Otto then described his brief stay in Banyuls sur Mer and his hike over the Pyrenees:

Then, for a few days, I had to wait in the little French border town [Banyuls sur Mer]. Beautiful country; peaceful people, vineyards and mounts of olive trees without end, an unbelievably beautiful blue ocean. I wanted to enjoy all this, but could do it only partially. What was ahead of me had me spellbound.

Saturday morning, at dawn, I set out. Was very hopeful, almost surprised that there was no fear in me. Briskly, I climbed on, in the brilliant early morning. Soon, there was the top of the mountain. A quick, strong handshake with my guides, a straight look into their eyes, then on I went downhill. Lost the trail, but should I worry about that? Did not care about the thorny bushes, the rocks—every so often I had to tell myself not to walk too fast, had to remember how you had warned me when I wanted to take off alone in the mountains. There, a dry creek that leads me back to the trail. After a five-hour hike I arrive at the border, get the stamp of entry, and off to the station. New problem: Spain no longer accepts French currency—what to do? Somehow I manage. A beautiful train ride through Catalogne, greetings on the right side of the snow-covered Pyrenees, to my left the ocean. It is singing in me. A new life begins. And my thoughts go forward, but also back, to those who are waiting.

He concluded with a brief description of his passage through Spain and the joy of seeing Eva's brother Erich and his wife Herta at the station in Lisbon:

Good luck in Barcelona—a seat for the following evening. Third-class carriage, is supposed to be strenuous, but what do I care about that! It's Sunday. I walk through the city, am amazed at the richness in the store displays, also sad about the evident naked misery right next to it.

Madrid the next morning. Had ordered a ticket at Cook's and was lucky again: a seat for the following evening, second class this time. That trip was a pleasure; I could even sleep. Now only one more concern: What would happen at the frontier? I no longer had the same amount of francs, had used some for traveling and living. The officer at the border was pleasant, and let me go. Only now I could really be happy—hardly noticed the ten hours until Lisbon. At the station, a radiant face, open arms: Erich. I could hardly believe it. Then I saw Herta and the others—they all looked happy.

Soon we sat down to eat—you were with us. Have to end now, the letter has to be mailed. How happy I am that now I am so close to you!

In a note to Eva from Lisbon on March 14, Otto made an urgent appeal for Eva's help in getting visas for Johannes Fittko and his wife Lisa[1] who had assisted him and other refugees with their escapes from France:

Something quick and short that is very close to my heart. Something must be done to get a visa for Johannes Fittko and his wife. . . . I don't know how far you can take this, or whether you're in a position to do anything, but I have promised him, as he essentially helped me to get here (I think you know how), that I would make every effort to assure that he is not forgotten over there. This man has already helped, in numerous cases, many people who were in my situation, and thereby continually risked that his own departure would be put in question.

Otto added the following note along the left margin of his letter: "45 people are over there already with the help of Fittko and the other friends in overcoming the same difficulties I just faced."

After finally receiving confirmation that Otto was in Lisbon, Eva wrote to him on March 14:

For the first time since the 9th of May, the burden on my heart dissolved, and I saw the world again with eyes that could see joy. It was such a beautiful, clear, sunny day. Many people saw me on my way to work—perhaps I appeared changed some-how. . . . How longingly, how full of love, I wait for the day when I will have you.

On that same day, Stern sent a note to Eva from Haverford, Pennsylvania:

I am very happy: That you have worked so nobly and success-fully; that we know Otto is in Lisbon; that your reunion pushes so close; that for once justice and love triumph.

This gives your life a new extraordinary and undying strength. You will know how to put it to use. Your gratitude will become work for the earth.

I have written a few lines this morning:

I lift my head, awakened
By a trilling from a bird never heard before.
There lay the land in snow.
And the morning sun rose.

Also on March 14, Eva reported to Eichler the positive results of her efforts to rescue their ISK colleagues.[2] This good news was tempered by Eva's report that the visa applications of their colleagues Nora Block

Platiel, her husband Hermann, and Nora's sister Herta Walter were being held up. The problem stemmed from the views about communism held by the husband of Nora's and Herta's sister who was already in America. Eva had enlisted the help of Paul Benjamin on these cases. In a letter dated March 12, 1941, Benjamin wrote to George Warren, head of the President's Advisory Committee: "I believe Miss Lewinski implicitly when she declares that these women have nothing in common politically with their sister's husband. . . . I am convinced that they, like Miss Lewinski, are high-minded, industrious people who are devoted to democratic principles and are worthy to be admitted to the United States."

But even with Paul Benjamin's strong support, Eva's efforts to obtain emergency visas in these cases would not succeed. The fact that the husband of Nora's and Herta's sister was known as a friend and defender of communists was enough to deny their applications. They would later escape from France to Switzerland with the help of René Bertholet.[3]

## Final days of waiting and Otto's grateful arrival

In her March 14 letter to Eichler, Eva expressed her happiness that it now appeared reasonable to hope that all, including Otto, would arrive. Eva urged Eichler not to give her too much credit for her work in seeking visas for their ISK colleagues:

> Willi: Please don't you, and don't the others, paint a false picture of what I have done here. Without Anna's and Klara's help and their old and stable relationships with exceptionally good and valuable people, I would have been able to do only a small fraction of what I did.
>
> So please: In case my impression is correct that you overestimate my work: Please adjust your judgment as follows, that all of us here, each in his position, have tried with all our strength to do all that was humanly possible to help our friends and our cause. Perhaps you might write to Anna? She is a really great person. And if she had not come up with this magnificent woman in Buffalo, Dorothy Hill, who more and more becomes our best friend, then many important connections would never have

come about. Through Dorothy came also the connection with
Mrs. Roosevelt, and many others. You understand, Willi, why
it is so important to me to write this to you. I would not want
to be unfair to these three able and helpful people for anything.

Eva ended this letter to Eichler by expressing her feelings about Otto's
arrival in Lisbon: "I am so happy to know he is out of the cauldron that
really could have brought something awful. I look very much forward
to living and working with him. By the way, he sends you his regards.
He was particularly pleased that you sent me the photos of him. All, all
the best, dear Willi, and the most heartfelt greetings!"

In a letter to Eva from Lisbon on March 21, Otto wrote that he still
had not received word that Eva knew he was in Lisbon. "I wait and wait
with impatience for a letter from you, for the first sign of life since weeks
ago. . . . I would so much like to read of your joy, feel your great joy,
after you know that I am here." He explained that he would likely have
to wait three more weeks before departing from Lisbon but observed:

> What is that compared to the many months that lie behind us?
> Now it is actually true. We will see each other, have each other.
> How indescribably wonderful that will be! Oh Eva, what a great,
> deep happiness it will be when you stand before me. I ask myself
> again and again: have I deserved that?

In Eva's letter to Otto written on the same day, she referred to Otto's
birthday on April 8 and asked him:

> What do I wish for you? Nothing that I do not wish for *us*.
> And that I can write that down after this hard year with a deep
> belief that it can become true—that is the most beautiful gift
> that could be given to us, to you and me.

Eva wrote a letter to Otto on March 24, hoping that it would arrive
in time for his birthday:

> I have a free hour, and tomorrow morning a Clipper will leave,
> and today I got your two good letters, the last from France, the
> first from Lisbon—and perhaps my letter will get there in time

First page of Otto's letter to Eva from Lisbon on March 21, 1941.

for April 8—so I have to quickly tell you that I love you and how happy I am when I think of you.

It is so unreal that I can write to you directly, that I can write your name, the good whole name on the envelope. I would like so much to do something nice for you, but I have been awfully busy the last few weeks, fortunately lately also with earning some money.

My dearest, now I almost feel as though we took the way over the mountains, through Spain, together. So clearly I see you stride out, hear you sing, see your eyes radiant—and at the same time I suffer because of all the misery.

She recalled her own feelings when she had to leave France and cross the Pyrenees and the ocean, leaving Otto behind:

> And then the climb over the mountains, without you, and the crossing of the ocean, without you, away from you—and I did not know where to send my thoughts to find you, I only felt: for me there is only to think of the past, not of a future.
>
> Oh my dear, and yet it was all right and necessary, and neither you nor I suffered in our inner life from it—sometimes I could cry with gratitude.
>
> I'll write to Gaby often. I love her, and know how hard her life is, and with what courage she masters it.

And she noted at the end of the letter, "How pleased I am that the blue book will come with you, and how I look forward to you!!"

On Eva's birthday, April 2, she wrote to Otto confirming her receipt of news that he would be departing from Lisbon on April 15. She asked, "Dearest, can that really be true?" She cautiously allowed herself to believe it. "I cannot yet completely grasp it, and yet there is something in me that gently allows me more trust that this year is really coming to an end." She told Otto that before going to work that morning, she bought flowers as his gift to her, "beautiful red roses." She then gave Otto updates about the current status of their other colleagues seeking to escape to America, noting that unresolved difficulties had still precluded the granting of visas to René Bertholet and his wife Hanna.

During this time, Eleanor Roosevelt was also being informed about the progress in Eva's visa cases behind the scenes. In a brief letter to Mrs. Roosevelt dated April 7, 1941, Sumner Welles reported, "I now take pleasure in enclosing a memorandum from the Visa Division indicating the action taken up to date" in Eva's pending visa cases.[4] The enclosed memorandum, dated April 3, 1941, was addressed to Welles from George Warren of the President's Advisory Committee. It listed the names of all of those to whom visas had been issued, including Otto; those whose cases had been approved by the Interdepartmental Committee on Political Refugees but were still "pending final action at the appropriate consular offices," including Hans Kakies; those whose cases were still "under consideration by the Interdepartmental Committee," including René and Johanna Bertholet; and those whose cases had been "disapproved after careful consideration" by the Interdepartmental Committee, including Nora Block and Herta Walter.[5]

With the help of U.S. officials such as Sumner Welles, Eliot Coulter, George Warren, and Hiram Bingham, First Lady Eleanor Roosevelt had fulfilled the commitment she had made months earlier to Eva, an unknown refugee, to try to help rescue Eva's endangered colleagues.

On his 41st birthday, April 8, 1941, Otto wrote Eva a short letter from Lisbon that was filled with anticipation of his departure. He spoke of two photos he had of Eva: the one she left for him with the note "pour toi" and another of her in the French countryside:

> Only eight more days, and I'll be on my way. The day is coming so close that we will be together again. I can hardly quite believe in it, and even over there, it will take some time to "realize" it, same as when I entered Paris, walked freely through the streets.
>
> Erich and Herta will be with you within a few days. It makes me very happy that it had been possible at the last minute still to get a place on the boat for Herta. But of course, you know all that now, and you'll know thousands of other things that they will have told you. . . .
>
> Many thanks for the flowers, my dearest, the real ones and the ones on the picture. They are the only decoration in my little room. Also your photo, the serious one. Heavy, almost sad do you look, and like a big question. But I still have another photo of you with me, the one at the cistern. I look at that when I want to see you cheerful, happy.

In a letter to Eva from Lisbon on April 14, Otto provided news of the sailing dates of other friends and told Eva: "Now this is probably the last letter I'll write you before we see each other again. Tomorrow evening, we take off." Otto departed from Lisbon the following day, April 15, 1941, on the Portuguese ship SS *Nyassa*.[6]

On April 30, 1941, shortly after his arrival in New York, Otto wrote a letter in French to Eliot Coulter, acting chief of the State Department's Visa Division, expressing his gratitude for Mr. Coulter's help in allowing him to enter the United States:

It is with true pleasure, after my arrival to the United States, that I express to you my great and sincere gratitude for the effective assistance you have given me. I know from Miss Eva Lewinski (and from Miss Dorothy Hill of Buffalo, whom I had the great pleasure of meeting here) all of the interest that you have shown me, and I appreciate it all the more because I recognize how the circumstances of my case could carry divergent interpretations at first glance.

I am very happy to have found myself here among close friends, finally again under a sun where one can breathe freely.

And I can assure you that this country will never regret the generous attitude that it has taken toward me and my friends.

In the hope of having the chance sooner or later to express all my gratitude to you in person.

Eva was also deeply grateful for the opportunity provided by those in this country who were willing to provide asylum for her and her colleagues. Sometime after her December 27, 1940, meeting with Eleanor Roosevelt in the White House and prior to Otto's arrival in New York in April 1941, Eva had a third brief meeting with the first lady. Eva described the impact of this meeting in her 1979 memoir "To Our Children":

Later on, I was able to see Mrs. Roosevelt again, this time in New York at the apartment of Miss Malvina Thompson, her secretary and friend, and she wanted more information in order to help a young writer, Hans Litten, prisoner of the Nazis, whose mother I knew, and who waged a desperate fight to save him. Again, Mrs. R's warm openness was extraordinary. She was concerned as a mother would be who wants to assist another mother to save her son. Our visit was short; she had to attend a meeting of the Save the Children Foundation, and she asked me if I wanted to come along to the place so we could talk some more in the taxi. In front of the house, a cruising cab stopped; she got in, and so did I, and driver said: "Hello Eleanor, how are you?" She smiled when she answered.

Perhaps by the time you'll read this, this episode might not seem in any way special to you. To me, the young refugee from oppression in Germany where fear of and submission to authority was a national characteristic, this was overwhelming. And this encounter did perhaps more than many another later experience to convince me that the United States was a country that I would come to love.[7]

Eva also noted that "none of the people who had issued financial affidavits of support [for the refugees Eva helped with visas] were ever called upon for financial help. All our friends, often through very hard work, were immediately self-supporting; some finished their often interrupted education and were able to do important work in their respective fields."[8]

On May 5, 1941, shortly after Otto's arrival in New York, Eva was given a half day off work to go to City Hall to marry Otto in a brief civil proceeding. Her brother Erich was the required witness. Eva recalled, "Then at the automat, we had lunch, and then I went back to work."[9] It is not clear what work she returned to on that day. While Eva worked to rescue her ISK colleagues, she needed money to help pay her rent. She initially took a job painting flowers on China plates for $12 a week. She was then hired to do clerical work "for an old Russian man" at a Jewish rehabilitation organization that provided vocational training to help impoverished Russian Jews.[10] She also worked extensively for the Emergency Rescue Committee.

Otto's arrival in New York and their marriage appeared to mark a happy ending to the challenging personal ordeals that Eva and Otto had each survived since their separation a year earlier on May 9, 1940. Unfortunately, Eva immediately faced another challenge: Willi Eichler would sharply criticize her decision to marry Otto.

As leader of the ISK, the group to which Eva had devoted nearly two decades of her young life at profound personal sacrifice, Eichler would take the position that Eva's decision to marry Otto was an unwarranted breach of the ISK's rules and of his trust in her. Under the circumstances, these charges could not have been more painful for Eva. She would explain and vigorously defend her decision to Eichler.

## 23. Eva's Defense of Her Decision to Marry Otto

Willi Eichler learned that Eva and Otto had married from other ISK members then in America including Erna Blencke, who was among the ISK's leaders. In a letter to Blencke dated June 6, 1941, Eichler wrote, "Now a word about Eva's wedding, which I heard about through your letter, although I don't know whether it even really happened. It is correct that, based on the reasons that were so far presented to me, I think it was the wrong decision." He added, "I have no idea why Eva did not at least tell me about the fact that she got married, although I guess that she thought this to be superfluous after she had also not shared the considerations that led to the decision." Eichler recognized that it may have been difficult for Eva "to articulate such considerations in a written letter," but he noted that "it appears as if you also had no chance to discuss the issue with her, although, judging from your letter, it was generally agreed that all of you [Blencke and other ISK members in America] wished to discuss the decision with her."

Blencke had stated in her letter that she was "convinced that [Eva] had serious reasons for taking this step." But Eichler countered, "I cannot imagine them at the moment, at least not insofar as there is certainly no serious reason for not discussing matters of this sort with your closest friends." He added, "The fact that these steps were not discussed appears to confirm the unfortunate fact that our relationships are defined by a lack of openness and understanding. A confrontation is avoided by presenting the others with a fait accompli because it can be assumed that no one will be inclined to discuss things that have already been decided and can no longer be changed."

In a letter to Eichler dated August 13, 1941, Eva answered his criticism. She began by conceding that her delay in writing and addressing "the conflict that has emerged between us" could only partly be attributed to the work that was keeping her busy. Eva noted that Eichler had recently received "detailed letters" about this from Blencke and other ISK members, some of which were known to her, and described her initial reaction to these letters:

ISK leader Willi Eichler. Courtesy of AdsD/Friedrich-Ebert-Stiftung.

> I immediately wanted to sit down and address the individual statements made in them, correct and reject them because I am convinced that they create a wrong image of the things they describe, partly because, by stressing certain less important things and leaving more important ones out, they must create an impression that was not intended by the author. At the same time, I am convinced that these letters, meant as contributions to aid our common understanding, were written with only the best intentions in mind. Because I cannot assume that my letters will not contain similar mistakes, I have lately not felt the courage to write at all.

Eva conceded that her delay in addressing this issue with Eichler was not justifiable. She then explained, in careful detail, why she made the decision to marry Otto and why she believed that the decision was consistent with ISK principles. Because of confidentiality concerns, she referred to herself in the third person, using one of her ISK pseudonyms, "Helene." She referred to Otto by his pseudonym "Tom," and she referred to Eichler in the third person by one of his ISK pseudonyms, "Bill."

Eva first addressed what she considered the "most important point" about the ISK commitment regarding marriage: "I have never been aware of the fact that any of us promised not to take a step such as the one Helene has taken [marriage]. The only—and important—thing that we agreed upon was that we would not do it for personal reasons, but only if more general interests made it necessary." She provided examples of such decisions that had previously been made for "general reasons," including the difficult decision that she should marry Stern if necessary to obtain a U.S. visa: "It was for such general reasons that Helene, as I wrote in my letter to you at that time, decided to form this bond with Luitpold [Stern]."

Eva explained: "It was only because of these general reasons that, in the case at hand, the step was taken so soon after Tom's [Otto's] arrival. The fact that taking such a step was in this case consistent with the wishes of the involved parties played only a subordinate role when the decision was made." She concluded: "I therefore regard the accusation against Helene, the charge that she coolly disregarded promises and resolutions, as not justified."

Eva then described in careful detail the process of her efforts to obtain visas for her ISK colleagues, including her contacts with Eleanor Roosevelt, and why it was necessary to disclose her personal relationship with Otto to American officials and to marry Otto immediately upon his arrival. Eva noted that Eichler had argued in one of his letters to Erna Blencke that Eva's mistake was that she had taken the first step of disclosing her special relationship with Otto to American officials. Eva responded to this contention—again referring to herself as "Helene" and to Otto as "Tom":

> The specifics of Helene's case were as follows: when she came here, she had to work on behalf of all friends, in the order of the cases' respective urgency. Because she did not know at the time whether Tom was still alive, no plans to work on his case were made at first; after all, one did not want to risk wasting the limited resources that were at hand. Shortly after her arrival here she learned through a telegram . . . that efforts to help Tom were now very urgently needed; and a few weeks later she heard that, how exactly remained unknown to her, he had escaped from the Nazis. . . . It was at this point that urgent measures were taken to obtain an affidavit, etc., all of it still without highlighting his personal relationship to Helene.

Eva explained that Anna Stein had introduced her to Dorothy Hill, who was "tremendously helpful" and had introduced Eva to Eleanor Roosevelt. Eva added that Hill had also obtained and at times even drafted the necessary documents for a number of their colleagues, including Otto. Hill had learned from Anna Stein about the "special relationship between Helene and Tom" and was adamant that Eva should disclose the relationship: "She thought it was completely wrong not to mention the nature of their relationship to the authorities, because in this particularly difficult case, naming familial reasons could be extremely helpful. At the same time, she [Hill] sent a letter of recommendation to the administrative authorities, in which she recommended Helene and also referred to her as Tom's fiancée."

Eva then explained the importance of the decision to disclose her relationship with Otto. She reminded Eichler of her earlier letter in which she had advised him that all submitted cases except Otto's had been approved:

In Tom's [Otto's] case, however, great difficulties emerged, which were caused and explained by the specifics of his case, and they began to take on such large political proportions, that the success of the whole endeavor hung by a thread. At this point, Helene decided to make use of both the good reputation, which she had by then earned, and her personal relationship with Tom, and to go directly to the officials in the State Department who were the source of the difficulties.

Thanks to the 30-minute conversation, or rather hearing, that she had to sit through [with Eliot Coulter, acting chief of the Visa Division of the State Department], accompanied by a good American friend [Paul Benjamin], as well as the belated good and open-minded impression Tom made at the consulate [in Marseille], he was not only granted a visa, but Helene's and her friends' esteem also grew.

Being familiar with the social customs here, Helene knew that her decision to have used her relationship to Tom when speaking to the authorities would have the practical consequences [marriage] that later indeed followed. However, she was convinced that she could take this responsibility, that it was indeed her duty, because this really was the only chance to have his case approved. She also believed him to be in danger, despite his good language skills, especially since his experiences with the Nazis, about which she had by then heard a few more details. Everyone who knew the situation here not only agreed that it was right to act this way, but encouraged us to do so whenever Helene or I hesitated.

Eva told Eichler that she was explaining this in such detail because it showed that it was "especially necessary in this case" to disclose her personal relationship with Otto, "which then, along with many other factors . . . made the following steps inevitable." She added:

> Just one more word on the reasons why all of those familiar with the situation deemed it necessary to accept these consequences shortly after Tom's [Otto's] arrival: around that time, a good dozen of our cases were under consideration at the administrative authorities, among them some very important ones such as the extension of Tegel's [Kakies] visa, and things were not moving forward. It appeared to be an excellent idea to combine Tom's arrival with a thank-you visit to the official [Eliot Coulter] in Washington, whom Helene had previously met to plead Tom's case. Such a visit would give Tom the chance to at once make a good impression and resolve any existing doubts regarding his integrity while also using the opportunity to try to plead for the still pending cases. Given the situation here, this was, however, only possible after having gotten married. And the intervention was of such urgency that no one wanted to be responsible for postponing it until after Helene and Bill [Eichler] had the chance to exchange letters.

Eva then tackled the tough question of why she had not notified Eichler in advance. Her answer was complex and revealing:

> What remains is the question why Helene, who had foreseen the necessity of all these steps, did not notify Bill in advance. And this in fact presents a point at which Helene cannot be spared earnest criticism. She was convinced, and rightly so, that she would not be able to discuss the content of this issue . . . and

that she would therefore here—as in many other cases—have to make a decision to the best of her knowledge and on her own. This fact, however, she should have of course disclosed.

At a point in time, however, when Tom's release still seemed like a miracle to her, she did not really dare to believe in his arrival before she actually saw him face to face. I don't know whether you know her personality as well as I. In a certain sense she is—you could say—superstitious or, to be more precise: she is a great pessimist, in the sense that she can only live and work if she is very well prepared that a project, in which she is objectively or personally involved, could have a bad outcome. If she has envisioned the possibility of such a failure in concrete detail and has consequently braced herself for it, she somehow feels better prepared and can therefore do whatever it takes to work towards a successful solution. And yet she does not, in earnest, believe in it.

I think this attitude can be seen as a method of self-protection: she is not sure how she could endure the severity of a bad outcome had she previously allowed herself to live in the hope of a good outcome. It was for this reason that it was obviously impossible for her in this case to overcome her own constraints and discuss the steps that would necessarily follow a positive outcome. She regrets this, blames herself and is aware of the fact that she should very much work on her—at least partly unreasonable—inner attitude.

Eva urged Eichler not to judge her shortfall too harshly. In this intensely personal explanation, Eva continued to refer to herself as Helene. She also questioned whether Eichler was really in a position to judge her:

Without wanting to excuse her [Helene/Eva] regarding this issue, I would like to say that I may be in the position to better understand her inner situation at the time and therefore do not judge her shortfall as harshly. As many others, whose exhaustion found a different outlet, she had a very rough year, and although she never complained, it nevertheless was very hard for her. I don't know, for example, whether anyone who did not witness the situation can imagine how much energy it cost her to leave Europe, at a point when she had to seriously reckon with the fact that Tom [Otto] may be awaiting a horrible fate, when she had to leave behind everything that she was attached to, people and work, and was faced with a task that, when she imagined what lay before her, went far beyond her own strength—a premonition that was indeed often later confirmed. From this point of view on the situation, which I very unwillingly address and which I only mention in order to try to shed light on the whole issue, I understand her behavior, although I admit, in just the same way that she does, that it was neither correct nor reasonable.

In light of everything Eva had experienced since May 1940, her understatement of her personal sacrifices for her colleagues is extraordinary—particularly knowing that it was written reluctantly in response to an accusation by her ISK leader that she had acted improperly and in her own personal interest by marrying Otto.[1]

Eva concluded with an apology to Eichler for playing a part in causing him to worry, but she repeated her conviction that his concerns were unfounded. Reflecting her ISK-taught belief that reason and Socratic dialogue could bring clarity to ethical disagreements, Eva concluded:

I think that this is all I should say about the matter at this moment. That I very much understand your concern, and that I am distressed by the fact that I have played a part in causing you to worry, you will have to believe, Willi. And yet I am convinced that your concerns regarding some of the most important factors are misconceived. I very much hope that we will at some later point have the chance to shed absolute clarity on our respective opinions, and maybe revise some of them.

The subject of Eva's marriage to Otto was but one part of a long letter that covered a host of other subjects relating to the ISK's current work. It was apparent that Eva in no way expected this issue to interfere with her commitment to the ISK and its political objectives. Eva did not retain this letter to Eichler, and she never spoke about this issue to her children, the authors of this book. It must have been painful for her. And it likely influenced Eva's later decisions about the degree to which the ISK should control her personal life.

# Part VI.

## Rescue Efforts and Work for the OSS in the Face of Personal Challenges

*The OSS mission in Bern served as a crucial conduit for communication between the French resistance and supporters in Britain and the United States. A primary channel that operated for most of the war was communication between "328" in Switzerland and "Eva" in the United States.*

—Historian Neal H. Petersen

*Secret and hazardous mission in ETO [European theater of operations]. Project involves considerable number of recruits capable of passing as natives of France and possessing background in labor or political movements in that country. Projected use of recruits is highly confidential.*

—Arthur Goldberg describing Otto's assignment with the OSS, February 21, 1944

# 24. Priorities: Eva's Rescue and Relief Work

The Emergency Rescue Committee (ERC) hired Eva as a case worker, initially part-time and then full-time. Throughout the war, Eva worked with the ERC and its successor, the International Rescue and Relief Committee (IRRC), to rescue and assist those still trapped in Europe. She also continued to work with organizations assisting elderly impoverished refugees in New York.

Eva barely mentioned her work for the ERC in her 1979 memoir, perhaps because she was so painfully aware that the doors to rescue of refugees in America were virtually shut, and so few were rescued compared to the millions of human beings who perished in the Holocaust. This cannot erase the fact that, despite overwhelming barriers, Eva and others at the ERC did everything they could to rescue endangered refugees. Eva's work with the ERC not only involved rescue efforts that became far more difficult as the war progressed; it also involved assisting with the transmission of funds for the relief of refugees in Europe. Documents in the files of the ERC and the IRRC reflect those efforts and the gratitude of those who received the assistance.[1]

In addition to handling many new cases, Eva's work with the ERC included her continuing efforts to rescue some of her ISK colleagues. To take one example, Eva had obtained a U.S. visa for Hans Kakies (aka Tegel) with the help of Eleanor Roosevelt, but Kakies was unsuccessful in his initial attempt to escape from France to Lisbon. Because some refugees who tried to escape from southern France over the Pyrenees had been captured, Kakies tried to escape by boat to Algiers in North Africa, from where he intended to travel to Casablanca and then to Lisbon. Unfortunately, he was stopped in Algiers, where he was interned in a camp, and during that internment his U.S. visa expired. The question of the extension of Kakies's visa was one of Eva's urgent cases pending before U.S. authorities at the time Otto arrived in the United States.[2]

Eva's work with the ERC on the Kakies case lasted many months. Despite the fact that Kakies had previously been granted a U.S. visa, his renewed application for a visa was rejected by the State Department. The ERC then sought to obtain a visa for Kakies to escape to Cuba. A Cuban visa was finally procured for him in November 1941, and he left Casablanca for Cuba on November 22.[3] Eva also worked on Kakies's appeal from the denial of his renewed application for a U.S. visa so he could move to America from Cuba. The President's Advisory Committee finally gave its "advisory approval" to the granting of a U.S. visa to Hans Kakies on August 3, 1942. That approval was cabled to the U.S. consul in Cuba, but there were further delays.

Kakies and his fiancée Erna Mros (who was already in America) wrote to Eva at the ERC and expressed frustration about the delays in his case. But Eva recognized that his move from Cuba to America was not an ERC priority. His life was no longer in danger. The ERC's priority at that time was trying to convince the State Department to rescue those who were then in imminent danger in Europe because of the French deportations of anti-Nazis. In a letter to Hans (then in Havana) dated September 1, 1942, Eva wrote: "We are, as you can well imagine, terribly worried about the situation in France—already a certain number of good friends and well-known anti-Nazis have been extradited. It is awful." And in a letter written on the same day to Erna Mros, Eva compared the situation facing Hans, now safe in Cuba and waiting for admission to the United States, with that of anti-Nazi colleagues who had been extradited by the French:

> During these last few days, I have been wondering whether we should ask the State Department again about the status of his case. But I then decided not to do it. As you know, the news from France is terrible, and we have tried everything to encourage the State Department to expedite decisions on cases in southern France. We now understand that they are giving priority to those cases, and that they intend to issue visas only in exceptional cases to those in this hemisphere. So it was better to let it go, as fortunately Hans was in no danger whatsoever.

I am sure that you agree with me. Some very good friends (so-cialists and other anti-Nazis, German, Austrian, Polish) have already been extradited, we just learned by cable. It is terrible, and I am afraid that we will not be able to do very much about it any more.

Hans Kakies left Cuba for Miami on September 8, 1942. In a letter to Hans dated September 23, 1942, Eva reminded him to thank those who had helped him, including the American citizen, Ward R. Whipple, who provided an affidavit guaranteeing financial support; Dorothy Hill, who had been an advocate on his behalf; and Frank Kingdon, chair of the ERC.

## Priority of rescue and relief work

As Eva continued to work tirelessly in New York to assist those in the most danger, she needed to respond to requests from her family in South Africa for financial assistance to support her ailing mother. As we have seen, shortly after Eva's arrival in America, she was able to correspond with her mother, who had moved to South Africa. Eva also began to correspond with her younger brother Rudi and younger sister Ruth, who were with their mother in Johannesburg. On April 4, 1943, Rudi wrote a letter to Eva's brother Erich and his wife Herta in which Rudi explained the hard wartime conditions faced by the family in South Africa and described the burden of supporting their mother.

Eva responded to Rudi in a letter dated May 31, 1943. Although written for Rudi, she addressed the letter to her sister Ruth, whom Eva barely knew at that time, because Eva could not be certain that Rudi would still be in Johannesburg when her letter arrived. He had joined the South African Army and was about to leave Johannesburg to serve with the Allied forces in North Africa and Italy. Eva tried to explain to Rudi that despite their separation and lack of contact during recent years, they shared a basic commitment: to defeat Hitler "and all the barbarous injustice he and his system stand for." Eva told Rudi, "You are in it up to your neck, and I admire you and think of you very much." She added, "We, although much farther away from the battlefields, are in it just as well, from another angle, and . . . have been in it all these years before the open war started." Eva expressed her hope that the day would come when they could exchange information about their mutual experiences. "For the time being, however, all we can do is probably to have faith in each other, and the certainty that, from whatever different angle, we work together to straighten out the same problem that faces mankind."

Eva went on to express her concern about her mother's ill health and the financial burden of taking care of her. Eva advised Rudi that "we will immediately inquire as to actual procedures for transferring money, and then Otto will send regularly about $20 a month. He will not send it monthly, however, but probably in one larger sum which is supposed to last for several months." Eva then tried to explain why she, Erich, Herta, and Otto had not previously offered to contribute to her mother's care and why they could not contribute more now from what Eva earned. In doing so, she provided a vivid summary of the economic challenges they had faced as refugees in New York:

You might, or might not, know in what situation we all arrived here: without literally anything except what we had on and what we could carry in a small suitcase over the mountains when we had to leave France via the mountains. You might remember that I arrived here first, and all the others were left behind, in daily danger of life, not the danger you face in battle, but the danger you face when helplessly caught in a trap. It was natural—as a matter of fact: it was the only possible thing to do—that I concentrated all my efforts on helping those left behind, and not on finding a suitable position. How hard that was, you certainly can imagine.

When eventually the others arrived here, their struggle was hard. You know, Erich was a good lawyer, and in France it had not been too hard for him to find a new way of earning his livelihood. But many years had passed, he had gone through a lot, and those first months or even year here were very hard for him. Earn a few cents an hour as a dishwasher, work for many months as shipping clerk in a publishing house, doing hard, dirty work—it is not simple for a young, healthy man—it probably was too much for someone of Erich's constitution and age. Anyhow, several months ago, he fell seriously sick (this is for you and Ruth, not for mother), with a heart disease. The doctor, when he discovered it, ordered him to stop work immediately. . . .

Herta is working very hard and courageously doing housework in other people's homes; and with his and their work and some help, they get along to earn their living and pay the doctor's bills.

Eva explained that Otto was working hard, but much of his earnings had been needed for Erich's illness and to provide financial help to rescue "friends in danger of life because they had stood for what we stand for." She noted that "in spite of his very hard work we are right now just in a position to pay our last year's taxes. He therefore can start now to help mother, but he could not do it before, as long as the other urgent matters were there." Eva expressed her expectation that Rudi and Ruth would understand that this use of Otto's money had been a priority: "After all, we knew that mother was being looked after, while on the other hand without his and other friends' help to those left behind in a trap, they would simply have perished."

Eva explained that rescue efforts had recently become nearly impossible. "Now, unfortunately, there is nothing that we can do anymore for those left behind but help to win this war as quickly as possible." But she added that they were still being called upon to assist those who had been rescued but needed financial help to survive: "When people rescued and brought here are old, have no family, no possibility to earn their living, fall sick—you simply cannot leave them alone. After all, there is a kind of close relationship that has developed during these years of common experiences and hardships and solidarity that makes the feeling of being a member of a very large family very strong." Despite this, she noted, "in the future it will be possible to send mother at least a little."

Eva also shared her concerns about Otto's health, explaining that Otto had also experienced tough times since the war began. "Otto does not look well at all, and it is possible that the doctor who is now examining his lungs, asks him also to take it easy and to do something for his health at least for some time." She noted that she had never been able to explain "what Otto went through between the time of the invasion of France and his arrival here, but you can believe me that it was the most strenuous experience—and dangerous for that matter—that has ever occurred to any of us. . . . So he might need more care than he did before."

Finally, Eva further described the circumstances that had precluded her from providing financial support for her mother. She explained that when she arrived in America, she "almost automatically was pushed" into doing social work to "help as many good people as possible." She noted that because the misery experienced by refugees did not stop, she had found it "awfully hard" to get out of continuing to do relief work, which did not provide much compensation. "But here also I feel that you understand and appreciate my attitude: as long as, with many efforts, people who stood for the right thing all their life long can be saved, it is our unshakeable duty to stand by them."

Unfortunately, Eva was not even able to follow through on the plan to send $20 a month from Otto's earnings to help with her mother's care. In a letter to Rudi dated January 24, 1944, Eva expressed her disappointment that the plan to send this money had become impossible. Erich had again fallen seriously ill and required surgery. All of their money was needed for his medical bills.

As a refugee in America, Eva had chosen to continue to work long hours with minimal compensation to help those whose lives were in imminent danger rather than seeking a better-paying job so she could help her mother. As a member of the ISK, this choice was painful but clear: to help those with the greatest need. Because of Eva's commitments and her brother Rudi's engagement in the war as a soldier, the financial burden of caring for Eva's mother fell primarily on her brother Ernst. In terms of physical and emotional support, Eva's younger sister Ruth, then caring for her three infants, became their mother's primary caregiver.

In her correspondence with her family in South Africa, Eva did not and could not mention certain other work she was doing in New York. While immersed in her rescue and relief work with the ERC, she had also been drawn into highly secret work with the new American intelligence agency established during World War II, the Office of Strategic Services, which later became the Central Intelligence Agency. Her involvement in that work would remain a well-kept secret until the authors of this book discovered and confirmed it.

# 25.  René-Eva Correspondence: Eva's Secret Work with the Office of Strategic Services

In 1942, Arthur Goldberg, a Chicago labor attorney who was the son of Russian Jewish immigrants (and would be appointed by President John F. Kennedy years later to serve on the U.S. Supreme Court), joined the newly created Office of Strategic Services (OSS) and was selected to head its Labor Section. The British formed a secret organization during the war known as the Special Operations Executive (SOE) to engage in espionage, sabotage, reconnaissance, and other special operations, including work with resistance groups in occupied and neutral countries.

Many secret records of the OSS and the SOE have now been declassified and made available to historians.[1] The previously classified material includes extensive correspondence and memoranda reflecting the efforts of the OSS and SOE to gather on-the-ground intelligence about wartime conditions in Europe. Among the OSS records are hundreds of documents referring to what some historians have called the "René-Eva correspondence": secret information transmitted from "René" in Europe to "Eva" in New York for use by the OSS.

"René" was often referred to in these documents by various pseudonyms including "Robert" and "agent 328." In his volume of messages from the Operational Records of the OSS at the National Archives, historian Neal H. Petersen observed:

> The OSS mission in Bern served as a crucial conduit for communication between the French resistance and supporters in Britain and the United States. A primary channel that operated for most of the war was communication between "328"

in Switzerland and "Eva" in the United States. Innumerable messages were passed, and funds were disbursed to Maquis, underground labor elements within France, and for the relief of French refugees in Switzerland via the 328 network.[2]

Some historians identified "René" and his pseudonyms as ISK member René Bertholet, the Swiss citizen who had been engaged in anti-Nazi resistance activities with the ISK and the International Transport Workers Federation (ITF) long before the war. But none had identified with certainty the person referred to as "Eva."[3] We now know that "Eva" is Eva Lewinski Pfister.

## Origins of the René-Eva correspondence

A letter found in the SOE files (in German) from "R. und H." (René Bertholet and his wife Hanna) to "Liebe Eva" (Dear Eva) dated October 24, 1941, describes initial efforts to establish a confidential method of communication between Bertholet and Eva in New York.[4] Bertholet advised Eva in this letter that because of the difficulties involved in exchanging letters by mail between Europe and America ("the letters go at least through Spain, France and Portugal where the danger of censors always exists"), they were looking into the possibility of finding a more secure method of communicating. Bertholet also advised Eva that he was enclosing letters to Paul Vignaux from Vignaux's friends in Europe.

Vignaux, a French trade union leader and professor at the Sorbonne, had met Eva and Bertholet in Paris and had reconnected with Eva when he arrived in New York in the summer of 1941. Bertholet asked Eva to advise Vignaux that his friends in the Christian Trade Union had been hit by the new laws in Vichy France regulating the labor movement and that "in order to build their work further, they need money."[5] He asked if it would be possible for Vignaux and his friends in the United States to collect money for resistance work in Europe. Bertholet suggested specific amounts to address the compelling need for this work and noted that "we don't want to lose any time." Bertholet advised Eva that he had already proposed to provide Vignaux's friends with 5,000–10,000 francs per month, an amount that would "serve to free up one or two of Vignaux's colleagues to organize the resistance work on a national basis within the Christian Trade Union sector."[6] Finally, Bertholet described in some detail how the money was to be transferred.[7]

In a now declassified OSS memorandum dated January 26, 1942, with the subject "Cable from Robert for Eva," Arthur Goldberg stated, "We are in receipt of the following cable from Robert for Eva. Will you be kind enough to transmit the context of the cable to Eva." Bertholet's cable (as translated by the OSS) is quoted in Goldberg's memorandum. The cable advised that except for the arrest of a French trade union leader, Léon Jouhaux,[8] the occupation of France by the Nazis "has had no effect on syndicalist movement."

> Information bulletins and clandestine papers continue to appear, advocating rejection of former Vichy supporters who have changed sides in Africa. The *Temoignages* [Testimony] was published in December. Police measures of repression increasing in severity, affecting *franctireur* and *combat* [French resistance movements/publications]. Movement being joined by many officers in hiding. Many workers taking refuge with peasants in the country from now prevalent labor conscription. Have maintained regular communication with France, but doubt that my regular trips can be resumed. . . . General war fatigue growing in Germany but masses still too apathetic. Although greatly concerned about postwar situation, and fearing dismemberment of Germany and an American-supported reactionary or Catholic government, the opposition is regaining courage.[9]

This January 26, 1942, memorandum appears to be one of the earliest in what would become an extensive flow of information from René Bertholet to Eva and the OSS. It is an example of the kind of on-the-ground information that Bertholet was able to gather from his extensive network of contacts in the resistance in Europe and send to Eva about the status of resistance efforts. In exchange, Eva would facilitate the transmission of funds from America to assist Bertholet's resistance and relief work.

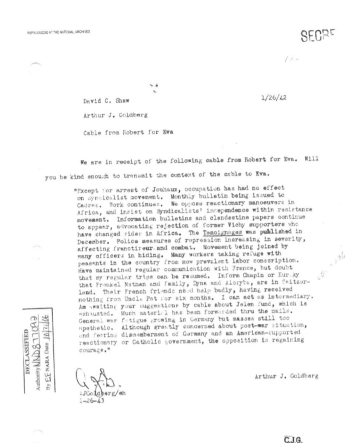

SECRE

David C. Shaw                                    1/26/42

Arthur J. Goldberg

Cable from Robert for Eva

   We are in receipt of the following cable from Robert for Eva. Will
you be kind enough to transmit the context of the cable to Eva.

   "Except for arrest of Jouhaux, occupation has had no effect
on syndicalist movement. Monthly bulletin being issued to
Cadres. Work continues. We oppose reactionary manoeuvers in
Africa, and insist on Syndicalists' independence within resistance
movement. Information bulletins and clandestine papers continue
to appear, advocating rejection of former Vichy supporters who
have changed sides in Africa. The Temoignages was published in
December. Police measures of repression increasing in severity,
affecting franctireur and combat. Movement being joined by
many officers in hiding. Many workers taking refuge with
peasants in the country from now prevalent labor conscription.
Have maintained regular communication with France, but doubt
that my regular trips can be resumed. Inform Chapin or Kurxky
that Frankel Nathan and family, Dyna and Aloryba, are in Switzerland. Their French friends need help badly, having received
nothing from Uncle Pat for six months. I can act as intermediary.
Am awaiting your suggestions by cable about Jelen fund, which is
exhausted. Much material has been forwarded thru the mails.
General war fatigue growing in Germany but masses still too
apathetic. Although greatly concerned about post-war situation,
and fearing dismemberment of Germany and an American-supported
reactionary or Catholic government, the opposition is regaining
courage."

                                                  Arthur J. Goldberg

AJGoldberg/eh
1-26-43

                                                      C.J.G.

OSS memorandum dated January 26, 1942, summarizing one of many
secret communications from René Bertholet in Europe to Eva in New
York for use by the OSS.

## The flow of René-Eva correspondence

On May 15, 1942, Eva wrote a letter (in French) to René Bertholet and
his wife Hanna about the ongoing arrangement to obtain reports from
them about the resistance in France.[10] Eva briefly reviewed the purposes
served by the reports they had previously sent, noting that they were
giving "exact information and documentation" about resistance activities
in France and were creating "interest in well-placed Americans in this
resistance and its importance." She noted that a bulletin prepared by "a
group of French unions, socialists and liberals" sought "to prove to the

American public that there is a basically democratic resistance in France, and it is not only the communists or the conservative nationalists who pursue resistance activity."

Eva further advised the Bertholets that "thanks to your excellent information . . . influential groups here are realizing more and more that this kind of resistance is the most interesting [and] is exactly what we had wanted." She noted that Bertholet "can thus tell our friends who are doing this work that it has already borne fruit."

Eva briefly reviewed the arrangement regarding the flow of this resistance information to America, noting the development of relationships with "representatives of the American labor movement," including some who "have come to important positions [an apparent reference to Arthur Goldberg] resulting in acceleration and facilitation of the arrangement we now have." She advised the Bertholets that "we are deeply interested here in the work of the resistance of the labor union-liberal-socialists in France. We think it is very important that this work become known here, and we want to help." She added, "We hope that in this way you have the possibility to send us reports about the resistance movement in a way that, for security reasons, you have not been able to achieve before. . . . I add that reports about other countries in Europe, about economic, social and cultural plans, are of equal interest.[11]

The information flow continued with a steady and high volume. Previously secret OSS documents reflect that Bertholet was sending twenty to thirty letters to Eva every month as of June 1942—a letter nearly every day.[12] When the flow of this information was interrupted at one point by American wartime censors who were intercepting mail sent from Europe to America, high-level OSS officials promptly took action. On June 25, 1942, the head of the OSS office in New York, John C. Hughes, sent a brief memo to F. Lamont Belin, conveying his concern that censors were holding up mail to Eva from Europe. This is one of the few documents in the OSS files that specifically identifies "Eva" in the René-Eva correspondence as Eva Pfister and reflects the importance that the OSS was placing on prompt receipt of this information at that time:

Mrs. Eva Pfister, of 40-40 Ebertson Street, Elmhurst, Long Island, has been receiving mail from Europe, chiefly from Switzerland, and she has been passing this over to individuals who deliver the same to our office.

We have reason to believe that some mail sent to her from abroad, photostated by the British censor in Bermuda and then released, has never been received by her. This would indicate that the American censor is holding up some of it, and, if possible, we would like to arrange that such mail be released for delivery to her with the least possible delay.

We are inclined to believe that if the censor continues to hold up certain mail, it will create some nervousness on her part and cause the steady flow of letters containing information to stop.

Will you please let me know if you can do anything about this.[13]

Belin responded to Hughes by memo dated July 3, 1942, noting that he had referred the inquiry to Colonel Cordeman, chief postal censor, who in turn had requested a "description of the material, the quantity, and the names of the senders." A document in the OSS files responding to this request described the nature and frequency of this information from Bertholet to Eva:

*Description of the material:*
Originals or copies of underground publications circulated in
    France
Typed copies of reports in French or German
Occasionally, but very rarely, photographs of documents
Letters accompanying above

*Quantity:*
All the above is mailed in separate letters of normal size and
    normal weight
Altogether 20 to 30 per month

*Names of senders:*
No name of sender ever on outside envelope
Letters are mailed generally from Zurich but sometimes from
    Geneva or Berne, Switzerland
Signature: R. or sometimes Jeanne, Anna or René[14]

In a letter dated July 14, 1942, Belin advised Colonel Corderman that the problem involved British censorship and had been resolved. He advised Corderman that "the British are fully aware of our wishes in this matter."[15]

Hundreds of pages of previously classified OSS memoranda in the National Archives summarize, in English, the correspondence between René Bertholet and Eva. The correspondence includes regular reports about the resistance situation on the ground in occupied France and elsewhere in Europe. It also reflects the regular transmission by Eva of funds from U.S. sources to Bertholet for his use in continuing resistance, rescue, and relief efforts in Europe during the war. A few examples of OSS memoranda summarizing the René-Eva correspondence are provided in Appendix B.

## The OSS's assessment of the ISK in planning to use German anti-Nazi refugees in the war against Hitler

Other German anti-Nazi émigrés were also offering advice and assistance to the OSS. Among them was Paul Hagen, the leader of the anti-Nazi German socialist splinter group Neu Beginnen (New Beginning) who had arrived in the United States in January 1940.[16] In April 1942, Hagen presented Allen Dulles with detailed proposals for the participation of German anti-Nazi refugees in organized underground activities. Dulles had been chief of the New York branch of the Office of the Coordinator of Information (the predecessor of the OSS) before the United States entered the war and then became the mission chief of the OSS office in Bern, Switzerland.

Hagen's proposals included building contacts with underground resistance movements in Europe, evaluating German publications, interviewing German prisoners, recruiting individuals for special "expeditions" to build ties with anti-Nazi trade unionists and socialists in neutral countries, and ultimately recruiting anti-Nazi prisoners of war for American intelligence work and having agents infiltrate Germany by parachute.[17]

These proposals were initially met with strong criticism and objections within the OSS. Some were suspicious that Hagen's group, Neu Beginnen, was a "revolutionary force" that envisioned a "German Soviet

Government."[18] Apart from this distrust of Hagen and Neu Beginnen, both Goldberg and William Donovan, the first director of the OSS, saw merit in Hagen's ideas. They were willing to override the ideological objections to working with socialists and began to discuss how to overcome obstacles to clandestine communications, including ways to circumvent American censorship. As historian Christof Mauch observed, "Hagen's agenda became a blueprint for the goals and work of the OSS Labor Division."[19]

Hagen envisioned a significant role for himself in these activities and proposed that he be named to a three-person German intelligence committee.[20] But he was too visible and controversial, and the OSS did not call upon him to assist with the implementation of his proposals. Indeed, throughout his life Hagen erroneously believed that the OSS had rejected them.[21]

Unknown to Hagen, the leaders of the OSS determined that other anti-Nazi refugees would be more capable of undertaking the clandestine activities he had proposed. It is not surprising that the OSS found that ISK members could be relied upon for this work. ISK members had always operated in the strictest secrecy and could be trusted to preserve confidentiality. They were not communists, and they had a valuable and current network of contacts with the European labor and resistance movements (including René Bertholet) and had demonstrated their voluntary and selfless commitment to anti-Nazi work for many years. In short, the OSS viewed the ISK as "extremely active" but "definitely anti-Marxist."[22]

In addition to his contacts with Eva in New York, Goldberg also met with Willi Eichler in London. Eichler introduced Goldberg to one of the ISK's contacts in the ITF.[23] Goldberg saw special value in the ITF, whose membership of railroad workers, sailors, streetcar conductors, and truck drivers could be excellent sources of information about military and political developments and could become involved in subversion and sabotage.[24]

As we have seen, the ISK had developed a long and close working relationship with the ITF during its prewar years of anti-Nazi resistance work in exile in Paris from 1933 to 1939. And ISK members, including Otto and René Bertholet, had also worked with the ITF during the Drôle de Guerre in conducting wartime sabotage of military trains. Goldberg's ideas about implementing resistance activities were nothing new to the ISK, and ISK members, including Eva and later Otto, were uniquely suited to assist the OSS in implementing them.

## Eva's work on the Sender Memorandum

On May 7, 1942, Goldberg sent a memorandum to Allen Dulles and George Bowden advising them of a luncheon conference he had with Toni Sender, a former social democratic member of the Reichstag in Germany, and Eleanor Coit, director of the Labor Education Service. Goldberg noted that "Miss Sender has a group of refugee labor leaders who . . . are very reliable and very well informed in the European labor situation." Goldberg recommended that the OSS "engage the services of the leading members of this group to make a survey of the current situation from the standpoint of the labor groups of the different countries in Europe."[25] This group of refugees prepared for Goldberg a memo, known as the Sender Memorandum, that discussed the role of labor in Germany and Nazi-occupied countries of Europe.[26]

On June 3, 1942, Dulles delivered the Sender Memorandum to Hugh R. Wilson, who served on the OSS Planning Board during the war.[27] In his transmittal memorandum, Dulles advised Wilson that "Arthur Goldberg tells me that the members of this group are prepared to cooperate in giving effect to the suggestions and proposals made in their memorandum." Dulles further observed that he is "more and more convinced that this is a field in which we can do really useful work."

The authors of the Sender Memorandum were listed on the first page in alphabetical order—Paul Kohn, Dyno Lowenstein, Eva Lewinski Pfister, and Toni Sender—with brief descriptions of their backgrounds.[28] The Sender Memorandum explained the potential importance of the labor movement in the fight against Nazism and fascism and of obtaining "a picture as accurate as possible of the European situation."[29] The memorandum observed that "with the rigid censorship in Europe it has been difficult—if not impossible—to gauge accurately the mood of the enslaved peoples in the laboring class, and the effect of fascist government measures on them. There are other sources for this information, and in a very systematic way they should all be tapped and used."[30]

The Sender Memorandum described the various sources of information from members of labor organizations, including those in exile working in the underground. Regarding underground movements, the memorandum suggested that "text and leaflets and newspapers should be followed" and that "the general situation in France, as far as resistance against the Nazis is concerned, should be investigated."[31]

The memorandum also addressed the importance of sending information to those in Germany who might be encouraged to resist Nazism. For example, it suggested that "news should be planned specifically for the navy yard workers at Lübeck; the women who lost their sons in Russia; the farmers; the Ruhr workers; the youth program; and so on." With insight gained from their years of anti-Nazi work, the four refugees who prepared this memorandum also observed the need to understand "what forces brought about Nazism and Fascism," and that "the spirit of hopelessness has been nourished among German workers by the fact that they do not see any other alternative to a Hitler victory but another, and perhaps worse, Versailles."[32]

The Sender group established the office of European Labor Research (OELR) to carry out the objectives of the Sender Memorandum. In proposing the establishment of this office to Allen Dulles on June 29, 1942, Arthur Goldberg noted that it would do its work "unofficially and without direct association" with the OSS.[33] The OELR produced a number of additional reports and memoranda in 1942.[34]

## Eichler's efforts to control the flow of Bertholet's information to the Allies

While the OSS was obtaining information from Bertholet through Eva, the SOE was also gathering similar information from Bertholet through Willi Eichler in London. A secret memorandum in the files of the SOE dated October 30, 1941, referred to "a contact in Switzerland" in whom the SOE was particularly interested because of letters he was writing to Willi Eichler in England. The memorandum explained that the SOE usually received translations of these letters "eventually from the Censorship" but urged that "it is rather important that we should receive immediate copies of any letters or telegrams" sent by this contact to Eichler. The memorandum noted that the name and address of the writer could not be given, "as he writes under a variety of names and addresses."[35] This "contact in Switzerland" was René Bertholet, most often referred to in the SOE's files by the pseudonym "Robert."

Another secret memorandum in the SOE's files dated November 7, 1941, discussed the lines of communication to be established between ISK leader Willi Eichler, "Robert," and the SOE. The memo noted that the SOE's ultimate objectives included arranging "for all communications between WILLI and ROBERT to pass through our channels and not through the open mail."[36] Assurance of strict confidentiality to protect those involved in resistance activities was of utmost concern for Bertholet in setting up these communications.[37]

During 1942, ISK leader Willi Eichler took steps to assume more control over the valuable flow of information from René Bertholet to the Allied intelligence organizations. Indeed, Eichler took the position in communications within the ISK that Eva had not received his approval to act as a conduit of such information for the American OSS. He sought to reduce Bertholet's correspondence to Eva in New York and to have such information directed to him in London for transmission to the SOE.

It is difficult to understand the reason for Eichler's attempt to reduce this significant flow of information to the OSS through Eva. Eichler certainly had political ambitions and was likely envisioning a significant role for himself in postwar Europe after Hitler's defeat. Bertholet's broad network of confidential sources, along with his dedication and discipline, produced the highest-quality intelligence information. Eichler may have thought that being the anti-Nazi German political leader in exile who controlled such information would enhance his influence with the Allies. Once again, Eva was placed in the position of having to defend her actions to Eichler.

A memorandum in the recently declassified files of the SOE dated February 10, 1943, titled "London Report No. 80/893" referred to an attached letter from "Mrs. Levinsky [sic]-Pfister" addressed to "Eclair" (the pseudonym regularly used by the SOE in referring to Eichler). The cover memorandum enclosing the letter stated:

> Apparently the relations between ROBERT [Bertholet] and our American friends are causing a certain amount of dissatisfaction in the small but compact I.S.K. group and the letter refers to it.

So far as we are concerned, we found among the New York members of this group, viz: the Pfisters (husband and wife), and Professor Vignaux—who joined them some time ago, the most cooperative spirit and frankness and we value this connection as the representatives of this group are among the few not concerned with the usual émigré squabbles and doctrinaire discussions.[38]

The referenced letter from Eva to Eichler dated January 26, 1943, provides important additional details about the genesis of the René-Eva correspondence. Eva informed Eichler that she had read the portion of his last letter to ISK member Erna Blencke about the relationship that had been established between Bertholet and "authorities here [the OSS]." She observed, "There are obviously quite a few misunderstandings and misrepresentations, and that's why I use this opportunity to tell you once more in chronological order how things happened and how they were agreed upon."

Eva began by explaining that before Paul Vignaux arrived in America in the summer of 1941, she and Bertholet had met him "quite often" in France when Vignaux also served as labor adviser of the French Ministry of Information. She noted that during the period from the collapse of France until his departure to America, Vignaux "had been instrumental in organizing the underground trade union movement." During that time, Eva explained, Vignaux had brought Bertholet in contact with Vignaux's friends.

Eva further explained to Eichler that when Vignaux arrived in America in the summer of 1941, "he immediately got in touch with us." She described Vignaux's reaction to information that Bertholet was sending to her in America:

When he [Vignaux] saw all the material that we had received from R. [Bertholet], he was very much impressed, all the more so as very often these were documents which he himself had either written or seen to it that R. [Bertholet] got them. Nobody else here had received any documentation about France at all, regularly and continuously. He told me at that time that he had had ample opportunity to think about R's [Bertholet's] and our group's [ISK's] work, and that he was convinced that

only we could make a contribution to the French labor movement, without which cooperation with America and England
was impossible.

Eva informed Eichler that "ever since that time, we have been closely co-
operating with V. [Vignaux], who by the way came here with a mandate
not only of his own trade unions, but of [Léon] Jouhaux [another French
trade union leader] as well." She assured Eichler that "R. [Bertholet] to
whom I wrote about it was very pleased about the cooperation which
was only the counterpart of his cooperation with V's [Vignaux's] friends
over there."

Eva then explained to Eichler that Bertholet had wanted to establish
a more secure way of communicating to Eva "so that more confidential information about the labor movement could also get here." She
told Eichler about early contacts established by Jef Rens with "some
Washington people for us, about which I wrote you at that time," but
that "nothing very much happened, because at that time the US was not
at war, and could not or would not do very much to help this special type
of work." The real contact, Eva explained to Eichler, "took place at the
beginning of 1942, through the intermediary of an influential member
of the American Labor movement who had become labor advisor of the
respective government agency [Arthur Goldberg]. A conference took
place, and it was agreed that the work of R. [Bertholet] and the French
labor movement which he represented interested greatly, and that people
here were prepared to assist it on lines which I explained to R. [Bertholet]
in my letter of May 15th, 1942, which was brought to him by messen-
ger, and of which I sent you a copy." Eva told Eichler that if he had not
received that copy, she would send him another one.

Eva advised Eichler that the arrangement had worked well for all concerned and had resulted in a regular flow of information: "R. [Bertholet]
and the other friends in France, ours as well as V's [Vignaux's], were
apparently pleased with this arrangement, because from that time on
they sent us regularly material, which was very much appreciated here."

Eva informed Eichler that Bertholet "also insisted on our trying to
get financial assistance from the American Labor movement, which we
did successfully several times." She added, "Since you never objected to
this approach, and since R's [Bertholet's] letter of October 20th, which
you forwarded to us, without any contrary comment, expressed exactly

our approach, we feel that you cannot possibly disagree with our general approach and the spirit of the agreement that was made here, such as I explained it." Eva concluded by telling Eichler that "for the time being, there is no mail being received from R. [Bertholet] here, but occasionally a few cabled notes reached us. It would of course be very helpful if you could let us have whatever material you should receive from him, for our and our friends' information."

Despite Eichler's desire to have Bertholet's information channeled to the Allies primarily through him, the OSS files reflect continuing correspondence between René and Eva through the end of 1944. Some of this correspondence reflected efforts by Bertholet to obtain funds for endangered friends (a few examples of which are provided in Appendix B). This correspondence was less frequent than in 1942, apparently due to Eichler's intervention. But some of the reduced frequency may also have resulted from the changing wartime conditions in France, including the Nazis' extension of their rule over the unoccupied zone following the Allied landings in Vichy French North Africa on November 8, 1942.

Numerous OSS documents reflect the continuing transmission of funds from Eva to "328" (Bertholet) to support French resistance work. For example, an OSS telegram of November 24, 1942, referred to "a long conversation with 328 . . . [that] confirmed his usefulness for contact with French syndicalist and labor organizations provided that his contacts can be maintained despite the present border patrol." The document also stated:

> 328 [Bertholet] stresses the fact that the French Labor organizations are reluctant to receive funds except from other labor organizations. Suggest that you consider the possibility that contributions be made by American Labor organizations. Provided that complete discretion as regards the method of transmission can be observed, we could pass on these funds through 328."[39]

And on August 16, 1943, "328" (Bertholet) sent the following message to "Eva":

> Received 50,000 for the Socialists, the CGT and the Christian Unionists. Many thanks. The reorganization of Socialist Party in France is making rapid headway. Newspapers like the *Populaire* are

being widely circulated throughout France. Comrades are thankful for the financial assistance which ought to be continued.[40]

Bertholet also continued to provide intelligence information throughout the war to Eichler in London for transmission to the SOE. In the records of the SOE, Bertholet was referred to initially as "Robert" and later as "Charles." Eichler was referred to primarily as "Eclair." A few examples of this Robert-Eclair correspondence are provided in Appendix B.

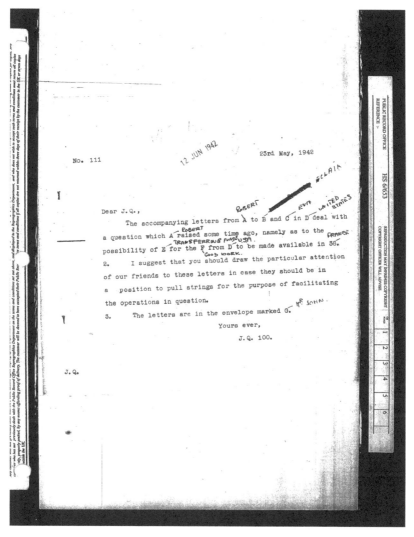

Sample SOE memorandum referring to Bertholet's request to have Eva transmit funds from the United States to support resistance efforts in France.

## The value of René Bertholet as a source of intelligence information for the Allies

Given the volume of information provided by Bertholet to the OSS in America through Eva and to the SOE in Britain through Eichler, it is apparent that Bertholet was considered a valuable communication link between the Allies and the resistance efforts in Europe. It is difficult to present a complete picture of René Bertholet. He acted with utmost discretion and anonymity, as did other ISK members, and little has been written about him.[41]

A Swiss citizen who grew up in Geneva, Bertholet had worked in Germany in the early 1930s against the rise of Hitler. After the Nazis took power in 1933, he had continued his dangerous work underground, necessarily engaging in "illegal" activities against the Nazi regime for which he had been imprisoned for over two years. Some of his work thereafter with the ISK and the International Transport Workers Federation, including his wartime work with Otto and Eva, has been described in this book.

Having been imprisoned by the Nazis, Bertholet was acutely aware of the need to preserve confidentiality. It was a matter of life and death—as was the need for the highest level of trust in his ISK colleagues. His neutral Swiss citizenship proved to be of special value; he could be a "border crosser."[42] Most of the ISK members in exile in Paris had been interned by the French and had difficulty obtaining exit visas. Bertholet and his wife were not interned and could continue to conduct their resistance and relief work across borders as Swiss citizens during the war.[43]

Bertholet was considered one of the SOE's "best and earliest agents."[44] Historian Dieter Nelles described Bertholet's unique importance to the SOE (translated here from German):

> For Division DF (clandestine communication) of the SOE,
> Bertholet undertook in 1941 and 1942 numerous courier trips
> between Lyon and Bern. He provided SOE agent Tony Brooks
> important contacts with French railway workers. Bertholet was
> an unusual agent. He refused any payment, and only occasion-
> ally and reluctantly accepted the reimbursement of high travel
> costs. "He has been able to establish contacts with my people

from Karlsruhe, Mannheim and Cologne to Hamburg," [Hans] Jahn wrote in March 1943. "R[ené] told me that many railroad presidents have bad headaches and I could be assured that much good work is being done."[45]

Historian Nelles also described the breadth of Bertholet's contacts: "Simultaneously with his work for the refugees, Bertholet tied together a network of contacts to the slow-growing union groups of the Resistance. In part from Vichy France, in part from Switzerland, he expanded these contacts and gradually created lines of communication to the occupied part of France, Italy, Belgium, Luxembourg, Austria and Germany."[46] Nelles quoted Eichler's observation in an internal report for the ISK

René Bertholet. Courtesy of AdsD/ Friedrich-Ebert-Stiftung.

in 1942 that Bertholet's reports were "recognized as so reliable and prompt that we have had confirmed by three governments that their own service does not deliver it so well."[47] Others commented on Bertholet's endurance. A colleague said, "Er schlief in Zügen [He slept on trains]."[48]

In his biography of Bertholet, Philippe Adant observed (translated here from German) that "it is virtually impossible to measure the value and the breadth of Bertholet's illegal work, even if one now feels an obligation to do so. How many people did he help to escape from the Gestapo? How many were able to survive thanks to his provision of material support? How much illegal material accomplished its goals through him? How much important information was provided by him? At the time, no one did an accounting; one had other concerns, and each was busy with his own tasks." Adant concluded: "Der Heroismus des Alltags (the heroism of everyday life), which was required of the members of the ISK and many others, cannot be expressed in numbers."[49]

It is evident from the OSS files that Arthur Goldberg and others in the Labor Division of the OSS recognized the reliability of Bertholet's information and of ISK members such as Eva. Later in the war, the OSS would also turn to members of the ISK to carry out efforts to infiltrate Germany by parachuting agents behind enemy lines. Otto would soon be asked if he was willing to take on such mission for the OSS.

But before that decision was faced by Eva and Otto, Eva would confront another problem. In 1943 while she was doing her secret work for the OSS and her continuing rescue and relief work for the Emergency Rescue Committee, several U.S. government agencies were prepared to deny her the right to continued refuge in America based on false accusations that she was a communist.

# 26. Three Big Decisions in 1943–1944

Three big decisions confronted Eva and Otto in 1943 and the beginning of 1944. Each would profoundly impact their lives: the decision by the U.S. government on Eva's application to extend her visa, the decision by Eva and Otto to have children despite the ISK's rules, and the decision that Otto should accept a request that he return to Europe on a dangerous secret mission for the OSS.

## Eva's application to extend her visa

While Eva was working secretly with the OSS and openly as a case worker for the Emergency Rescue Committee (ERC), she applied to extend her own U.S. visa in 1943. As revealed in records released by the FBI in response to requests under the Freedom of Information Act (FOIA), Eva's application for an immigration visa at that time was met with vigorous opposition.[1]

Eva had been given an initial extension of her temporary visa until October 21, 1943. Her application for an immigration visa in 1943 was first considered by the "Interdepartmental Committee Number II," composed of five federal agencies: the State Department ("State"), the War Department ("War"), the FBI, the U.S. Immigration and Naturalization Service (INS) ("Immigration"), and the Office of Naval Intelligence ("Navy"). This committee issued an opinion on March 10, 1943, unanimously recommending "unfavorable action" on Eva's application.[2] The committee stated that "the applicant, by reason of her birth in Germany, is an alien enemy and as such excludable unless some benefit is seen in the regularization of her status."[3] It is apparent that the committee disregarded Eva's years of anti-Nazi work and was unaware of her clandestine work with the OSS.

The committee further noted that "one of the intelligence services has furnished a report concerning sponsor [Benjamin] Zevin which indicates he is secretary of the Cleveland Civil Liberties Union. This information may well be considered derogatory." Benjamin Zevin, one of Eva's sponsors for this application, was an executive with the World Publishing Company in Cleveland.[4]

On May 17, 1943, the "Interdepartmental Visa Review Committee A" interviewed Eva.[5] In response to a question, Eva informed the committee that her brother Erich had been a member of the Association of Free Germans for some time but had resigned as a member over a year earlier.[6] Following that interview, the committee recommended withdrawal of the case "pending the receipt of a report concerning the International Rescue and Relief Committee, the employer of the applicant, as well as a report on the Association of Free Germans."[7]

On the afternoon of October 5, 1943, the Visa Review Committee met again to consider Eva's application. The minutes of this meeting show that four of the five members of the committee (State, War, FBI, and Navy) recommended against granting an immigrant visa to Eva, and only one member (Immigration) recommended in favor of her application.[8]

The opinion of the majority of the committee provides a sobering example of how bits and pieces of information can be used to create a distorted picture of a refugee. The stated reasons for the majority's recommendation against granting Eva's application included her involvement in rescue and relief work for the ERC, erroneous input from an unidentified FBI informant that she was a communist, and suspicions about her sponsor.

The majority noted: "Reports have been submitted by one of the intelligence agencies which indicate that this individual has been active in connection with the ERC since her arrival in the United States and in that connection, has interested herself in Communists who are seeking entry into this country."[9] The State Department's representative added his own sharp attack against Eva's affiliation with the ERC by targeting the work of Varian Fry in Marseille:

> Particular attention may be invited to the information con-
> cerning Varian Fry, who was sent by the Emergency Rescue
> Committee to France and who established in Marseille the
> Comité Americain de Secours, with which the applicant [Eva]
> was affiliated. Mr. Fry was arrested by the French police and
> expelled from France for his activities. In about June 1942 the
> French police raided this office in Marseille, arrested all the
> personnel and seized all the equipment. . . . The activities of
> this office were a source of considerable embarrassment to the
> American Government representative in France.[10]

It is a sad irony that the State Department was using Eva's work with the
ERC in New York and Varian Fry's rescue work in Marseille as reasons to
deny Eva's application. As noted earlier, Fry was posthumously honored
and named "Righteous Among Nations" by Israel's Holocaust memorial Yad Vashem in 1996 for his rescue work in Marseille. At the award
ceremony in Jerusalem on February 2, 1996, U.S. Secretary of State
Warren Christopher apologized for the State Department's treatment of
Fry. Christopher stated that "regretfully, during his lifetime, his heroic
actions never received the support they deserved from the United States
government, particularly the State Department."[11]

The majority opinion also relied on an unidentified "confidential
informant" to support the erroneous conclusion that Eva was a communist: "As late as January 1943 one of the intelligence agencies [the
FBI] was furnished with a list of individuals described as former German
Communists, which included the name of Eva Lewinski."[12]

The majority opinion further challenged the credibility of Eva's sponsor. "Information has also been furnished concerning Benjamin David
Zevin, which indicates that this individual has continued to employ a
Communist regardless of the fact that he is familiar with the individual's
affiliation with the Communist Party. It would appear, therefore, that
he definitely cannot be relied on when the best interests of the United
States Government are under consideration."[13]

Finally, the majority opinion included the separate comments of
the State Department's representative to "emphasize his belief that the
presence of this alien in the United States is particularly inimical to our
national security." He asserted, "There is not the slightest doubt in the
mind of this representative that she is a rabid Communist." The majority

concluded that "this granting of an immigration visa to this applicant at the present time would not be consistent with the best interests of our Government and disapproval is therefore recommended."[14]

In sharp contrast, the dissenting opinion of the INS's representative stated that "in so far as the record is concerned, there is no evidence that the applicant is a Communist or that she has been personally associated with any known Communist party or organization." He added, "It seems desirable to permit this applicant to change her status to that of permanent residence, particularly in view of the consideration that her husband is a legally admitted alien and has declared his intention to become an American citizen. Furthermore, the record indicates that this applicant has been actively engaged in anti-Nazi activities."[15]

Fortunately for Eva, the administrative Board of Appeals agreed with the dissenting opinion and found in favor of Eva's application. A memorandum dated October 22, 1943, provided the following "Excerpt from opinion of the Board of Appeals" summarizing its reasons for finding in favor of Eva:

> The Board is impressed by the record which this applicant has made in refugee work and by the commendations which she has received. It also noted with interest the FBI report of July 9, 1943 setting forth the Cleveland Press story on her anti-Nazi activities. The record indicates that the applicant has two brothers serving in the British Army. It also indicates that she is herself now on the staff of the International Rescue and Relief Committee, an association whose directors include some outstanding American citizens. The Board finds benefit in the applicant's abilities and in allowing the maintenance of family unity. The applicant's record and the excellent support contained in the file give satisfactory evidence that she may be granted this permit with safety. Accepting the reasons of the USIS representative in Committee A, the Board recommends that the permit be granted.[16]

Only partial information is available about the sources of the false accusation that Eva was a communist. FBI director J. Edgar Hoover had written to the State Department's Visa Division on July 9, 1943, with a "Supplemental Report" about Eva.[17] That report reveals that one of the

reasons for this accusation was Eva's support for the visa applications
of Nora Block, Herta Walter, and Hermann Platiel. The FBI's report
quoted the following statement from a Visa Division memorandum:

> "The cases of Nora Block and Herta Walter were recommended
> for refusal because both were sponsored by Leo Gallagher,
> their brother-in-law, who is an American Communist in Los
> Angeles. The case of Hermann Platiel, who has recently married
> Nora Block, is now presented for formal consideration for the
> first time."
>
> "The person who is pressing for a favorable consideration
> of these cases is Eva Lewinski, who entered the United States
> in October, 1940, under the sponsorship of the American
> Federation of Labor and who has subsequently sponsored a
> number of Social-Democrat refugees, including several rec-
> ommended by the President's Advisory Committee. Her own
> integrity is vouched for by Mr. Paul Benjamin, Secretary of
> the Buffalo Council of Social Agencies, who is well known to
> Mr. George L. Warren. Miss Lewinski has interviewed Mrs.
> Roosevelt on behalf of these aliens and a number of others, and
> Mrs. Roosevelt has passed on their names to Mr. Welles for in-
> formation and action."[18]

Interestingly, the FBI's July 9, 1943, report also advised the State
Department that Eva was receiving information from Europe, apparently unaware that this was information that Eva was secretly obtaining
for the OSS from René Bertholet:

> A confidential source advised on September 27, 1942, that Mrs.
> Eva Pfister . . . received mail from Zurich, Switzerland, contain-
> ing extracts from French and German newspapers and other
> reports relative to the situation of the Jews in Europe and the
> general effect of the war on the people of captured countries
> (62-62736-2-13072). . . .
>
> A confidential source on May 1, 1942, advised that Mrs.
> Eva Pfister . . . was the recipient of clandestine anti-Nazi liter-
> ature. Some of her associates in the United States and Europe
> and probably she herself apparently constitute a group who are

working to unite the French people, particularly labor, against their present government. . . . (62-62736-2-3267)[19]

Finally, the FBI's report advised:

A reliable confidential source on January 29, 1943, furnished this Bureau with a list of individuals whom he described as former German Communists. Included on this list is the name of Eva Lewinski. (100-200123-4: Bob M.).[20]

The FBI did not identify the "reliable confidential source" referred to as "Bob M." But a document that was released in response to a request under FOIA provides important insight into the nature of the list of alleged "former German Communists" he provided to the FBI. It was a list of over 150 names of exiled anti-Nazi Germans who were asked by 8 of those on the list, including Paul Tillich and Eva, to cosign an anti-Nazi declaration dated January 30, 1943.[21] This declaration marked the tenth anniversary of Hitler's assumption of power in Germany and denounced the brutal Nazi regime that had "brought disgrace over Germany and immeasurable sorrow over the entire world." On the top of this list, the informant had typed the following message to the FBI: "All names in the following list which are not followed by a parenthesis remark by me are Communists, fellow travellers or Communist stooges." Next to some of the names, the informant had typed his notations in parentheses, such as "Socialist," "innocent Socialist," "nothing known concerning him," "completely innocent," and "right-wing German-American."[22]

Eva's name was among the many anti-Nazis on this list that did not have any such notation from the informant. While some of the more than 150 German anti-Nazis on this list were (or had been) communists at some point in their lives, many of them—including Eva—had not. Among the many other names in the same category as Eva on this list (i.e., without any "exonerating" parenthetical notation from this informant) were Albert Einstein, Thomas Mann, Heinrich Mann, Lion Feuchtwanger, and Paul Tillich.

It is deeply disturbing that such a list of German anti-Nazis—prepared and used by exiled Germans to express their strong and united condemnation of the Nazis—would be used by the FBI to support the majority of the Visa Review Committee's recommendation to deny Eva's application. And it is disturbing that the FBI and the majority of the committee relied on the notations of this informant who indirectly and falsely accused Eva of being a communist. It is reassuring that the INS representative and the Board of Appeals rejected that accusation.

Years later, the FBI acknowledged its lack of confidence in the reliability of the information produced by this informant, "Robert M":

> On January 29, 1943, a confidential informant who has furnished *both reliable and unreliable information in the past* furnished a list of names of persons whom he described as communists, fellow travelers, or communist stooges. Included on this list was the name of Eva Lewinski (not further identified). (Robert M; 100-200123-4).[23]

The U.S. policy of excluding all refugees who were communists was based on the understandable fear of bringing anyone to America who would advocate or participate in the violent overthrow of our system of government. That blanket exclusion did not apply to those affiliated with socialist organizations, but the distinction was easily blurred as evidenced by the response to Eva's application to extend her visa in 1943.

Although beyond the scope of this book, it bears noting that thousands of Germans, Jewish and non-Jewish, actively opposed and resisted the Nazis before and after Hitler assumed power in 1933. Most of those were members of the German Communist Party or were socialists affiliated with the German Social Democratic Party or various smaller socialist splinter groups such as the ISK, Neu Beginnen (New Beginning), and the Socialist Workers Party. Virtually all of these German anti-Nazis paid dearly for their active political resistance against Hitler. Most were forced into exile. Others were hunted down by the Nazis and incarcerated in prisons and concentration camps, where many were tortured and killed by the Nazis. Because of the Cold War that emerged from the ashes of World War II, historians in Western bloc countries were generally reluctant or unwilling to recognize the personal sacrifice, suffering, and loss of life of socialists and communists in the fight against Hitler.

We do not know if any of the representatives on the Interdepartmental Visa Review Committee or the Board of Appeals were secretly informed of Eva's role in obtaining intelligence information for the OSS from René Bertholet when they considered her application to extend her visa in 1943. As part of a response to a FOIA request and appeal, an index card was found that provides a hint but not an answer. The card refers to a specific 1943 document in the files of the INS, but the document could not be located. The missing document is described as follows:

> 23/9562 PFISTER, EVA LEWINSKI: Office of Strategic Services Washington, D.C., requests that citiz [citizenship] appln [application] be expedited. 3/9/43[24]

The request by the OSS to the INS in this missing document in March 1943 might have been a key factor in the INS representative's dissenting vote on the Visa Review Committee in support of Eva's application and in the ultimate ruling by the Board of Appeals in Eva's favor in October 1943.

Another document includes subsequent input from the OSS to the FBI about Eva. In a letter dated January 12, 1944, the director of the OSS's Research and Analysis Branch, transmitted to the FBI one copy of a secret memorandum titled "The German Political Emigration."[25] This OSS memorandum (declassified and released in response to a FOIA request) does not refer to Eva's work with the OSS. However, it does provide summary descriptions of the various German political groups in exile, including the ISK, and clearly distinguishes the ISK from the German Communist Party. The OSS memorandum accurately refers to the ISK as promoting "non-Marxian Socialism" and states that "in the United States Miss Eva Levinsky-Pfister and Erna Blencke are the two best known members of ISK." Although the FBI received this information from the OSS a few months after the Board of Appeals had granted Eva's application for an immigration visa in October 1943, it appears likely that the OSS weighed into the process in favor of Eva through some secret channel.

Of course, there is no way of knowing what would have happened to Eva if the committee's recommendation to reject her application had been affirmed by the Board of Appeals in 1943. When her temporary visa expired on October 21, 1943, would America have given her a further extension of her temporary visa or tried to deport her to Vichy France for further deportation to Nazi Germany?

Eva did not have access to all of this information about the deliberations of these Visa Review Committees, including the false statements made about her. Those false statements would certainly have disturbed her, but they likely would not have changed her positive impression of America. The unsuccessful and unfounded opposition to the extension of her visa would not have outweighed the gratitude she felt for the help she had received from individual Americans such as Dorothy Hill and Paul Benjamin; organizations such as the Jewish Labor Committee, the American Federation of Labor, and the ERC; government officials such as Sumner Welles, Eliot Coulter, George Warren, and Hiram Bingham; and, of course, First Lady Eleanor Roosevelt. Above all, Eva was moved by the warmth, openness, and lack of blind deference to authority that she saw in these Americans who were willing to help her.

## The decision to have a child

During these years of intense immersion in the ISK's work in Europe and America, Eva never lost her deep desire to have children. This desire was revealed in her earlier writings—perhaps most clearly in the poems she had written in Paris and in her letter to Otto about her admiration of the mother in *The Grapes of Wrath* ("And that mother—the incarnation of love that never tires—how I would like to become like her!!"). Yet her commitment to the ISK and its battle against the Nazis—and the passage of time—were conspiring to foreclose that for her.

In Eva's letter to her brother Rudi and sister Ruth in South Africa on May 31, 1943, in which she had explained why she and Otto and her brother Erich had been unable to provide financial assistance to her mother, she had also commented,

> Apart from all the trouble and hard things of life, I personally know that I am very privileged, because Otto and I, we know that there are few people who are so happy together, and can stay together at least for a while. Otto is over draft age, and will therefore, since he is working in a defense industry, probably stay at home for the duration. What comes after that is in shadow, as far as we are concerned—we don't exactly expect an easy time—but about that in one of my next letters. Anyhow, the uncertainty of the future, and some other concerns, have up to now prevented us from building a family of our own—and

>sometimes I fear that time will make this provisional decision a permanent one.

Eva obviously was not free to speak openly about the tension she felt all those years between her desire for a family and her political commitment to the ISK with its idealistic, ethically driven focus on assisting others in need. During the past decade of Eva's life, this had meant her total commitment to the fight against fascism and deferring any thought of having children.

As revealed in Eva's writings, she was both remarkably rational and deeply emotional. From her reports to ISK leader Willi Eichler and her correspondence with government officials seeking to obtain visas, we see an unusually strong, disciplined, and rigorous thinker with an extraordinary work ethic. From her private diary entries and letters to Otto, we see a person with a profound emotional need to love and be loved—a person moved by poetry, nature, and music.

These tensions in her inner life were obviously affected by all she had endured: the loss of her father when she was eight; her difficult relationship with her mother, at first relating to her as an adult friend when only a child, and then being told to back away and act like a child; her childhood experiences with anti-Semitism toward her father before his death and toward her by her best childhood friend in school; the demands and restrictions of her early ISK training that resulted in an emotional shutdown that nearly caused her death; her separation from the first person she truly loved, Rudi L., because of her forced exile to Paris; and the burdens of war, from the internment in the Vel' d'Hiv and behind barbed wire at Gurs, to months of uncertainty about Otto's fate, to the duty call to go to America an ocean away from Otto and her adopted home of France, to her frantic work in New York to help rescue others while knowing that multitudes of innocent human beings in Europe were being abandoned and "deported" by the Nazis.

Having survived all of this, Eva's desire to have a child with Otto remained strong. As she had experienced with her decision to marry Otto, Eva knew that a decision to have a child would likely be viewed as a selfish betrayal of ISK principles by her friends in the ISK who had educated her, with whom she had worked so closely for so many years and whom she still respected deeply. But after much thought, Eva reached her own conclusion that the ISK's rule against having children was ultimately flawed. She hoped that she could have a dialogue with her ISK teacher Minna Specht and ISK leader Willi Eichler about this. Eva wanted to try to convince them that it would be in the best interest of the organization to change this rule so those women who wanted to have children would not be foreclosed from productive work with the ISK.

But Eva did not wait for a change in the ISK's rule. She was running out of time. Eva's and Otto's desire for a child was too great to sacrifice. In the summer of 1943, they finally made the decision. Eva became pregnant; and despite a war-torn world, they looked forward with hope to the birth of their first child.

## The decision that Otto should participate in a dangerous OSS mission in Europe

At the beginning of 1944, ISK leader Willi Eichler asked Otto if he would be willing to go back to Europe to participate in an anti-Nazi mission. In her 1979 memoir, Eva briefly described that request and its terrible timing:

> Once more, we had to make a far-reaching decision. I was expecting our first child when Otto was asked by friends in Europe if he would volunteer again, and to that effect join the American Army in a special unit which concerned itself with strengthening the anti-Nazi forces behind the lines. His experience after his capture in Luxembourg, his knowledge of languages, his personality, seemed to indicate that he could again do very useful work towards the defeat of the Nazis.
>
> We were torn up about this. It had taken a great deal of thought to finally reach the decision to have children, and to look forward to a life of our own, after the war. We both agreed that Otto could not say no, and that he was morally obligated to go. So, he enlisted, went into training, and was to be sent overseas just as the baby was due.

In a brief letter to Eichler dated February 1, 1944, Otto confirmed his agreement to participate in this mission, stating simply: "Thanks for your letter. This is just a short note to let you know that I agree to participate in the work that you mention. The necessary steps are now being taken for my coming over which will be arranged through my induction in the Army."[26] Otto was willing to rely on Eichler's judgment without knowing any details about the mission: "I quite understand that it was not possible for you to explain more in detail the nature of the work; and since you say that it is politically along lines which we can accept, I feel that this is a sound enough basis for my decision." Otto concluded, "I hope that we will be able to discuss the work and many other problems soon directly."

It is clear from the René-Eva correspondence that the new Labor Section of the OSS, headed by Arthur Goldberg, was eager to tap into the intelligence resources of anti-Nazi political refugees from Europe and had been doing that with Eva and others since 1942. Otto's mission, as initially envisioned by the OSS, was very different and involved high risk: he was to be dropped by parachute behind enemy lines to assist the anti-Nazi underground as the Allied troops pushed into Germany.

Otto's OSS personnel file is now declassified.[27] A one-page form dated February 21, 1944, signed by "Arthur J. Goldberg, Major, AUS," stated that "Pfister, Otto (civilian)" was to be "inducted in District of Columbia." Typed under the heading "Intended Assignment (Location and Job Description)" was the following:

> Secret and hazardous mission in ETO [European theater of operations]. Project involves considerable number of recruits capable of passing as natives of France and possessing background in labor or political movements in that country. Projected use of recruits is highly confidential and urgent.

The form stated that Otto's "Language Facility" is "French and German," that "special OSS training will be required," and that he had already been interviewed. Under the heading "Additional Essential & Special Qualifications," Goldberg wrote:

> a) Language qualification is unusual, involving native fluency or sufficient degree of proficiency to permit development of such fluency; b) physical condition must be good; c) willingness to undertake, on a voluntary basis, hazardous duties overseas is essential; d) geographical knowledge of the country involved is important.

Goldberg concluded: "This man possesses these unusual qualifications to a high degree and is urgently needed."

Otto's mission was to infiltrate enemy-occupied territory as a *civilian* agent, not as a uniformed soldier. Yet the decision was made that his return to Europe for this mission would be facilitated if he was sent as a soldier. As noted in a document in his OSS personnel file, "He was recruited during a period when transportation was extremely tight for civilians and for this reason it was decided to enlist him in the Armed Services in order to expedite his transportation and to avoid other questions having to do with his alien status."[28] His enlistment in the U.S. Army encountered some initial hurdles.

Although Otto's background made him uniquely qualified for the special requirements of his OSS mission, the U.S. Army had to make exceptions to its usual qualification standards to allow his induction. He was too old: "he was placed in the Army although he was considerably over-age [forty-four years old] and was not otherwise subject to such service."[29] It is understandable that such an exception could be made without being conspicuous. Otto looked significantly younger than his age.

Otto also had been very nearsighted since his early childhood and needed to wear thick corrective glasses. Without them, he could not see clearly beyond a few feet. When Otto was examined for enlistment at Fort Myer, Virginia, on April 10, 1944, his vision was determined to be a "disqualifying physical defect." A memorandum seeking a waiver stated that "it is now desired to obtain a waiver of the physical defect discovered in the physical examination at the earliest possible date."[30] The memorandum presented the following reasons for the waiver:

> Mr. Pfister is intended for a secret hazardous mission for which he possesses qualifications which cannot be duplicated. Further training for this mission and the execution of the mission itself requires that he have military rather than civilian status. The nature of the mission is such that defective vision is not a material consideration and will not interfere with the projected mission.

One cannot help but wonder why defective vision was not considered a material consideration for the proposed mission of parachuting behind enemy lines—given the risk and dire consequences of losing or breaking his glasses. However, the OSS obviously believed that the risk was outweighed by the potential benefit to the mission of Otto's special qualifications.

Despite the uncertainties still facing Eva and Otto at the end of 1943, the anticipation of their first child brought them joy. The following year when Otto was in Europe with the OSS, Eva wrote to him and recalled "those late Sunday afternoons" in the winter of 1943 when they sat together in their small apartment in New York listening to chamber music concerts on radio station WQXA:

> And we were sitting in our music corner, our hearts often overflowing with happiness, because the music—it was Beethoven—touched us at the innermost feelings, and we were together, one in our hearts, and we lived with gratitude and humbly towards the day when our child would be with us, our child that was growing in me, and filled my heart with an almost unknown tenderness towards every living being.[31]

# 27. A Devastating Loss

In her 1979 memoir, Eva stated simply,

> Our baby lived only for a few hours: an accident at birth—and
> we had wanted her so much! Otto's sailing orders were delayed
> for a week. Then he had to go.

Anticipating that Otto would be leaving for Europe, Eva bought a
diary so she could write to him about the baby in his absence. The first
entry in this diary was written on May 11, 1944, while Otto was away
in OSS training in Virginia—a month after the death of their child and
about a month before he would leave for Europe:

> Into this book I had wanted to write for you, Otto, for you to
> read later, the small and big events out of the life of our child.
> Now life has rejected our child, and only very slowly I find my
> way back. You will have to leave nevertheless. And although I
> fight against it, revolt, argue with fate, and make it hard for you,
> you are right that in reality I agree with your decision, respect
> you all the more because of it, and would not have it any other
> way under the circumstances.
>
> Something so awfully hard has intervened in our life, so
> unspeakably hard. Yet, when I ask myself, seriously and hon-
> estly, if I would not have wanted to start on this path, had I
> known how it would turn out, I can say without hesitation
> that I would not have wanted to have missed the experience of

these last ten months for anything in the world. This experience with its sweetness and hardness has made another person out of me, makes me understand life and people differently, more fully. How my, our, life is going to continue; how I am going to be strong enough to be the friend and companion you need in the coming times? If and when am I going to have you again? So many big, heavy questions for which there are no answers.

A few weeks later, on May 25, Eva wrote another diary entry directed to Otto after receiving a letter from him. She assured him that "the hard events of the last weeks brought us, if that is possible, even more closely together." She reflected on their decision to have a child. "Now it's been almost a year since, after many thoughts back and forth, we took the decision and the courage to have a child." She acknowledged that all the reasons that had kept them from having a child were still valid: "these times that require one's total strength to cope with; the responsibility towards the child whose justified demands for attention and care might partially be neglected if, as we are determined, we will continue to be available for our work." And she recognized that some of their ISK colleagues who "have chosen such a hard life . . . will not understand how we can think of ourselves." Eva then listed the countervailing forces that had resulted in their decision. "But on the other hand: the longing that is becoming more and more burning for the child that will result from a union of you and me. The certainty that we cannot wait much longer. And the growing confidence that we will be able to give our child enough good things, that in spite of all difficult external circumstances, it will grow into a straight, good human being. We decided, especially after the doctor strongly encouraged us. But we did not need that any more; our decision had been made."

The months that then came—you will forget them as little as I ever will. How well I felt and looked. How confidence and trust returned, and love to others. But above all, the sacred experience of the new being that was growing inside me. How I felt life for the first time. How it got stronger from week to week, more lively, so that towards the end real waves could be seen and felt in my abdomen. How we loved our little one, when it stretched and moved in all directions at once. How also you loved me, me, your wife who was now to become the mother of your child!

Then came the request for you to leave, and thus the first heavy obstacle, with which we had grappled before, became suddenly cruelly real and imminent. I believe we stood up to the test, both of us. Me too, although I revolted more against the thought that the unity of the three of us was to be torn apart before we could have given it a firm content. As hard as all that was: the only consoling factor in it was the tiny human being that was growing in me, part of you and me, that would remain in me while you were gone, that would wait for you when you would come back to us.

Eva ended this diary entry by describing her feelings as her "hour came closer":

I learned new things every day, learned to be alone, to spend the night without you, to fight my fear. To my surprise and that of others there was no fear in me of the delivery. And again and again, almost to the last day, new decisions that tested our determination to put personal wishes in back of the objective needs. We passed the tests again and again; but it cost us a lot, so much inner strength.

April 11th came. You were in Washington; I was expecting your call at night. During the day I had worked as usual; did the laundry, cleaned up the apartment, wrote your 1940 story. Late in the afternoon, it started. Erich comes, Herta, I call the doctor. It is still too early to go to the hospital; labor has to become much stronger. But during the night I will probably be ready. I don't go to a meeting. Herta stays with me. Around 9 o'clock, the phone: you are at the station! Soon you are home, happy with me how well everything seems to work out. We sleep for a few hours. Labor is getting stronger, and towards morning, at around 5 a.m., we get ready to go to the hospital. The drive in the cab through the cold, rainy night into the dawn; you are holding my hand; we are calm and happy.

It took months before Eva could bring herself to write the next entry in this diary. Otto had departed for Europe. On August 19, Eva wrote about the pain of their separation, her fear for his life, and her constant thoughts about the loss of their child:

> Almost three months have gone by since I last wrote. In the meantime, you had to leave, and it's been over two months that we are separated by the ocean. And I have to get used to life with fear for your life; to the waiting from letter to letter, to the moment of coming home after work when the heart stops for a second while the eyes look for the feared telegram; to being alone with the fear; to the will to go on living, to the courage for hope. It is possible, but very, very hard, sometimes so that one feels one cannot carry the burden any longer.
>
> And in addition to everything else, again and again, with the same bitter pain, comes the memory of the tragedy with our child, not wanting and being able to accept fate, the search for the cause, for guilt, living through again every minute of the night of April 12th to 13th. I know it makes no sense; yet I cannot ban thoughts and memory. If you were here, we would talk about it occasionally, we would carry the load together. If you were here, perhaps our second child would already grow. Oh why, why did we have to be hurt so badly?

In the same diary entry, Eva then described in heartbreaking detail the night that Marianne was born and died, as if she believed that writing it down for Otto would somehow relieve the pain of "living through again every minute of the night of April 12th to 13th." She first described her desire for support during the difficult early hours of labor:

> You know how much, even under ordinary circumstances, a friendly gesture, a warm word, mean to me. During that night it almost became a need for survival. The nurse was overworked . . . and nobody else was there because they had sent you away. So I was all alone in these hard hours. And when the pains became heavier, seemed almost unbearable, then I called out for my mother, very softly, so as not to disturb anyone. I don't

know, do not remember, if I called for you; I believe that in those hours one needs one's mother.

When her labor intensified, Eva rang for the nurse who came only after a long wait. Eva asked the nurse please to call her physician, Dr. Kautsky.[1] The nurse refused. Eva then experienced "hellish hours" with bleeding and severe pain, "fear to hurt the baby, begging, imploring the nurse to call the doctor . . . not the courage to demand . . . endless loneliness."

Shortly before 6 a.m. the head nurse heard her cries, and Eva was immediately transported to the delivery room, "bright, clean light, a nurse, an assistant physician." Eva felt calm—relieved to be surrounded by people. "They say to hold back, the doctor would be there right away—there he is; they put the mask in front of my face, I only hear how my doctor comes quickly, hear myself cry out . . . but no more pains, I am relieved."

As Eva felt the baby being born, Dr. Kautsky called out, "Why does she bleed so much?" She then heard "from far away, regular clapping, but no baby's cry" and asked if something was not right. At that moment the baby cried, and the other doctor said, "It's a lovely little girl, a little Eva." For a moment, Eva was filled with happiness: "calmness, peace, limitless gratitude to all those who had helped me."

But she sensed that something was wrong. "Slowly consciousness returns as though it was standing next to me, and asks me: 'Why doesn't your first effort go to the attempt to open your eyes, to see your child, your, Otto's child?'"

> Only when I am on the stretcher, in the elevator, I open my eyes, and see the nurse hold my little girl, a little bundle, and she makes a noise—happily, tired, I close my eyes, am being put into a bed, am resting, resting.

Dr. Kautsky called Otto, and he came to her hospital room. Eva wrote in her diary:

> Whatever we lived through together—what can equal this moment, where we hold hands, in greatest, purest happiness, in

deep, humble gratefulness. How we feel rich. In the bed next to me is a young woman. She had her baby yesterday, her husband is in the army, and did not get any leave. You can be with me.

You try to see the baby. They put that off until the afternoon, when you'll come back, to me, to us.

You are leaving, I fall asleep, in deep, happy exhaustion; in the nursery, the newborn babies cry; one of them is our daughter.

Then Dr. Kautsky came back to Eva's room. He told Eva not to be concerned, but "there had been some breathing difficulties at birth, and in order to be quite sure, he had called a pediatrician in consultation—there is no reason to be afraid; the pediatrician would soon come in himself and report to me in detail." Here, Eva's diary ends. When Eva translated this diary years later, she added:

That is the end of the diary. Unbelievable how it brings those hours back. I never saw the baby. They wanted to prosecute the nurse; I felt there was no point—it would not bring the child back. Later, I was told that Marianne was a healthy baby. She had aspirated blood (my blood) at the moment of birth. . . . I was also told that everything had been done to return her to normal breathing—to no avail. As a consolation, they told me that deprivation of oxygen at the moment of birth would leave irreparable brain damage.

In a letter dated May 25, 1944, Eva's sister Ruth wrote from Johannesburg, "We all learned the sad news about your baby Eva. We all were very shocked about it but those things are not in our hands. I hope you have not lost confidence in starting again when time has come for you again." Commending Eva on her "courage to be a mother" and noting that "my turn will come when this war has come to an end," Ruth then turned to the declining health of their mother and the burden it had created for her and others. "For more than two months, Mother has been in bed. She is a very sick woman. I only hope she is getting better soon. It would be horrible if she has to suffer like this for a longer time to come." In a letter dated June 4, Eva's aunt Rahel (her mother's sister), who also lived in South Africa, expressed her sympathy for the loss of Eva's child and her separation from Otto. Attached to that letter was this note from Eva's mother:

> My Darling daughter Ev. I would have written to you earlier if my health had been better. I can't tell you in words how sad I am about your grievance. I know so well how you were longing for a baby. Please, my Ev, write to me about everything and I wish you best, best health my Darling. Also all the best for Otto. He must come back to you very soon and in best health. Don't forget to give him my love when you write to him. Please give me his address. Send all my love to our good "Erichen" and my good "Hertakind." The doctor has been here just now. He comes twice a week. Today I have to stay in bed because I got another injection . . . and bronchitis still troubles me but it is better. If I only could better sleep, my sleep is bad even with drugs. Well, we must hope for better. Ev, I like your snaps [photos] so much. I am longing to be together with all of you my dear children. Keep well. With 1000 heartfelt kisses and all my love! Your Mother

Eva returned to work shortly after Otto's departure. In a June 22, 1944, letter to her brother Rudi who was serving with the Allied forces in North Africa and Italy, Eva noted that there was "much work, and as much help as possible to others seems at this time the only thing for me to do—you understand that, don't you?" And by letter dated July 26, Eva told her sister Ruth that she was "up and working again." Eva added, "It has been a very hard blow; and when you say that it required courage in the first place to have a child now, I can only say that I need all my courage now where I am alone, and could not have the child. You see, I am not young anymore, and that begins to amount to very much in connection with this whole problem. Well, let's hope that the war may be over soon, and our men come back—then life may begin once more."

The individual case files of the International Rescue and Relief Committee (IRRC) (the successor to the Emergency Rescue Committee) confirm that Eva was back at work in the summer of 1944.[2] Correspondence from one file provides a poignant example of her work at that vulnerable time. In a letter dated July 10, 1944, to Dr. Ernst

Jurkat of Princeton University, Eva wrote, "You, no doubt, will be interested to know that we just got a cable from Switzerland containing the following information: 'Dora Jurkat is liberated from camp, lives now at Criens with son. Mother Theresa Bergass arrived in Switzerland several weeks ago. Money arrives regularly via Quakers. We pay the necessary difference for their maintenance.'" In Dr. Jurkat's reply to Eva dated July 25, he expressed his gratitude that the IRRC had made it possible for his wife and son to be reunited:

> It was with great pleasure, that I received your letter of July 10th informing me about the cable you have received from Switzerland regarding my family. . . . I certainly am very grateful to your organization for paying the necessary difference for the maintenance of my family thus making possible that my wife can live in liberty and together with our son. The separation of mother and son was a constant worry for me knowing how much it means for both of them to have each other.[3]

One can imagine the combination of gratification and grief that Eva felt from her role in helping bring a mother and child together at that time. Eva's rescue and relief work was part of her continuing embrace of the ISK-driven duty to do what she could to help others in need. That work also helped relieve the pain of the loss of her child and her second separation from Otto.

# Part VII.

## Separated Again

*Chérie—mon petit, Paris has fallen! Just in this moment I hear it, and maybe only you (surely only you!) can feel what I am feeling in this moment.*
—Otto's V-mail message to Eva on August 23, 1944

*Chérie—I just turn on the radio: Paris liberated! Can you imagine how I feel?*
—Eva's V-mail message to Otto on August 23, 1944

# 28. Otto's OSS Mission and Eva and Otto's Wartime Correspondence

Otto had joined the OSS at the end of February 1944. He had received training at Fort George G. Meade in Maryland and at another unidentified OSS location in Virginia. As he recalled, "With a group of other prospects, I was taken to a secluded facility in Virginia for telescoped military training and for special instruction for the task that was before us: to be dropped behind the lines in Europe to join and help the antifascist underground."[1] Otto was inducted in the U.S. Army in Washington, D.C., on May 9, 1944. The U.S. government expedited the granting of U.S. citizenship to him, and he received his Certificate of Naturalization on May 25, 1944.

## Otto's return to Europe: a lifesaving change in assignment

Following the death of Eva and Otto's first child on April 13 and the completion of his OSS training, Otto was shipped to London on June 12, 1944, where he engaged in further OSS training. To Otto's surprise, however, it was determined that he would not be able to participate in the parachute jumping course:

> After crossing the Atlantic, in the stifling, overcrowded holds of the *Queen Elizabeth*, we reached our quarters in London. The buzz-bomb attacks were in full swing, and when we lined up the next morning in the street, one of our men was killed by a fragment. We started to go through some more training courses. One was parachute jumping, taught by a British outfit. Prior to

Otto's Certificate of Naturalization dated May 25, 1944.

this course, there was a very thorough physical check-up, and I was not accepted. I was told that, although in perfect health, considering my age (44), the British authorities did not want to assume responsibility for me doing this work.[2]

Otto's age was likely the explanation he was given for this decision, but other factors were apparently also considered. A document in Otto's now declassified OSS personnel file about his eligibility for additional "hazardous duty pay" contains another explanation: "The only reason why Pfister did not go on the mission for which he was recruited was that the area to which he was to be sent was overrun and the mission, therefore, was not capable of being initiated. Pfc. Pfister did render a very valuable function in assisting both Lt. A. E. Jolis and Capt. Richard Watt in Field Bases C & D, respectively, in preparing agents for penetration projects in Germany."[3] This document does not provide any details about the "area to which he was to be sent" and by whom it had been "overrun." The invasion of Normandy began on June 6, 1944, and Otto arrived in London three weeks later, on June 29.[4]

Willi Eichler later gave Otto yet another reason for the change in his mission. In a letter to Otto shortly after the war, Eichler explained that "the primary difficulty was that they did not want to let you out of the Army here [in London], and we, on the other hand, did not want to commission any soldier with such a delicate mission, such as the one Jupp [Kappius] had."[5] Otto had been inducted into the army to facilitate his transportation to Europe for this mission, but apparently he could not be released from the army to perform it as an independent ISK member. Instead, other ISK members such as Julius "Jupp" Kappius, who were not affiliated with the U.S. Army, would perform the mission envisioned for Otto.

Whatever the reason, this change in Otto's assignment may have saved his life. The danger of dropping by parachute behind enemy lines to organize and engage in espionage and resistance activities at that point in the war was enormous. In an interview, Arthur Goldberg later recalled that he personally accompanied refugees who had volunteered to serve as OSS agents to the airplanes that would carry them to their drop targets. When asked if he "had any sense of the kind of odds they faced," Goldberg replied simply, "Very bad. I didn't think they could make it. And I used to tell them that. They were much braver than I."[6]

Kappius (alias "Jack Smith"), would later be dropped by parachute into Germany in September 1944 on a mission like the one also initially intended for Otto. The purpose of the mission (referred to as "Downend" in OSS code) was for Kappius to organize an underground network of trade unionists in Germany's Ruhr region "to foster resistance against the Nazi regime, carry out acts of sabotage in strategically important war plants, build up a network of agents, and use subversive operations to wear down German moral."[7] Kappius encountered serious difficulties but survived his mission.

## 1944 correspondence while Otto was in war-torn Europe

Of course, Eva was unaware of any details about Otto's OSS assignments. On June 28 she wrote to Otto that "the news was good this morning: Cherbourg free, authority handed over to the mayor, Governor Poletti doing a thorough cleaning up job in Rome—all that made me somewhat hopeful. When am I going to hear from you? I am with you with all my love."

In a letter to Otto on July 1, 1944, Eva referred to a special secret they shared: she was pregnant again. "Another week is gone. No news from you. No change in my condition—I still don't tell anybody about it for fear that our hopes may not materialize. Still, I feel I ought to tell Herta, but up to now I just was not able to. Oh Ottoli, help me believe that we can have a child, and that this time I will be able to give him enough strength to live!" Eva asked Otto not to be worried and assured him, "I try hard to do alright and to remain the way you want me to. If only I knew how you are."

On July 4, Eva expressed her joy at finally receiving a cable from Otto. She reported to Otto about a letter she had received from her mother in South Africa, the first one after her mother had learned of the death of their child. Eva noted that her mother "was of course terribly upset" and advised Otto that her mother's health "is rather badly shattered." Eva added, "I am worried, and feel unreasonably guilty that we had to add to her worries."

On July 9, Eva informed Otto of sad news about their secret:

> My heart is hurting very much that it has to cause you pain once more. But we have to take it, and although it is even harder than I had expected it to be, I promise you to get over it. So there will be no child when you are back, and strange and exaggerated as it may seem, the pain is almost as great as on April 13th. Also, I was quite alone when it happened. Herta had left in the morning for Wellesley. . . . Finally, I talked to Dr. Gottschalk . . . and she told me to lie down, be very quiet—at the beginning it looked as though it might perhaps stop. But at night it began again, and all day today, so there can be no doubt that it is out. . . .
>
> Please, Otto darling, you must not worry about me, although I know that it is hard on you, this news. Physically I am alright, and otherwise I am sure I will get over it. . . . Now I am looking at your picture, and it is a little bit as if you were holding my hand, and strength and faith and confidence are coming over me, slowly.

Eva then expressed her concern about news she had received from South Africa that there seemed to be something wrong with her mother in addition to her heart condition. And in a V-mail message to Otto the following day, Eva explained that her brother Rudi, then serving with the Allied forces in Europe, had just advised her by letter that their mother had recently been in critical condition with her heart and diabetes and had "nearly not pulled out of it."[8]

Otto's first long letter to Eva from Europe was written in German, in part on July 14 while in a hospital in London and in part after his recovery on July 22. Otto explained that when he first arrived in London, he was hospitalized with high fever and pain and swelling where he once had an operation on his thyroid. He assured Eva that he had now recovered and sent greetings from their ISK colleagues in London, including "Vic" (one of Willi Eichler's pseudonyms). Otto also described his "cheap but very clean room" that was outside the city (over an hour commute by train and bus to his training) but "undisturbed by Hitler's flying bombs." Confirming that he had not yet received any of Eva's letters, Otto then asked Eva about their secret:

> But now to you, my love, it always comes into my mind how it will be decided, baby or not. Perhaps you have already sent a letter that will let me know more . . . but I still wait for a sign of life from you. . . .
>
> I think so often about you, my love, and our home. It is something wonderful to be with a person to whom one can tell everything, get it all out; one hardly knows to treasure it fully when one has it. And then I am completely without your hands, your face, and you. And *my* hands are alone; my arms long for you and my lips want to tell you how much I belong to you.
>
> How much joy it would give me to see your writing, what you have written, what you think, what you feel. I love you so, Evali!

Eva's letter to Otto dated July 17 included an encouraging comment from their close friend Marie Juchacz:[9]

> Marie wrote me the other day from Wellesley, after she had heard that I had gotten your cable. She said: "It is bitter for you to be thrust apart. It is good to know that you are but one in your way of thinking and acting. You have chosen a very, very

painful happiness. But don't be afraid, don't lose your courage; I am convinced that you will grow, and that later on you will not want to miss even the very painful elements of this period of your life."

Eva added her encouragement to Otto. "You will miss me, as I miss you. But both of us, we will make it. Because we know that the other being is ever present, because we know that the way we decided was basically right, and we would not want it otherwise."

Eva's letters to Otto often included her observations about the course of the war. In a V-mail message dated July 20, 1944, Eva explained her reaction to news of the unsuccessful attempt by German officers to assassinate Hitler that day:

> You can imagine how excited we are about the news of the *Attentat* [assassination attempt] against Hitler. I had a feeling since late last night, when I heard over the radio that telephone communications with Berlin had been interrupted, that something was bound to happen. What a shame the bomb or whatever it was missed Hitler! Every minute that he disappears earlier is a gain for mankind.

And in a letter dated July 26, Eva reflected further on this unsuccessful assassination attempt:

> Chéri, and what do you think of the news? When it first happened, that is when I had the first inkling of what might happen from a little dispatch over the radio, we all were very excited, and thought that the end of Hitler and his system and the war might really be within reach. Now it looks a little different.
>
> Certainly none of the top officers who revolted can be called our friends, and in order to have peace in the long run, they must disappear just as much as Hitler and his gang must. But the fact that they obviously do not believe any longer in the possibility of a German victory must be considered of the greatest importance, and reflects, I am sure, the war weariness of the bulk of the German nation, at this time, with the exception of the Nazis themselves who know that their time is up anyhow.

The generals tried the trick in order to save their own necks, and there are certainly a number of potential Badoglios among them.[10] But I don't believe that history can be stopped very easily. And once things begin to crumble at the top, repercussions down below the rank and file will probably follow. And all depends upon their coordination, political wisdom and determination to clean house.

But of course, the end of the Nazi war machine may still be quite a ways off, and I think we have to count with the possibility that before they are doomed, they will try to bring as much misery upon mankind as they possibly can. How I wish we could talk about all this, you and me. But then, maybe it is right that this is not the time to talk, but to do the things you do. I love you, Otto, you know?

Turning from the assassination attempt to hopeful personal signs, Eva commented in this letter on "our avocado" plant. She observed that it was "quite a miracle how the plant has grown since you left. Believe it or not: it is now about 27 inches tall, has real leaves, and is growing every day." She advised Otto that she did not yet want to plant it in a garden but that "a larger pot is certainly soon necessary." She concluded, "I like this plant which still is not very beautiful, but so strange and vigorous."

In a brief letter to Eva on July 22, Otto reported that he saw Eva's brother John, who was then serving in the British Army, and noted that his wife and child were well.[11] In a V-mail message on July 27, Eva expressed her joy on learning of this. "I was so happy, but couldn't help the tears—you understand me, don't you?"

Otto's V-mail message to Eva dated July 27 confirmed that he had finally received Eva's prior letters, including the July 9 letter with news of her miscarriage. "Chérie, I feel so well how hard it must have been for you to realize that there will not be a baby this time. But I think like you: Maybe a little later better conditions will give better hope that everything is going alright. And don't think it is too late."

Otto provided more details about his meeting with Eva's brother at Welwyn Garden near London. "One evening, I got out of the train in Welwyn and there he stood, waiting for me. . . . He is almost the same as six years ago, looks young, strong in his British uniform, and has the same optimism in his eyes like in the time of Paris." Otto told Eva that

Otto in U.S. Army uniform with Eva's brother John in British Army uniform.

he and John had been able to spend one afternoon and evening together, and although the time "was of course too short to tell each other all that happened the last six years, we could at least have a general impression."

In a V-mail message on July 29, Eva wrote about "Hitler's awful, cruel, indiscriminate attacks" against suspected traitors in the wake of the assassination attempt. "It often keeps me wide awake at night, and never leaves me." This failed coup by officers in Hitler's army had a deep impact on Eva, and she would have more to say about it.[12]

In early August, Dorothy Hill invited Eva, her brother Erich, his wife Herta, and Marie Juchacz's husband Emil Kirschmann to spend two weeks of vacation at Dorothy's home in Wollaston, Massachusetts, to escape a heat wave in New York City. In a letter to Otto on the first day of that vacation, August 5, Eva noted that "it is so stifling hot that it is almost unbearable" even though Dorothy's home was "only three blocks from the ocean." Eva described a swim she took that day:

> It is kind of a bay, and the water is quite still, no waves at all, just like a big, big lake. But the water, very salty, carries you without you making any effort at all, cool, refreshing . . . it was heavenly.

I felt I was back in Montauban, swimming in the river. Although the surroundings were so different, something in myself reacted the same way: I was so close to you, and happy, a confidence spreading, a trust that everything will turn out right, that the time is not so far away when we again will live together, experience the beautiful and the hard things of life as one. I felt the same way when swimming in the Tarn river [in Montauban], and never again was the confidence there so alive as it was today in the ocean.

Eva reacted to news of the progress of the war in French towns she knew so well. "We follow the news eagerly, as you can imagine. The advance in France is stupendous, and when I think of Granville, Mont St. Michel, St. Malo, Nantes, my heart beats faster. What may our friends in those parts of France feel, do today? Sometimes it really feels as though the day of the final breakdown of the Nazis and Wehrmacht are near, and then better things can begin again."

Eva then offered her harsh condemnation of those German officers who had so belatedly attempted to assassinate Hitler:

In a way, although it sounds cruel, I do not think it was bad that the Wehrmacht did not succeed, and that the Nazis took those drastic steps [Hitler's retaliatory killing of suspected traitors] to reduce the power of the traditional—military and economic—war lords so a job is done, or at least begun, that has to be done, and all the better that it happens now, and not after the defeat. Because I am afraid that after the defeat there might be too many who "had said all along" that "after all, the Army was always opposed to Hitler, and brought about his crush—so why not accept their cooperation." And then everything might start all over again, and the war might end with the foundations laid for the next one. And if there is one thing that frightens me more still than all the horrors of this war, it is this idea.

In a V-mail message to Otto on August 6, Eva described a prophetic dream in her first night on vacation at Dorothy Hill's home:

If the old saying is true that whatever you dream the first night at a strange place will become reality, we need not worry. I dreamed of you: you came back to me even before I expected you and everything was as before. And there were children—our children—I love you Ottoli, my heart is all filled up with you.

On August 9 in a V-mail message written in French, Eva commented on the rapid advances of the Allied forces in France. "If this continues, Paris will soon be liberated." And in her letter of August 15, she wrote that she just heard on the radio the news about the landing of the Allied troops in southern France. "You can imagine how I feel. I know this will bring the end of the war so much closer. I know how many hearts in France today will beat faster. But how much suffering this implies! Really, I feel stronger and stronger that every bit of force and imagination ought to be employed to make this war the last war."

Eva then asked Otto, "Now, that you know a great deal more facts, do you think that your, our decision [that Otto accept the mission to return to Europe] was right?" She added, "I do not question of course the necessity and rightness of our decision as long as we did not know more about the facts. But I would very much want to know—would feel relieved—whether you *now* think it is worthwhile. Can you let me know?" Eva ended this letter by telling Otto how he eased her pain, even though he was away:

A while ago, I had a little talk with you, looking at your picture. I was feeling lonesome and terribly sad—it's now four months since our *Kindlein* [baby] was born and died, and I still can't accept it, still am looking for a cause that brought it about, and that did not have to be. The hospital, the nurse, my shyness not to insist on getting the doctor on time. So many things came back to my mind as though they had happened yesterday. But then you said, through the medium of that little snapshot, "Evali," you said, "you must not look backwards. I will soon be back with you, and then we'll build a future." Ottoli, I believe you, and I'll keep strong and fit for that day.

Writing on the same day, Otto told Eva that he was walking that afternoon "through the small, peaceful streets near Hyde Park" and saw the open door of a small public library. He observed that "libraries are a sort of common ground all over the world. This one wasn't much different from the one we have around the corner in the Bronx. Only a little darker and a bit sleepy." Otto commented on the progress of the war:

> The news, coming out this afternoon, of the allied landing in South-France, gives a new crescendo to the conviction that only little time is left to Hitler's modern barbarism. And soon we will be able to see how strong and renewed the movement for human liberty will set in. Let's hope it will!

At the end of the letter Otto exclaimed, "Oh! How I liked the news about the avocado! Strange, how much such little things may mean."

## The liberation of Paris

In her letter of August 17, Eva wrote that the "news continues to be very good, the advance towards Paris is amazing, and the casualties in Southern France seem to be light, at least at the beginning of the campaign."

The following day, Eva told Otto that she had just finished making little parcels for him and for her two brothers, Rudi and John. "It is so little that we can give you, but if you know with how much love it is sent, it certainly will mean something." The process reminded Eva of her mother:

> When making those parcels . . . I thought of mother. You know, when we were still going home from time to time, we used to imagine things, and to tell each other what we would like to do if all of a sudden we were to be very rich. And then mother said that her dearest wish would be to have in her apartment one little spare room, with nothing in it but a table, chair, shelves, empty boxes, wrapping material; and enough money so that as often as she liked she could send her loving "Päckchen" [little packages] to all her children all over the world, and if possible to all their friends. She then did not realize how much "all over the world" we would be one

day—oh, it is so terrible to think of her as being desperately ill, and not able to help her!

Eva then expressed her excitement about the impending liberation of "our Paris":

> The news keeps me wide awake. As far as we could make out from the radio this morning, we seem to be quite close to Paris. Orléans, Chartres, Étampes—how many memories are connected with these names. And to think that our Paris will soon be free again, the "faubourg" Issy les Moulineaux [suburb of Paris where they had lived]—it makes me wish to be there with you. If only many of our friends live to see this, and stay on to see the reconstruction of a decent way of life and participate in it! I do think though that hard fights are still ahead before the war is over.

In a brief V-mail message on August 23, Otto wrote:

> Chérie—mon petit,
>
> Paris has fallen! Just in this moment I hear it, and maybe only you (surely only you!) can feel what I am feeling in this moment. Of course, we were waiting for it, but still, "c'est a peine a croire" [it's hard to believe]. And how much happier I would be if you were with me in this unique hour, only you (and I) know it.

And at the same moment in New York, Eva sent an excited V-mail message to Otto:

> Chéri—I just turn on the radio: Paris liberated! Can you imagine how I feel? I just had to write you right now before going to the office—I know this very minute you'll be thinking of me and all the things that unite us so closely. Let's hope, work, pray—that the bell will ring for the liberation of all Europe, and the reconstruction of a better world.
>
> I love you, Otto, with all my heart.

But in her August 25 letter, Eva's elation about the liberation of Paris was dampened by news of "bitter fighting still raging in Paris":

> I think that the blow was hard to assimilate by everyone who had been so overwhelmingly happy about the liberation of Paris. And I am wondering why. Because, of course, there can be no doubt that Paris will be liberated in the near future, that the Nazis will be driven out. There will be so much more loss of life, and that is terrible. The obvious confusion that brought about the premature news is also discouraging, because one thinks immediately how the Nazis will try to make use of this and to divert attention from their real defeats.

Eva pointed to what she saw as one of the most hopeful aspects of the liberation of Paris:

> I think the thing that made the whole news so unbelievably good (and why then the disappointment was so great at first especially for us) was that, according to what we first heard, Paris was liberated by the uprising of the people. That made us proud, and more hopeful for the future of France and Europe than one had ever dared to be before. . . . I have come to the conclusion that there is really no reason yet to be discouraged. Because the fundamental fact that the people stood up has not changed. Only, they were not strong enough to do away with the enemy. The news of the enemy giving up after so short a fight was too good to be true. And we have to accept the hard fact that nothing in this struggle is being won without going the whole bitter way of a deadly fight.[13]

Eva then shared her bleaker view:

> The news of these last days of the tremendous advances of the Allies in France, the news of the crumbling of German resistance here and there, made us all too optimistic. And I have found the way back to my old, more pessimistic outlook that nobody is giving anything away, and that, although I have no doubt as

to the final outcome of the struggle, we better be prepared for very bad things before we are through with it all.

I am writing this at my lunch hour at the office. Just now a girl comes back with a paper saying that Paris is now definitely liberated. But it does not seem confirmed yet, so I am holding back my hope until the real confirmed news comes through.

The next day, Eva was finally able to write to Otto, "Now Paris is free and all the joy when we first heard it has come back into my heart." She also told Otto that she received a V-mail from her brother John "from 'somewhere in France,' dated Aug. 13. He was alright, had come by quite a few sad and terrible sights and was very, very busy." She wondered, "Maybe by now he is already in Paris? Notre vieux, cher Paris! [Our dear old Paris] It is just too wonderful to think of Paris being free, being herself again!"

In Otto's letter dated August 26, he noted his receipt of some of Eva's prior letters and answered her question about their "decision":

Yes, I think even *now*, our decision was right. It would be too complicated to explain in detail why, but this is the way I feel.

I haven't had much time and "tranquillité" to talk much with Vic [Eichler] about what you call "our way of life." I told him once how and why we decided to have Marianne. He listened with comprehension but there was no time to go "au fond des choses" [get to the bottom of things] and I hardly think this is the right moment to have this kind of conversation because everyone is too busy.

Otto closed this letter by telling Eva, "While writing, I am listening to good music, something like our good old WQXR, and my mind and my heart are going back to our little music corner, with Toscanini on. . . . And your beautiful hands are in mine. . . . I am sure the day will not be too far away when we can do this again. I hold you close to me."

In a V-mail of August 29, Eva expressed her deep gratitude:

You know, chéri, these days I realize ever anew how very rich we both are—to have each other, and to be secure and at home with each other. . . . It is strange. I feel that life has been and is very hard, cruelly hard to us, and often I miss you so I think I cannot stand it. And at the same time I feel privileged and happy to know you are there, and I am there for you.

This sounds all very confused, but certainly not to you who understand every inch of my being and feeling. I love you, Ottoli.

## 29. The War Drags On, Reports on Nazi Atrocities, and Another Personal Loss

Casting a pall over the news of the Allied advances were reports of Nazi death camps. In a letter to Otto dated August 31, Eva observed that "the news that came from Poland is terrible. Did you see the story contained in the enclosed article? Those inhuman, terrible things will cast their shadow all the way into the future—and how can it be otherwise, I am asking myself often." The article referred to by Eva in this letter was not preserved, but news accounts about the death camps in Poland were available at that time from various sources, including *Life* magazine.[1]

In this same letter, Eva described a gift she just received from their friend, artist Theo Fried: "the sketch he made of you with the harmonica. It now hangs in the bedroom on the small wall next to the window, you know, where you had hung the drawings for our child. . . . It is so much you, the part of you that I love so, the part that can quote Rilke and have that look—Oh Otto, do come back to me soon!"

In her letter to Otto on September 5, Eva again commented on the rapid progress of the Allied troops. "Three days ago I wrote you that it looks as if the battle of Belgium were now to begin, and now the battle of Belgium seems to be over. Brussels, Anvers free, Luxembourg on its way to be free—as you say: all those names 'look at you like old friends.'" Eva updated Otto on news she received from her brother Rudi about her mother's condition:

Rather bad, pitiful news about mother. Her condition got worse and worse, and eventually they decided to amputate one leg from the knee on. Mother took it very bravely . . . but the week afterwards everything looked just terrible, with very little

Theo Fried's drawing of Otto playing the harmonica.

hope left. . . . He says that her tremendous will to live and see us all again is the greatest possible help. . . . Imagine mother suffering so, and I here, so far away, letters taking unreasonably long to get to her, and not able to do the least thing to make things easier for her. It is so inhuman, so cruel.

She then asked, "You do agree, Ottoli, don't you, that I send mother some money, when they ask for it. With one exception, when I sent it to her, I put the money that I am getting from the War Department in the bank every month. But I am sure it is alright with you that we help mother with the little we can. D'accord [agreed]?"

In her letter to Otto dated September 9, Eva turned again to news of horrific Nazi crimes:

> When reading the horrible accounts of what the Nazis did to the Jews in the Polish ghettos . . . I was wondering how much of these facts were known to the German people at large. I am still convinced that most of them don't know the smallest fraction of it, and still, they'll have to know it in order to understand the general feeling against them. I don't know whether the broadcast sends these facts into Germany. But I think after Germany's defeat, it would still be a task to tell them the story of what has been done. Nothing but mere facts, strictly checked, without exaggeration or propaganda. But bring home to them the whole horror so that it shakes up even the most indifferent. Oh, I know, this is probably quite impracticable—as you said . . . when things are too terrible, people in a kind of self-protection just don't want to notice, shut themselves up, try to forget what they knew, not to believe what they are told. But still, deep inside me I feel that a way must be found to make it

impossible, not only by force, but morally as well, that human beings perform or tolerate such crimes.

In the same letter, Eva described in detail the account she received from her sister Ruth in South Africa about their mother's condition, including the amputation of her leg. Eva told Otto, "You can imagine how I feel today. I decided, on the basis of Ruth's letter in which she says that the illness cost tremendous sums, to cash the two Army checks of this month, and to send mother again $100. I'm sure you agree, dearest."

After completing his additional OSS training in London, Otto had traveled to France in late August 1944 as the Allies were advancing to Paris. He later recalled that "while the Allies closed in on Paris, my outfit also crossed the Channel, and we reached that city a week after the Liberation, the population still showing exuberantly their gratitude."[2]

Otto with fellow American soldiers on their way to Paris in August 1944.

Given the secrecy of his OSS work, Otto's letters provided very little information about his activities. In a letter dated September 5 (and continued on September 19, 1944), he informed Eva that he was "now somewhere in France, and extremely busy." He then described his visit to the place in Paris where he and Eva had met nearly a decade before:

> Of course I passed on the 28 [Boulevard Poissonnière]. There is still the old name on the windows. I saw the concierge, and learned that John [Eva's brother] was there the day before! I left him some words and think it isn't impossible to see him.

Otto noted the names of some of their friends who were imprisoned and others who had been "deported by the Nazis." He also let Eva know that he had "no trace" from Gaby yet. Regarding other wartime news, Otto noted that "it's hardly possible to keep pace with all that's happening. How long will it last? This is everybody's guess. Anyhow, you can imagine how I felt when I heard that Luxembourg is free!" Otto ended this letter: "Chérie, do you know how much I love you? Do you realize how intensely I would like to have again one of our quiet and exquisite Sunday breakfasts with you? . . . And don't worry, I am fine and confident."

Eva's brother Ernst wrote to Eva from Johannesburg on September 9, 1944. It was not an easy letter for him to write. Ernst had been the first of Eva's family to move to South Africa, and he and Eva had not written to each other for the past ten years. Their lack of communication was due in part to their war-imposed separation and in part to that episode many years earlier when Eva, as an eighteen-year-old in Germany, had felt betrayed by Ernst. As described earlier, Ernst had set up a job for Eva in 1928 in the record shop owned by his unmarried friend and secretly paid her salary in the hope that she would develop a relationship with his friend, abandon her early involvement with the ISK, and lead a more "normal" life.

When Ernst finally broke the long silence with this letter, he described in detail the "agonizing pain" their mother was suffering. But he also assured Eva, "Fortunately, her will to live remains as strong as ever. . . . There were days—many of them—where the best one could hope for was for her to be spared further suffering. But now, we do hope and pray that she will be able to fulfill her strongest wish to see her children again." Ernst praised their younger sister Ruth for the care she was giving to their mother while also caring for her three young children. He asked Eva and her brother Erich to write to their mother "as often as it is physically possible," but he cautioned, "Please do not under any circumstances ever mention anything that may give her cause to worry." In other words, Ernst was urging Eva not to share with her mother her feelings about the loss of her child and her worries about Otto in Europe. Near the end of the letter Ernst wrote, "As I have not written to any of you for more than ten years, I think that just before finishing off, I will give you a very short description of us here." He then described his years of hard work to earn money for the family and their mother's care under difficult circumstances.

In a short note to Otto on September 10 Eva wrote, "Beautiful music on the radio, and also the announcement that the Allies entered Luxemburg . . . how I wish I could be near you!!" And in her letter of September 13 she told Otto, "I am glad about what you tell me of your and Vic's [Eichler's] conversations about our 'way of life.' Of course, I don't think that it should be discussed now. But it is good to know that you don't feel that all doors are closed between him and us—I don't think so myself." She ended this letter:

> What a safe feeling I had when you told me that wherever you may have been, you listened to music such as we like it, and you came back to our corner, and all the things that are connected with it. Ottoli, I so wish that a time might come soon when all the values in life will be in the forefront again, when one will have the possibility and the right to enjoy beauty and music and love and nature—and each other.

In a brief letter on September 20 Otto told Eva, "Of course I agree with what you say about sending money to [your] mother. If only she would gain again strength and health." Otto also noted that he was happy that Eva had received the drawing from Theo. On the same day, Eva wrote with concern about some of their friends in France:

> Oh, and the many names of friends that you tell me about—how I see them all, how I see you, finding this one and the other! . . . Am very curious to know how you found Vieilledent. . . . How did it happen that the Vidalencs were deported to Germany? . . . And what about Victor and Henriette—did you find them, are they alive, not deported? . . . Have you seen any trace of Jose? Is there still the old concierge at Issy? Any news about Gab? Mousy? And good old Guerret—do you think you will have a chance to look him up or write him?

She also commented about Otto's return to the vegetarian restaurant where they first met:

> How strange it must have seemed to you to see the old name at the windows at 28 [Boulevard Poissonnière]! And see the old

concierge—did she recognize you right away? Is Pierrette still there? But she is probably a young woman by now, and not the young little girl we used to know!

In her letter on September 23, Eva reminded Otto of their special Sunday mornings in the Bronx:

How beautiful they used to be, our Sunday mornings, do you remember? It is a lovely autumn day, very cool, sunny, clear, transparent air. If you were here with me, you would probably already be impatient with me for sitting here and writing, and not ready to go out in the sun. Where would we go? To the Bronx Park probably, down the path towards the river. And then to the lovely place, you remember, with all the exotic little plants in the rocks where once you talked with the Italian guardian, and tried hard to convince me that it would not be right if I took one of the little plants—I did not, but wanted very much. And then we would sit in the sun, look at the green and brown and gold all around, occasionally be sad when someone with children would pass by—but probably not too sad, because we would have each other, and would have hopes.

Her thoughts then turned to the continuing fighting. "The war news keeps me in its grips these days. And I cannot keep from thinking day and night about these boys at Arnheim, for six days and nights without sleep, fighting, dying, hoping—In a way it all, the war and all it implies in terms of human suffering, is much nearer to me since you went away—you understand that, don't you?"

On September 27, Eva told Otto more of what she read about the story of the men at Arnheim who eventually had to surrender. "I can't get rid of the fear that despite everything we are not through yet, that a very hard fight is ahead, and that until the final defeat of the Nazis, they may have had time to eliminate every decent being in Germany." She enclosed "a little drawing of Marian Anderson" and asked Otto "do you remember when we heard her at the Metropolitan Opera? 'Sometimes I feel like a motherless child.'"

On October 4 Otto wrote, "Terrible what you write me about your mother. Send more money. I think it is necessary." Eva's mother wrote to Eva on October 9. She briefly described how she was dealing with her pain and expressed her hope and prayer that "our three good boys [Otto and her sons Rudi and John] will come home from the war very healthy and very soon."

In Eva's short letter to Otto on October 10, she commented on the photograph she received from him with Otto in uniform along with her brother John's wife Jeanne. "Before me I have now not only you, as my 'GI Joe,' but I also have your hands, your beautiful, strong, clean hands in which I had trust and which I loved almost before I loved you." And in a letter dated October 12, she wrote:

> Today is a double anniversary: four years ago I arrived in this country, not knowing anything about what had happened to you. And six months ago our child was born . . . and I could not keep it, we could not. O chéri, time does not seem to heal very much I am afraid. Last night it was as if I lived through that night six months ago again, even physically. And it is hard to be alone at such moments. But eventually morning and light did come, and your letters, and work and activity, and life goes on. Do you know how I love you, Otto?

Eva also commented on news from her sister Ruth about their mother's wish to see all of her children. "Ruth says that mother showed an indomitable spirit through all these times, and often, when she, little Ruth, almost gave up, mother carried on, and there is just one motor that keeps her going: that is her wish to see us all again. Ruth says that we should consider it very seriously whether we think after the war we can manage to come to them and be with mother. Well, the war is not over by a long way—but I hope we could make this wish of mother's come true, don't you?"

That wish would not be fulfilled. On October 16, Ruth sent a Western Union telegram to Eva with the news that their mother had passed away. On the same day, Eva's brother Ernst wrote a short letter to Eva in which he openly shared his grief. "I cannot believe we have lost her. Eva, Mother was to me always all that is noble and good. I have had continued love from her, far more than I deserved." He informed Eva, "I thought you would like to know that I brought some flowers in your name to her grave."

In a short letter to Otto on October 17, Eva wrote:

I do not know how to say this to you, and only you can realize how my heart is hurting, and how I would want you with me: this morning a cable arrived from Ruth—our mother died yesterday. I feel all burnt out, have no words. Our child, and now our mother. Let me be with you, Otto, let me hold your hands, fast, come close, close to me. Your strength and your love are everything. Je t'embrasse, et suis remplie d'une tristesse immense [I embrace you, and am filled with an immense sadness].

Two days later, Eva wrote to Otto about "the terrible reality of the fact that our mother is no more. . . . It is so cruel, and leaves a terribly empty space." She told him that she looked at a photo of the "good, good face" of his mother, who had died many years earlier. Commenting on both of their now-deceased mothers, Eva wrote:

If only in their lifetimes we could have made things easier for them. But Ottoli, they knew that we loved them, and that we could not help so many, many things. You know, when one all of a sudden realizes after how relatively short a time a door is finally closed, life ended—one is sorry for every minute wasted that could have been used to give love.

In her letter of October 22, Eva shared her innermost thoughts with Otto about him, religion, death and the progress of the war:

If you could be home with me this afternoon! The sun is coming in through the windows of our bedroom, the sky is of a transparent light blue, the trees are almost bare of leaves, but here and there in the garden some flowers look at you, remnants of the summer. And in the house our plants are strong and healthy, your pictures look at me, and some books that are friends. . . .

And for hours music as we like it: Mendelssohn violin concerto . . . Marian Anderson with old songs that bring tears to your eyes; and now a Beethoven symphony. You are very, very close to me, my dearest; this is home to me because you built it, because every corner of it breathes of our life together. . . .

And when it is quite still around me and in me, in a silent way without words I pray for you, for us—I could not say that to anybody else but to you, and you know it, know why.

This morning I listened for a while to the Ethical Culture Society address about the differences of real sincere religious feeling, and dogmatic sectarian formalism. He also said some deep honest words about the meaning of death. I thought of how it would have interested you to listen, how you would have sat there, in our music corner, and listened with that expression of concentration, of good will.

Eva's thoughts returned to the fighting in Europe:

The war is puzzling me, you know. Hitler's last appeal to the German people, the creation of a "Volkswehr" [people's army] was accompanied by an acknowledgement of weakness and defeat such as I have never heard of before. He does not pretend that all the sacrifices he is asking for are necessary for victory. Victory is out, even he admits; and the only goal remains a "livable peace." One would think that after such a frank admission of defeat, it would begin to crumble. But it does not; they fight on, for all we know, like devils; and if Aachen is to set a pattern for things to come, then very bitter fighting is ahead.[3] And still I am convinced that the great majority inside Germany would want the war over as soon as possible.

Why then do they fight on, why do the soldiers in Aachen who want to surrender not turn their arms against their officers who refuse the ultimatum? Maybe the answer is that the more than ten years of terror have so destroyed every inch of confidence in each other that nobody dares to get out of his isolation, to make the link with his neighbor, his fellow at the front, and not be alone anymore in his will that it may end. Only when that happens, when there are not innumerable isolated individuals, but everyone becomes part of a unit—small as it may be—could we hope for any result. But when is that going to happen? Sometimes I am scared, frankly scared for what the future has for mankind.

Otto's letters to Eva provided only the barest information about his location and nothing about his activities. In her letter of October 24, 1944, Eva told Otto, "It would be wonderful if I had just an inkling of the part of the Continent you are in right now." On the same date, Otto wrote vaguely that "once more we are going somewhere else."

In a long letter to Eva on October 30, Otto noted that his address had changed from "1st EXP. DET" to "FIELD BASE 'C'." He assured her, "Now don't get worried about this field base, it is way behind the lines, somewhere in Belgium, not far from the place where I used to see Jef [Rens]." Referring to Paris by its nickname "Paname," Otto expressed his disappointment that he had to leave Paris before he could look into questions Eva had raised about some of their colleagues. He explained that he had asked one of their friends in Paris to try to find the answers.

Otto then advised Eva of "hard news" he had already learned about the deportations, imprisonments, separations, and deaths of some of their friends in Paris. "Lisa Jacobi and her two children have been deported by the Nazis the 2 February 1944. Since then no news from them. Her husband is still prisoner in Germany. Terrible!" He gave Eva the "bitter news" that the father of one of their friends in New York named Reine "was taken by the Nazis, but since he was sick, they put him in the Rothschild hospital, from where he came into a 'hospice.' There he died." Advising Eva that he could not get more details, he asked her to tell Reine how deeply sorry he was. Otto also reported "another hard and bitter fact: Peskin has been deported in January 1943. His wife is in Switzerland, his brother and wife are in Paris and so are his two sons."[4]

Otto then asked Eva if she could help locate funding for a children's relief organization in Paris called the "cantine populaire," a grassroots soup kitchen sustained by the Comité des Juifs de France (Committee of French Jews). "Of course, they badly need funds, especially because they plan to create a 'Maison d'Enfants' [Children's House] for 3000 parentless children (to begin with). I didn't promise anything to them but to write you about their hard needs, and I think if anything can be done, it should be done quickly."

In Eva's letter of November 3, she expressed her happiness that Otto had been able to contact people who had worked with the printing shop that the ISK had used in Paris so many years ago. "That you could get hold of some of the people of rue Vieille du Temple is wonderful, and has created, together with their paper, quite a joy among their people here. . . . Did you notice that their paper, one of them, was printed in our old printing shop, rue de Ménilmontant 32?"

The progress and horror of the war as well as Otto's safety dominated Eva's thoughts while he was away. But other questions burned in her mind and heart: What would the end of the war mean for her and Otto? Would Eva need to return to Europe to continue her political work with Otto and her ISK colleagues? Or would Otto come "home" to her in America to start a new life?

# 30. Questions about the Future as the Allies Battle in Europe

In her letter of November 5, Eva sought reassurance from Otto about the future. She began by describing their "Sunday late afternoons last winter" when they sat in their music corner listening to Beethoven, filled with happiness and gratitude as they anticipated the birth of their child. She then posed her question:

> I wanted to talk to you about something that has been on my mind for quite a while. It concerns our future. I know, as things are, and with the little we know, it would be foolish to do any real planning. But I would like to be sure that you still feel as when you left: that we will both try, at the earliest possible moment after the war, to come back to each other, and if this moment is not years and years off, and conditions are just bearable, to have a child. It would make things easier for me if I knew that that is what you also want, or whether anything new has come up that made you change your mind.
>
> Perhaps it is nonsense to bring this up. But in a way I have to. You see, I feel quite strongly that after the war there *might* be—I am sure that there *will* be—conditions that open innumerable tasks for every one of us, and that this may go on, from one task to the other, without ever coming to the moment where one might feel that now one had the right to stop for a little while.
>
> And on the other hand, we have both come to a point, as far as age and strain are concerned, where we cannot postpone

indefinitely the fulfillment of our deepest desire, without acting irresponsibly towards the child. Or maybe, should we admit that it is already too late now, that we have let the moment pass when it was possible? I refuse to believe it, perhaps because it means so much to me and, I feel sure, to you, and because I am convinced that my love will be strong enough, and so will yours, to make it up to our child that we are not as young as we ought to be.

You don't have to write much about this; just tell me that you feel the same way about our future as you did before. You know that is one of my great weaknesses—to need confirmations once in a while.

In closing, Eva attached "a tiny little new leaf of our avocado that fell off," noting that "the real ones are ten times its size, but you can see its texture and shape."

The election of Franklin Roosevelt was the subject of Eva's November 8 letter to Otto. She told him that she had spent the prior evening with Marie Juchacz and her husband Emil Kirschmann listening to the returns on the radio and that she was thinking of Otto all evening and deep into the night.[1] She reported that "the results this morning look even better than they did last night. It looks as if isolationism had received a thorough beating and, what may be more important, that Roosevelt now has a solid majority in Congress." Eva then noted, "I must admit that only last night, when I looked at the Encyclopedia before the returns came in, I began to really understand the mechanics of it all." She asked Otto, now an American citizen, "Did your vote get here in time?"

On that same day in Europe, Otto had just received Eva's earlier letter about the death of her mother. He wrote:

Oh, Chérie, I feel how hard and bitter must be the loss of mother for you, how ardently you had hoped she would be able to see all her children again.

But if I fully understand when you say, "a door is closed, life ended, and one is sorry for every minute wasted that could have been used to give love," I know better than anyone else how little time you ever wasted, how entirely you gave always your time to what you are so convinced to be your first duty.

> Chérie, how intensely I would like to be with you in such
> hard moments, to hold your hands, to share your sorrow, to let
> you feel my own!

In Eva's November 10 letter, she first expressed her joy at seeing
the photos from Otto, including the one of him in the jeep. She told
Otto that he looked cheerful "but tired, as if many hours of sleep were
missing badly." Eva then noted that the news about the death of Reine's
father was terrible and explained her difficulty in breaking the sad news
to Reine. Responding to Otto's request for funding for the Cantine
Populaire, Eva informed him that she had given this information to
her friend Samuel Estrin of the Jewish Labor Committee (JLC).[2] She
assured Otto that the JLC already had an application pending to transmit funds and that funds were available. She lamented, "3000 parentless
children—and that is probably only part of all there are in France! What
a terrible responsibility for mankind! Anyway, as far as financial help is
concerned, they are going to get it, and soon now since new regulations
concerning contact to France make it much simpler."

In Eva's letter to Otto on November 16, she quoted from her sister
Ruth's letter about their mother's last days. Eva was grateful to learn that
their mother did not suffer and "looked beautiful and peaceful when she
died." Eva ended the letter by alerting Otto that Eichler and Bertholet
(using the pseudonyms "Vic" and "Roger") had asked her whether she
would give up her job and join them in their work in Europe. She told
Otto that she would try to explain "the most important pros and cons"
as she saw them in her next letter. She concluded: "In any event I do
not intend to make any change without consulting with you—they
know that, and I think they don't object. So now you know that this is
occupying my mind considerably, in addition to everything else."

On November 19, Eva commented on the Allied offensive and
asked, "Is this going to be the big push that will shorten the war? Will
any help be forthcoming from forces within Germany? And what is it
going to mean in terms of individual suffering!" Returning to the question about her future, she expressed concern about whether she should
follow Eichler's suggestion. She again told Otto that she preferred to
write about it some other day and assured him that she would not decide anything without him. But she reminded him: "What I wrote you

some time ago about my deep, deep desire to be together with you as soon as possible after the war, and to have again a child, enters into my decision a great deal."

In a V-mail message the next day, Eva noted that "the news is good—just listened to the radio, and keep my fingers crossed. There seems to be a real break-through towards the Rhine." And the following day, Eva observed that "it must be unbelievably hard fighting, especially in the north which seems to be the most important part of the battle. How I am waiting for a sign of a real crack inside [Germany]! I am more and more convinced that unless such a thing happens, the prospects for the future are as dark as can be, I mean the political outlook."

In her letter on November 25, Eva reported on news "that the First Army has come through the Hürtgen forest, after a 10 day 'tree to tree' fight. I realize, or at least try to, what that fight, in cold and humidity and mud, means in human terms, and the clippings from 'Stars and Stripes' which you sent helped to realize it better. Still, I am hopeful on the military part of it, not in the short term though, unless it breaks *in* Germany."

Two days later she wrote, "Last night I went to a concert—Budapest String Quartet, Mozart, at Town Hall. It was beautiful, unearthly beautiful, but I missed you terribly. . . . One thing will make you glad: The Jewish Labor Committee has obtained a license, and has sent 7000 f. to la Cantine Populaire in Paris. Good? They, especially Estrin, send you warm regards."

In a letter dated November 29, Eva turned back to the question about her future. She expressed her hope that she would hear from Otto soon about this and confessed that she was "more and more hesitant" about taking a new position in Europe. "I am afraid that the new position might entangle me still more with things that I don't really agree to. And you know me well enough that once I have accepted a position, I feel responsible for it and a certain loyalty to the job, and am not free any longer. Well anyway, maybe the whole thing will not work out. As I told you before, one of the important considerations for me is not to do anything that would postpone our reunion. Alright?"

Eva then described a conversation she recently had with a friend of an ISK colleague, "a very nice, sad man, with intelligent, but deeply discouraged and hurt eyes." She explained that after talking about the general war situation, "we touched on more personal things, and it appeared that his wife and one daughter had to stay behind in Poland, that one year ago he had heard indirectly that they were still alive, and since then nothing, nothing but the general reports about what had happened to Jews in Poland." She asked,

> Can you imagine how I feel, Ottoli, every time when I am face to face with such a horrid thing that has been brought about by the Nazis and the inability or unwillingness of the others to check them in time? Then I understood the look in his eyes, this look of hopelessness—and still, the man is not hopeless, he carries on what he thinks is right to be carried on.

Eva also told Otto about a wonderful book she was reading that impressed her deeply. "It is the new one by Ernie Pyle, war correspondent, who does not describe the big battle, or the strategic plans, or the political rifts and currents, but very simply what war means in terms of human suffering, and human comradeship, and human suffering again and again."[3]

During these months of separation, Eva worked long hours on relief work with elderly refugees and with the Emergency Rescue Committee. On December 6, she apologized for not writing much that week. "It is just that I have too much to do these days, and when I get home late at night, I am rather tired, and not good to write a real letter anyway. You know, some weeks, things seem to pile up, and this is the third evening in a row where I will not get home before very late."

In a letter on December 7, Otto also apologized. Acknowledging that Eva had been waiting a long time for a real letter, he explained: "I have been busy the last three weeks. A job to be done in limited time, with limited means and yet interesting enough to try to squeeze out every little bit of the offered possibilities." He noted that he was now again "not far from Paname [Paris]," and while he was waiting for new directions he could "take some time out to look quietly" at her letters, her "wonderful, exciting letters, and try to answer all the little and big things."

Otto's writing was interrupted at this point, and he began writing again, in the same letter, two days later:

Dec. 9, I had to stop; Vic [Eichler] came in the door and with him Roger [Bertholet]. They just came from Roger's place. Vic left yesterday, but R. is still here for some days. You imagine how happy we all were to see each other.

They told me of course about the project concerning you. And in this very moment I got your letter . . . with the note about the same question, and your promise to write more about it in your next letter. Now I am waiting intensely for this next letter. I know there are "pours et contres" [pros and cons].

But my first reaction was, and is still, that I would be foolishly happy if you could be on the same soil with me, on the same Continent, and that (who knows!) maybe some way or the other we could see each other, and *maybe* even *work together* for a while.

But I don't want now to say more about that. I just want to get this in the box for you and hope I will soon get your next letter.

Along with updating Otto about her recent contacts with friends, Eva happily informed him in her letter of December 10 that she had been invited to attend the opening of an exhibit of drawings by their friend Theo Fried that would include his sketch of Otto playing the harmonica, "the sketch where you ride on the chair, and where the movement of your foot is so well caught that you hear it all, the music and the rhythm." She also told Otto that she would be seeing Jef Rens the following Tuesday, noting that Rens was on his way back home and that she was looking forward to the visit.

The next day, Eva received a letter from her brother John who was "somewhere in France." In a brief letter to Otto that day, she wrote:

[John] gives me Gaby's and Mousy's addresses, which made me very glad, and I sat down right away at my lunch hour and began to write to Gaby. In case you don't have it, here it is: Gaby Cordier, 44 rue Curiol, Marseille. Mousy: Helene Perret, 52 rue Remesy, Toulouse (isn't that the old address where Theo and Ansze lived?). I think you might want to write to Gaby—and if you hear from her before I can have an answer, do let me know how she is, and whether she has found some personal happiness—I wish it for her so very much.

Eva noted in a brief V-mail message to Otto on December 13 that she had seen Jef Rens the day before and they had a good long talk. She also told Otto about the exhibition of Theo's drawings: "beautiful drawings, some of which you would have loved; and our 'harmonica player,' in a corner, is very much alright, from every point of view."

In a brief V-mail message on December 16, Otto raised the question about Eva's future. He told her, "I still am waiting for the letter in which *you* give your impression about the problem." Noting the delays in delivery of mail, Otto explained that he was sending this by V-mail "because I think you will get it quicker than Air-mail and I am afraid you will get my Christmas wishes too late."

That same day, December 16, 1944, the German Army launched a surprise attack to the west through the dense forests of the Ardennes in Belgium, France, and Luxembourg. This began the Battle of the Bulge that resulted in the highest number of American casualties of any operation during the war. In this last desperate military move, Hitler sought to take control of the Belgian port of Antwerp; split, encircle, and destroy four Allied armies; and force a favorable peace treaty. The battle would last until January 25, 1945.

Eva's letter of December 18 addressed two critical subjects: the disturbing news of the Nazi offensive that she first heard the day before, and the question of her future work. She expressed her fears and worries about the offensive, telling Otto that she was glad to know he was back near Paris. But she added, "Of course how can I know where you are now?" She recognized that it was "certainly too early to say anything definite about [the offensive], and we know by far too little."

> The fact remains . . . that in spite of everything, they have been able to gather enough strength to launch such a thing, at a time when one does not understand how they can carry on at all. They are hard, bitter things that we are up against, and not only on the fighting fronts. And you certainly understand, Otto dearest, that tonight I cannot talk too much about what I feel, in this connection, nor very much about any other things close

to our heart. The thought, the possibility, that this terrible war might be prolonged, and before it is ended, the ground stones laid for the next one, takes every wit out of me.

Eva informed Otto about her receipt that morning of his letter that had been interrupted by the visit from Eichler and Bertholet, again referring to them by the pseudonyms "Vic" and "Roger." She explained that his letter "made me so very happy, especially at the beginning, when it looks as if that were going to be *the* real letter. But then, of course, when you tell me who interrupted you, that was another surprise, which in a way made up for the letter not yet being the real one. I am so glad you could see Roger and Vic." Eva wrote:

> You must in the meantime have received my different letters about my work, and I am glad that Roger and Vic told you their side of it. I am still very hesitant about it, for many reasons, the main being that I know so very little about what I am expected to do in detail, about the degree of freedom etc. Of course, being geographically nearer you is a great point in favor of my accepting. But on the other hand, it might not be possible at all to get together, and our home-coming to each other might even be postponed—and that is one thing that, if humanly possible, I don't want to happen.
>
> And the general situation and trends don't make me very enthusiastic about it all. What do Roger and Vic think about it? I regret very much that I did not hear much from them about it beyond their wish that I come and join them which is very vague. There is also the technical question of being able to go at all where again I have my doubts as to its possibility, and its price.
>
> I wish we could talk about it all—by the way, after your talk with Vic and Roger you probably have more elements on hand to judge the pros and cons than I have at this time. And so I think I would say that if you advise me to go, I'll do it. Or is that making things too easy for me and throwing too much of the responsibility into your lap? It's all so difficult!
>
> I'll have to stop now—it is getting too late. I am thinking of you constantly, and am waiting to live with you again, with

all the strength that is in me. Keep well, my dearest, and let me hear from you as soon as you can and as often as possible. A real letter from you means life to me.

In a V-Mail message to Otto on December 20, Eva confided that she listened to the news "with so much anxiety." "If I only knew where you were right now! I wish before Christmas is here, I will have a letter from you—these days are hard to take, with so much memory of things past and the present so dark, but I will not lose courage, not for you."

## Otto's assignments with the OSS

The correspondence between Eva and Otto reveals little about Otto's work for the OSS. Even apart from their correspondence, available details of his work remain sketchy. Secret OSS travel orders retained by Otto provide some information. A November 12 travel order states that Otto was "directed to proceed to the city of Antwerp, Belgium . . . for the purpose of delivering a highly confidential message to M. Camille Huysmans, the Mayor of Antwerp. He is to remain in Antwerp until M. Huysmans delivered to him a message to be delivered to this organization, and thereupon he is to return to his proper station." A December 1 travel order directed Otto to proceed to Paris again on or about December 3, 1944, on temporary duty for approximately seven days "for the purpose of carrying out the instructions of the Commanding Officer." No details on this Paris assignment were provided.

Otto's next travel orders reveal his location during and after the Battle of the Bulge. Otto was ordered first "to proceed on or about 21 December 1944 on temporary duty for a period of seven (7) days to Headquarters, 9th Army." He was then directed "to proceed on or about 8 January 1945 on temporary duty for a period of approximately seven (7) days to Field Analysis Unit, United States Army, 1-3 rue Belliard, Brussels, Belgium." Both of these orders were "for the purpose of carrying out the instructions of the Commanding Officer." Otto was then directed to proceed on or about January 21, 1945, and on or about February 4, 1945, for periods of approximately ten days each to another military location "for the purpose of special duty involving PW [prisoner-of-war] interrogation and for the purpose of carrying out the instructions of the Commanding Officer."

Otto later recalled that he went to Luxembourg following his first trip to Paris. "I drove by the field outside Kehlen where, four years earlier, I had sweated over my cover story, and where I had hidden my passport, under a heavy rock. I found the spot, but not the passport. The rock was gone."[4] He described the nature of his work in Belgium during the Battle of the Bulge:

> Next, we went to Belgium. During the Battle of the Bulge, I interrogated German prisoners of war in a stockade. Many of them were young; some still held stubbornly to their Nazi indoctrination. . . .
>
> I was sent to Antwerp, where I was to interrogate Belgians who had been deported to Germany as forced labor. Every summer, they were allowed to return to their homeland to help with the harvest. Many had left Germany only a short while back when overtaken by the advancing Allies; and so they had fresh information about many things our organization [the OSS] needed to know.
>
> They were sent to me by leaders of Belgian Labor organizations, and most of them were very eager to talk. Alone, I had a big "office" in an abandoned maternity hospital where, for weeks, from morning to evening, I asked my questions. I even learned to smoke at that time—offering a cigarette helped quickly to warm up the conversation.[5]

The purpose of Otto's interrogations was to obtain information that could assist OSS agents in their espionage and infiltration programs. Precise details were needed to allow agents to infiltrate German cities without detection. An OSS "Interrogation Guide" given to Otto contained the following Introduction:

> [M]ake two assumptions: 1) that you are going to the place your informant comes from and that you have to supply yourself with all the general and special knowledge necessary to make you suspicion-proof; 2) that you know nothing about these

things at all and you must get everything necessary out of your informant—forget what you already know!

The "Interrogation Guide" provided a detailed outline of questions to be asked about the informant's life: where he lived, what he ate, what he did in his spare time. The guide included questions about the informant's city, the addresses and streets that had been bombed out, and details about all means of travel, number of foreign workers, and police controls. In the case of an informant whom the interrogator judged to be reliable and trustworthy, additional questions were to be asked about potential "safe addresses," that is, "addresses of people who are anti-Nazi, decided and willing to work against the Nazis or at least give a hand in the fight against the Nazis, and who may be approached by us for help, information, or leads."[6]

A separate OSS document given to Otto, titled "Safe Addresses," provided further instructions on the specific information to be obtained on this subject. The final paragraph required the interrogator to provide his "estimate of the informant":

> How did you contact him? What sort of recommendation were you given with respect to him? What has he done or what is he doing against the Nazis? Does he impress you as a man of intelligence and good judgment? Is the other information he has given you apparently reliable?
>
> *Note*—you *must* answer these two questions: 1) Why do you consider the informant to be absolutely reliable and trustworthy? 2) If you were going on a mission would you be willing to go to this "safe address"?[7]

The "Interrogation Guide" included questions to be asked of the informant about identity papers, travel, military status, and occupation, noting: "Get full details here, remembering always that your report may be used to build up a cover story." The guide also included "subjects of particular interest," such as details about the armed forces (discharge, deferment, and furlough process and papers), the Gestapo, Organization Todt,[8] foreign workers, and "certain occupations about which we know little."[9]

Otto's assignment in Belgium was not without danger. He recalled:

Regularly, I crossed a big, busy square right at noon (I always
heard a carillon ring the noon hour) on my way to eat. That day,
having an urgent report to finish, I went later. When I came

**German V-Bomb Hits Belgian City.**   Dead Belgian civilians lie in the streets as military
personnel (left) and two priests (right) survey damage caused by explosion of a German
V bomb in a main intersection in a Belgian city.

**Belgian Civilians Killed by Rocket Bomb.**   Bodies of Belgian civilians, killed by the explosion of a German rocket bomb, on December 2nd, lie amid wreckage at a main street intersection in a Belgian city. This photo was made a few minutes after the bomb blast.

Page of article with photos of results of buzz bomb attack in Antwerp (retained by
Otto in his "OSS" folder).

to the square, a horrible view opened up: dozens of dead and wounded on the pavement, hit by a buzz bomb right at noon! At that time, Antwerp was still hit regularly every day almost every hour.[10]

In a brief letter on December 21, Otto informed Eva that he had been writing to a number of colleagues and friends and hoped "to let them have a word for the New Year, but I am afraid there is not time enough." He explained that he was now receiving mail by "special courier and he doesn't run so often." He expressed his hope that "the mail will be in before Nöel, that will be my loveliest Xmas gift." He also hoped that Eva had received his packages with gifts for others in time.

Eva commented further on news of the Nazi offensive in a letter on December 22. "No matter what the outcome—the immediate result for the boys out in the field, and for the civilian population in those countries just liberated, is something hard to grasp in all its meaning. I can't stop thinking of these civilians in Belgium, in Luxemburg, what they must feel, what this must mean to them." She then shared some personal news: "In spite of all this, Christmas is nearing, and in spite of how I felt anyhow, and especially now after all the news, I did the things that one is supposed to do before Christmas, bought presents, wrote letters, cards, tried to pick out the right things for everyone, tried to create some joy." After noting the titles of books she bought for close friends, Eva told Otto that she had sewn something special for Marie Juchacz "according to an old pattern of mother's."

> I thought about it a while, and found out that I would not want to do that for anybody but [Marie]—somehow she reminds me of mother although she is entirely different. And her children are away, and she does not know whether they are still alive; and she almost never talks about it, is so courageous.
>
> I often feel that of the love and care that I could not give to mother while she was still among us, and that her children cannot give to her, I want to make up a little to her. Do you understand me, Ottoli? She loves you so much.

After describing her gifts to others (including small gifts sent from Otto), Eva admitted, "I did keep for us the little vase which you did not say explicitly that you want to give away. I love it. The other day I had two tender, small roses in it, and it looked very delicate and beautiful. Now I have a little branch of pine in it which makes it look like Christmas."

## Eva's year-end letters

As always, the year-end holidays were a time of reflection for Eva—perhaps more so in 1944 than ever. In a letter to Otto about their challenging year, Eva wrote:

> Now Christmas Eve has come. I am in our home, the home that we built together, and that we love. Your pictures are before me, some pines in vases, some candles on the bookcase. But you are not here. And my thoughts don't even know where to look for you. But my heart knows that in these hours, if you are at all free to yourself, you are with me, and all that unites us, lives as strongly in you as it does in me.
>
> There was no letter. But I know I am not the only one without mail these days. The hearts of many, many of our friends beat faster when we think of you. . . . And if I could give anything to help you, to be with you, that would be the greatest joy and comfort. But no, my only contribution at this time can be to remain courageous, not to lose myself in self-pity, not to forget for a moment the millions of others who are in similar situations, to remain strong for you, and to keep up hope.
>
> You, dearest, you are the only one to whom I can say that there are moments in my life where I feel again that I can, and that I must, pray. Not in words. But for instance now, they are playing a Mozart piano concerto over the radio, and everything that is good for me becomes free and goes out, toward someone, something that created greatness and beauty without bounds. It is impossible to put in words what I feel; but you see, Ottoli, I am so sure that you understand me anyway—and that is probably the deeper reason why I love you as I have never loved anyone.

Eva assured Otto that she would not be alone this Christmas Eve. She would go with her brother Erich and his wife Herta to spend the evening with Marie Juchacz and her husband Emil, and they would be joined by Samuel Estrin and Theo Fried. Eva confided:

> I like them all, and sometimes am inclined to forget that every one of them has his pack to carry. Marie who never found the other being as you and I have found each other; who loves her children very deeply, and who does not know today whether one or the other are still alive. She never speaks about it, but I often feel what happens inside her. And Emil who will probably think of his companion who had to leave him so suddenly.[11] And Herta and Erich—separated from their boy now for over five years.
>
> I know all that, and my heart goes out with love to all of them, not in every instant but now. And still, what has struck us this last year does not become easier therefore. I cannot help but think, and feel again, every emotion of our Christmas last year, our deep silent happiness about our child growing in me, our being together, so one. We had sent a cable to mother so she may get it on the anniversary of father's death. I, with our child coming, was closer to my mother than I had ever been before.
>
> And then our child had to go without my even taking her once in my arms. And mother had to go, and I was not there. And you are far away, and nobody can know, today less than ever before, when this war is going to be over, when and after how much endless suffering.

Eva then reflected about what they both had chosen to do in their lives together. She offered her own judgment:

> Ottoli, it is all very, very hard. But the part that we could influence with our will—I would not want it differently. You have decided, and so have I, to go the hard way, to do what we think was our duty. And even though we realize only too well that our individual action does not change the course of things one way or the other (and we know it more painfully every day as the political situation develops), we did individually all we could. And we did it as one which makes us very, very rich. True, there were moments when I lost faith in my strength, when I

struggled against you and the right decision. But you held fast, held me fast, and so I came back to what I had always accepted.

I think, as a facet of this year, we can say, without being pretentious, that we do not have to be ashamed of ourselves. I am very proud of you, Ottoli, and I promise you that I will use these months where you are far from me so that I will become more worthy of you.

Eva then shared a fond memory:

I have been thinking so much these days and nights about how it all came about that we met, and about so many wondrous things that happened to us. One beautiful memory is connected with an evening late in Paris, in the Tuileries, when all of a sudden you began to recite our Rilke (translated from German):

We want, when it again becomes a moonlit night,
to forget the sadness of the large city
and go out and press against the fence
that divides us from the broken-down garden.

Who would know it now, who met it during the day:
with children, light clothing, summer hats,
who knows it so: alone with its blossoms,
the ponds open, lying without sleep.

Figures, that stand mute in the dark,
appear to rise up gently,
and stonier and stiller are the light
figures at the entrance of the avenue.

The paths lie as untangled strands of hair
next to each other, quiet, of one purpose.
the moon is on the way to the meadow;
the fragrance flows off the flowers like tears.
Over the quiet fountains
still stand the cool traces of their play
in the night air.

Eva closed the letter, with the last sentence in French: "Ottoli, I love you because you taught me to love, to love the other's soul and body, to embrace his entire being. Let us wish and pray to be permitted that I may give you all the happiness that you deserve. Je t'embrasse, mon Otto, mon aimi—et aussi que le jour ne soit pas trop loin ou je puisse te donner notre enfant—embrasse-moi, tiens-moi serre contre toi—je t'aime [I embrace you, my Otto, my love—and also hope that the day will not be too far off when I can give you our child—hug me, hold me tightly next to you. I love you]."

In her special New Year's letter to Otto, Eva again reflected on the impact of the events of 1944:

> This year that brought us so much sorrow to our hearts is now almost over. I have so often thought about it all these last days, and there is no getting around it—it has been so painful that one was asking oneself: how can life go on? But it did go on, again and again. And I must be true and, above all, "not exaggerate," as you would say: there have been, besides the hard things, also the most happy, exalting moments last year where we were as close to each other as one can be.
>
> Do you remember, the first three months, what we felt, we who had almost become three? When we decided that you had to leave, this feeling of being so completely in agreement with each other, with what we believed in? When you came home for your weekend passes, our quiet nights beside each other, the tremendous tenderness to each other, to our child? The wonderful moments when we heard the other's voice over the telephone.
>
> Then the night when through the rainy cold early morning the taxi brought us to the hospital. You held my hand. I felt peaceful, happy, not afraid. And then the next morning when you first came to me, kissed my hand, held it, your eyes so full of love, of fulfillment, of gratefulness—Ottoli, in spite of everything that came afterwards, these moments have become part of our life too, nothing can ever take that away from us.
>
> Then the following months, with the terrible hopelessness and tiredness in my heart slowly, slowly melting away, only because of your love that held me up, that stood with me, by me, that did not let me down for a moment although you

had been let down so cruelly, because you had so wanted our child, more than you ever put it into words, and I had given it to you for an infinitely small moment of happiness only, and then it went away. How I loved you these months, how I loved your goodness!

Eva told Otto how much their correspondence meant to her and why they should remain grateful:

And even since you are away, there are moments of happiness that you give me. With your letters, with a word here and there that touches my heart deep, deep inside, with everything that comes from you to me, but also with everything that comes from me to you. When I can write you as I like to, when it flows out of me, when I feel a close communication with you—then also I am happy—So, let us not be ungrateful to the year that is coming to an end. If at all possible, it has brought us still closer to each other than we were before. Although far from each other, we know where we are at home, entirely at home, and peace. And that is so much more than many, many can call their own.

She then shared her most fervent hopes for their future and that of humanity:

I do wish and pray that the next year may bring us together again, may permit us to work and live together, may help us to fulfill the greatest desire of continuation of our lives. And may [it] let us construct, and not destroy, or defend against destruction. When speaking out these hopes that are in my heart, that I want to cry out, but cannot, they sound very much in the air, not at all down to earth.

As the world looks at this end of the year, it does not seem realistic at all to hope for more than a cessation of hostilities, to hope for the real foundations to be laid for a real peace which is of course impossible without economic justice. But if we could not hope, and work for it, everyone in his or her little way, to come true, life would really not be worth living.

Eva told Otto that for Christmas, Emil gave little "poems" to everyone along with his presents. The words he gave to Eva were in essence
"Against my belief, life is stronger than death." Eva pondered the meaning of these words:

> I have thought about that much lately, whether or not it is so
> or the other way, and I think I slowly come to the conclusion
> that he is right. If that is so, then the good forces in man can be
> made stronger than the evil forces, and then a time can come
> where peace is stronger than war, construction stronger than
> destruction. I am quite sure that that is your fundamental belief
> too, Ottoli, and that is why you always carry on so cheerfully,
> confidently, although the present developments and surround-
> ings would indicate the strongest possible trends to the contrary.
> Am I right?

Eva confessed that "although it sounds perhaps silly, this has become,
since I started to write, a rather important, rather solemn hour which
has made many things clearer in my mind than they had been before."
She concluded:

> I think it is true when I say that I do believe in a future, that I
> believe in our future. You and your love and the deep security
> it gave me, brought that about. You know that, Ottoli, have
> known it all along. But in this hour I have to say it again. And
> because of this force in you, and because you made me see the
> world differently—because of this I feel it is right for us to
> have children.

# PART VIII.

## HOPE RENEWED

*The other day I sought an expression of what I feel we, you and I, mean to each other. And I could find no other than to say: we are at home in each other. To be able to say that in all honesty is ultimate happiness to me, and I cannot conceive of any other.*

—EVA'S LETTER TO OTTO ON JANUARY 7, 1945

*Ottoli, I'll have to learn many, many things for our child, many of the light, happy things of life, stories, songs, plays. But I don't think I have to learn love.*

—EVA'S LETTER TO OTTO ON FEBRUARY 4, 1945

# 31. 1945: Signs of Spring as the War in Europe Grinds to an End

For unknown reasons, Otto's letters during 1945 are missing from the wartime correspondence that Eva and Otto so carefully retained. But Eva's letters illuminate their separate paths through the end of the war.

Eva's first letter of 1945 to Otto, written on January 4, was notably upbeat. She announced that "the mail has been wonderful since yesterday" and listed the dates of the letters she had just received from him. She also had news for Otto about significant new obstacles that would prevent her from accepting Eichler's proposed new "job" for her in Europe—obstacles that, in her heart, must have lifted her spirit:

> I have not heard anything definite yet, but it looks as if we better do not count too much on [the new job in Europe] for the present. There is a general regulation according to which wives of service men serving in the same theater of war may not be employed by a government agency overseas (in the same theater of war). At least that is how I was made to understand—there were, of course, other difficulties in addition to this.
>
> I may be told more about it soon, and will let you know then. But as I see it, we better discount it for the time being. It's a pity in many an aspect, because I would have loved to be again with Roger (Bertholet) and his wife. But the problems were not negligible either, and probably growing as things look here now. Anyway, there is nothing that anybody can do about it, and so we have to take it.

Eva admitted the personal benefit of this. "As far as our personal interest is concerned, I still think that we have more of a chance to come together again at the earliest possible moment if I stay at home and wait for you." In noting another factor weighing against her return to Europe at that time, the question of citizenship, Eva stated: "Of course it would be better to have that settled first, and I have a strong impression that that is one of the real difficulties preventing me from going. . . . I still have one more year to go [to be eligible for U.S. citizenship], you know that, and there are no possibilities whatsoever to shorten that period, none at all, because that is the law."

Regarding Otto's visit with René Bertholet, Eva said, "I was so glad to see that you had a good time with Roger. I had to smile a little when I saw his OK as far as our personal plans for the future [having children] are concerned, but it is nice all the same. When you see him again, give him my—well, not love, but friendliest regards, and my love to his wife."

In her January 7 letter, Eva told Otto that Fritz [Friedrich] Adler had sent her a letter that Otto had written to Adler.[1] She noted, "He was obviously very pleased, and I was much more than that, deeply moved that you had written him, and how you had written." She explained:

Among our friends, close and less close, he certainly has the greatest stature and moral personality. I become more and more convinced of that the more I have to do with him. And that's why I am doubly glad that your letter to him has found such an easy tone of implicit mutual understanding, and that you make so plain that you see the great dangers of our time just where he sees them.

You see, one of the main things he believes in is to speak out what is, and not to fool himself and others, to see all one does and to judge it from the deepest principles we believe in. And you do just that in your letter, you show that you have a sense of proportion, that you don't overestimate trends and possibilities.

Eva also described her feelings about a book she had just read in which the author spoke of love. She offered her own thoughts about that subject:

When one lives with each other, struggles together, goes together through the wondrous experiences of moments of purest happiness, and periods of deepest sorrow, only then one's own person becomes an entity, and the other's person becomes an entity, only then the entities become one.

The other day I sought for an expression of what I feel we, you and I, mean to each other. And I could find no other than to say: we are at home in each other. To be able to say that in all honesty is ultimate happiness to me, and I cannot conceive of any other.

Eva ended the letter with her description of a recent visit with friends, including a young woman, Nora Nackel, and her six-and-a-half-year-old daughter. She explained that she had agreed to the visit despite the fact that she was "somewhat scared": "you see I am as yet not sure of my reaction or rather my capacity of controlling my emotion when I am with other people's children, and I hate to show too much of it." Having brought the child a gift, "a lovely book with delicate designs, and a story to it, about 'the elegant elephant,'" Eva happily reported to Otto, "My 'elephant' proved to be quite a success, and for the first time since many, many months, I was perfectly at ease with a child, and so was she."

After the child went to bed, Eva spent a quiet evening talking with Nora and her mother Marianne Welter as well as Marie Juchacz and "another woman . . . about 50 years old, beautiful, tall, looking somewhat like Minna [Specht] or Mary [Saran]. She had been a teacher at one of Marie's schools for labor social work in Berlin, and is now a professor at the school of social work in Cleveland." Eva described the evening:

And there we were, sitting around a little tea table, talking, mainly about social work and its problems that the woman from Cleveland sees in all their sharpness, about this country, about many, many things. It's hard to put into words what made for the atmosphere of the evening. It was probably un ensemble [a combination] of elements. . . . But the fact was that I was as relaxed, and interested, and alive as I had not felt for a long time, and that, had it not been so very late when I got home, I would have written you about it right that evening. Because you know, Ottoli, nothing becomes quite mine before having told you about it, having shared it with you.

Later that same day, Eva wrote to Otto about a concert she had attended. It was "beautiful—so much more alive than the same music over the radio or on records. I especially enjoyed the 'Kleine Nachtmusik' which I had never heard before at a concert hall, but which I, we both, know so well and love. You were with me, I saw your face, your expression, at the tender, gracious movements of Mozart."

In her January 15 letter, Eva praised Otto for writing letters to their friends, noting that they had each called her and "everyone seems to be extremely pleased that you write them, and how you do it—in spite of everything you say, you *have* a capacity of expressing what is on your mind and heart, and people feel that strongly." She gently encouraged him to write more to her: "Only you understand that a real letter from you to me, I mean a quiet letter on the 'longish' side would be something wonderful." She then told Otto that a letter he had previously sent had touched her deeply:

> It is almost as if I feel your heart beat, feel the mood you were in when writing the letter, see you, your face that I love so, your hands, those strong expressive hands. . . . Do you remember our first night in Chevreuse when my first gesture of love and confidence was to put my hand in yours?

Eva informed Otto that many men in the shop in which he had worked in New York had left for the army during the past year. That shop made wood patterns for war production. Eva noted that one of Otto's coworkers had said "flattering things" about the kind of man Otto was, and when his mission in Europe was complete, he should tell his superior officer that a vital war job was "eagerly awaiting" him in New York.

Eva then described an incident that moved her deeply. It involved her work helping impoverished elderly refugees from Europe, many of whom could not speak English and needed financial assistance:

> Kate Duncker, you know, one of my old people, was ill and had to be taken to a city hospital on Welfare Island.[2] I went there to look after her and to make the necessary financial arrangements. I had never been there before—the most terrible misery concentrated on this one island where obviously only the poorest of the poor, those who have nothing, nobody left, go. I talked to

the social investigator, an elderly rather sickish looking colored woman, with a beautiful, warm human face. She took down all the facts, how old they were, what they lived on, when they got here, what they had been doing before, who I was and why I was interested, what my committee [the Emergency Rescue Committee] was and so on.

When we were through with the routine, she told me what and how we would have to pay. And I got up and made ready to go. She gets up too. And instead of the conventional "good-bye," she looks straight into my face, takes my hand, shakes it with warm frankness, and says in a deep voice which still rings in my ears: "We know what sorrow is, your people and mine. I should not talk about it, better forget it; but with you it is different—you are sympathetic, you must have gone through much—have you been down South? Some things are terrible, over there, where our boys fight—but here too." I will never forget the expression on her face when she said this first sentence, the sound of her voice, the feel of her bony, strong hand in mine.

In a brief letter on January 20, Eva referred to news of the Russian offensive and again expressed her hope that Germans would finally rise up and stop the war. "Although one better reckons with a long hard fight, it is not entirely unreasonable to think that the explosion inside Germany really could happen any minute now. Oh, how I am waiting for that. Because I am more convinced than ever that the longer it lasts, the worse will be the chances for a reasonable peace, and so my ardent desires for the killing to take an early end are linked with the little hope that is left for the winning of the peace."

Eva asked Otto in a V-mail message on January 22, "Did you know that Hanni had been deported . . . Terrible!" And in a short letter on January 25, Eva told Otto about "a tragic, pitiful letter from Aunt Rahel, mother's sister, written shortly after the news of mother's passing had reached her." Eva confided, "Oh, Ottoli, I so often feel a guilt because I could not do anything to help mother when things became so terrible. But it was really not possible these last years. You understand, Ottoli, more than anybody else, why I am attached to the work with my 'old' people [relief work for refugees]. In a way I try to make up to them who are helpless and alone what I could not do for mother."

In her January 28 letter, Eva expressed concerns about Gaby:

> You never told me whether or not you heard directly from Gaby.
> I wrote her a long letter to her address in Marseille that John
> gave me. But that letter of course may take very long to get
> there. Will you let me know when you hear from her? I so want
> to know that she is alright, and happy, if possible.

Eva then noted the news on the radio that Beuthen and Kattowitz had
been taken and that the industrial region of Upper Silesia seemed to
have been given up. "I really can't see how they can go on for long, the
Nazis, I can't. But then we have thought that it could not go on for quite
a while, and somehow or other it always did continue, so we better don't
count too much on an early end even now when so much points to it.
But I do wish it were near, with every fiber of me!"

Before closing this letter, Eva told Otto about a concert she would
attend in which Lotte Lehmann would be "singing songs of Schubert,
Hugo Wolf, Brahms." Eva noted that Lehmann "reminds me of our
mother, partly because mother used to sing all these songs and they are
part of my warmest and most harmonious childhood memories; but in
a way she also looks a little like mother. . . . You will be with me, Ottoli,
as you always are when beauty and sorrow and love touch my heart."

In her letter of February 3, Eva informed Otto that she had sent a
parcel with the things he had requested: olives, chocolate, coffee, nuts
and almonds, soup. She teased Otto about sending her clippings without
any accompanying word. "I mean, with you I can be honest, and not
try to pretend that a 'clipping letter' brings exactly as much happiness
as a real letter. But now, please, don't conclude that you should change
anything. Do just as it is best for you, and you know that next to your
being with me, your letters mean life to me, and when there can be no
letters, then a sign that you are safe and well, of recent date and as often
as possible, is the next choice." She closed this letter by describing a
difficult visit with a friend and her seven-month-old baby:

> When I held the little fellow in my arms, [his mother] busied
> herself outside the room, and so I did not have to hold back my
> tears. Chéri, do you really believe I will ever again hold our own
> child in my arms? I say "again," and in reality I never even laid

eyes on our child's face, only on the little bundle in the nurse's arms. It gives me confidence and strength to know that you believe in it—sometimes I need much strength, much strength.

Eva shared another poignant experience with the child of a friend in her letter of February 4. The little girl, Marianne Mayer, was to stay over with Eva as their parents went out, but shortly before they were to leave, Marianne declared that she did not want to stay:

> Not that she did not like me—she did not know about that. But she did not know me yet; maybe she would stay some other time when she had gotten to know me better. . . . I went in to her, she was in the bedroom reading some books, and told her that it was quite alright, we would be together some other time when we knew each other. I don't know what it was—all of a sudden she warmed up, and said that after all she would like to stay.
>
> So she did, and I don't think she regretted it. We prepared dinner together—she making a "soufflé-omelette," I the rest. Then she asked me whether I knew a mystery story, or could make up one; she would begin to tell me one. I was frankly scared, my head was quite empty; finally I remembered some story in Colliers, and believe it or not, I successfully told my mystery story. Then it was the turn for jokes, and then games (find out what object of the room the other has in mind); then for her to pick out what bed she was to sleep in . . . then the bathtub, and finally, tired, sleepy, I kissed her goodnight, tucked warmly in clean sheets.
>
> And I have to come to you, Ottoli, to share it with you, it all, the sweetness and bitterness, the uncertainty, the fear, the feeling of warmth and protection when I see her in your bed. Ottoli, I'll have to learn many, many things for our child, many of the light, happy things of life, stories, songs, plays. But I don't think I have to learn love.

In Eva's short letter of February 8, she reported on a note she had received from her brother Rudi, who was fighting with the Union of South Africa along with other British Commonwealth forces. Eva was corresponding regularly with Rudi by V-mail and sending him packages.

She was worried when she had not heard anything from him for a full month. "It's just a short note, saying that he was in quite a tough spot, but that now he has plenty of time, is looking forward to books I said I would send—do you think he may have been wounded? He had been in the frontline all the time, last time wrote about his 'foxhole,' and how they had tried to cheer it up with the help of our Christmas cigars and coffee. . . . Anyway, it gave me the creeps, and I am only glad that his letter is of so recent a date." Eva also commented on news she had just heard: "still 'heavy resistance, bitter fighting' on all fronts, despite the tremendous advances still a long war ahead. When, when are they going to give up, to break up!"

Eva turned to the beauty of a winter morning in the Bronx in her letter of February 9:

> This morning especially I would have wanted you to be here. There had been plenty of snow during the night and when look-ing out of our bedroom window, it was as in a fairy tale. Not that we did not have much snow before. But this had been, for the first time, the quality of snow clinging to the branches, to the telephone wires, to every little outstanding thing outside, and so nature became alive in a pure way, every line more clear, more distinct, more beautiful. And with that a clear pale blue sky, the smoke out of the factory chimney . . . also clean and white, everything transparent—it was so beautiful I cried a lit-tle, and thought of that other Sunday, last year, where you per-suaded me to take out my mountain boots, and where off we went, to our Bronx Park, into the loneliness of snow and trees and ourselves—do you remember?

Eva then told Otto, "Nothing new at all about the changing of my job, nothing from here, not a word from Bill [pseudonym for Eichler] or Roger [Bertholet]. I think the whole thing is stalled for the time being, and nobody seems to be able to do anything about it. Maybe it's just as well." She ended the letter with an update on the avocado plant. "It is now standing on the window sill, before my desk, and almost as tall as the window. And my big problem is where to put it within a few weeks, when it will have outgrown the window . . . you remember how we wanted something to grow out of the 'Kern' [seed], and how patient you were when I was already about to throw it away, or not to water it anymore? And when all of a sudden it began to live, just at that time you had to go."

On February 12, Eva reported that "they just announced over the radio that the meeting of the three [Franklin Roosevelt, Winston Churchill, and Joseph Stalin at Yalta to discuss the reorganization of postwar Europe] is over, and from what I can gather without having seen their declaration, it does not look so bad, at least as far as their decision is concerned to stick together." In a brief letter on March 1, Eva commented with caution on more good news about the progress of the war. "Today Krefeld, Trier were taken, and it really does not seem as if anybody were following Goebbels' and Hitler's frantic appeal to fight till the death. Oh, if this were only true! . . . As long as they are determined to fight for every ruin, as they did in Aachen, it can still be a terribly long, agonizing fight."

## Signs of spring, longing for an end to the fighting

In her letter of March 4, Eva sent Otto special thanks for a letter in which he "wrote of spring coming, 'the kind of spring you and I love so much,' of the 'wide field with the winter seeds eagerly pushing up,' of how you miss me 'so that it hurts.'" She then shared another special experience with music. "We went to the Frick collection on Sunday afternoon where there was a beautiful piano concert of Mozart and Schubert (we must do that once, when you are home again—it is one of the most beautiful accomplishments in New York, these concerts at the Frick collection)."

On March 6, Eva wrote, "Cologne has fallen, and you can imagine how I feel. But still, they keep on fighting and one cannot understand why, how. Sometimes it drives me crazy to think of this senseless, useless waste of human lives and values. Didn't you think that Eisenhower's appeal yesterday found the right tone? I think it did, and I wish with all my heart that it will be listened to, and followed."

In a short note to Otto on March 7, Eva thanked him for his "good, warm, loving, lovely letter" and added:

Glad you had news from Gaby. I did not hear from her yet at all, but I hope she did get my letter that I wrote as soon as it was possible. No, I am not afraid any longer, you know that. Give her all my love when you see her, and tell her about us. And tell her also how very much, how deeply I wish for her the same happiness as we found it.

On March 10, Eva wrote, "The news these days since the [Allied] crossing of the Rhine has so electrified me that I just could not sit down quietly and write you as I so wanted to do." She promised to write him a "real letter" tomorrow. The following day, Eva began a longer letter by telling Otto that she had found it difficult to sit down and write, even though "all day long I was with you, all my thoughts, all my heart." She explained:

> It was one of those days where the sadness about things in general and particular, keeps so hold of one's heart that one can do nothing against it—anyway when one is alone, and the only person on earth towards whom one could and would let oneself go for a little while, and sadness and sorrow would melt away, and one could breathe freely again, is not there; and to put that burden on him in a letter seems cruel, and one cannot do it because it can be put on paper only when it is somewhat passed.
>
> So I had to let go, read the "Times" for hours . . . listened to the radio, reports, and music. And just now I had a good cup of coffee, and a long look at your picture, and things begin to be right again.

Eva described the news of the Allied crossing of the Rhine: "the tremendous accomplishment of these few men who made this extraordinary use of the ten minutes before the bridge was blown, but also the limitations of the crossing at this particular spot, the hardships of the terrain on the other side." She again lamented the fact that the German soldiers still put up resistance:

> If only they would realize that they are being driven to certain death by this group of gangsters who want to put off defeat only to put off the day when they will have to pay for the terrible misery they have brought upon the world. . . . Of course, nobody knows how efficient the terror machine still is. In some article

of today's papers, I read a sentence to the effect: "A soldier will fight on as long as he knows that fighting means possible death, and stopping to fight means certain death." And that is probably terribly true, because the sense of self-preservation is certainly the strongest instinct in every human being. But the moment ought not to be far where just this sense of self-preservation should bring them to stop it all.

Eva described for Otto an Emergency Rescue Committee meeting "where the head of the displaced persons Division of UNRRA [United Nations Relief and Rehabilitation Administration] who had just returned from Europe addressed the meeting. . . . It was very impressive, but a terribly sad story which he had to tell." She also referred to "a report from Anne O'Hare McCormick of the NY Times who is back from Europe, and who gave her impressions not in figures or economics or military strategy, but rather in terms of people, especially children, what war and occupation and liberation and war again has done to them, the look on their faces, these old little people of five and six years of age who have seen things that one should not see in a life time." Eva concluded: "I wish with all my heart that the military defeat of the Nazis were here, that at least killing and destruction on a mass scale stops, that then one can again, probably under the most appalling conditions, but yet again think in terms of construction, of giving help, of making good, of bringing back life."

As Eva looked to the end of war to bring back life, she wrote to Otto on March 18 about signs of spring emerging in the Bronx Park:

Today is a real spring day, not damp, not sticky, warm, yet so that one looks for sunny spots outside with pleasure. We [Herta and I] went to the Bronx Park, and on very few bushes, one or two trees, the buds began to burst, tiny little leaves were showing. Here and there some spots of fresh green grass, but as a whole everything is still in the process of preparing itself for spring, working from deep inside, but the outside still grey, dry. Yet you feel new life coming everywhere, and I miss you, Otto.

Eva then told Otto about a letter she had received from Bertholet, before Bertholet had seen Otto. The letter "interested me very much, especially the part in which he tells me of his work with Regina [Kägi] and of his urgent need to participate in something constructive, something helpful, bringing relief for the greatest misery, after these awful years of destruction and war."[3] This appears to be the work that Bertholet and Eichler wanted Eva to do with them in Europe, and it presented a profoundly difficult choice about her future: whether she should continue to commit her whole life to assisting others in great need or pursue her personal desire to have a child with Otto. She carefully reminded Otto what was most important to her and again sought his reassurance:

> I so understand him [Bertholet], and I would want to help in this if there were any possibility. But it does not seem as if there is for the time being. So it will have to be postponed for a later date, and maybe then we know also what your assignments are going to be, and we can again plan together. That is, in spite of all my urge to help, the thing that is closest to my heart. You don't blame me for it, Ottoli?

In a letter the following day, Eva thanked Otto for the "wonderful," "loving," "generous" letters she recently received from him. She wrote, "Yesterday I told you of the first signs of spring that I noticed in Bronx Park. Today I have your letter in which you describe spring where you are. I know it is the same thing with you: these first, tender beginnings of new life, one wants to live them together." She happily described the continuing growth of the avocado that "will soon be the tallest in the family." And she asked, "Did I tell you that once I picked a tiny little leaf plant, like a little rose, from the rock garden in the Bronx Park? I just could not resist, and it was very, very little, not bigger than the tip of my little finger. I planted it, and now there are all around it three or four new little ones, and they all stick happily together. Oh, Ottoli, you don't mind my telling you about these things that might sound ridiculous in this world of war and terrible happenings. But yet, they are part of our world too, and I feel that you understand in what spirit I write you about them."

In a brief letter of March 27, Eva told Otto that "this has been a day not only of much work, but of great excitement—the news from the front, Eisenhower's statement that the [German] Armies on the West Front are broken, and in addition to that for an hour in the late morning unconfirmed announcement of impending peace—all that made for a rather hectic day." She went on:

> But I just can't close it without coming to you, without sharing with you what I feel now, when, even to my pessimistic eye, the end of organized Nazi resistance is in sight. With it the end of untold misery and destruction. This is something so great that for a moment it overshadows the tremendous problems of the future—you understand me, don't you, dearest? Oh, how I wish I were near you now, to live this with you.

Eva's eye was not pessimistic enough. The ultimate Allied victory was by now a virtual certainty, but the fighting, death, and destruction would continue.

Eva's sister-in-law, Herta, was ill and facing an operation on her thyroid in New York in early April. Eva took care of her while Herta's husband Erich worked in Hartford. In a letter on April 1, Eva wrote, "This morning, Easter Sunday, warm, clean spring air, sunshine, tomorrow my birthday, a week from today yours, and heart so full of longing and love for you that sometimes I think I can't hold it any longer." She told Otto that Erich was staying with Herta "so it was alright for me to go away, go where we two are closest to each other. And that's where I am sitting now, after a long walk to all the places we love: in our Botanical garden."

> It is indescribably beautiful, with a shy, tender, clean beauty, full of promise and life. And I miss you more than I can say. My eyes and my heart are still full of this new green that is so fresh that it seems almost golden; full of the wonder of one tree near the river under which I stood for a while; proudly, delicately, it stretches its arms, with innumerable buds, standing erect, like candles. And one of those buds, just one on the whole tree, had just released its treasure to freedom and life of its own: a full bunch of well-formed leaves stretched towards the sun, still a little crumpled, still sticking together, but full of strength and vitality.
>
> And then our rock garden; it is still closed; but I went around it and through the gate, and above it I saw those bright yellow daffodils coming out of the grass; a bush, far away, full of

deep violet blooms, another one overflowing with festive white
flowers. And then all the little things . . . a little bird resting
confidently on the side of the path; one, two butterflies, very,
very small, but oh so alive; the sun coming through the green
veil of the trees; the air so good to breathe, deep, deep. And
Ottoli, with every one of these emotions, you are inseparably
linked, you and our life together and our love for each other
and our love for the wonder of life. You will come back to me
soon, Ottoli?

Eva told Otto that she was going with Erich and Marie Juchacz that
afternoon "to Carnegie Hall, to the Matthaeus-Passion, conducted by
Bruno Walter—Erich and Herta's gift for my birthday." And she added,
"Tonight, when everybody has gone to bed, I will open your gift which
has been on my desk for over a week. I will read your letters, and be
with you."

Otto's birthday gift to Eva was a book of Rilke's poems. He also
arranged to have Emil bring twelve deep red roses to Eva with a card
from Emil that read "Rote Rosen von Otto [red roses from Otto]." Eva
thanked Otto for both gifts in a letter of April 3 and told him, "Till
late in the night, I read a page here, a page there, and felt close to you
as if you were bending your head over the same pages with me." She
also told Otto that the performance of Bach's *Matthäus Passion* was "in-
describably beautiful": "For the first time I understood the full tragedy
of the story of Christ. . . . [B]efore going to the concert, I got out the
Bible and read . . . with great profit, only wishing to have you near. Oh,
and that music—it really does not seem of this earth any longer—the
last chorus: 'Sleep thou sweetly sweetly sleep. Rest, thou weary tortured
body.' It sweeps you away, away to all those you love, and who could not
stay with you—We must hear it together when you are home again."

After taking Herta to the hospital on April 4, Eva told Otto in a
letter that day, "I don't like hospitals, never did, and especially not now."
She thanked Otto for his recent letters and told him how pleased she
was that Otto had seen Kramer (the ISK's pseudonym for Hans Jahn)
and that he had sent her greetings. She sent Otto regards from a friend
who was having her twenty-fifth birthday that day and noted, "Do you
realize that was my age when we met, and that it is exactly ten years ago

that that happened? What tremendously rich ten years you have given me!" She rued the fact that the war still raged. "It's going at tremendous speed, but why, why, are so many still fighting? To prolong this agony is really criminal."

In her letter to Otto on his birthday, April 8, Eva expressed her love and hope for their future together:

> You must feel how intensely I am with you since this day began, how all my capacity to love, and all my thoughts and feelings are concentrated on and in you, how I wish I could be with you, were it only for a moment, just hold your face in my two hands. . . . Let us hope, and have confidence in our future together, and in the meantime keep our chins up, and give our best to each other, and to the things we believe in.
>
> And above all, keep well, my dearest, bleib mir gesund [stay healthy for me], as mother used to say, our mother who loved you so. This morning I looked at both their pictures, your mother's and mine. Your mother would also have loved me Ottoli, had she known me, her eyes seem to tell me that. You have her eyes . . . you know, those honest, straightforward, good eyes that I love so.

Eva shared her dismay about the war:

> The war goes on. It is amazing on the one side, the progress that is being made everywhere, and the relatively ineffective resistance. But on the other hand it is terribly depressing that it has to go on that way, that piece by piece has to be gotten by fighting, that there is not enough strength left to get any substantial help from within, other than passivity. . . .
>
> I just talked about it with some friends . . . and we all agree that even with the most pessimistic outlook none of us had thought this could have happened. We obviously, all of us, have greatly underrated the strength of this total terror machine, and also the degree of fatigue and hopelessness that must pervade those who wish it were over but have no strength left to do something about it.

Eva closed this letter with many questions for Otto about friends in Europe, including whether he had heard from Gaby again. She attached to the letter a petal "from one of the roses that I got from you for my birthday."

In an April 10 letter Eva noted, "Hannover taken, Wien [Vienna] almost, Bremen approached—how long can it still last?"

## The death of Roosevelt and the end of war in sight

On April 12, 1945, Franklin D. Roosevelt died at his retreat in Warm Springs, Georgia. This was also the anniversary of the death of Eva's first child. In a letter to Otto on April 12, 1945, Eva wrote:

What I would give not to be alone tonight! The terrible shock of Roosevelt's death; the war drawing to its end; and this night, the night of April 12 to April 13, in which a year ago our deepest hope was fulfilled and, almost before we had realized it, finally taken away. There is not proportion between these three things, and yet every one of them is scarcely bearable.

I don't know; perhaps I'm just an egocentric, petty woman who cannot forget her small sorrows at a time when the world is shaking. I don't want to be that; and yet, the agony of the thing that happened to us a year ago is as burning and alive as if it had happened yesterday. And that I don't want to unburden it to anybody, makes it harder yet. That is the reason, Ottoli, why I talk to you about it. Just tell you what you know anyhow. Get comfort from you, compassion and understanding. My heart, my soul need that sometimes, because they are so hurt, and alone.

Roosevelt—I think he was a *good* man in addition to being great, and that is why so many of us will sense a feeling of personal loss. For him the end may have been wonderful: to have accomplished so much, to have given himself so entirely, to be sure that he has done his share, that the end of the killing is near—he could very quietly close his eyes and go to rest. But for us, for all the people, for the solution of the problems to come—I don't see yet how the loss can be compensated.

And where may you be this night, Otto? Perhaps you are so busy that it passes without letting you come to yourself. But if you have time now, I know you too will think back, and you will think of me. Then you must know that you are not alone this night, that I am with you with my thoughts and heart. My heart, full of sorrow, but also full of deep grateful love. And of good will. Do you feel that, my Ottoli? Let me rest with you, let's both be again at home in each other.

In a short letter on April 14, Eva noted that "it cannot be long now before the end of the war will be declared—what are we going to feel far from each other at that moment, Otto, my dearest!" She told Otto, "I did not write you yesterday, but you know that I lived every moment of that day a year ago, with you, and it hurt very much to be so alone. But I stood it, somehow, and life goes on."

News about the war was the focus of Eva's brief letter on April 18:

This terrible report about Buchenwald which I enclose made me sick day and night; and when I think of all these things, I just don't know how everything is going to go on. I must talk more about it some other day, but I want you to get the report as soon as possible. Then tonight the news that Ernie Pyle was killed in action. And I am wondering why it is that the best ones have to go. And late tonight, reports on the radio about stiffening resistance everywhere—can you explain to me how that is possible? I give up to understand.

In her letter of April 20, Eva wrote that "they announced the capture of Hoyerswerda" where Otto had been held in the Nazi prisoner-of-war camp in 1940. She told Otto, "My thoughts are with you more than ever. How long is it to last still? And why, why do they fight on?"

She also described an exhibition she had attended the night before "in memory of the fighters and victims of the Ghetto—you remember, it was two years ago that they opened their desperate fight in Warsaw. Horrible pictures which keep you awake all night, bring despair, and shame, to your heart." And she asked, "How will we all ever be able to atone for this that we could not prevent from happening?" Eva praised those who presented the exhibition, including "a moving address by La

Guardia. . . . But the pictures—they haunt you, together with these Buchenwald reports. . . . Tell me Ottoli, how is it possible that human beings like you and me—they were children not so long ago—could lose themselves in such abject depths?"

In Eva's letter of April 22, she reported that she read the morning paper. "It makes me sick and almost despairing of mankind":

> Of course we knew that there were concentration camps in Germany with unprecedented horror and cruelty. But never before has the story been told with all its details and on this mass scale, as it is now. All the reports sound only too true, and the delegation of Congressmen and publishers that has been invited to visit these camps, by Eisenhower, is another indication that there is no exaggeration, and that it is just the truth that is being told, and brought home.

Eva then observed something missing from these reports that she found deeply disturbing:

> In all these reports, nobody or scarcely anybody, says that many of these camps, especially Buchenwald, had been organized by the Nazis against their political enemies from within. . . . Not that this would change the atrocity of these deeds; but the fact that some Germans suffered with them together with the others is another proof that there were decent human beings in Germany who tried to do something against these criminals. And their tragedy, our tragedy, is that they were unsuccessful in their attempts, and that these attempts are meeting with a dead silence from the civilized world.
>
> The reporters seem to be convinced that the large part of the German population did not know what happened in those camps. . . . That they are being shown now, without sparing them, is, I think, the only right thing to do. Because they have to realize what has been done in their name in order to understand the feelings of the world against them. But I wish the full story would be told, to them and to the world, and credit given where it is deserved.

Eva described the current fighting in the streets of Berlin. She also observed that "the Ruhr pocket was finished off rather quickly. But there one had the impression that the civilian population and parts of the Army were sick and tired of this murderous senseless fighting, and did something about it. While at other spots the SS terror still holds them all in their grip. Oh, how I wish it were over, over once and for all!"[4]

Eva noted that her brother John, on his way back to his base, "saw Gaby for several hours in Paris, and as happy as their reunion was, he says it was very hard because their feelings towards each other are still so very strong." She asked Otto again,

> Did you hear from her [Gaby] again? She is in Lyons now, says John, working at a newspaper, and I am afraid she might not have gotten my letter that I had sent many months ago to her Marseille address. Anyway, I have not heard from her directly yet, and I wish I would. Tell her, when you write or meet her that I wrote her a long letter, and that I'll write again as soon as I get a good address, and that I hope in the meantime to hear from her, and that she may be well.

Eva shared some important news with Otto in her letter of April 23:

> I must tell you what happened today. On my way to the office, in the subway, I was, as usual, reading the "Times." On page 5 another of those horrible accounts about Buchenwald which I begin to read. . . . And then, at the end of the second paragraph, the news that electrifies me, that Kautsky's brother [Benedikt Kautsky] is alive. . . . I was thrilled as I had not been for a long time. . . .
>
> It is great on so many accounts: first I knew how Kautsky was worried about him, did not believe him alive anymore. He was last supposed to be in Oswiecim (Auschwitz), and everybody knew that most of the prisoners were killed there. When months after the liberation of O. [Auschwitz] by the Russians no word of or about him had come out, Kautsky gave up hope. And now this news.

But on a more general ground: he is the first leading Austrian or German Anti-Nazi who is thus found alive—and is it too daring to hope that he will not be the only one? And then also: even though many of them will have perished, at least he is there who was with them, and who can testify as to their presence, to their sacrifice. But what this man must have gone through in the years from 1938: Dachau, Oswiecim, Buchenwald—it is terrible beyond imagination.[5]

Otto's assignments with the OSS at this time are unclear; only sketchy information can be pieced together. A travel order to Otto dated April 24, 1945, directed him "to proceed for a period of approximately seven (7) days to Brussels, Antwerp and Paris, for the purpose of carrying out the instructions of the Commanding Officer." Another travel order directed him "to proceed on or about 30 April 1945 from their present station to London, England, reporting upon arrival to the Commanding Officer, Hq & Hq Dot, O of Strategic Services, for station and duty." His specific assignments are not described. Otto also traveled with his commanding officer into Germany as the war was coming to an end. As Otto later recalled, "In the meantime, our troops had crossed the Rhine. Soon after that, I went with my C.O. [Commanding Officer] on a special trip to Aachen, Köln [Cologne], and Godesberg. We drove our jeep through the rubble of those towns—the destruction was horrendous."[6]

In a brief letter on April 28, Eva told Otto that Erna Blencke was pleased to get a letter from him "and found it very interesting, also what you told her of your trip." Eva wrote:

You can imagine that I am, we all are, eager to hear more about it—the destruction seems to be terrible. . . . Did any friends survive? The news of the military development since yesterday is amazing—the junction which of course everybody had expected, but yet, when it was officially announced, one quite realized the bigness of it. The dash into Austria, the capture of Augsburg, the revolt in München [Munich], the surrender of Dittmar.

On May 1, Eva wrote, "I had thought that today would be peace day. That does not seem to be so. But it surely can't last any longer, and this total disintegration must be followed, it seems to me, by total collapse. Did you hear more about what happened in Munich?" She then returned to her most pressing personal questions: "And when am I going to hear from you? When will there again be a common future, a planning together for us? I am very eagerly waiting for your letter, for what decisions the next days and weeks will bring."

## VE Day

In a V-mail message on May 2, Eva wrote, "Dearest, this is just a note. The news these days—Mussolini killed, Hitler dead, Berlin fallen, peace with Himmler or fight goes on, Italy surrendered—it is almost too much to remain quite sane. And I miss you."

On May 7, 1945, a day earlier than the official VE Day, Eva marked the Allied victory in Europe by writing to Otto:

> That we cannot live these hours together is something that is and will remain heavy on my heart. But I know we are so one in feeling and reacting that our thoughts most likely have been going along the same lines—an immensely heavy load off one's chest that at least in one part of the world the killing is over. That the horrors of the concentration camps are of the past, really and irrevocably, that the gates and the barbed wire have opened to those most courageous fighters; and that those who perpetrated these crimes will not go unpunished, that at least some of the worst of them have already disappeared, don't breathe any longer the same air as we do.
>
> But also the tremendous tasks ahead, and the ever-mounting difficulties that are opposed to a lasting peace based on a mutual confidence, and on a solution to the economic problems on an international scale. But I am getting very impatient, quite upset as a matter of fact, with all those who say resignedly that we are heading towards the next world war. Of course I know all the problems, but if only part of human endurance, and suffering, and capacity to go beyond oneself, would be employed towards creating peace rather than perfecting war, I think it could be done. And anyway one has no right to give up—there would

be no sense in living if it really were that hopeless. I know that you think, you feel the same way, and I know I love you more than anything else in the world.

This was my VE Day: it began with your wonderful, loving letter . . . with the long quotation of Rilke with which I largely agree. . . . When I got off the subway, electricity was in the air, paper flying from all the windows, people gathering in the streets, a man saying: "This seems to be it alright; but my boy is in the Pacific, so what does it mean to me?" And I rushing to the office . . . someone had just heard it over the radio, it was official, they had surrendered. One has an urgent need to communicate with others who feel as you do in such moments. . . . I tried to telephone one or the other of our friends: Estrin, Marie, Hans, Erna—But no line available.

So off we went to Times Square. People were coming, streaming in from everywhere. . . . Their faces were glowing with an inner light. With the exception of some, here and there an older woman, with tears in her eyes, and strain all over—and you could see that her boy won't come back.

When we came back to the office, there was a little let-down about the announcement not being official although the surrender was official—but now they just announce that Pres. Truman, Churchill and Stalin will make the official announcement simultaneously tomorrow morning at 9 a.m.

So now everything is clear, and I am home, listening to the radio, being very much alone, but really not alone because you fill my heart, you are so present, I am proud of you, and if you would walk in right now, my love could not be greater than it is now.

Eva told Otto that she would "just drop a line" to her brothers John and Rudi: "how I wish for them that this means going home for good!" And she returned to her pressing question: "What it will mean for you and me, I don't dare to guess; but I do hope that the next days or weeks will bring me an answer." Ending the letter, she wrote:

Dearest, this *is* a great day, a day of the deepest importance, a day which throws into man's lap opportunities and a challenge

as had not been given him for very, very long. Although I realize only too well that the individual's effort is less than a grain
of sand—you have given so generously of your best. And I am
proud of you. My deepest wish is for the times to come now
that we may be able to throw our bit in together, in unison,
and that our common life may have a continuation, may go on
after us. I love you.

# 32. A New Life

Following VE Day, Eva had been hoping—and beginning to believe—that Otto was on his way home. But in Eva's letter of May 11, 1945, she referred to a letter from Otto that must have been deeply disappointing to her. She told Otto that his letter of May 3 "makes one thing clear . . . that nothing has been decided as yet as to whether or not you will ask for a discharge [from the army], or whether you will, after consultation with friends, apply for a new assignment. And that means that we have to be patient for a little while longer, which I promise you to be, dearest." Eva then presented the reasons she believed Otto should ask for his discharge.

Eva first assured Otto that she did not want to push him into doing something he did not want to do, or hold him back from doing what he thought was right. But because they were not together to discuss this, she told Otto that if he decided to stay in Europe and accept a new assignment, she wished he would explain fully the reasons for his decision: "As far as I can see, the cons are very much stronger than the pros, and I would like to understand as much as possible your decision."

Eva then presented her own views. She conceded, "There is of course a strong personal element in it, and I do not for a moment wish to disguise it." But apart from the personal element, she told Otto that because the war in Europe was over, their "contribution to any constructive work" could best be made independently—not as part of Otto's continuing work with the U.S. Army and the OSS:

> You enlisted for the duration of the war in Europe, you are over
> 42, and the Army regulations say plainly that it is up to you to

ask for your discharge. I don't think that anybody would feel that you neglect a duty if you take this opportunity now. And what you, what we, do later on will depend upon possibilities that offer themselves, once you are back in civilian life.

Eva then weighed the benefits of Otto's return against his possible future contribution with the army in Europe. She told him that their "interests of being together, of planning to live and work together, have a much heavier weight" than they did before the military victory in Europe. "This phase is over, and whatever anyone can do now, we should not have any illusions about its having any far-reaching importance. . . . Therefore the time has come now, I feel, where our interest to work together can be put forward strongly, even if it means that temporarily you or I will not be at a place where we can be of some value."

Eva noted that it was difficult to explain all of this in writing, but she did not want to miss an opportunity to make their interest in being together as clear as possible. "I realize of course that I can judge the situation from here only, and that some angle of it might look different from your end. But not the general principle . . . and I would need very strong arguments indeed in order to be convinced that another course is called for." She concluded:

> Chéri, with all these dry words—do you feel how I love you, how I miss you, how these days when I thought you might walk in at any moment, I was and looked [like] a different person, how hope and energy and confidence came back to me? Maybe I should not say this because it might look as if I tried to influence you. You know that . . . whatever you decide, I will carry on, schlecht und recht (bad and good). But I would be a miserable hypocrite if I did not admit that in a deeper sense, only life with you is life for me. Do you understand me?

Eva did not have to wait long. In her letter of May 13 she wrote, "This minute I get your cable saying that you will probably be home within a month. Can you imagine how I feel, how relieved, how grateful."

Otto had been offered a commission if he would sign up for another year of service with the OSS, but he respectfully declined. As he later recalled:

I was only too eager to go home. And before long, I was crossing the Atlantic again, back to New York.

On October 1, 1946, Kathy was born. Eva wrote in her 1979 memoir:

> Impossible, without going into too many details, to describe our joy about and with you children. Kathy, when I saw you first, and held you, it was the most beautiful experience in my life, that made everything right, seemingly forever.

Of course, this decision to have a family against the dictates of the ISK and to make a new home in America was not an easy one. On December 17, 1945, Eva wrote a letter to Minna Specht, her beloved and respected teacher at the Walkemühle and the ISK's founding educator. Eva tried to explain why she no longer could support some of the restrictive rules of the ISK. She first noted that she was sure Specht would understand that "it is not disloyalty when I and some other former students of the school [the Walkemühle] do not wish to see much of our experiment repeated." She assured Specht that she was not "rejecting the foundation of our educational work." Instead, Eva wanted to explain the serious limitations she saw in its practical application. Above all, she wanted Specht to understand her disagreement with the ISK's view that a meaningful commitment to its important work precluded its members from marriage and having children:

> Today I firmly believe that a close and lasting relationship with another human being who has the good fortune to find such a companion, does not interfere with work but rather makes it more productive. That for most women, at a particular point in their life, it lies in the interest of their personal development and the retention and development of their psychological strength, to have children; that this only temporarily disrupts work, and seen over the long term as a result of the organic development of their strength, more springs out for the work than by a constant sapping of strength in the breakdown of this development.

Eva further observed that it was obviously a difficult task to bring one's obligations to society into accord with the obligations to a new child, but she argued that "we must be successful in this task, if we in any way believe in the future possibility of a cultivated life for the broader masses, in the possibility that a woman does not need to choose to lead her life either as a housewife and mother, or as a fighter who artificially suppresses her natural instincts and is in constant battle with herself." Eva recognized that "naturally, each woman will have to make her personal decision and have to answer to her own conscience." But she expressed her deep concern that a person should not be pushed into making this decision at an early age, as the ISK had done with Eva and others:

> If someone, as a mature person, with complete awareness of the situation and of herself, makes the decision to forego motherhood, I have great respect for that. What I find dangerous, however, and thus for the future reject, is that young people who cannot fully comprehend the consequences of their decisions because they simply do not know what either the fulfillment or the denial means for their lives, make such decisions. That is indeed what we have done, even though never explicitly but in substance. We therefore, each in our own time and way, had to resolve a conflict in our conscience as events stormed in on us in their full strength—a conflict that I believe people should not impose without emergency.
>
> Please do not misunderstand me, Minna, I am not urging that the task of education is to structure lives as far as possible to be without conflict. That is not possible, for the conflict between desire and duty is always there, and people should learn as young as possible to develop their strength and to be ready to do their duty in developing conflict situations. But in order really to be ready and capable, and not only in words, one must also understand the strengths of desires, one must really live and experience the strengths and significance of natural drives, like love, motherhood—and the significance they have in general and in one's own special life—in order first through the building of these strengths to reveal the necessary strength for the fulfillment of duty.

I firmly believe that the person who has affirmed these new obligations for the lives of herself and her companion can also be ready for the challenge, and I equally believe that it is the task of education to make people capable of this readiness. Readiness also to devote oneself to a full life; not readiness for asceticism—of which normal human beings are not capable, without taking on such harm that even for work only insignificant strength is left over.

Minna Specht. COURTESY OF AdsD/ FRIEDRICH-EBERT-STIFTUNG.

Eva urged her former teacher to understand why she had tried to explain her position:

> Now, when you have read these inadequate sentences, Minna, you will understand why I hesitated so long before I even wrote. I have so little time that even this was written in haste, and thus almost necessarily will create new misunderstandings. I believe one should think about these things in depth and calmly in the not-too-distant future, not in self-defense or accusation, but rather with effort, really to draw the right conclusions that come from our experiment that we, ourselves, you as teacher, we as students were engaged in. But in the exchange of letters, this is hardly possible. On the other hand, after your letter that was so warm and full of understanding, I wanted in no case to gloss over these things that have indeed remained unexplained for so long, and somehow stand between us. So please understand this as a humble attempt to explain my position.

Eva obviously hoped that through the kind of open and reasoned debate she had learned at the Walkemühle, both Minna Specht and Willi

Eichler would ultimately be convinced that she was not abandoning the ideals of the ISK to which she had dedicated such a huge part of her early life. Based on her letters to Eva in response, it appears that Specht understood and respected Eva's views but did not fully accept them.

Eva remained convinced that her decision to have children was the right one for her. A year and a half later on April 29, 1947, Eva wrote again to Specht. She began: "At this moment, the baby is asleep after a somewhat stormy morning. I have completed my most pressing work; however, two packages still sit here that still need to be completely tied up." She added, "Katherine's laundry is still not washed. And this after-noon I need to go into the City to discuss a few things in the [Emergency Rescue] Committee. Katherine will then stay home with a young woman whose child comes to me from time to time when her mother needs to go out."

After setting this scene, Eva assured Specht: "the chronic lack of time and a much more difficult to achieve mobility to free up myself for other things—these are to date the only serious problems that have emerged in connection with the baby." Advising Specht that she had "agonized and struggled so long with the preliminary question whether one can assume the responsibility of having children," Eva wrote:

> Today, that question has been answered for me, positively, and I would give a lot if I could sometime explain all my reasons for this to you and others who are involved in bringing up and educating young children. I will not try to do that now; but because you asked me whether I was content, I want to tell you: not only content, but infinitely grateful and happy, actually for the first time I have become a complete person. To see how, out of the tiny, helpless being, a person very gradually emerges, how a body, nerves and senses develop and grow, and gradually spirit and will develop—I find to be a constant wonder.
>
> I am convinced that this growth in its decisive elements follows its own rules, but within that framework it is the task of parents and educators to create the conditions that allow this de-veloping human to become healthy and straight and complete in body and character. That nature may have given her a minimum of healthy conditions and possibilities to develop; that other circumstances beyond our control do not destroy everything

(social catastrophe, war), and that we ourselves might have the capability to help her become a person with inner and outer sensitivities toward public life—these are our shared thoughts and wishes in connection with our child.

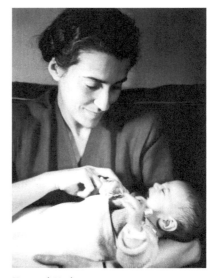

Eva acknowledged the need to organize her life with the mutual help of others "so that we do right by our child, but we are not completely devoured by those efforts." And she conceded that "a certain measure of real limita-

Eva and Kathy.

tions is unavoidable in the early years." She enclosed a small picture of Katherine, "taken on our first outing to the green, when she was just six months old. I think as far as one can now see, she has gotten a lot of Otto's nature: cheerful, open to other people, very receptive to friendliness, purposeful when she gets something in her head that she wants." Eva noted that she and Otto were not "completely absorbed with thoughts, worries and joy" about their child. "Sometimes I wish that one could be

Otto and Kathy.

so fully absorbed; but the state of the world naturally does not permit that. From that, I have answered your question whether we have totally withdrawn, whether we keep in touch with old friends. That contact has, of course, not been severed."

With firm belief in the core values that she knew they shared, Eva concluded:

That we today consider some aspects of our philosophy as subject to challenge, that we have answered some questions of personal lifestyle in different ways than we previously did, does not touch on what is, for me, the most essential: to find new ways and methods to live a correspondingly ethical life. I am convinced that many of our first efforts were good and unassailable. Many, however, I would not want to see repeated. Many should have been decisively broadened. Each of us who participated in this educational experiment will measure it in retrospect based on his experiences and new insights; I consider it as all of our duty to undertake together an assessment of the experiment. In that sense, therefore, I am here with you and will be here, as long as what is unthinkable for me does not seep in: that dogmatism takes the place of critical reason and an examination of the past gets condemned as heretical. . . .

I must finish now; the little baby needs to eat soon. Minna, I think about you so often, about your difficult life, and from all my heart I wish that something from our enormous efforts will take root in the stony ground.

# Epilogue

Eva and Otto lived in their small flat at 1830 Anthony Avenue in the Bronx near the Grand Concourse and E. 176th Street. They struggled to make ends meet. Otto used his woodworking skills to earn a living, and Eva experienced the joys of watching little Katherine grow. On March 29, 1948, Eva gave birth to identical twins, Tom and Peter. It is difficult to fathom the radical change in Eva's life: the abrupt transition from more than a decade of total commitment to fighting fascism and aiding victims in a war-torn world, to the challenge of caring for two infants and a toddler in New York with no extended family to help, supported only by Otto's meager wages.

The physical chores were overwhelming at times, but Eva felt "a perceptible change" in those first few years with her children in New York. "Now we no longer seemed to be just refugees, stranded there. A tenuous sense of belonging to a new community started to develop." Neighbors who also had young children helped her. "Our three flight walk-up apartment in the West Bronx, with one bedroom, was really not adequate for comfortable living with three children—the carriage, the apartment building's washing machines in the basement, clothes lines on the roof. Without mutual help among neighbors one could not have made it, and this fact became the new pattern of our lives—we no longer were strangers among strangers."[1]

Eva applied for her U.S. citizenship in 1946. As part of that process, the U.S. Immigration and Naturalization Service requested information from the FBI about Eva on April 8, 1946. In its response on June 20, 1946, the FBI commented that Eva had come to its attention in 1942

Eva's Certificate of Naturalization dated July 25, 1946.

and 1943 in connection with her efforts to obtain an immigration visa and had been described as a "prominent member" of the ISK—an organization that "has been said to be both anti-Communist and anti-Nazi."[2] Eva became an American citizen on July 25, 1946.

Somehow, Eva and Otto eked out a living. But Otto became convinced that a small apartment in New York City was not the best place to raise their children. Just as he had moved from Munich to Rome in 1920 and from Italy to France in 1926, Otto longed for a new start—this time in California, with its mild weather and natural beauty. He became convinced that he, Eva, and their children could have a healthier, better life there. The decision to move to California was not easy for Eva. She had lived and worked in New York for a decade and had developed close ties with refugees and colleagues who had worked with her during the war. But Otto and other refugee friends who had recently made the move to Los Angeles convinced her. With the savings they managed to accumulate, they were able to purchase a one-way flight to Los Angeles in 1950 for the whole family. Kathy was three and a half years old, and the twins were two.

## The early years in California

Another refugee couple who had moved to California, Ola and Werner Vorster, helped Eva and Otto locate an apartment in the San Fernando Valley, then an emerging suburb of Los Angeles.[3] Otto had made furniture for their apartment in New York that could be sent in pieces to California and reassembled. Eva recalled that "when finally our furniture came parcel post, we gradually had what we needed most urgently, acquiring refrigerator, and beds, and other things that could not be sent, second-hand."

Otto quickly found a job making custom furniture. A friend of the Vorsters, Rudy Brook, immediately offered to take Otto to and from work until he could buy a car. Rudy was a Jewish refugee who was then working as a landscape gardener in Los Angeles, though he had completed his legal studies in Germany before 1933. Eva later described the generous assistance they received from Rudy and his wife Eva. "From the first, they acted as though they were family, and in many ways that remained so and became stronger, as the years went by." Of course, Eva and Otto could not get along in Los Angeles without a car. They were able to afford a 1939 Packard that cost a few hundred dollars. Otto was the only one who could drive, and he needed the car for work. "So," Eva recalled, "during the weekdays, we had to stay put, and since we experienced a real heat wave shortly after having arrived in June, the first weeks and months here were not happy." She later conceded, "If we had any money at all, I would have urged Otto to go right back—I was much more lonely and isolated here than I had ever felt in New York. But of course, that was out of the question; we stayed on, and gradually things got better."[4]

After a brief stay in the small apartment, Eva and Otto were able to buy a new house in Canoga Park, located in the northwest corner of the San Fernando Valley, then a rural area filled with groves of orange, lemon, almond and walnut trees and fields of strawberries and asparagus. The three-bedroom, one-bath, ranch-style house was on a half-acre lot that had once been part of a walnut grove. It cost $10,000, affordable only because the GI Bill allowed them to make a small down payment with a thirty-year mortgage at 4 percent. Eva later described the first night in their new home:

That first night, you all in bed, Dad and I were sitting in the empty living room; we looked around it and at each other, visualized the wall—now bare—covered with bookshelves, and how you would play in the big yard—now nothing but dirt, and we felt that this would be a good home for us all. And it became just that.[5]

In addition to three mature walnut trees that remained on the lot, Otto planted young fruit trees—a Santa Rosa plum, two peaches, and an apricot—along with two almond trees. Eva soon learned to make and preserve jam from the fruit they produced. Otto also planted three small pine trees in the front of the house. He would observe over the years how they were growing like the children. And he planted and carefully tended rose bushes that soon offered a profusion of fragrant roses for Eva.

For ten years, Eva devoted most of her time to being a mother. These were deeply happy years for her. She no longer had the time or felt the need to maintain any diaries, but she continued her correspondence with her family in South Africa and Europe and with colleagues in New York and Europe, using the typewriter that had been given to her by Maurice Abravanel upon her arrival in America.

Otto was soon able to start his own small business as a cabinetmaker. He had no desire to employ workers to assist him and to leverage his income. Instead, he leased space, along with another independent cabinetmaker, in a small shop on Cochran Avenue near Pico Boulevard in Los Angeles. There Otto worked long hours, six days a week, making custom furniture for wealthy families in Los Angeles and Beverly Hills. He liked being his own boss, and he was a demanding one. He was driven by pride and discipline to create furniture that met his own high standards of craftsmanship, precision, and beauty, standards developed from decades of learning as an apprentice in Munich and in cabinet shops in Rome, Nice, and Paris. He did not make much money; his income was barely enough to make ends meet. Yet Otto found deep satisfaction in his work. He later reflected:

You know, I was so fortunate to always love my work. Well, not quite always. When I was 14, I had a hard time to accept that I should be only an apprentice cabinetmaker, while all, or almost all, of my friends went to "higher" education. To push a cart through the streets of Munich in working clothes (with a blue apron) delivering work and fetching material was somehow degrading. I knew that I could have done well in school. It took me some time to make peace with the plane and saw and glue and find that there could be deep satisfaction in building something out of wood, even sometimes something beautiful.

Later, working in Italy, and finally for many years in Paris, I learned an enormous amount of woodworking and loved my trade more and more.

Now, I realize how what once was seemingly a tough lot not to have fulfilled my yearning for so-called position in life, turned out to be a good thing in disguise. I continue to build things, keep young with my tools and my never-ending projects. I still get up in the morning, eager to be out in the shop to see things grow. Welch ein Glück [What good fortune]![6]

Their house was quickly filled with furniture crafted by Otto. The walls were graced with prints of paintings by van Gogh and Cézanne, drawings by Käthe Kollwitz, and original paintings by Eva's and Otto's dear friend from Europe, Theo Fried. All of this art, including the least expensive paper prints, was mounted by Otto on wood with frames he carefully crafted in mahogany, walnut, or pine. The living room was soon lined with shelves upon shelves of books written in French, German, and English—books about art, architecture, ancient history, philosophy, and literature including, of course, the poetry of Rainer Maria Rilke. The array of art books offered prints of other artists they loved, including Rodin, Michelangelo, Degas, Bonnard, and Barlach.

It was not easy for Eva and Otto to adapt their European backgrounds and experiences to southern California in the 1950s. They saved enough from Otto's limited earnings to introduce their young children to music, paying for private lessons on the piano and string bass for Kathy and on the violin for the twins. Kathy continued with her instruments until she was fourteen, but the twins gave up their violins in favor of baseball gloves at the age of eleven. Instead of classical music, the children began to listen to popular music on the radio and on 45-rpm records. They watched popular shows on a small used black-and-white television set.

Whatever disappointment Eva must have felt about these cultural influences, she kept it inside. She fiercely supported and encouraged the assimilation of her children into American life. Eva and Otto spoke English with their children and reverted to their native German or to French only during periodic visits from European friends, family, and colleagues or when keeping secrets from their children about holiday gifts.

Eva and Otto remained deeply interested in political developments in the world and in their adopted America. They closely followed the election between Adlai Stevenson and Dwight Eisenhower in 1952. The couple observed with concern the Joseph McCarthy hearings in the 1950s, admired the hopeful young Kennedy family in the early 1960s, and supported those who marched for civil rights. Eva and Otto were able to buy a used piano, and Eva played it often, filling their home with the sounds of Mozart, Bach and Beethoven.

Eva kept careful track of the limited family income and expenses in a small notebook—balancing the figures each month. She sewed some of her children's clothing. Annual vacations were spent with a week of camping at what became Eva's and Otto's beloved Sequoia and Yosemite National Parks. Eva often commented that the pine-scented air at 6,000 feet was perfect for her. Otto made new American friends, playing his harmonica around the campfire and singing folk songs in Italian, German, and French.

After the move to California, Eva and Otto were finally convinced that the twins, too skinny and frail, needed the benefit of more protein from meat. Eva reluctantly began to add small portions of meat to family meals. Dinners always included a salad of fresh lettuce and tomatoes, often with thin-sliced cucumbers, and dressed with oil, vinegar, simple spices, and lemon—as it likely had been prepared in the Restaurant Végétarien in Paris in another world in another time.

Eva and Otto remained uncommitted to any formal religion, and they did not seek to raise their children according to the doctrines of any church. They initially explored the Ethical Culture Society, an ethical, educational, and religious movement in America premised on the belief (consistent with that of the ISK) that learning to live in accordance with ethical principles is necessary to lead a meaningful life. They may have read about Albert Einstein's comment on the seventy-fifth anniversary of the New York Society for Ethical Culture in 1952 that the idea of "ethical culture" embodied his personal conception of what is most valuable and enduring in religious idealism. Einstein observed that "without 'ethical culture' there is no salvation for humanity."[7] For a brief period, the young family attended Sunday meetings of the Ethical Culture Society of Los Angeles.

At the urging of a neighbor, Eva began playing the organ at the local Methodist church, and the family attended some services there, especially to hear music on Easter and Christmas. Then for several years the family attended services at the local Unitarian church, whose members in the Unitarian Service Committee had made extraordinary contributions to rescue and relief work for refugees in France and Portugal during the war.[8] The Quaker religion was also interesting to Eva and Otto, and for a brief period the family attended services at a local Quaker church.

But regular churchgoing never took hold. It became clear to their children over time that Eva's and Otto's true religion was the love and hope they drew from the miracles and beauty of nature and the capacity of human beings to reason; to create art, literature and music; and to help others. Despite (or because of) the events that had shaped their early lives, they held onto the belief that the good in humanity could and would prevail over the evil. They believed in the existence of a God as creator of the miracles of nature and life, but they could not accept all of the doctrines of any formal religion.

Eva and Otto celebrated Christmas. It was a special holiday for the young family: the pine fragrance of the Christmas tree fully decorated in the living room, the fire in the fireplace on Christmas morning, the anticipation of gifts, and the music—the beautiful carols with themes of peace on earth, love, and hope. Money was always scarce, and gifts were few but carefully chosen, often hand-crafted by Otto. As evidenced by Eva's prior writings, Christmas and the year-end were times for reflection, gratitude, and hope for the future.

The two refugee couples who had helped Eva and Otto when they arrived in California, the Vorsters and the Brooks, also had young children, and the families regularly celebrated holidays together. At the gatherings of this "extended family" of immigrants, the European parents played classical music on the piano, violin, and cello. They engaged in animated discussions about current political issues at the dinner table in their German accents, often slipping into their mother tongue. To their

young American children who eagerly left the dinner table to play outside together, all of this was part of the unusual and vaguely understood
backgrounds of their parents.[9]

Eva and Otto encouraged their children to do well in school, and
the children were all expected to pitch in with regular household chores.
The twins regularly accompanied Otto for full days of work at his shop
on Saturdays and during the summers—sweeping the sawdust on the
floors, cleaning the shop's bathroom, sanding, rolling dowels and operating the drilling machine. When the twins were at the shop, Kathy
stayed home with Eva to help her with work around the house. The three
young children observed and experienced the satisfaction that comes
with hard work.

For many years while the children were young, Otto sat on a wooden
stool in the hallway outside their bedrooms every night and played
German music on his harmonica, an instrument he had played throughout his life. He played beautifully, some lively folk songs, some delicate
classical pieces, as the three children drifted to sleep. He always ended
these "good-night songs," as he called them, with a poignant rendition
of "Taps" that he had learned in the U.S. Army.

Young family at home in the San Fernando Valley.

## Eva's visit to Germany to see her brother Erich

Eva's brother Erich had struggled to find meaningful work in America and always intended to return to Germany to assist with the rebuilding of that country. He and his wife Herta were also anxious to reunite with their son Tom (Theo), then a young man who had married in England and whom they had not seen for eight years. After visiting their son in England, they returned to Kassel, Germany, in 1947, where they had lived when forced to escape from the Gestapo in 1933. Erich then served as a devoted and highly respected judge in Kassel. He became the *Landgerichtspresident* (president of the State Court) of Hessen and a member of Hessen's Constitutional Court, and he presided over a number of trials of former Nazis.[10]

Like Eva, Erich retained his conviction that the appreciation of music and art is vital to human development. As he helped rebuild the judicial system, he also contributed to the cultural revival of Kassel. He supported the reestablishment in 1949 of the Volksbühne (People's Theater) and supervised it until his death. He worked closely with Lotte Lenya to promote the production of the European premier of one of

Kurt Weill's American musicals, *Lady in the Dark*, which opened in Kassel in May 1951 with the German title *Das Verlorene Lied* (The Lost Song). Erich was also one of the initiators and the vice chairman of the Gesellschaft Abendländischer Kunst des XX Jahrhunderts (Society for Western Art in the 20th Century) that evolved into the world-re-nowned international contempo-rary art exhibition in Kassel, the *documenta*.[11]

But Erich had suffered serious health problems while in exile. In addition to the struggle to earn a living, his years in New York were burdened by deterioration of his

Eva's brother Erich in Kassel in 1950.
COURTESY OF AdsD/FRIEDRICH-EBERT-STIFTUNG.

health, including his hospitalization and near death in 1943.[12] In the fall of 1955, Eva left her young family in California for several weeks (Kathy was nine, and the twins were seven) and returned to Germany for the first time in twenty-two years to see her ailing brother. "We both knew he was nearing the end and so did his beautiful, courageous Herta. And yet, we were able to feel joy and gratitude that we could be together once more."[13] Erich died of a heart attack on February 16, 1956, at fifty-eight years old, just five months after the closing of the first *documenta* in Kassel.

## Eva's teaching career

The first ten years in California with Eva at home and Otto working came to an abrupt end when Otto needed an emergency eye operation. He could not work for several months, and Eva suddenly needed to provide for the family. She began working night shifts on blueprints at Rocketdyne, an aerospace company, and applied to college. After her early life of struggle in the fight against the Nazis, Eva commenced her American college education at age fifty, first at a local community college and then at California State University. She earned a bachelor's degree, a teaching credential, and a master's degree.

Eva became a foreign-language teacher in public schools, where she taught students at the junior high and high school levels. She never strayed from her belief in the importance of education and embraced her role as a teacher. She later reflected:

> I don't want to talk much about my years of teaching—times have changed so much, and so have attitudes about education, that to bring my experiences into context and not seem hopelessly romantic about it, I would have to go much too far for the purpose of this writing. I do want to say, though, that I was basically very happy during those years, doing what I felt it was in my nature to do. In spite of all of the criticism that is unleashed today against our educational system, in spite of the disillusionment that so many in my profession experience, I still am convinced that education—reaching out to young people—points to one of the best long-range solutions to social problems.

It was always easy for me to relate to kids, because I basically liked and respected them, and could often anticipate and accept the many crazy detours that some had to take before knowing more or less who they were. Somehow, I never felt wasted, and often, I was so gratified about the young people's response that I thought I got more out of our relationship than the other way around. That today there is contact, and with some, friendship, with a few of these people, many years after I had been their teacher, is another of those rewards for which I am grateful.[14]

At the age of sixty-five—then the mandatory retirement age for teachers—Eva had to step down from teaching. Her students and colleagues did not want her to retire. It was difficult for her to leave teaching when she felt she still had much to give.

Eva turned again to her writing. Working on the old typewriter given to her by Maurice Abravanel in October 1940, sitting at the old desk that Otto had made for her in New York, she wrote the 1979 memoir "To Our Children." She encouraged Otto to write sections about his experiences, and she began to translate some of the important diaries and correspondence from her life in Europe in case it might become interesting, at some point, to her children and grandchildren. Eva briefly described her reason for writing the memoir:

At some point, it probably will mean something to your children, and help them come to an understanding of their own personality, by knowing something of the continuity and diversity of all the strands that made them. And to you three, with our never ending love.[15]

## Contact with Eva's family in South Africa

Eva maintained regular contact with her family in South Africa through an exchange of correspondence, birthday and holiday greetings, and observations about world events. Eva's sister Ruth visited Eva and Otto in New York shortly after the war, and Ruth visited the Pfister family in California in 1961 with one of her daughters, Charlotte. Eva's brother Rudi and his wife traveled to California years later, and Ruth's other

Eva with her sister
Ruth in New York
after the war.

daughters Yvonne and Vivian also visited. Eva and Otto traveled to
South Africa once in 1972. In addition to connecting with family, they
visited Soweto, and Eva shared with her family and friends the sadness
and despair she felt in witnessing the inhumanity of apartheid.[16]

## Contact with Otto's family in Munich

Otto's parents died in Munich, his mother in 1933 and his father in
1943. Of course, Otto had no contact with his father or his sisters
during the war. But shortly after the war ended, Otto reconnected with
his sisters by sending them packages with food and clothing they desperately needed. The son of Otto's sister Dora, Carl-Otto, wrote a letter
to Otto on April 12, 1948, in which he thanked his "Lieber Onkel"
(dear uncle) for a package they had just received from him. Carl-Otto
briefly described what he had experienced in the past five years: After
becoming a German soldier in Munich when he was seventeen years old,
he had engaged in the bitter fighting in Russia in 1944, where he was
captured and placed in a prisoner-of-war camp six hundred kilometers
east of Moscow. During the year and a half he was in the camp, he was
nearly worked and starved to death by his Russian captors. He managed
to survive and returned to Germany after the war.

Eva was hesitant to connect with Otto's family in Munich. Many years later in 1968, Eva and Otto made a trip to Europe. Eva met Carl-Otto, along with his wife Trude and their two young daughters, Sabine and Caroline. Eva was drawn to Trude's warmth and strength as a young mother, and Trude loved and admired Eva. They developed a close friendship and corresponded regularly for the rest of their lives.[17]

## A final move

In 1981, Eva and Otto moved to a retirement community in Camarillo, California, in Ventura County, about thirty miles north of the home in which they had raised their children. This was not easy for Eva, but the heat and air pollution in the San Fernando Valley had become a burden on Otto's health, and she ultimately agreed with his desire to make this change.

Soon their small condominium in Camarillo was filled with the furniture made by Otto, the familiar wood-framed prints of paintings and drawings on the walls, and the shelves of books. Otto converted the garage into a woodworking shop, with machines, clamps, planes, and carefully stored hardwoods that he used to make furniture for his children's growing families.

Camarillo became a special place for Eva and Otto's children and grandchildren to visit. The area resembled the open spaces, orchards, smells, and sounds of the family's early years in the San Fernando Valley. Eva could again buy fresh strawberries from the local farms.

## A final parting

Otto suffered a stroke in August 1985. As Eva had always done during difficult times, she began to write again, starting what would be the last of her diaries. In the initial days following his stroke, Otto was conscious but partially paralyzed. Eva and their three children were in the hospital at Otto's side. Peter told Otto that he needed to recover so he could teach Peter the Italian language as he had promised. Kathy reassured Otto that she had been watering his plants, and he mumbled that he "had been wondering about that." In her diary entry on August 21, Eva noted that "when the children say that they love him, he says: 'That is evident'—'evidentemente.'" Eva then wrote:

> When I hold his right hand, he lifts it, and kisses mine. When we leave, he says "Va bene."

These were Otto's last words before he slipped into a deep coma. Kathy, Tom, and Peter returned to their homes, and Eva stayed with Otto, watching and hoping for some sign that he could hear her. He never regained consciousness. Eva recorded her thoughts and feelings each day. Shortly before he passed away, Eva wrote this simple prayer for him:

> Lord, let him go gently through this long night.
> The days were long, but full of love, strength, and accomplishment.
> Love of family and friends, of children, of nature, of beauty, of
>     work; of poetry and music, and of history.
> Zest for living and exploring, for building and constructing
>     and improving.
> Desire for healing wounds, for alleviating suffering and hunger;
>     for human dignity and peace.
> Now the time is coming for him to rest, and for us to let him go.
> He and we need help and each other.

On September 11, Eva wrote in her diary,

> The breathing seemed less labored. His heartbeat was very fast, saw the pulse where the collarbone is. It got slower, and slower, until I did not see it anymore. I went to the nurse, not really believing what I thought I had seen. Stethoscope—nothing. Her arms around me: "He is gone." "Could this be a mistake?" They took me out where the reality struck me so hard that I could not conceive it.

The next day, Eva wrote a brief summary of Otto's life, a personal obituary for family and friends (provided in full in Appendix C). She concluded: "He was a whole man, secure in his identity; he loved people and he loved life."

Following Otto's death, Eva's health began to fail. Her loss of hearing impaired her ability to communicate with others, including her grandchildren. She worried about her capacity to remain independent. Her greatest fear was to become a burden to her children. And as she struggled

with her health and her life alone without Otto, she continued to make periodic diary entries with reflections about life and death. At times, it seems that her diary entries were again directed to Otto, the man she had met in Paris fifty years earlier who was now finally separated from her.

As Eva watched other friends grow old, infirm, and incapacitated, she recognized that the way Otto had died was a blessing. She confessed that at times when Otto was in a coma, she had wished that he could die. But she noted in her diary entry on October 2, 1985, that "every moment of seeing him warm and breathing was a gift and when it finally stopped, I did not want to believe it. I'll never forget those four weeks." And when another friend passed away after a difficult illness shortly after Otto's death, Eva wrote in her diary that she could "not help crying" and feeling for her friend's wife and daughters, and observed, "Living is hard, dying is harder, to be left behind is perhaps the hardest."

Eva was grateful that her children were able to help her through difficult times, but she had an intense desire to avoid imposing on them. In a diary entry a few months after Otto's passing, Eva described telephone calls with Kathy:

> There were some good talks with Kathy over the phone. She is unbelievably sensitive and understanding. Unfortunately, she often catches me at a low point, and so she gets the brunt of my depression or whatever it is that bothers me, and then I feel guilty to have burdened her.[18]

Eva wondered what she should do with the letters and documents they had managed to preserve from their early lives. In a diary entry on October 27, 1985, she noted that she was "trying hard to sort things out, and find[s] it very hard and slow." She added that she "came across a box of old letters (1941 etc.), Otto and me, Stern and me" and asked, "What to do with all these letters? I have no idea; don't want to throw them away yet, but eventually will probably have to, so they are not a burden for the kids."

Fortunately, she did not discard the letters. On December 11, 1985, she noted in her diary that "there were a few days where I could think more calmly and positively about our life together; grateful that we had so much, not angry that it ended." Yet she still grieved and struggled with what to do with the papers:

> But then, the emptiness comes back, and also memories that are not so good—about things I wish I had said or done when I did not, or could not. I still try to put order into all those folders, with letters and copies of a lifetime, and don't know how to go about it; what to discard, what to keep, and how.

Eva often described in her diary how much her visits with her three grown children and their young families meant to her: Kathy in Amherst, Peter in Berkeley, and Tom in Los Angeles. When Eva visited Kathy in Amherst in 1986, Kathy asked if she could do a videotaped interview of Eva's experiences of internment and escape from southern France in 1940. On July 6, 1986, Eva reflected about this interview in her diary, "I felt totally negative about it; but when I realized that it seemed to mean a great deal to her, I agreed. . . . So we did it and it was not bad at all, not self-conscious or embarrassing. At some point in their lives, it may mean something to the children and grandchildren to have that record."

In August 1986, Eva was also interviewed in her home in Camarillo for a German television documentary. Speaking in German, she responded to questions about her experiences in Camp de Gurs, her escape over the Pyrenees, and her efforts to rescue others in America with the help of Eleanor Roosevelt and as a case worker for the Emergency Rescue Committee.[19] Eva noted, "The interview went alright; but the whole thing was strenuous, and although it was a good experience, I was glad when it was over."[20] When the interviewer and camera crew had finally left she wrote, "Now I am back to my silent home. This month, with all the acute memories of Otto's going, is hard."

The fact that this interview occurred in August—one year after Otto suffered his stroke—was an added burden. As we have seen throughout Eva's life, anniversaries of important events were times of reflection for her, a seed likely planted by the death of her father when she was just eight years old. Eva noted in her diary entry on August 21, 1986, "I have just been re-reading the notes I made during Otto's illness and dying; the memory is so vivid, and so is the sadness. But I lived through this year, and now think more of Ann's baby that should come soon—hope all will be well."

Ann, the wife of Eva's son Tom, gave birth to Eva's seventh grandchild on August 25, 1986. Her final grandchild arrived in 1987. Eva's diary is full of descriptions of the joy that her eight grandchildren gave to her.

At 11 p.m. on September 10, 1986, the eve of the first anniversary of Otto's death, Eva wrote:

> The year is almost over that Otto died. I just lit a candle. Its gentle flickering makes me think, think of the last moments of his life when the pulse beat at his throat became quieter and slower, and then stopped. I also remember my childhood when mother would always have a candle on the day of Dad's death, and leave it on until it burned out. There is something peaceful about that light.
>
> Peter just called. I love him very much.
>
> At the end of the year, I begin to feel much more reconciled, and at peace. Grateful that we could be together, even when we were apart, these many years. Thankful that he had the time here [in Camarillo] which he loved; . . . the core of his being was never altered, the great love with which he embraced the children and me, and so much beside us.
>
> His dying also was gentle, and for that I am very grateful. I realize too that I am learning to be alone.

In her diary entry the following day, Eva noted that she received "a beautiful card from Kathy" and calls from Kathy and Tom, "so I was touched by all three of our kids."

## Final reflections

Even as she adjusted to Otto's death and to living alone with her increasing health limitations, Eva's mind remained active and reflective. She continued to correspond with her relatives in South Africa and Europe and with friends who had shared pieces of their past lives in Europe and in New York. From regular birthday and holiday greetings to periodic long letters, Eva's writing reflects the special closeness earned from the hard times they had shared, along with reflections on current political and social issues.

Shortly after Otto died, Eva had received a poignant note in French from Gaby Cordier expressing her feelings upon learning of Otto's death:

> I am so saddened by your news that I can't express it in words. So many memories come back, so alive, so unbelievably present that they have become part of myself, part of what I have made of my life. . . . Life was hard in those times, in the historical context. But how happy we were about the deep understanding among us![21]

In a lengthy diary entry two years later, on January 28, 1987, Eva sadly reported that she had received news of Gaby's death. Eva wrote:

> We had known Gaby well during those years in Paris 1933 to 1938, and kept in touch by letters, although only intermittently. Once, we visited her in Paris. . . . We had lunch at what had been the Restaurant Végétarien—now a Chinese restaurant. . . . Our meetings were brief, reluctant to pick up on what had been. But it was good to see her again.

After describing Gaby's anti-Nazi work together with Eva in Paris, Eva noted that Gaby and Eva's younger brother Hans had fallen in love during those years in Paris and that Gaby had become pregnant. Eva explained that Gaby had an abortion because she and Hans shared "their absolute determination that under the circumstances in which they and we all lived, she could not have the child." Eva lamented, "I can never forget her hopelessness and quiet suffering about that decision. I felt with her, yet no one had any doubt then that it was the right decision."

Eva then explained that following the Nazi invasion of France in 1940, Gaby had been able to "help many to escape from the occupied zone to Vichy France, often at great risk for her life," because she was Swiss and remained free to travel in France. Eva described how Gaby had helped Otto escape from occupied Paris to unoccupied southern France and reflected on the impact of the brief intimacy between Gaby and Otto at that time:

> She met Otto again after he had gotten out of the Prisoner-of-War camp in Germany and arrived in Paris to find that I and almost all of our friends were gone. He had to get out into the unoccupied zone. Gaby took him across [the demarcation line] in the middle of one night, and it was a miracle that they were successful. In the ensuing exhilaration about the freedom that now was theirs, a great closeness flared up between them, and thankfulness. But also bad, sad feelings toward me, and what their closeness would mean to me when they would tell me about it.
>
> I was able to accept this when much later they told me about it. And that is one of the things in my past about which I feel good—that petty bitterness did not destroy me and our relationship.
>
> Another thing for which I am grateful is that, much later when Otto got so desperately ill, I wrote to Gaby about it, and our correspondence which had been there, but over long intervals, became much more solid during the last years and months of her life. Now that she is gone, that feeling of not having to be sorry over neglecting a dear friend means much to me.[22]

Eva's diary includes comments about books she had recently read, noting that Kathy had suggested many of them. Eva also contributed to an article commemorating her friend, Marie Juchacz. Eva wrote about the struggle of attempting to be "a woman and a mother who could not be satisfied with a fulfilled life of her own, but who . . . worked for a place in society for all who suffered injustice."[23]

Eva never lost her idealism and hope for world peace. In a diary
entry on November 25, 1985, she wrote:

> I went to a Public Issues Forum . . . and that turned out to
> be the most uplifting evening I have spent in a long time. A
> film was shown made by a group World Beyond War, filmed
> simultaneously in Moscow and in San Francisco; and what
> the speakers (leading cardiologists in Moscow and at Harvard
> Medical School) said, how they looked, the Russian and the
> American audience—beautiful and concerned faces, a Russian
> and an American children's choir—all of that said more than
> any preaching and harangue could do that we are all one—one
> people, one world—and that we all will learn to live together,
> or we'll die together.
>
> It was as simple as that, totally un-hysterical and it inspired
> hope. I have felt for a long time that with the means of de-
> struction at hand, war has become obsolete, and have said that
> sometimes, always feeling timidly right, yet perhaps too naïve
> and unsophisticated. Now to hear that view expressed calmly by
> noted, competent people who seem determined to spread this
> truth, was an inspiration to me.
>
> I would so have wished that Otto could have shared that
> evening with me.

In a diary entry on January 28, 1987, Eva commented that she had
reread her 1979 memoir. She observed that it is meaningful "only in a
very limited way" and added, "Since I had wanted to be factual, not too
personal, not sentimental, it is in parts rather barren, should perhaps
be 'fleshed out.'"

Eva died abruptly on May 9, 1991, in a car accident after apparently
suffering a heart attack while driving. No one else was injured. She was
eighty-one. Eva had written and spoken openly to her children about her
belief that death is part of life, that she accepted this and was comfortable
with it. She loved the drawings of the German artist Käthe Kollwitz. In

the year before she died, Eva asked Tom and Kathy to read a letter from a book of letters written by Kollwitz to her children. Kollwitz wrote:

> Do not misunderstand what I am writing today and do not think me ungrateful; but I must say this to you: my deepest desire is no longer to live. I know that many people grow older than I, but everyone knows when the desire to lay aside his life has come to him. For me it has come. The fact that I may or may not be able to stay here a while does not change that. Leaving you two, you and your children, will be terribly hard for me. But the unquenchable longing for death remains. If only you could make up your minds to take me in your arms once more, and then let me go. How grateful I would be. Do not be frightened and do not try to talk me out of it. I bless my life, which has given me such an infinitude of good along with all its hardships. Nor have I wasted it; I have used what strength I had to the best of my ability. All I ask of you now is to let me go—my time is up. I could add much more to this, and no doubt you will say that I am not yet done for, that I can write quite well and my memory is still clear. Nevertheless, the longing for death remains. . . . The desire, the unquenchable longing for death remains. I shall close now, dear children. I thank you with all my heart.[24]

Tom told his mother that he thought the passage was depressing. Eva assured him that it was not.

Death is part of life. After the winter comes the spring. In describing her first encounter with Otto at the Restaurant Végétarien in Paris in 1935, Eva noted that they both loved the poet Rilke. It is fitting to close this epilogue with Rilke's words:

Spring has come again. The earth
is like a child that knows poems by heart,
many, o . . . . For the vexation
of long learning she gets the prize.
Her teacher was strict. We liked the white
in the old man's beard.
And now we may ask what the green, the blue
is called: She knows it, she knows!
Earth, having holiday, lucky earth, play
now with the children. We want to catch you,
happy earth. The happiest will succeed.
O, what her teacher taught her, the many things,
and what stands printed in roots and long
difficult stems: She sings it, she sings.[25]

# Afterword

Our learning process while researching and writing this book produced a number of "stories within the story"—about how we learned of information that was not known to our parents or, for reasons we believe we now understand, our parents chose not to tell us. These discoveries differed in gravity and impact on us. Each was a meaningful surprise.

## Otto's anti-Hitler gramophone recording in 1936

Our parents told us that our father had been involved in distributing anti-Nazi literature while working with the Internationaler Sozialistischer Kampfbund (ISK) in Paris. We recall our father telling us, when we were very young, that some of the anti-Nazi material was on paper so thin that it could be swallowed if he were captured. In fact, Otto had retained some of that delicate paper, and he would carefully unfold it to show us how thin it was. As children, we were intrigued with the idea that our father would have had to eat secret papers to avoid getting caught by the Nazis.

In the course of our research, Peter discovered that Otto's voice was used on anti-Hitler phonograph recordings produced by the ISK in Paris and smuggled into Germany. We were able to obtain the transcript of one of these recordings from historian Ursula Langkau-Alex, a senior research fellow at the International Institute of Social History in Amsterdam. As described in Chapter 7, the recording strongly encouraged Germans to vote "no" in the March 29, 1936, referendum in which Hitler sought ratification of the military occupation of the Rhineland.

We were also able to obtain a digital recording of the actual *sound* of this gramophone recording that has been preserved in the Bundesarchiv in Koblenz, Germany. It was stunning for the three of us to listen to the clearly recognizable voice of our father on this recording, predicting in 1936 that the result of Hitler's aggression and provocations "can only be war" and that Hitler "will rattle his saber so long that he will unleash a world conflagration." It was also sobering for us to learn that the Nazis considered this recording to be an act of high treason, adding to the danger that Otto faced when he was captured by the Nazis in May 1940.

## Otto's anti-Nazi sabotage work during the Drôle de Guerre

We knew from our parents that Otto was taking some kind of anti-Nazi materials to Luxembourg on May 9, 1940, and was captured by the Nazis when they invaded the following morning. Because our parents told us that Otto had been involved in distributing anti-Nazi literature while working with ISK members in Paris, we assumed that he was making the trip on May 9 for that purpose.

But we never asked our parents for answers to any of the following questions: What had our father done in continuing to work against the Nazis after his release from French internment at the beginning of February 1940? Who was he meeting in Luxembourg on that trip of May 9? What was he was delivering? Why was he in such serious danger if he fell into the hands of the Nazis?

During our research, Peter found a chapter in a book by Jef Rens, a Belgian labor leader, titled "René Bertholet et Otto Pfister."[1] Rens described his encounters with Otto and René Bertholet as being "among the most unique that I had in my life."[2] We were shocked when we read Peter's translation of Rens's vivid description of his first meeting with Otto in Rens's office in Brussels—a meeting in which Otto quietly opened his heavy briefcase and showed Rens the bombs.

This was an unsettling revelation for all of us. Our father had always been a gentle person, a lover of peace. We felt that our parents were open with us about their early lives in Europe, both in conversations and in their 1979 memoir. We knew that our father had participated in resistance efforts against Hitler for years in Paris, but we had never heard anything from our parents about bombs.

Much of the information presented by Rens in his book corroborated other facts we knew, but not all of it. So, we searched for more information to confirm or refute what he had written about Otto's activities during this period.

We first looked again, more closely, at the writings our parents had left for us. In an early draft of her memoir, Eva described Otto's internment by the French at the beginning of the war in September 1939. Following his release from that internment, she explained, "He *participates actively in the war against the Nazis.* He travels, sees and helps people who work against the German war machine. *Each of these trips is fraught with danger.* The last one he takes is the morning before the 'Blitzkrieg'—he is in Luxembourg and I am not to know whether he survived until much later when I am in America" (our emphasis).

We also found a brief but clear statement in a memoir written by Tom Lewinski, the son of our mother's brother Erich. Tom wrote that after being released from internment by the French, Otto took up "active sabotage work against the Germans."[3]

Why had our parents chosen not to volunteer information to us about the specific nature of our father's resistance work during this period? Perhaps they wanted to remain true to the ISK's commitment of strict confidentiality, a commitment that the group had once considered essential to the resistance work and the survival of its members. We also assume that our parents wanted to shield us from knowledge that our father had been compelled by circumstances to participate in such violent activities on behalf of the French government—even though this was during a time of openly declared war between France and Germany and the target was the Nazi war machine.

Still, it was unsettling to learn that our parents had not revealed this to us, and we wanted more information. As explained in Chapters 7 and 8, we learned more about how ISK members worked closely with the International Transport Workers Federation (ITF) in anti-Nazi resistance efforts before and during World War II. In our further research about the ISK-ITF relationship, we found numerous references to Hans Jahn as not only a leader of the ITF but also an active organizer and participant in sabotage efforts against Hitler's war machinery. Such activities, with the assistance of the ISK, increased dramatically during the Drôle de Guerre.[4]

Putting these pieces together, Peter recalled that our father had made a vague reference in the 1979 memoir to the name of the person he was going to meet on May 9 in Luxembourg. He reviewed our father's description of his May 1940 trip to Luxembourg: "*I arrived in Luxembourg, went to Hans J., unloaded my anti-Hitler material.*" "Hans J." had to be Hans Jahn, and the words "unloaded my anti-Hitler material" now had a clear and chilling meaning.

We did not have much hope of finding any contemporaneous French records of the ISK's collaboration with the ITF and the intelligence unit of the French Army, the Fifth Bureau, in their efforts to sabotage Nazi war matériel transports during the Drôle de Guerre. We assumed that any such documents would have been included in the bonfires of documents destroyed by the French government before the Nazis marched into Paris.[5]

Given that British intelligence had also been involved in these sabotage efforts by the ITF at that time, we wondered if British documents still existed with information about this activity. As explained in Chapters 8 and 25, the Special Operations Executive (SOE) was the secret British agency involved in espionage and sabotage operations before and during World War II. We discovered that many previously confidential SOE files had been released to the public in recent years and that a private British company had microfilmed many of those files. An index to these files revealed three microfilm reels relating to the ISK and its collaboration with the SOE as well as an SOE file titled "Johannes Jahn."[6] The documents in this SOE file provided vivid confirmation that Jahn was involved in blowing up German trains during this period.

## The French village that gave refuge to Eva

As described in Chapter 10, Eva's experience in the small farming village immediately after her release from Camp de Gurs in June 1940 had a strong and lasting impact on her. She was able to stay there for only two weeks, because the line of demarcation was set and the village was just within the zone to be occupied by the Nazis. However, the willingness of these poor villagers to accept her group of endangered German refugees with kindness and generosity gave her hope in the worst of times. As she explained in her 1979 memoir, Eva had not written the name of the village in her diary or correspondence (so she would not endanger the villagers) and could not recall it. This led to her comment: "If I have any regrets about things not done in my lifetime, it is that I was never able to find that little village again, and give thanks to the people, or to their children or grandchildren, who had been so unbelievably good to us."

When Kathy planned our trip to France in 2011, she had several objectives: to visit the memorial at Camp de Gurs where Eva was interned by the French government because of her German origin in May and June 1940; to visit Montauban, where Eva and others in her ISK group stayed for several months waiting for news about U.S. visas that might allow them to escape; and to hike over the Pyrenees on the same path taken at different times by Eva and Otto. But Kathy's plans were further driven by a special mission: she wanted to try to identify and visit that small village that had given refuge to Eva. If possible, she hoped to bring some resolution to the regret Eva had expressed in her 1979 memoir that she had forgotten the name of the village and had never been able to convey her gratitude to the villagers or their heirs. Kathy hoped that if we could find this village, someone might still be alive who was a child when Eva was sheltered there.

Eva's sister-in-law Herta, who had been with the group of ISK members in the village, told Eva that she believed the village was named "Senlies," but we could find no village with that name and wondered if she had meant Salies de Béarn, a town near Gurs. Kathy noticed that Salies de Béarn was also the return address on the letter Eva wrote to Stern from the village. However, Salies appeared much larger and more urban and prosperous than the small farming village that Eva described.

In a short diary entry written on June 24, 1940, during the time when she was in the village, Eva had written what appeared, on close examination, to be the letter "C" (not the letter "S") in front of the date. Because Salies de Béarn was exactly on the line of demarcation, Kathy thought it was possible that what we called the "mystery village" may have been a small village whose name began with a "C" that was in the occupied zone just west of Salies de Béarn. She obtained and reviewed detailed local maps of the area around Salies and identified several villages that fit that description. Kathy then wrote to their mayors, briefly describing our mother's history during that time and asking if they had any knowledge that could help us locate the village. Jacques Bargell, former mayor of the village of Castagnède, responded that he would be happy to meet with us when we were visiting the area.

To our amazement when we met with Jacques, he said that he had talked with various people in his village and thought that his village, Castagnède, was the one that our mother had described. Even more surprising, he told us that he had found a "witness": Rosine Fontanieu, who had lived in Castagnède all her life. Rosine remembered that when she was seven years old, a group of German women, with a few children, stayed in the village but had to leave when the Germans came. Jacques then told us that she remembered watching the women as they left the village on foot and described a specific detail: Rosine had told him that one of the women was elderly and had a broken leg and was pushed down the road in a *poussette* (baby carriage). Eva had described this same detail to us in her 1979 memoir. We were stunned. Considering the timing of the encounter (just before the arrival of the Nazis in Castagnède), the location and nature of the village, and Rosine's recollection of this group of women, we believed that we had found the village.

Jacques then took us to meet Rosine and her husband Georges in their home in Castagnède, where we sat around their beautiful wooden table and talked with Rosine about her memories. She recounted her recollections of that time as a seven-year-old, including her memory of the elderly woman in the *poussette.* Rosine said she always wondered what had happened to the women after they left Castagnède. She remembered that the people in the village wept when the group left—and, for very different reasons, wept again when the Germans arrived soon thereafter.

So, on September 25, 2011, sitting together in Rosine's home in the French countryside seventy-one years after our mother had found refuge in her small village, we were able to convey to her the gratitude that Eva had never been able to communicate herself.

Our trip to southern France in 2011 also allowed us to visualize the places referred to in our parents' writings: the memorial at Camp du Gurs, with its replica of the grim barracks contrasting sharply with the beauty of the countryside and the Pyrenees rising in the background; the train station and graceful bridges over the Tarn River in Montauban; and the "little border town," Banyuls sur Mer, from where Eva and Otto both began their separate escapes over the Pyrenees. And our hike together

Tom, Kathy, and Peter on the trail over the Pyrenees in 2011.

over the Pyrenees allowed us to see the "vineyards and mounts of olive trees without end, and unbelievably blue ocean" as described by Eva in her account of her crossing. Having made the strenuous hike ourselves over the roughly marked trail now named for Walter Benjamin, we could see and feel the "brilliant early morning," the "top of the mountain," the "thorny bushes, the rocks" that both of our parents had experienced under such different circumstances over sixty years earlier.[7]

## FOIA requests for records about the granting of U.S. visas to Eva and Otto

On our behalf, Tom sought records about our parents from various U.S. government agencies under the Freedom of Information Act (FOIA). The process was frustrating at best. In essence, the initial agency responses advised us that no such records could be located. We therefore had to pursue several administrative appeals.

A ruling on one of the FOIA appeals directed the FBI to conduct a further search for the documents we requested. The FBI in turn directed other agencies to search again for the requested records. Ultimately, we were able to obtain copies of a number of important documents about the granting of Eva's visa that we had not found elsewhere.[8]

Our discovery of records pertaining to the government's consideration of Otto's visa case was especially difficult. Eva had retained in her files a copy of a letter with some intriguing information about the process involved in the U.S. government's consideration of Otto's visa application. That letter, dated January 22, 1941, was from Undersecretary of State Sumner Welles to Eleanor Roosevelt's secretary, Malvina Thompson. As explained in Chapter 21, it revealed that Otto's case had been reviewed by an Inter-Departmental Committee composed of five different U.S. agencies. Referring to this letter in our initial FOIA requests, we sought records from each of the agencies comprising this committee. Initial responses to these requests advised us that no such records existed or that if they existed, they had either been destroyed or could not be located.

After several administrative appeals and thanks to the help of Mary Kay Schmidt of the National Archives, we finally received a copy of the minutes of the meeting in which the committee reviewed Otto's case. Those minutes explained the committee's suspicions about the credibility of Otto's story of his capture and release by the Nazis and directed that Otto be interviewed again by the U.S. consul in Marseille.

As explained in Chapter 21, it is difficult to understand the delays of the American consul in Marseille in following the direction of Welles to conduct an "expedited" examination of Otto and report by telegram back to the State Department. Based on Otto's correspondence to Eva, it is apparent that someone in Marseille was either negligently or intentionally delaying that process. We were eager to obtain any records about the further examination of our father by the U.S. consul in Marseille, the report of that examination to the State Department, and the further consideration of his case by the Inter-Departmental Committee.

Index cards were ultimately produced in response to our FOIA appeals that identified telegrams between the Marseille consul and the State Department that likely would have helped explain the reason for these delays. Those telegrams also would have identified the official (or officials) at the Marseille consul who interviewed Otto. To our disappointment, however, the telegrams themselves could not be located and apparently were destroyed by the State Department and/or the FBI. The National Archives informed us that the FBI had "thoroughly 'weeded' the files some years ago."[9]

Finally, our pursuit of administrative appeals under FOIA resulted in the release of the disturbing records described in Chapter 26 about

Eva's application for an extension of her visa in 1943—in which the State Department's representative urged the denial of her application based on the false accusation that she was a "rabid Communist"—as well as release of later records about the granting of her application for U.S. citizenship in 1946.

## The identity of "Eva" in the René-Eva correspondence

After our discovery of the information about our father's participation with René Bertholet in the effort to sabotage Nazi trains during the Drôle de Guerre, we continued to be intrigued with Bertholet and his work with our parents. In a book by Susan Subak, *Rescue & Flight: American Relief Workers Who Defied the Nazis,* we found a passage—and a key footnote—that led to our discovery about Eva's work with Bertholet and the Office of Strategic Services (OSS) in New York during the war.[10] Dr. Subak described Bertholet and referred to his contact in New York known as "Eva":

> [Daniel Bénédite's][11] link with the New York office was the bold operative René Bertholet, OSS code number 328. Bertholet had been an acquaintance of Varian Fry, and upon his return to New York, Fry had relayed to U.S. Government contacts the idea that Bertholet could be a very useful source to them. . . . René Bertholet and his wife Hannah . . . concerned themselves with developing a large information network from their base in Bern with resistance and labor groups in France and elsewhere. In their large network, they had a particularly key friend in New York known as "Eva." Eva was in touch with the OSS and may have been on the staff, but her or his identity was highly secret. . . . Allen Dulles considered René Bertholet's information absolutely vital and was willing to use OSS codes to send letters and cables back and forth between "René" and "Eva."[12]

Our suspicion that "Eva" might be our mother was heightened by Subak's further speculation about her identity in a footnote:

> "Eva" may have been German but certainly was comfortable in the French language and used it for correspondence. The person

. . . may have been Eva Wasserman, who worked for a time at the International Rescue and Relief Committee office in New York. . . . It is also possible that Eva was Eva Levinski [*sic*], who worked with Toni Sender and Dyno Loewenstein in advising the labor division of the OSS.[13]

Subak based her speculation that "Eva" might be our mother on the memorandum that was jointly submitted by Toni Sender and others, including Eva Lewinski, to Allen Dulles on May 27, 1942 (the Sender Memorandum described in Chapter 25), and the source she cited for the existence of that memorandum was a book by Dr. Christof Mauch, *The Shadow War against Hitler*.[14]

Mauch's book provided further important hints but no clear answers. Mauch furnished helpful background on the formation by the OSS in 1942 of the Labor Section, headed by Arthur Goldberg, and explained the nature of the Sender Memorandum.[15] He noted that the goals of the Office of European Labor Research were described in the Sender Memorandum and cited the specific locations in the National Archives where the Sender Memorandum and related documents were located.[16] Mauch also referred to "Agent 328," who was providing critical secret intelligence information to the Allies at the end of 1944. He acknowledged that he did not know the identity of Agent 328 but guessed that it might be René Bertholet.[17]

A book written by historian Neal Petersen, *From Hitler's Doorstep: The Wartime Intelligence Reports of Allen Dulles, 1942–1945*, contains many references to secret wartime correspondence between "328" and "Eva." Petersen's book is essentially a reproduction of actual messages based primarily on the operational records of the OSS (Record Group 226) at the National Archives that had recently been declassified. Messages in Petersen's book referring to "Eva" and "328" shed some light on the extent and duration of this correspondence and the nature of the information exchanged. But Petersen never identified the "Eva" in this correspondence.

We contacted Dr. Mauch and advised him of our research into our parents' early lives and our review of their papers. We asked if he might have retained the Sender Memorandum and other records from the OSS files that he had gathered in his research. While we were in southern France on our trip in 2011, we received an e-mail message from Dr. Mauch that contained both bad news and good news. The bad news was that he no longer had copies of the extensive OSS documents he had obtained in his research for his book, and researching the OSS files would be "very, very difficult, almost impossible." The good news was that Dr. Mauch confirmed from his recollection of the documents that our mother was the "Eva" in the OSS records and that she was corresponding regularly with René Bertholet. He explained in his e-mail:

> I remember the name Eva Lewinski Pfister very well from many records. Usually only a code name was given or Eva Lewinski was just called Eva. And yes, there are telegrams and messages going back and forth to René Bertholet. I think Eva was a key figure in the whole network of Dulles' more labor-oriented informants.

Dr. Mauch also made the following observations about our parents:

> You absolutely have to keep the records of your parents. This is so important. . . . How sad I never got to know them—I did an OSS oral history project in the 1990s, and what a pity I could not keep the records. . . . At any rate: you can be very proud of your parents, very proud. They were among the best anti-Nazis. . . . They were good people. If only there had been more around like them.

So we now knew that Dr. Mauch believed that "Eva" was our mother and that "328" was Bertholet. But we still wanted to obtain OSS records from the National Archives that would confirm this. We contacted Susan Subak and explained our parents' background and our recent discoveries regarding our mother's involvement with the OSS—including the references we had found in her book, *Rescue & Flight*. Dr. Subak graciously agreed to review the OSS documents from her prior research files and undertake further research for us of the OSS records at the National Archives.

In a memorable e-mail message, Dr. Subak sent us a preliminary report on her research. She attached some key OSS documents she had found that referred to Eva Lewinski and stated: "I have no shadow of a doubt that 'Eva' is your mother."

This research from the OSS files caused us to probe into the possibility of also finding previously classified records from the Special

Operations Executive (SOE) about Bertholet's role in providing similar information to the SOE through ISK leader Willi Eichler in London. That led to our further discovery of a treasure of recently declassified files of the SOE.

In reviewing these SOE files on microfilm at the Cecil H. Green Library at Stanford University, we not only found many examples of what we have described as the Robert-Eclair correspondence in Chapter 25 but also discovered the crucial letter from Eva to Eichler in which she defended her involvement with the OSS by describing the genesis of that secret arrangement.

## Further reflections about the ISK

The core belief of the ISK was that a good life could not be lived unless one is fully committed to helping others in greater need. That belief, based on reason and ethics, produced an organization of remarkable individuals—of Jewish and non-Jewish origin—who were willing to sacrifice their personal comfort and safety to engage in an early and active fight against the evil of Nazism. In that sense, the ISK is a remarkable example of German resistance and human goodness during a time when so many people and organizations turned their heads away from evil until it was too late for the millions who perished.

We have described the nature of our parents' work with the ISK largely through their own writings. We had heard bits and pieces from them about the ISK. We knew that Eva had been involved with the group from a very young age and that Otto began working with the ISK after they met in Paris in 1935.

We also sensed that our mother had deeply ambivalent feelings toward the ISK and some of its most basic tenets, though she never discussed with us in detail the group or her disagreements with it—nor did we know enough to inquire. It seemed that issues surrounding the ISK had a powerful effect on our mother, but we were not sure how or why. In our quest for a better understanding of our parents and those times, we learned more about both the ISK and Eva's relationship with it. In that process, we discovered the tensions between Eva and the ISK and found them to have been far more difficult than we had imagined.

Most important, we discovered the correspondence between our mother and Willi Eichler in the archives of the Friedrich-Ebert-Stiftung

in Bonn that revealed (after identifying the many pseudonyms) how
Eichler had criticized Eva for her decision to marry Otto and how she
defended that decision. We also discovered how Eichler sought to control Eva's involvement with the OSS. The strain in her relationship with
Eichler was part of a much deeper tension between our mother and some
of the ISK's principles and personal demands that she ultimately rejected.

We also learned that Eva was not the only devoted ISK member
to be criticized for questioning the ISK's leadership. For example, Paul
Bonart and his wife Bertha were expelled from the ISK in 1938 after they
criticized Eichler for failing to recognize the increasing dangers faced by
ISK members who remained in Germany. Bonart, a German of non-Jewish heritage who was married to a member of the ISK, had remained in
Germany after 1933 and participated in the ISK's anti-Nazi work there.
He was among those who were imprisoned by the Nazis and successfully
resisted Nazi pressure to provide information about ISK members. As
the danger from Hitler's terror apparatus increased, Bonart and his wife
were able to escape from Germany, first to Paris and ultimately to the
United States. While in Paris in early 1938, Bonart and his wife tried to
convince Eichler that the ISK's resistance work in Germany had become
futile and fatally dangerous to ISK members.[18]

According to Bonart, Eichler was deeply disappointed in the critical report that he and his wife presented at that time in Paris. Eichler
found it unacceptable that they were giving up on the ISK's basic strategy—which was to continue working with the network of ISK members in Germany to develop effective protests, resistance, and ultimate
revolt by the Germans against Hitler. Bonart acknowledged that there
"was no doubt in Bertha's or my mind that Willi and his friends had
dedicated their lives to the defeat of Hitler." But Bonart questioned why
Eichler was so critical of him and Bertha when they had never questioned Eichler's personal integrity and commitment.[19] Bonart described
the pain felt by his wife, who had dedicated years of her young life to
the ISK: "The rejection by her closest friends, the accusation of being
disloyal, depressed her deeply. It took her more than a year to find a new
direction and meaning for her life."[20] Yet, despite this negative personal
experience with the ISK, Bonart retained the highest regard for the ISK:

> In spite of its flaws, the ISK attracted hundreds of the most
> dedicated, ethically committed, and courageous human be-
> ings I have ever known. After the war, most of them returned

to Germany and joined the Social Democrats in the task of rebuilding the country. They held positions as elected representatives of Federal and State Governments, mayors, newspaper editors, writers and educators. It is safe to say that all of them were highly intelligent, honest, and committed public servants.[21]

Bonart was right about the contributions of ISK members after the war. To take a few examples, we previously described the work of Eva's brother Erich as a judge and patron of the arts in postwar Germany. Willi Eichler returned from England to Germany in 1946 and he helped to rebuild the postwar Social Democratic Party (SPD). Eichler served as a member of the Bundestag from 1949 to 1953 and as a member of the SPD's Executive Committee for over twenty years. He was one of the leading contributors to the development of the Godesberg Program, the SPD's new platform that was ratified at an SPD convention in the town of Bad Godesberg (now part of the city of Bonn) in 1959.[22] Eichler also continued his publishing work, founding the magazine *Geist und Tat* (Spirit and Action) and serving as its editor until his death in Bonn in 1971.

After the war, René Bertholet quietly devoted the rest of his life to helping those in need. He continued his relief work in Europe as people struggled to survive in the rubble of war. In 1949 he moved to Brazil, where for the next twenty years he worked with poor communities. He first participated in the creation of a colony of five hundred landless people in Paraná, Guarapuava, and then established a cooperative in Pindorama, Alagoas. Bertholet died in 1969 at the age of sixty-two.

In the fall of 1945, Minna Specht was the only German invited to attend an international conference in Zurich on the plight of children suffering in the wake of the war. In 1946 she returned to Germany, where she headed a private school until 1951. She also became a member of the German Commission for UNESCO and worked with the pedagogical institute of UNESCO in Hamburg. Together with Martha Friedländler, Specht also edited a pedagogical publication that offered alternatives to Nazi-era authoritarian approaches to the raising and education of children. Specht died in 1961.

Tom Lewinski, the son of Erich and Herta who had been separated from his parents throughout the war because of their total commitment to the ISK, was able to overcome that adversity and had a successful life with his family in England. But his separation from his parents was a poignant example of the personal cost of dedication to the ISK. In his brief tribute in the postscript to his book about his father, he wrote:

> My father Erich Lewinski was an extraordinary man. If I have misjudged him, that is because I did not really know him, that is because at several crucial periods of our lives his priorities lay in other directions.
>
> There are many who cannot see the wood for the trees. There are also those who see the wood very clearly, but fail to recognize the individual trees.

We know how Eva struggled with the consequences of her choice to engage in rescue and relief work in New York for others in dire need, consistent with her commitment to the principles of the ISK, rather than seeking a better-paying job that would allow her to assist her ailing mother in South Africa. As Eva was aware, that choice imposed a huge burden on her brother Ernst and sister Ruth, who struggled to make ends meet and sacrificed much to care for their mother. As a young woman in Germany, Eva did not like Ernst's focus on material success. Such a focus seemed inconsistent with the ISK's basic premise that a meaningful life required an active commitment to ease the suffering of the many in need. But Eva later came to appreciate deeply how people such as Ernst and Ruth, who did not devote their lives to an attempt to remedy injustice in the world, endured great personal sacrifices to help those in need who were closest to them.

Finally, we cannot ignore other unsettling aspects about the ISK's political philosophy that stretch beyond the scope of this book. For example, the ISK's view of the need to educate an elite group of political leaders—rigorously trained to make ethical decisions for others through reason and Socratic dialogue—is fundamentally inconsistent with a belief in the ability of all people, whatever their education and training, to make proper political decisions by exercising their right to vote.[23] To ISK members in the 1930s, the electoral victories of Hitler's Nazi Party confirmed their views of the dangers of democratic decision-making—but Hitler's assumption of power was due to many other factors, including weak democratic institutions and traditions in Germany at that time that were unable to provide a check against Hitler's assumption and abuse of power.

Despite the profound flaws of the ISK, we have not come across anyone—among our parents, other ISK members, other socialist groups at the time, and even individuals at high levels in the intelligence services of the United States and England—who was not impressed by the intelligence, ethics, idealism, trustworthiness, and profound courage of these ISK members. That is both high praise and high caution. Even the best of people and intentions can be blind to some truths and can cause pain. The ISK must ultimately be judged in the light of the group's impact on the fight against Nazism and on the personal lives of its members—a subject that is worthy of further historical study and reflection.[24]

## A palette of grays

There is much to be learned from all of this, and the lessons are not simple. Eva and Otto met at a time when the extremes on both sides of the political spectrum viewed complex human problems in simplistic and extreme terms, producing unparalleled human suffering. Their story reveals the complexities confronting those who seek to understand the truth and to live ethical and meaningful lives.

In addition to exposing complexities in evaluating the ISK, the story of Eva and Otto reveals the dramatically different faces of America at that time. America was a place of asylum and freedom for a small number of endangered refugees who, like Eva and Otto, were offered opportunities in America that were unheard of in Europe. But it was also a nation that shut its doors to the multitude of Jewish and non-Jewish political refugees who lost their lives in Nazi death camps. We see the selfless assistance of American citizens and groups, including Dorothy Hill, Paul Benjamin, the Jewish Labor Committee, the American Federation of Labor, and the Emergency Rescue Committee. We see how First Lady Eleanor Roosevelt and government officials such as Eliot Coulter and Hiram Bingham used their power and influence to assist refugees despite an environment of understandable wartime fear. But the story also exposes U.S. government officials who did whatever they could to oppose and resist efforts to rescue endangered victims of Nazi persecution.

We also see the different faces of France during the war. On one hand, it was the country of refuge for those political opponents of Hitler who had to escape from Germany after 1933 and from Austria and

Czechoslovakia in 1938. It was the small village in southern France and the welcoming city of Montauban that provided shelter and safety for Eva and her small group after their release from Camp de Gurs. And it was the French resistance fighters throughout the war. On the other hand, France was also the country that interned Eva and other refugees in the Vel' d'Hiv and Gurs and was complicit with the horrors of the Vichy government's roundups and deportations of Jews to the Nazi death camps.

And we see the vastly different faces of Germany before and during the war. We know all too well the unmitigated evil of Hitler and of the many Germans who eagerly followed his descent into inhumanity. We also know that there were some Germans, Jewish and non-Jewish, who committed their lives to *actively* opposing Hitler and that they did so knowing that they faced the real risk of imprisonment or death after 1933. We will forever struggle in assessing the responsibility of those Germans who opposed Hitler but did not actively resist because they feared the consequences of such resistance for themselves and their families. And we cannot help considering the moral culpability of German children who grew up in the 1930s, such as our cousin Carl-Otto, and were conscripted as teenagers to fight for the Third Reich.

We must also grapple with unsettling questions about personal decisions and their consequences: What if Otto had not decided to leave Munich in 1920 to live in Rome? Hitler's early political successes were in Munich. He appealed to a population that was struggling with the humiliation of its defeat in World War I and with the burden of reparations and economic hardship. As a poor young worker who was frustrated because he could not pursue his education and a better life, how would Otto have reacted to the rise of Nazism if he had stayed in Munich? Of course, we can never know the answer, because Otto's move to Italy and then to France transformed him. It opened up his world.

Other personal decisions also had enormous consequences: Eva's decision to join the ISK and her later wrenching decision to escape to America so she could rescue others, Eva and Otto's decisions to have a child against the rules of the ISK, Otto's decision to accept the request that he join the U.S. Army and return to Europe with the OSS, and Eva and Otto's decision to remain in America after the war. To what extent were these decisions compelled by events beyond their control, and to what extent were they creating their own destinies?

Most important, however, we draw strength from seeing in the story of Eva and Otto a meaningful triumph of love, reason, and courage in an era of unprecedented hatred and brutality.

Examining the infinite hues of gray in seeking to understand the large and small riddles of life is a formidable challenge but also offers infinite beauty. In Otto's February 12, 1941, letter to Eva, when he was still stranded in southern France and Eva was in New York, he included a poem by Rainer Maria Rilke. That poem, translated from French, refers to the color gray:

> Along the dusty path
> The green becomes almost gray.
> But this gray, only slightly,
> Has in it shades of silver and blue.[25]

Mindful of the humility exemplified by our parents' entire lives, we submit that the story of Eva and Otto, when carefully examined, reveals unusual levels of meaning and beauty.

# Acknowledgments

Many have assisted and encouraged us along the way. We give special thanks to those who spent hours reviewing early drafts of the manuscript and provided thoughtful comments. They include Judge William Alsup, Richard Gabriele, Terence Renaud, Marshall Small, and Susan Subak.

Scholars who had done related research and writing also graciously and generously assisted us. Dr. Subak had written a fascinating book, *Rescue & Flight: American Relief Workers Who Defied the Nazis,* that gave us important clues about Eva's secret role with the Office of Strategic Services (OSS). Dr. Subak then helped us with further research on this issue at the National Archives. Jack Jacobs, professor of political science at John Jay College and the CUNY Graduate Center, shared documents he had gathered in his research and writing about the role of the Jewish Labor Committee in rescuing political refugees and about experiences of women refugees in exile, including Eva. Historian Christof Mauch provided encouraging responses to our inquiries about Eva's role with the OSS. Marion Kaplan, Skirball Professor of Modern Jewish History at New York University, reviewed our book proposal and excerpts from our manuscript and provided insights and warm encouragement. Documentary filmmaker Pierre Sauvage shared information on his project about Varian Fry's efforts to rescue endangered refugees in Marseille. Scholar John F. Sears, who is currently writing a book, *Eleanor Roosevelt, Refugees, and the Founding of Israel,* invited us to his home in western Massachusetts, where we exchanged documents about Eva's contacts with Mrs. Roosevelt. And Michael D. Jackson, visiting professor at Harvard Divinity School who wrote a moving article about Walter Benjamin's ill-fated attempt to escape over the Pyrenees in 1940, helped

445

prepare us for our own hike on the same trail in 2011 and encouraged us as our project progressed.

A number of individuals at archives and libraries helped us with our research. Mary Kay Schmidt at the National Archives was the key to our ultimate success in obtaining important records we requested under the Freedom of Information Act. Sabine Kneib of the Friedrich-Ebert-Stiftung (FES) in Bonn, Germany, located files with correspondence involving Eva. She also helped arrange a meeting for us in Bonn with Karl-Heinz Klär, who had previously done research at the FES about the Internationaler Sozialistischer Kampfbund. We thank Claude Laharie and André Laufer of the Amicale du Camp de Gurs for their input in response to our inquiries about the history of the camp, for publishing the French translation of our article about Eva's experience at Camp de Gurs in the *Bulletin de l'Amicale*, and for posting the article on the Amicale's website. Finally, Jodi Boyle helped make our review of the Emergency Rescue Committee's early files at the M. E. Grenander Department of Special Collections & Archives at SUNY–Albany productive and enjoyable.

We thank Tom Brokaw for his interest in the story of Eva and Otto and for reviewing the manuscript. Tom's family has a long association with the International Rescue Committee (formerly the Emergency Rescue Committee) that continues to perform vital work for endangered refugees throughout the world. We also thank Carol Larson for reviewing the manuscript and sharing her thoughts about Eva, her former high school teacher.

Kathy's close friend Betsy Hartmann, author of several books and professor emerita at Hampshire College, gave us valuable advice about the daunting process of seeking to publish this story. We are also grateful for the feedback and encouragement we received from other friends and colleagues of each of us including Rob Barrett, Nancy Bekavac, Jim Boyce, Terry Bridges, Vincent Brook, Megan Callaway, John Crewdson, Joyce Duncan, Marlena Ekstein, James Garrett, Sam Gladstone, Melvin Goldman, Paul Goldstein, Marie-Hélène and Scott Hammen, Ann Craig Hanson, Heidi and Jeff Jacobs, Shirley and Gary Lange, Natasha (Vorster) and Joe Levine, Heija Martin, Jennie McKenna, Davina Miller, Michael Odenheimer, Greg and Candace Osborn, Barbara Pearson, Rosalind Pollan, Patty Ramsey, Paul Roberts, Patricia Romney, Ken

Schoen, Renee Spring, Janet Taft, Jim Wald, Gerry Weiss, Paul Wiley, and Bob Wynn.

Our primary goal from the beginning of this project was to preserve the story of our parents' early lives so it will be available to scholars, teachers, students, and general readers. We are therefore deeply indebted to the two institutions that have made it possible for us to achieve that goal: the Purdue University Press for deciding to publish this book and the U.S. Holocaust Memorial Museum for agreeing to preserve our parents' papers and make them accessible for future research. Our heart-felt thanks go to Justin Race, Katherine Purple, Kelley Kimm, Chris Brannan, and Susan Wegener of the Purdue University Press for their in-variably thoughtful and responsive input as we worked our way through the publishing process. And we are grateful for the time and sensitive input of Judy Cohen, Grace Cohen Grossman, Rebecca Erbelding, Sara Bloomfield, and others at the U.S. Holocaust Memorial Museum who encouraged us to preserve our parents' papers and their story.

We received loving encouragement from our extended family in South Africa: our cousins Yvonne, Vivian, and Charlotte (daughters of Eva's sister Ruth). Our cousin Tom in England (the son of Eva's brother Erich) inspired us with his strong interest in our project but sadly passed away before it could be completed; his daughter Kay has provided her support and encouragement throughout. And we thank our cousin Carl-Otto (the son of one of Otto's sisters) and his loving wife Trude for their deep interest in and support of our work. Sadly, they both passed away in Munich while we were working on this project, but their daughters, Sabine and Caroline, carry forward their love and respect for Eva and Otto.

Finally, we thank Kathy's husband Neil, Peter's wife Bonnie, and Tom's wife Ann for their substantive input on the manuscript and their encouragement and patience throughout. We thank Tom's son Ben for his time and expertise in providing technical assistance for our prepa-ration of the manuscript. And we thank all of our children, Ben, Dan, Eliza, Franklin, Julia, Monica, Sam and Tim, for understanding the importance of this project to us and to them.

# Appendix A.  Summary Backgrounds of ISK Members on Eva's List of Applicants for Emergency Visas

The original typed version of this summary has the following note in Eva's handwriting at the top: "Submitted to the President's Advisory Committee by Eva Lewinski 52 West 68th Str. SUsquahana 7-7344, and by Miss Dorothy Hill, 22 Oakland Plaza, Buffalo."

1. *Pfister, Otto, born on April 8, 1900, at Munich. Cabinetmaker and interior decorator.*
Has done on close relation with French, Belgium and Luxembourg trade-unionists underground work from different borders into Germany, especially during the war. Has been captured by German military authorities at Luxembourg's invasion, was prisoner in Germany for several months. Germans did not realize his identity. So he succeeded in coming back to France. He is now in the unoccupied part of France and must soon leave so the Gestapo may not put its hands on him.

2. *Lewinski, Erich, born on January 1, 1899, at Kassel, and his wife Herta, born Voremberg, born on October 9, 1897 at Grebenstein. Lawyer.*
Has been a well-known Anti-Nazi-lawyer in Kassel, had to flee when Nazis came to fetch him in his office. In Paris he opened a restaurant that gave much money to rescue emigrants and to anti-Nazi-work. His public activity against the Nazis was known everywhere in the emigrants' movements. Just now we learn that Nazis in Paris had raided both his apartment and his office. Although extremely exposed himself, he is helping for months other refugees in Marseille to get out of France.

*3. Kakies, Hans, born on June 1, 1906, at Berlin. Social worker.*
Has done trade union underground work in Germany till 1937. Then he had to leave, threatened by imminent arrest. Went then to Holland, where he continued in close relation with Edo Fimmen, Secretary of the International Transport Workers Federation, and with Wilhelm Spiekmann, Secretary of the International Employees Federation, underground work against Nazi Germany. Fled to France before German invasion of Holland and is now in a French internment camp near Marseille.

*4. Blencke, Erna, 42 years old, born in Magdeburg. Professor of mathematics.*
Has done underground trade union work in Germany till 1938, as a district leader, after having lost her place as professor. Had to leave Germany when the big trial against our friends began in which she was included. Collaborated in Paris actively at propaganda-work against Nazism, in connection with the French propaganda-secretary.

*5. Albrecht, Eugen, 39 years old, born in Hannover. Employee.*
Has done underground trade union work till 1938, was then arrested for one year, and for several weeks put into irons, to get out of him names of his friends. He stayed silent, was released provisorily. After his flight to France, he collaborated at an Anti-Nazi publishing house, now closed by the Nazis in Paris, which published among others the book of Irmgard Litten: "Beyond tears." He also participated actively at trade union work of German and Austrian refugees in Paris.

*6. Block, Nora, born on January 14, 1895, at Bochum. Lawyer. And her sister: Walter, Herta, born Block, about 48 years old, born at Bochum.*
Has been a well-known Anti-Nazi lawyer at Bochum, and had to flee when Nazis came to power. In Paris she has been a secretary of Leopold Schwarzschild, and later on, for the last years, director of the social service of the biggest emigrants-relief-association. She is known in the emigrants' movement as a courageous fighter against Nazism, who continued her activity in helping others even while in the concentration camp. Is now in the southern part of France.

*7.  Peiper, Gisela, 32 years old, born at Berlin. Teacher.*

Was dismissed as a teacher after the Nazis' rise to power. In spite of big danger because of being Jewish she participated actively at underground trade union work in Hamburg. Was arrested in 1937, released after several months. Went then to Austria to continue underground Anti-Nazi work. Arrested again, she just escaped before the Nazis invasion of Austria. Participated in Paris at Anti-Nazi youth-movements.

*8.  Timmermann, Frieda, born on August 7, 1907, at Hamburg. Dressmaker.*

Participated until 1939 at underground trade union work in Germany, by establishing contacts between underground groups of different cities and districts in Germany. Left Germany only at the very moment of her being arrested. Is a typical example of a simple German woman devoted with all her personality to the fight against the Nazism.

*9.  Amelung, Irmgard, born on October 8, 1911, at Bremen. Teacher.*

Has done underground trade-union work in Bremen until 1938, and progressive educational work against the German war-aims. Had to leave Germany in 1938 because of danger of imminent arrest. In Paris she collaborated at an Anti-Nazi-publishing-house, as did M. Eugen Albrecht (5).

*10. Bertholet, René. Born on April 29, 1907, at Geneva. Journaliste. His wife Johanna, born Grust, born on January 24, 1901, at Hannover.*

Bertholet, a Swiss citizen, helped in 1933 to organize with the International Transport Workers Federation underground trade union work in Germany. Was arrested for two and a half years of prison. After his release he collaborated at French Trade union movement and as a journaliste for *Le Peuple*, the daily of the French Trade Unions, under the pen-name of Pierre Robert. During the present war he continued propaganda against Nazi Germany, at the Belgium, Luxembourg and Swiss border, in connection with Pfister (1). His wife is one of the best collaborators of the cause of freedom and justice.

# Appendix B.  Examples of René-Eva and Robert-Eclair Correspondence

## René-Eva correspondence

The following examples of Office of Strategic Services (OSS) memoranda summarizing correspondence and documents sent by René Bertholet to Eva for transmission to the OSS give an impression of the nature of these materials.

*"Memorandum for OSS" regarding "Information from RENE" dated July 31, 1942*

The following documents have just been received from René and relate to the movement of resistance in France:

1. Rassemblement des Forces de la Libération. Grave warning to patriots to look out for spies and secret police.
2. Pourquoi nous mourons de Faim? [Why are we dying of hunger?] Claims that with the connivance of Vichy, Germany commandeered from July, 1941 to April 1942: 92,600 head of beef; 55,000 sheep; 31 million liters alcohol; 11 million liters brandy; 13 million liters vermouth; 166 million liters wine; 18 million kilos vegetables and fruit; 23 million kilos grapes; 31 million kilos potatoes; 15 million kilos almond cacao; 700 thousand kilos green coffee; 2,300,000 quintals of WHEAT, all in car lots, to which must be added far

greater quantities of foodstuffs consumed by the Germans in the country, the countless truckloads and millions of parcels of food sent to Germany by them.

3. Address by DAUPHIN-MEUNIER on lamentable condition of French prisoners in Germany, including the workers.

4. LE TIGRE, clandestine sheet, May 5, 1942.

5. Number of press directives of German censorship.

6. Tract circulated in region of Aix-en-Provence during May.

7. Leaflet urging French workers to sign up to work in Germany.

8. Pamphlet on anti-Semitism issued by French Christian socialists, circulation 25,000.

9. Leaflet against persecution of Jews circulated clandestinely in 15,000 copies.

10. Leaflet circulated by clandestine papers containing de Gaulle's declaration, reported well received.

11. Leaflet inciting French workers to sabotage German war production, 100,000 copies distributed.

12. Article on the Pope distributed by Catholics of Montauban and Toulouse.

13. Leaflet with photo of starving Russian prisoners circulated by COMBAT.

14. LE FRANC-TIREUR, June, 1942. Circulation 18,000.

15. LIBERATION, July, 1942. Circulation now 35 to 40,000. Also issue of June 24, 1942.

16. COMBAT, June, 1942; LIBRE FRANCE. Paper published by French students.

17. Circular of Christian Syndicalists against recruiting French workers for Germany.

18. Letter of Christian Syndicalists to Pétain.

19. Report on Communist disturbances in Marseille May 30th.

20. German report by Dr. Weizman on complete failure of food rationing system in France.

21. Vichy Labor Dept. invitation to Christian Syndicalists delegation to Laval, and their reply refusing to take any such political action.

22. Quotations from articles in Paris Revues.

23. Letter July 7, 1942, Léon to Vignaux.
24. Leaflet circulated by COMBAT urging French workers to remain in France and refuse to accept German inducements.
25. Patriotic leaflet on 14th July.
26. Leaflet to French workers urging demonstration May 1st.
27. Article on New Religious Front in France.
28. Letter July 6, 1942, from Secretary of State for Industrial Production at Paris to all organizations of industrialists ordering dissemination in all plants of Laval's appeal for workers to sign up for Germany.
29. Letter in Russian to KURSKI and mimeographed Hebrew sheet circulated by associates of the "Bund" in France.

Covering letter from René to EVA dated July 28, 1942, is likewise enclosed. Note that article entitled "Ou va la France?" sent with last batch of papers was not written by Fernand de Brinon but by Francois Poncet, former French Ambassador to Germany.[1]


*"Memorandum for O.S.S." from Bern, August 7, 1942, "Subject: Documents from René re conditions in France"*

The following documents have been received from René and are destined for Eva:

1. Copy of clandestine sheet published by Catholic Republicans, date apparently in June, 1942.
2. Report on address by German Prof. Grimm in Marseille June 8, 1942.
3. Leaflet distributed by "COMBAT" among workers in vicinity of Aix-en-Provence.
4. Leaflet "Thou shalt not be Hitler's Slave" circulated among workers by "France-Liberté" advocating refusal to heed Laval's appeal for workers to go to Germany.
5. Copy of a circular of the Légion indicating dissatisfaction with efforts of Legionnaires.

6. 2 reports on recruiting of French workers for Germany: July 6, train with 690 left for Dijon. 130 from Nice and 180 from Toulon came in special cars attached to regular train. Of 380 from Marseille 200 were natives from Africa. Only 60% were French, and of them 40% negroes.

7. Telegram June 4, '42, to Marseille Police re posters of Légion urging enlistment for Russian front.

8. Copies of communist tracts from Marseille.

9. Various notes of information for Marseille press in June.

10. Series of censor's orders to French press, in Free Zone.

11. German order relative to return of refugees to Alsace.

12. Various reports from Germany and Poland.

13. Declaration of clandestine Italian Socialist Party against Italian preparations for military occupation of Tunis, Corsica, Nice and Savoie.[2]

*Memorandum from Arthur Goldberg to David Shaw dated March 25, 1943 entitled "Message for Eva" (Example of Efforts to Provide Relief Funds for Refugees)*

We are in receipt of the following cabled message from Switzerland for Eva:

The family of Ryba Nathan are very thankful for the transmittal of the twelve thousand nine hundred. The Nathan family wishes you to tell Kursky that Peskin, Stark, Dobin, Honikman, Madame Jelin and Dr. Bonchewskyan and son have been deported. Their family, which is staying in France, is in great danger. Kursky is requested by Nathan to send the equivalent of $6000 in order to save them by means of the same channel and me. Will you please inform Sascha that Baccia has safely arrived here. Anschi desires some news of Theo. Although the difficulties are increasing the work continues. Will you kindly inform us if you receive the important documentation on French resistance which we are giving to Sam [reference to Uncle Sam, the U.S.].[3]

*OSS document dated April 2, 1943, titled "Material for Eva, 328 [Bertholet]" (apparently a translation summarizing "Press Bulletin of Fighting French, No. 78, Mar. 11, 1943")*

The deportation of young French [laborers who were sent to Germany to support the war effort] is nothing but conscription, in collusion with the old Sadist of the Hotel Sévigné at Vichy and the arch-liar Laval, who hates the truth. The truth is that these youths are being sent for the most part to the German étape in the East. Orders which have been seen mention Danzig, Königsberg, Silesia. French conscripts are being dispatched to the depots of the Wehrmacht, and so, brigaded with German troops they will be helpless; they will be ordered to the massacres of the Eastern Front to fill the gaps in the ranks of the Nazis.

Laval says there are a million of these youths of the classes of 40, 41 and 42. Making allowances for exemptions, etc., that means 700,000, or 45 to 50 new divisions presented by Laval in a fortnight to his Berlin Master. These youths have been delivered to Nazi recruiting offices, where they are examined, passed and deported in less than 10 days.

Let our British and American allies ponder this as well! These thousands of young men would not have left had they had the slightest hope. On the one hand there were the political intrigues in North Africa, the suspicion of collusion between Pétain and certain persons in Algiers patronized by Gen. Eisenhower, and on the other hand the tremendous disappointment caused by the failure to establish the Second Front after so many months, despite so many promises and oft repeated boasts that all was absolutely ready. The net result is that France has lost classes of a million men who could have supplied the Allies with a magnificent army. Once again the United Nations have lost the race against the Axis. It is high time, indeed, that the Allies learned the importance of audacity and decision.

At Lille 23 German officers were killed at the Casino, and German quarters were attacked by patriots with bombs and grenades. In Paris several buildings were attacked by them and in the rue Laborde sentinels guarding a garage were killed and all military trucks were burned. All patriots escaped.

At the Renault plant 5,000 out of 15,000 workers were conscripted.

Extensive railroad sabotage is reported from Paris-Batignolles, Bethune, at St. Cyr-en-Val, Macon, between Lille and Valenciennes, and at Sedan.

Official French documents relative to the evacuation of Marseille and vicinity. A zone 300 kilometers from the sea is proscribed, all through the collaboration of French authorities. Railroad authorities have issued special orders for patrol of lines constantly to prevent sabotage.[4]

## Examples of the "Robert-Éclair" correspondence for the Special Operations Executive (SOE)

*Brief typed letter in the SOE files dated May 23, 1942, from "J.Q. 100" to "J.Q."*

This letter would be meaningless if it did not include handwritten notations for the reader to understand the references. The source of these notations (shown below in brackets) is unknown. Even with the notations, the message is not completely clear. It appears to refer to Bertholet's efforts to have funds transferred from the United States to support resistance efforts in France, which was also referred to in the René-Eva correspondence:

> The accompanying letters from A [Robert] to B [Eclair] and C [Eva] in D [United States] deal with a question which A [Robert] raised some time ago, namely as to the possibility of E [transferring funds] for the F [good work] from D [U.S.A.] to be made available in 38 [France]. . . . I suggest that you should draw the particular attention of our friends to these letters in case they should be in a position to pull strings for the purpose of facilitating the operations in question. . . . The letters are in the envelope marked G. [Mr. John].[5]

*SOE Memorandum from "X/G" to "AD/X" Dated September 20, 1943,*
*Listing Messages Received by Eichler ("Eclair") from Bertholet ("Charles")*

This memorandum included reports about reactions to the fall of
Mussolini ("joyfully welcomed"), the efforts by the Nazis to crush dissent
("S.S., S.A., and H.J. are being trained with most modern equipment for
stamping out demonstrations, strikes, etc. Every second man must be
regarded as a Nazi agent"), the resistance of foreign workers at Siemens
("[r]oughly 75% foreign workers at Siemens whose alleged laziness is certainly deliberate"), and sabotage efforts within Germany ("Considerable
sabotage on works and communications especially during raids. Also
anti-Nazi wall inscriptions. All this much hushed up."). The document
also included the sobering assessment "The Nazi machine is still firmly
in hand. Hopes [for rebellion] lie in hunger, bombardments and serious
military defeats."[6]

# Appendix C.  Eva's Memorial Summary of Otto's Life

Otto died on September 11, 1985, at the age 85. To you who have known him for many years, what follows will not tell you anything. Those of you who are newer friends may be interested in knowing more about his early years.

He was born a child of a Catholic bricklayer and his wife, in Bavaria. In spite of intelligence and excellent performance at school, an academic career remained out of reach financially. He would have liked then to become a bridge builder. That was also not to be. Instead, he became a cabinetmaker's apprentice, and later the master craftsman that he was until the end of his life.

At age 20, he left home and Germany and went to Rome, where he worked at his trade, learned to love the Italian language, music, opera, art, and the people.

When Mussolini took over, he did not want to stay—he cherished freedom too much. So he went to France, to Paris, again using his skill and love for wood. There he met Eva, a Jewish political refugee from Germany. They met at her brother's (a former lawyer) vegetarian restaurant, and in spite of different backgrounds, they discovered how much they shared: love of freedom, of nature, of poetry, and of art. It became for both a bond that lasted close to 50 years.

Otto, a man of integrity, would not just proclaim his opposition to Nazi oppression; he acted accordingly, by participating in the underground work against Hitler. In the course of this, he was captured by the German army which had just invaded Belgium and Luxemburg. In a situation where many of us would have given up, he survived, with a

French identity made up while crouching alongside the road on which the German army was marching to their early victories.

He survived a prisoner-of-war camp, came back to France, the main part of which was now occupied by Germany, to find that he had lost everything, and that Eva had found asylum in the United States, from where she tried to bring other endangered refugees to safety.

Among them was Otto, thought lost, but who had survived. They were finally reunited in New York; he worked again at his craft, and soon their first child was born. The baby did not live; the pain of this loss was great. However, Otto, in total agreement with Eva, had earlier enlisted in the OSS [Office of Strategic Services], and four days after the loss of their baby he was sent overseas where he served as an American soldier in England, Belgium, and France. His unit followed the army that liberated France, and he was back in Paris, the city that he had loved so.

Finally, the war over, he came home, to have a family which seemed a miracle to him and Eva, then to move to California where again he made beautiful furniture, and many friends.

The three children grew up, to Otto's and Eva's never-ending joy. They finished their educations and built their own careers and families. The old house in the Valley where they had lived for 30 years now became too large, and he took the initiative for the move to Leisure Village.

Here, he spent the last four years of his life, and they were happy years. Good air; new friends; swimming and biking; and work in his beloved shop, which many villagers saw and liked. He loved to show the shop to whoever wanted to see it; he loved to teach whoever wanted to learn, including his grandchildren, to make "dove-tails." He felt good here at home, with every bit of furniture made by his own hands. He whistled and played the harmonica; he liked to sing German, French, and Italian songs; he loved to read and to recite poetry; he played chess.

Yet, he kept abreast of the world, and of new ideas. He contributed as much as he could to any cause that he deemed worthwhile: the fight against injustice, hunger, pollution, war. He was a whole man, secure in his identity; he loved people and he loved life.

September 12, 1985
Camarillo, California

# Notes

## 1. Childhood in Goldap

1. Except as otherwise noted, all quotations in this chapter are from Eva Pfister and Otto Pfister, "To Our Children," unpublished memoir (Los Angeles, 1979), 1–12.
2. After World War I ended, Erich and Ernst came back, physically unharmed. Erich returned to the university to continue his study of law. Ernst worked in Berlin as a civil engineer and soon would be sent to South Africa by his firm.

## 2. Study in France and at the Walkemühle

1. Unless otherwise noted, all quotations in this chapter are from Eva Pfister and Otto Pfister, "To Our Children," unpublished memoir (Los Angeles, 1979), 41–52.
2. One translation of the group's name is "International Socialist Action Group," but this translation and others such as "International Socialist Vanguard" do not provide a meaningful sense of its philosophy, purpose, and impact.
3. Historical studies of the ISK written in German include Werner Link, *Die Geschichte des Internationalen Jugend-Bundes (IJB) und des Internationalen Sozialistischen Kampfbundes (ISK), Ein Beitrag zur Geschichte der Arbeiterbewegung in der Weimarer Republik und im Dritten Reich* (Meisenheim am Glan: Hain, 1964); Heiner Lindner, "Um etwas zu

461

erreichen, muss man sich etwas vornehmen, von dem man glaubt, dass es unmöglich sei," in *Der Internationale Sozialistische Kampf-Bund (ISK) und seine Publikationen* (Bonn: Friedrich Ebert Stiftung Historisches Forschungszentrum, 2006); Karl-Heinz Klär, "Zwei Nelson Bünde: Internationaler Jugend-Bund (IJB) und Internationaler Sozialistischer Kampf-Bund (ISK) im Licht Neuer Quellen," *Internationale Wissenschaftliche Korrespondenz zur Geschichte der deutschen Arbeiterbewegung* (1982).

Other helpful sources of information in German about the ISK's philosophy and resistance activities include Sabine Lemke-Müller, *Ethik des Widerstands, Der Kampf des Internationalen Sozialistischen Kampfbundes (ISK) gegen den Nationalsozialismus: Quellen und Texte zum Widerstand aus der Arbeiterbewegung, 1933–1945* (Bonn: Dietz, 1996); Sabine Lemke-Müller, "Kritische Philosophie und aktuelle Politik, Ein Gespräch mit Susanne Miller," in *Zukunft der Demokratie in Deutschland, ed. Andrea Gourd and Thomas Noetzel* (Opladen: Leske + Budrich, 2001), 125–30; Martin Rüther, Uwe Schütz, and Otto Dann, *Deutschland im ersten Nachkriegsjahr, Berichte von Mitgliedern des Internationalen Sozialistischen Kampfbundes (ISK) aus dem besetzten Deutschland 1945/46* (München: K. G. Sauer, 1998), Einleitung, 1–22.

Works in English about the ISK (and its predecessor IJB) include Leonard Nelson, *Politics and Education*, translated by W. Lansdell (London: Allen & Unwin, 1928); Walter Struve, *Elites against Democracy: Leadership Ideals in Bourgeois Political Thought in Germany, 1890–1933* (1973; reprint, Princeton, NJ: Princeton Legacy Library, 2017), 186–215 (examining the philosophy and early political work of Leonard Nelson); Christian Bailey, *Between Yesterday and Tomorrow: German Visions of Europe, 1926–1950* (New York: Berghahn Books, 2013), 86–113 (considering the ISK's role in the history of European integration). See also the Afterword in the current volume, with citations to biographies and memoirs of other ISK members.

4. Eva later commented about a book published in honor of Specht's eightieth birthday, Helmut Becker, *Erziehung und Politik* [Education and Politics]: *Minna Specht zu ihrem 80. Geburtstag* (Frankfurt: Verlag Öffentliches Leben, 1960): "Each time I open it, and especially when I read again the contributions written by some of my former friends who were students at the Walkemühle at the same time as I had been, I am moved by

the wealth of memories it brings back." Eva and Otto Pfister, "To Our Children," 48.

## 3.  Anti-Nazi Work in Germany

1. Unless otherwise indicated, all quotations in this Chapter are from Eva Pfister and Otto Pfister, "To Our Children," unpublished memoir (Los Angeles, 1979), 52–55.
2. *Der Funke* was the ISK's primary publication in Germany before Hitler assumed power in 1933. In February 1933, the Nazis prohibited the further distribution of *Der Funke*.
3. E. Prelinger, A. Comini, and H. Bachert, *Käthe Kollwitz* (Washington, DC: National Gallery of Art and Yale University Press, 1992), 182.
4. The socialist splinter groups included, in addition to the ISK, Neu Beginnen (New Beginning) and the Sozialistische Arbeiterpartei (Socialist Workers Party), headed by Willi Brandt.
5. Antje Dertinger, *"Every Farewell Is a New Beginning": Erich Lewinski, a Biography*, translated by Tom Lewinski from the original German manuscript *"Die Drei Exile des Erich Lewinski"* [Erich Lewinski, Three Times Exiled] (Gerlingen: Bleicher Verlag, 1995), 42–53.
6. T. Lewinski, "What Happened to the Lewinskis?" (unpublished memoir, 1987), 20–23.
7. Ibid., 25.

## 4.  Early Years in Exile

1. Leaders of the German Socialist Party (SPD) fled to Prague and established headquarters in exile there. When Hitler invaded Czechoslovakia in 1938, they too fled to Paris. The SPD group in exile referred to itself as SOPADE.
2. Heiner Lindner, "Um etwas zu erreichen, muss man sich etwas vornehmen, von dem man glaubt, dass es unmöglich sei," in *Der Internationale Sozialistische Kampf-Bund (ISK) und seine Publikationen* (Bonn: Friedrich-Ebert-Stiftung Historisches Forschungszentrum, 2006), 51.
3. Eva Pfister and Otto Pfister, "To Our Children," unpublished memoir (Los Angeles, 1979), 58.

4. Tom Lewinski, "What Happened to the Lewinskis?," unpublished memoir, 1987, 27–31 (quoting from an account written by Erich Lewinski's wife Herta).

5. Ibid., 31–32.

6. Ibid., 34–36.

7. Eva and Otto Pfister, "To Our Children," 60.

8. Lewinski, "What Happened to the Lewinskis?," 36.

9. The small groups of ISK members who remained in Germany after 1933 also financed their underground anti-Nazi activities by working in vegetarian restaurants in different cities in Germany. Lindner, *Der Internationale Sozialistische Kampf-Bund*, 51; Karl-Heinz Klär, "Zwei Nelson Bünde: Internationaler Jugend-Bund (IJB) und Internationaler Sozialistischer Kampf-Bund (ISK) im Licht Neuer Quellen," *Internationale Wissenschaftliche Korrespondenz zur Geschichte der deutschen Arbeiterbewegung* 18 (1982): 327.

10. Eva and Otto Pfister, "To Our Children," 61.

11. Eva's Paris diary tells a personal and poignant story of her relationship with Rudi during this difficult period. Only a few examples of entries from this diary are included in this book. We have translated these diary entries from the original German.

12. Eva's unpublished 1970 draft memoir.

13. The following is the original German version of this poem:

> Ich sehe auf die Bäume in der grossen, lauten Strasse.
> Es ist ein heisser Sommertag.
> Grün sind die Blätter noch, aber verstaubt und matt.
> Und wenn der Wind sie streift, fallen sie ab,
> Müde, hilflos, wie im Herbst.
>
> Und ich sehe mich.
> Ich bin jung. Warum fehlt mir die Kraft?
> Immer öfter steift grundlose
> Traurigkeit meine Seele,
> Und Tränen fallen, kaum zurückzuhalten.

Eva later translated some of these poems into English, and we translated others.

14. Saint-Malo is beautifully described in the novel by Anthony Doerr, *All the Light We Cannot See* (New York: Scribner, 2014).

15. Granville is a small harbor town on the coast of northwestern France about ninety-five kilometers by train from Saint-Malo.

## 5.  Childhood in Munich

1. Except as otherwise noted, all quotations in this chapter are from Eva Pfister and Otto Pfister, "To Our Children," unpublished memoir (Los Angeles, 1979), 25–32.
2. Lina died in 1927 at the age of nineteen.

## 6.  "Education" in Italy and France

1. The quotations in this chapter are from Eva Pfister and Otto Pfister, "To Our Children," unpublished memoir (Los Angeles, 1979), 33–40.
2. Theodore Fried, born Jewish in Hungary in 1902, was an artist who had moved from Budapest to Vienna in 1924 and from Vienna to Paris in 1925. He met Otto and Eva in Paris, where they began what would become a lifelong friendship. When the Germans invaded France in May 1940, Fried fled to Toulouse in southern France and later escaped to America.

## 7.  Anti-Nazi Work in Paris

1. Heiner Lindner, "Um etwas zu erreichen, muss man sich etwas vornehmen, von dem man glaubt, dass es unmöglich sei," in *Der Internationale Sozialistische Kampf-Bund (ISK) und seine Publikationen* (Bonn: Friedrich-Ebert-Stiftung Historisches Forschungszentrum, 2006), 50. See also Karl-Heinz Klär, "Zwei Nelson Bünde: Internationaler Jugend-Bund (IJB) und Internationaler Sozialistischer Kampf-Bund (ISK) im Licht Neuer Quellen," *Internationale Wissenschaftliche Korrespondenz zur Geschichte der deutschen Arbeiterbewegung* 18 (1982): 322–23.
2. Lindner, "Um etwas zu erreichen," 49–50.
3. Ibid., 46; Werner Link, *Die Geschichte des Internationalen Jugend-Bundes (IJB) und des Internationalen Sozialistischen Kampfbundes (ISK), Ein Beitrag zur Geschichte der Arbeiterbewegung in der Weimarer Republik*

*und im Dritten Reich* (Meisenheim am Glan: Hain, 1964), 141; Christian Bailey, *Between Yesterday and Tomorrow: German Visions of Europe, 1926–1950* (New York: Berghahn Books, 2013), 87.

4. Lindner, "Um etwas zu erreichen," 50. This group of ISK members in Germany later took on the name Unabhängige Sozialistische Gewerkschaft (Independent Socialist Union, USG). Hellmuth von Rauschenplat, who assumed the name Fritz Eberhart, first headed the USG.

5. Ibid., 51. See also Klär, "Zwei Nelson-Bünde," 324–28.

6. Bernd Sösemann (ed.), *Fritz Eberhard: Rückblicke auf Biographie und Werk* (Stuttgart: Franz Steiner Verlag, 2001), 115–21. Sösemann's description of the ISK's resistance efforts in Germany is largely taken from descriptions in Fritz Eberhart's "Arbeit gegen das Dritte Reich," Berlin 1980 (Beiträge zum Thema Widerstand), and from Werner Link's work on the ISK, *Die Geschichte des Internationalen Jugend-Bundes (IJB) und des Internationalen Sozialistischen Kampfbundes (ISK)*. Sösemann writes that the ISK had developed into a "master of conspiracy" (*Fritz Eberhard*, 115). See also Wolfgang Benz, *Geschichte des Dritten Reiches* (München: Verlag B. H. Beck oHG, 2000), 120, translated by Thomas Dunlap as *A Concise History of the Third Reich* (Berkeley: University of California Press, 2006), 124–25.

7. Sösemann, *Fritz Eberhard*, 115–21.

8. Ibid.

9. Ibid., 115n15 (citing numerous other works also referring to the creative resistance efforts of the ISK).

10. Antje Dertinger, *Every Farewell Is a New Beginning: Erich Lewinski, a Biography*, translated by Tom Lewinski from *Die Drei Exile des Erich Lewinski* [Erich Lewinski, Three Times Exiled] (Gerlingen: Bleicher Verlag, 1995), 79; Lindner, "Um etwas zu erreichen," 48.

11. Bailey, *Between Yesterday and Tomorrow*, 98; Lindner, "Um etwas zu erreichen," 64.

12. Bailey, *Between Yesterday and Tomorrow*, 98; Dertinger, *Every Farewell Is a New Beginning*, 80.

13. For example, Eichler used several names, including Martin Hart; Gerhard Kumleben used the name Francois Gerard; and Heinz Kühn used the name Hendrik H. Frans. Bailey, *Between Yesterday and Tomorrow*, 112–13nn72, 75, and 84. Remarkably, Eva managed to retain some original issues of the *Warte*, and they are among the papers we have donated to

the U.S. Holocaust Memorial Museum. The fragile pages now break to the touch. The Friedrich-Ebert-Stiftung in Bonn, Germany, also has issues of the *Warte* in its archives.

14. Lindner, "Um etwas zu erreichen," 50–51, 89.
15. Ibid., 89.
16. Ibid., 51, 89.
17. Dertinger, *Every Farewell Is a New Beginning*, 81.
18. Ibid.
19. Lindner, "Um etwas zu erreichen," 89.
20. Eva Pfister and Otto Pfister, "To Our Children," unpublished memoir (Los Angeles, 1979), 63.
21. Dertinger, *Every Farewell Is a New Beginning*, 80.
22. Lindner, "Um etwas zu erreichen," 58.
23. Bailey, *Between Yesterday and Tomorrow*, 103. German historian Antje Dertinger notes that Eichler "suspected some intrigue by the Communists who wanted to halt any further cooperation between the non-Communist groups which Eichler had initiated." Dertinger, *Every Farewell Is a New Beginning*, 83.
24. See, e.g., Sabine Lemke-Müller, *Ethik des Widerstands, Der Kampf des Internationalen Sozialistischen Kampfbundes (ISK) gegen den Nationalsozialismus: Quellen und Texte zum Widerstand aus der Arbeiterbewegung, 1933–1945* (Bonn: Dietz, 1996), 151–57, describing the work in exile of the following women who were members of the ISK: Minna Specht, Grete Henry-Hermann, Maria Hodann (Mary Saran), Erna Blencke, Hilda Monte (Meisel), Eva Lewinski, Änne Kappius (Ebbers), and Anna Kothe.
25. Dertinger, *Every Farewell Is a New Beginning*, 83.
26. For background on Karl Frank (alias Paul Hagen) and Neu Beginnen written in English, see Terance Renaud, "The German Resistance in New York: Karl B. Frank and the New Beginning Group, 1935–1945," undergraduate thesis, Boston University, 2007, and "'This Is Our Dunkirk': Kark B. Frank and the Politics of the Emergency Rescue Committee," student essay, Boston University, 2009.
27. Ursula Langkau-Alex, *Deutsche Volksfront 1932–39: Zwischen Berlin, Paris, Prag und Moskau; Zweiter Band: Geschichte des Ausschusses zur Vorbereitung einer Deutschen Volksfront* (Berlin: Akademie Verlag, 2004–2005), 104–5.
28. Ibid., 104 (translated from German).
29. Ibid., 105. See note 41: BA/K, R60 II/56, file 1, "Criminal case file

against unknown concerning preparation for high treason" (translated from German). See also ibid., 104n39, referring to letters to Ursula Langkau-Alex from Dr. Suzanne Miller dated December 15, 1982 and January 7, 1983, and to Erna Blencke as sources for the identification of Otto as the speaker on the recording.

30. The photograph of this recording, along with digital copies of the sound, were provided by the Bundesarchiv in Koblenz, Germany.
31. Lindner, "Um etwas zu erreichen," 55–56 (translated from German).
32. Ibid., 56.
33. Ibid.
34. Philippson Judgment, English translation, 6–7.
35. Ibid., 17.
36. Ibid.
37. Ibid., 13.
38. Ibid., 18.
39. Ibid., 20–21. The court in the Prawitt case observed that splinter groups such as the ISK cannot be considered "in an isolated fashion." The court emphasized the danger of German vulnerability to the influence of the highly educated Philippson's "production and dissemination of inflammatory writings." See also H. W. Koch, *In the Name of the Volk: Political Justice in Hitler's Germany* (London: I. B. Tauris, 1989), 63, 63n79, citing BDC VGH (Berlin Document Center, Volksgerichtshof) Judgment 19.1.1938 ("Splinter groups of the KPD were persecuted with equal fervour: 'in spite of their relatively small numbers they must not be underestimated'").
40. Others who were named in the judgment as participants in Philippson's treasonous activities include Hans Prawitt from Hamburg ("sentenced by judgment of December 7, 1937 to 6 years' imprisonment"); Walter Brandt from Hamburg; Max Mayr from Kassel; Wilhelm Ebert from Magdeburg; Fritz Hartmann from Cologne; Swiss citizen Marie Öttli; Mr. and Mrs. Josef and Änna Kappius who fled; Berta Turnier from Hannover, Frieda Arnold from Bremen, and Richard Bauernsass from Kreidlitz bei Koburg (all of whom "were sentenced in connection with the present criminal case"); Karl Melzer from Magdeburg (sentenced to eight years' imprisonment); Alfred Dannenberg from Hannover, Ludwig Linsert and Hans Wehner from Munich, Hildegard Schulze from Braunschweig, and Marie Broeker from Syke, District of Hoya ("sentenced in connection with these criminal proceedings to one year

of imprisonment"); Mr. and Mrs. Krueger, members from Berlin who "regularly met once a month in the apartment of the Accused and later in the apartment of Mr. and Mrs. Krueger"); Erna Braesicke, Walter Probst, Alfred Kubel, and Heinrich Breves ("who likewise have been sentenced in connection with the present criminal proceedings"); Eduard Rhode from the Magdeburg discussion group; Kurt Pfotenhauer from the Weimar group ("who has likewise been sentenced in connection with the present criminal proceedings"); Fritz Seidestueker and Hugo Schmidt from Eisenach; and Lisbeth Katholy from Leipzig "who has fled."). Philippson Judgment, English translation, 9–10.

41. Paul Bonart, *But We Said "NO!": Voices from the German Underground* (San Francisco: Mark Backman Productions, 2007), 147–54.

42. "Wir Erinnern an Julius Philippson," Ottostadt Madgeburg, http://www.magdeburg-tourist.de/media/custom/698_6203_1.PDF. Rabindranath Tagore (1861–1941) was a Bengali writer, poet, and philosopher who won the 1913 Nobel Prize for Literature. Tagore's writings express sympathy for the poor and promote universal humanistic values.

## 8. War Begins

1. Eva Pfister and Otto Pfister, "To Our Children," unpublished memoir (Los Angeles, 1979), 62.

2. Eva retained a small notebook of handwritten poems from Stern that must be the one she describes here.

3. Eva and Otto Pfister "To Our Children," 62.

4. The rest of Otto's family remained in Germany during the war. We later came to know the son of one of Otto's sisters (our cousin) and his family well.

5. To our knowledge, very little has been written about this anti-Nazi sabotage effort during the Drôle de Guerre. We describe further in the Afterword how we initially discovered this new information and then confirmed it.

6. Jef Rens, "René Bertholet et Otto Pfister," in *Rencontres avec le siècle* [Encounters with the Century], translated from the Dutch by Jean-Pierre Orban (Gembloux, Belgium: Editions Duculot, 1987).

7. Ibid., 103.

8. Ibid., 106. With the declaration of war against Germany in September 1939, the French intelligence operations were reorganized. The Service

de Renseignements (Intelligence Service) became the Cinquième Bureau (Fifth Bureau) of the French Army. See Ernest R. May, *Strange Victory: Hitler's Conquest of France* (New York: Hill and Wang, 2000), 287.

9. Ibid., 107–8.

10. S.O.E. Archives, HS6/642, Operations of Johannes Jahn (1936–1940), S.O.E. Germany No. 102 ("SOE/Jahn file"). These declassified SOE documents are available on microfilm at the Cecil H. Green Library at Stanford University: *Special Operations Executive, 1940–1946: Subversion and Sabotage during World War II, Series One: SOE Operations in Western Europe* (from Adam Matthew Publications). Information about the ISK's involvement with the SOE can be found in Part 3: Germany, 1936–1945, reels 28–30.

11. SOE/Jahn file, 12B.

12. Ibid.

13. Ibid.

14. Ibid., 11A.

15. Germans use *Du* for "you" (rather than the formal *Sie*) with children, family, and close friends.

16. This is an apparent reference to the primary ISK publication in Paris at that time, *Die Warte*.

## 9. Eva's Internment

1. Press release dated May 12, 1940, quoted in full in French in Denis Blanchot's afterword, "La premiere 'rafle' du Vél d'Hiv', un orphelin de l'Histoire [The First Roundup at the Vel' d'Hiv, an Orphan of History]," in Lilo Petersen, *Les Oubliées* [*The Forgotten*] (Clamecy, France: Jacob-Duvernet, 2007), 193.

2. Ibid. (translated from French).

3. Parts of this diary were translated into English by Eva, and the remaining parts were translated by us. This diary was difficult for Eva to reread at a later point in her life. In her memoir, her description of her experience in the Vel' d'Hiv and in Camp de Gurs began as follows: "The months spent in those camps were so full of emotion that it is difficult to think or write about it even now. Not knowing if I would ever see Otto again, not able to talk about it, I kept a diary."

4. "Stern" is Austrian poet Josef Luitpold Stern. "Hanna" is ISK member

Johanna Fortmüller Bertholet, René Bertholet's wife. "Mousy" is Hélène Perret. "Nora" is Nora Platiel, born Nora Block. Nora had studied law in Göttingen, represented those accused of resisting Hitler before 1933, and worked with the ISK group in exile in Paris, where for a period of time she shared a small apartment with Eva and ISK supporter Hélène Perret. All were Eva's colleagues in Paris.

5. There are different estimates of the number of women interned in the Vel' d'Hiv at this time. Petersen, *Les Oubliées*, 60, 165–73 (referring to estimates of 5,000 but concluding, after extensive research, that the exact number will never be known because documents that might have revealed that number were destroyed); Stanley Meisler, *Shocking Paris: Soutine, Chagall and the Outsiders of Montparnasse* (New York: St. Martin's, 2015), 152 (estimated 4,000–5,000); Elizabeth Young-Bruehl, *Hannah Arendt: For Love of the World* (New Haven, CT: Yale University Press, 1982), 153 (noting that the number of German women transported from the Vel' d'Hiv to Camp de Gurs from Paris and its suburbs was 2,364).

6. Petersen, *Les Oubliées*, 59–64. See also Lisa Fittko, *Escape through the Pyrenees* (Evanston, IL: Northwestern University Press, 1991), 8–15 (first published in German as *Mein Weg über die Pyrenäen, Erinnerungen 1940/41* [Munich: Carl Hanser Verlag, 1985]); Meisler, *Shocking Paris*, 152; Young-Bruehl, *Hannah Arendt*, 152–53.

7. Claude Lévy and Paul Tillard, *La Grande Rafle du Vel' d'Hiv, 16 juillet 1942* (Paris: Robert Laffont, 1967).

8. Petersen, *Les Oubliées*, 165–84.

9. Eva translated a number of the letters she wrote to Stern, with the heading "Some Letters to a Friend." She explained: "This translation has the following background: Josef Luitpold Stern, an Austrian Social democrat, educator, and poet, became a very good friend of ours during the emigration years in Paris, Southern France, and America. After the war, he returned to Austria—a very old man—and was still able to see part of his work published in Vienna. The title of this publication is *Das Sternbild* (Europa Verlag, Wien). These excerpts are from the Fifth Volume: *Hall und Widerhall vom eifrigen Leben*. (*Sound and Echo of an Active Life*), pages 26–30."

10. Videotaped interview of Eva Pfister by Kathy Pfister, 1986.

11. Regarding the origin of Camp de Gurs, see Petersen, *Les Oubliées*, 69, 196; Claude Laharie, *Le Camp de Gurs, 1939–1945, un aspect méconnu de l'histoire de Vichy* (Pau: Société Atlantique d'Impression à Biarritz,

1993), 9, 15, 75–120. Regarding the number of internees at the camp during this period, see Petersen, *Les Oubliées*, 167–68; Laharie, *Le Camp de Gurs*, 138–43, 363.

12. Laharie, *Le Camp de Gurs*, 236–47; Petersen, *Les Oubliées*, 171; Donald Lowrie, *The Hunted Children* (New York: Norton, 1963), 60–72; Michael Dobbs, *The Unwanted: America, Auschwitz, and a Village Caught in Between* (New York: Knopf, 2019).

13. Leharie, *Le Camp de Gurs*, 35–54 (describing in detail the physical structure of the camp); Petersen, *Les Oubliées*, 9–14, 69; Lowrie, *The Hunted Children*, 60–72 (providing a detailed firsthand description of the structures and conditions in the camp as he observed them as a relief worker beginning in November 1940); "Holocaust Encyclopedia," United States Holocaust Memorial Museum, www.ushmm.org/Gurs (describing Camp de Gurs). See also the website of Amicale du Camp de Gurs, www.camp gurs.com, an organization dedicated to preserving the history of the camp.

14. Ibid.

15. Petersen, *Les Oubliées*, 9–14, 67–72; Leharie, *Le Camp de Gurs*, 38–44 and chaps. 9–12. See also Hanna Schramm, *Menschen in Gurs: Erinnerungen an ein französisches Internierungslager (1940–1941)* [*Humans in Gurs: Memories of a French Internment Camp, 1940–41*] (Worms: Georg Heintz, 1977) (French edition Hannah Schramm and Barbara Vormeir, *Vivre a Gurs: Un Camp de Concentration* [Heintz, 1979]; Fittko, *Escape through the Pyrenees*, 33–40; Lowrie, *The Hunted Children*, 60–72.

16. Elliot Arensmeyer, who worked with the Amicale du Camp de Gurs and gave lectures in New York City on the history of the camp, reported that during this period of internment the postmaster in the small village of Gurs was sympathetic to the internees and made a special effort to ensure that their mail was picked up and delivered to them. Kathy Pfister's interview with Arensmeyer, May 2012. See also Fittko, *Escape through the Pyrenees*, 39 (describing the lifting of restrictions on sending and receiving mail).

17. Gaby Cordier, Hélène "Mousy" Perret, and Hanna (Johanna Bertholet) were not interned because they were of Swiss, not German, origin.

18. This is a reference to Otto's return from internment by the French in Camp Cepoy at the beginning of February 1940.

19. Eva Pfister and Otto Pfister, "To Our Children," unpublished memoir (Los Angeles, 1979), 65.

20. Leharie, *Le Camp de Gurs*, 143; Petersen, *Les Oubliées*, 168–69.

21. Leharie, *Le Camp de Gurs*, 143n42; Petersen, *Les Oubliées* (includes some

quotes from Eva's diaries as well as references to the internment of German American political theorist Hannah Arendt at the Vélodrome d'Hiver and Camp de Gurs during this period); Hanna Schramm, *Menschen in Gurs*; Fittko, *Escape through the Pyrenees*.

22. Leharie, *Le Camp de Gurs*, 15; "Témoignages" [Witnesses], Amicale du Camp de Gurs, http://www.campgurs.com/le-camp/témoignages/; "L'Histoire du Camp" [The History of the Camp], Amicale du Camp de Gurs, http://www.campgurs.com/le-camp/lhistoire-du-camp/; Petersen; *Les Oubliées*, 179–80.

23. Petersen, *Les Oubliées*, 179–81 (translated from French). Instead of the term "undesirables," a more appropriate description of this period at Camp de Gurs would be "the period of internment by the French government of women of German origin, including those women of the German resistance who had been actively engaged in anti-Nazi work while in exile in France during the period 1933–1940."

## 10.  Eva's Refuge

1. Except as otherwise noted, the quotations in this Chapter are from Eva Pfister and Otto Pfister, "To Our Children," unpublished memoir (Los Angeles, 1979), 65–70.

2. Letter dated June 23, 1940, from Eva in "Salies-de-Béarn (Basses Pyr.)" to Stern in Montauban.

3. This journey and our discovery of the village are described in the Afterword.

4. Letter dated June 27, 1940, from Eva in "Escou, pres d'Oloron (Basses Pyr.)" to Stern in Montauban.

5. Letter dated July 1, 1940, from Eva in "Escou, pres d'Oloron (B. Pyr.)" to Stern in Montauban.

6. Telegram dated July 7, 1940, from Eva in Oloron to Stern in Montauban.

7. Elizabeth Young-Bruehl, *Hannah Arendt: For Love of the World* (New Haven, CT: Yale University Press, 1982), 156 ("Montauban became a meeting point for escapees from camps all over France because the mayor of the town was a socialist and expressed his opposition to the Vichy government by housing former prisoners"); Erich Lewinski, "Von der Menschenwürde [Of Human Dignity]," in *Leonard Nelson Zum Gedächtnis*, eds. Minna Specht and Willi Eichler (Frankfurt, Göttingen: Verlag Öffentliches Leben, 1953), 271–290 (translation into English by Tom Lewinski); Benson Varon, *Fighting Fascism and Surviving Buchenwald: The Life*

*and Memoir of Hans Bergas* (n.p.: B. Varon, 2015), 10–13; Concours National de la Résistance et de la Déportation 2008, "L'aide aux per-sonnes persécutées en France pendant la Seconde Guerre mondiale: Une forme de résistance," Ville de Montauban, www.Montauban.com/connection_resistance/document5.pdf. As the war progressed, one of the notable resisters in Montauban against the Vichy government's collabo-ration with the Nazis was Monsignor Pierre-Marie Théas.

8. Antje Dertinger, *Every Farewell Is a New Beginning: Erich Lewinski, a Biography*, translated by Tom Lewinski from *Die Drei Exile des Erich Lewinski* [Erich Lewinski, Three Times Exiled] (Gerlingen: Bleicher Verlag, 1995), 88–89.

9. Lewinski, "Of Human Dignity," 8–9.

10. Ibid.

11. Videotaped interview of Eva Pfister by Kathy Pfister, 1986.

12. Letter dated November 2, 1940, from Eva to Willi Eichler. Eva wrote this long letter to Eichler three weeks after her arrival in New York, reporting on events that she and her ISK colleagues experienced following the Nazi invasion of France in May 1940. Other parts of this letter are discussed later in this chapter and in subsequent chapters.

13. Videotaped interview of Eva Pfister by Kathy Pfister, 1986.

14. Dertinger, *Every Farewell Is a New Beginning*, 93, quoted in Helga Haas-Rietschel and Sabine Hering, *Nora Platiel, Sozialistin, Emigrantin, Politikerin: Eine Biographie* (Köln: Bund-Verlag, 1990), 113.

15. Letter dated November 2, 1940, from Eva to Willi Eichler.

16. See Chapter 15. See also Tom Pfister, Peter Pfister, and Kathy Pfister, *Eva and Otto: America's Vetting and Rescue of Political Refugees during World War II* (Los Angeles: Pfisters, 2017).

17. The formation of the Emergency Rescue Committee and the work of Varian Fry are described in Chapter 15.

18. Letter dated November 2, 1940, from Eva to Willi Eichler.

19. Dertinger, *Every Farewell Is a New Beginning*, 100–101.

## 11.  Otto's Capture and Imprisonment

1. Jef Rens, "René Bertholet et Otto Pfister," in *Rencontres avec le siècle* [Encounters with the Century], translated from the Dutch by Jean-Pierre Orban (Gembloux, Belgium: Editions Duculot, 1987), 109–10. Rens did not provide further specifics about his plans with Otto on that fateful day. Instead, he went on to describe the origin and nature of his

anti-Nazi sabotage work with Otto and René Bertholet during the Drôle de Guerre. As Rens explained, "My purpose here is not to pick up the thread of events that have shaken our history in this summer of misfortune, but only to discuss my meetings with these two exceptional men who were René Bertholet and Otto Pfister."

2. Shortly after arriving in America in 1941, Otto made notes in German about what happened to him on this trip to Luxembourg, describing his capture by the Nazis and how he managed to survive. We no longer have the original German notes, but Eva transcribed and translated them into English in their 1979 memoir. Except as otherwise noted, the quotations in this chapter are from Eva Pfister and Otto Pfister, "To Our Children" unpublished memoir (Los Angeles, 1979), 72–88.

3. Before we embarked on our research for this book, we had always assumed that the "anti-Hitler material" referred to in Otto's description was leaflets and other anti-Nazi publications, and we did not know the identity of "Hans J." See the Afterword in this volume.

4. Eva later noted "This is where Otto's notes end." The subsequent descriptions of Otto's further imprisonment and release by the Nazis are from his recollections. Eva and Otto Pfister, "To Our Children," 84.

## 12.  Otto's Return to Paris

1. Except as otherwise noted, the quotations in this chapter are from Eva Pfister and Otto Pfister, "To Our Children," unpublished memoir (Los Angeles, 1979), 88–89.

2. Jef Rens, "René Bertholet et Otto Pfister," in *Rencontres avec le siècle* [Encounters with the Century], translated from the Dutch by Jean-Pierre Orban (Gembloux, Belgium: Editions Duculot, 1987), 115.

3. Letter dated November 8, 1940, from Otto to Eva. This letter was originally written in French, and Eva later translated it into English.

4. Ibid.

## 13.  Eva's Escape over the Pyrenees

1. Videotaped interview of Eva Pfister by Kathy Pfister, 1986.

2. Eva Pfister and Otto Pfister, "To Our Children," unpublished memoir (Los Angeles, 1979), 71.

3. Letter dated November 2, 1940, from Eva to Willi Eichler.

4. Lisa Fittko, who assisted Walter Benjamin and many others with the crossing of the Pyrenees in 1940–1941, described her efforts to help the struggling "Old Benjamin" to endure the strenuous hike through the mountains into Spain in her memoir. Lisa Fittko, *Escape through the Pyrenees* (Evanston, IL: Northwestern University Press, 1991) (first published in German as *Mein Weg über die Pyrenäen, Erinnerungen 1940/41* [Munich: Carl Hanser Verlag, 1985]), 103–15. Benjamin's crossing is also described in detail in an article by Michael Jackson, distinguished visiting professor of world religions, Harvard Divinity School, "In the Footsteps of Walter Benjamin." *Harvard Divinity Bulletin* 34 (2006). See also Sheila Eisenberg, *A Hero of Our Own: The Story of Varian Fry* (New York: Random House, 2001), 93–95.

5. Eisenberg, *A Hero of Our Own*, 165–69. See also Fittko, *Escape through the Pyrenees*, 145–47, describing Breitscheid's and Hilferding's refusal to cross the border without a French exit visa because they considered it "incompatible with their position as statesmen to leave by an illegal method" (based on reports from Varian Fry and Fritz Heine).

6. These were members of the Falange, the fascist movement in Spain under General Francisco Franco's regime.

7. Eva did not explain this reference to lost luggage. Apparently, those who escaped illegally over the Pyrenees at this time were able to arrange to have their luggage shipped across the border by train. Jackson, "In the Footsteps of Walter Benjamin."

8. Kathy Pfister's 1986 interview of Eva.

9. Marianne was one of the women who had been with Eva in Camp de Gurs and helped her explain their circumstances to the mayor in Castagnède when they initially arrived.

10. Eva is apparently referring to the Great Lisbon Earthquake on November 1, 1755, that nearly destroyed Lisbon and the surrounding area.

11. Except as otherwise noted, the quotations in this chapter are from Eva's diary entries written on the dates noted.

12. HICEM is an acronym of *HI*AS, *I*CA and *Emi*gdirect. HIAS continues to provide assistance to refugees. Tragically, the opposition to such assistance was one of the hateful motivations of the shooter in the massacre at the Tree of Life Synagogue in Pittsburgh on October 27, 2018.

13. Born in Vienna, Austria, in 1879, Friedrich (Fritz) Adler initially studied chemistry, physics, and mathematics and became a professor at the

University of Zurich, where he knew Albert Einstein. Adler gave up his scientific work and became actively involved in the international trade union movement and socialist politics, serving as secretary-general of the Social Democratic Party of Austria from 1911 to 1914. His fight against the war policy of Austria-Hungary in World War I led to his assassination of the minister-president of Austria in 1916. Released from prison during the revolution of 1918, Adler served as secretary of the International Working Union of Socialist Parties in 1921 and as secretary-general of the Labour and Socialist International until 1940. He and his wife fled to the United States in 1940.

14. This letter and list were obtained from the files of Jack Jacobs, professor of political science at the John Jay College of Criminal Justice at the City University of New York. Professor Jacobs obtained the document from the Jewish Labor Committee Collection, Robert F. Wagner Labor Archives, Tamiment Library, New York University.

## 14.  Eva's Voyage from Lisbon to New York

1. Jef Rens, "René Bertholet et Otto Pfister," in *Rencontres avec le siècle* [Encounters with the Century], translated from the Dutch by Jean-Pierre Orban (Gembloux, Belgium: Editions Duculot, 1987), 111.

## 15.  Eva's Daunting Task

1. Videotaped interview of Eva Pfister by Kathy Pfister, 1986.
2. Audiotape of interview of Eva in early August 1986 for a German television documentary about refugees who had escaped from Nazism. The interview was conducted by Karin Alles of Hessischer Rundfunk, which produced a documentary in November 1987 titled *Das Letzte Visum, Fluchtgeschichten anno 1940.*
3. Kathy Pfister's 1986 interview of Eva. Eva's living expenses in New York were likely paid initially by the ISK and/or the JLC, but she soon paid all of her living costs with income she earned from various jobs.
4. Born in 1903, Maurice Abravanel grew up in Lausanne, Switzerland. He then lived in Germany, where he pursued his interest in music from 1922 until 1933. When Hitler assumed power in 1933 Abravanel moved to

Paris, where he lived from 1933 to 1936 and served as music director of Balanchine's Paris Ballet. In 1936 he moved to New York as the youngest conductor that the New York Metropolitan Opera had ever hired. In 1947 Abravanel was appointed director of the Utah Symphony Orchestra, and between 1954 and 1980 he was the music director of the Music Academy of the West in Santa Barbara.

5. Videotaped interview of Eva Pfister by Kathy Pfister, 1986.

6. Eva's brother Erich Lewinski, who was then working in Marseille with the ERC, sent this cable to Eva about Otto.

7. Rafael Medoff, *FDR and the Holocaust: A Breach of Faith* (Washington, DC: David S. Wyman Institute for Holocaust Studies, 2013), 2; Charlotte R. Bonelli, *Exit Berlin: How One Woman Saved Her Family from Nazi Germany* (New Haven, CT: Yale University Press, 2014), 5.

8. Historian Jack Jacobs carefully researched and described the development and implementation of this extraordinary process aimed at rescuing endangered political refugees. Jack Jacobs, "A Friend in Need: The Jewish Labor Committee and Refugees from the German-Speaking Lands, 1933–1945," *YIVO Annual* 23 (1996) (abridged English translation of *Ein Freund in Not: Das Jüdische Arbeiterkomitee in New York und die Flüchtlinge aus den deutschsprachigen Ländern, 1933–1945* [Bonn: Forschungsinstitut der Friedrich-Ebert-Stiftung, 1993]): 391–417.

9. Letter dated February 28, 1940, from the president of the AFL, William Green, and the secretary-treasurer of the AFL, George Meany, to the "Officers of National and International Unions, State Federations of Labor and Central Labor Unions." Wagner Archives, Tamiment Library, New York University, Jewish Labor Committee Collection 1934–1947, Box 9.

10. Jacobs, "A Friend in Need," 393. This delegation was composed of William Green, president of the AFL; Isaiah Minkoff, executive secretary of the Jewish Labor Committee; David Dubinsky, president of the International Ladies Garment Workers Union and treasurer of the JLC; and Alexander Kahn, general manager of the *Forverts* (Forward), a Jewish daily newspaper that supported trade unions and democratic socialism.

11. Ibid., 394–95, 410, 415nn15, 57. Eleanor Roosevelt also supported efforts to rescue endangered political refugees during this time. Austrian socialist leader Joseph Buttinger (aka Gustav Richter) reported on a meeting he had with Eleanor Roosevelt in late June 1940 along with Joseph Lash and Willy Mueller about steps to be taken to rescue anti-Nazi

political refugees in Europe. See "Joseph Buttinger Report on 'Attempts to Organize Assistance for Political Refugees in France and England,' June 26–27, 1940," Selected Digitized Documents Related to the Holocaust and Refugees, 1933–1945, Eleanor Roosevelt Papers, Franklin D. Roosevelt Presidential Library & Museum (hereafter FDR Library).

12. Jacobs, "A Friend in Need," 393–95 (and authorities cited). See also, e.g., Doris Kearns Goodwin, *No Ordinary Time: Franklin & Eleanor Roosevelt; The Home Front in World War II* (New York: Touchstone, 1994), 100–101 (and authorities cited); Gregory Wallance, *America's Soul in the Balance* (Austin, TX: Greenleaf Book Group, 2012), 170–71, 231 (and authorities cited).

13. Letter dated July 3, 1940, from W. Green to Hon. Breckinridge Long, Wagner Archives, Tamiment Library, New York University, Jewish Labor Committee Collection 1934-1947.

14. Letter dated July 3, 1940, from Breckinridge Long to William Green, President, American Federation of Labor, Wagner Archives, Tamiment Library, New York University, Jewish Labor Committee Collection 1934–1947.

15. Jacobs, "A Friend in Need," 395–97. Rudolf Katz, secretary of the German Labor Delegation, provided names of prominent members of the German Social Democratic Party in exile; Paul Hagen was there to advocate for refugees with ties to Neu Beginnen; and Joseph Buttinger of the Austrian Revolutionary Socialists was there to vouch for the endangered Austrians. Hedwig Wachenheim, a former member of the Prussian Diet who had immigrated to America in 1935, also played an important role. Her criteria for endorsing Germans for these lists included those who were in immediate danger of being turned over to the Gestapo and excluded anyone believed to have been a communist or "fifth columnist."

16. Ibid. These lists are preserved in the Wagner Archives, Tamiment Library, New York University, Jewish Labor Committee Collection 1934–1947.

17. Jacobs, "A Friend in Need," 397.

18. These lists included: Rudolf Breitscheid, a leading member of the German Social Democratic Party who also served in the Reichstag during the Weimar Republic; Rudolf Hilferding, a leading German socialist theorist who served as minister of finance during the Weimar Republic; Marie Juchacz, one of the first female members of the German Social Democratic Party, the first female member of the Reichstag to make a speech before any German parliament, and a founder of the

Arbeiterwohlfahrt Committee (Workers Welfare Institution); and Friedrich Stampfer, a social democratic leader and journalist who served in the Reichstag during the Weimar Republic.

19. Jacobs, "A Friend in Need," 398.

20. National Archives, Record Group 59, Visa Division, General Visa Correspondence, 1940-45, 811.111 Refugees/254I, Box 149 (obtained through FOIA request and appeal). Attached to this list is another six-page list with the heading "In France." It contains the same names as in the telegram with brief descriptions of the occupations of each, including the following: "LEWINSKI, EVA, journalist and trade unionist."

21. In 2002, Secretary of State Colin Powell presented a posthumous award to Bingham on behalf of the American Foreign Service Association for his "constructive dissent" in assisting refugees, often in defiance of restrictive immigration policies. In 2006, the U.S. Postal Service issued a stamp honoring Bingham as a "Distinguished American Diplomat." And in 2011, the Simon Wiesenthal Center presented a posthumous Medal of Valor to Bingham for helping to save the lives of endangered refugees during his service as vice consul in Marseille. See also Robert Kim Bingham Sr., *Courageous Dissent: How Harry Bingham Defied His Government to Save Lives* (Greenwich: Triune Books, 2007); Robert Kim Bingham Sr., "Hiram ('Harry') Bingham Homepage," www://hirambinghamrescuer.com.

22. Letter from Eva to Willi Eichler dated November 2, 1940, original written in German. All quotes from this letter are from a translation by Eva.

23. Ibid.

24. Ibid. Karl Frank generally referred to himself in the United States as Paul Hagen and is referred to in this book as "Paul Hagen" or "Hagen." Joseph Buttinger also used the name Gustav Richter and is referred to in this book as "Joseph Buttinger" or "Buttinger."

25. Rather than having direct input in New York City on the selection of their ISK colleagues in the special visa list process, Stein and Deppe had been working in Cleveland and Buffalo to gather affidavits to support visitor's visas for a handful of endangered ISK members, including Eva. See letter dated August 23, 1940, from Maria Halberstadt of the League for Human Rights in Cleveland, Ohio, to John Winant, director of the International Labor Office, describing the status of this effort with attached drafts of affidavits, John Winant Papers, Box 178, Appeals for Refugee Aid, FDR Library.

26. Buttinger's wife, Muriel Gardiner, moved to Europe after graduating from Wellesley College in 1922 and studied in Oxford and then in Vienna, where she received a degree in medicine from the University of Vienna. She met and married Buttinger in Vienna and became actively involved in antifascist underground work. Gardiner used the code name "Mary" in her underground work that she described in her memoir. Gardiner claimed in 1983 that she was the character "Julia" in Lillian Hellman's memoirs *Pentimento* (1973) and in the movie *Julia* based on a chapter of that book. Gardiner's role in the resistance was more recently explored in Sheila Isenberg, *Muriel's War: An American Heiress in the Nazi Resistance* (New York: Palgrave Macmillan, 2010).

27. Terence Renaud, "The Genesis of the Emergency Rescue Committee, 1933–1942" (undergraduate thesis, Boston University, 2005). This essay along with Renaud's essay "'This Is Our Dunkirk': Karl B. Frank and the Politics of the Emergency Rescue Committee" (student essay, Boston University, 2009) provide a detailed historical account of the formation and work of the ERC.

28. In 1942, the ERC joined with the American branch of the International Relief Association, an organization that had been formed at the suggestion of Albert Einstein in May 1933 to aid the families of political prisoners in Germany and political refugees from Nazi terror. The name of the newly combined organization was the International Relief and Rescue Committee, which later changed to the International Rescue Committee (its current name).

29. Donna F. Ryan, *The Holocaust & the Jews of Marseille* (Urbana: University of Illinois, 1996), 141; Renaud, "The Genesis of the Emergency Rescue Committee, 1933–1942."

30. Varian Fry's book *Surrender on Demand* (Boulder, CO: Johnson Books/ U.S. Holocaust Memorial Museum, 1997), first published by Random House in 1945 after his return to the United States, preserved his recollection of his work in Marseille. A number of biographies have been written about Fry, including Sheila Isenberg, *A Hero of Our Own: The Story of Varian Fry* (New York: Random House, 2001); Carla Killough McClafferty, *In Defiance of Hitler: The Secret Mission of Varian Fry* (New York: Farrar, Straus, and Giroux, 2008); Andy Marino, *A Quiet American: The Secret War of Varian Fry* (New York: St. Martin's, 1999). Emmy Award–winning documentary filmmaker Pierre Sauvage and the Chambon Foundation he founded have done extensive work in preserving

and communicating the legacy of the work done by Fry and those who assisted him. Sauvage is creating a documentary film, *And Crown Thy Good—Varian Fry in Marseille*, about Fry and other Americans involved in rescue work in Marseille at that time.

31. Jacobs, "A Friend in Need," 398–401.

32. Mordecai Paldiel, *Saving the Jews: Amazing Stories of Men and Women Who Defied the "Final Solution"* (Rockville, MD: Schreiber Publishing, 2000), 62. According to Paldiel, "[Fry] was to coordinate his work with Dr. Frank Bohn, who was on a similar assignment, on behalf of the AFL (American Federation of Labor)—known as the Dubinsky list, and which was geared to rescue members of the former German Social Democratic party, now stranded in France and in danger of being turned over to the Gestapo." David Dubinsky, an American labor leader (president of the International Ladies Garment Workers Union), worked with Isaiah Minkhoff as treasurer of the JLC on these efforts by American labor leaders to rescue members of the labor movement in Europe who were threatened by the Nazis.

33. Jacobs, "A Friend in Need," 399.

34. Antje Dertinger, *Every Farewell Is a New Beginning: Erich Lewinski, a Biography*, translated by Tom Lewinski from *Die Drei Exile des Erich Lewinski* [Erich Lewinski, Three Times Exiled] (Gerlingen: Bleicher Verlag, 1995), 106–7, 109 (photo shows the following "advisors to Varian Fry's Emergency Rescue Committee—Marseilles, 1940": Erich Lewinski, Fritz Heine, Jacques Weisslitz, Daniel Bénédite, Heinz Ernst Oppenheimer, Hans Sahl, Marcel Chaminade, and Maurice Verzeanu).

35. Fry, *Surrender on Demand*, 14.

36. See, e.g., David S. Wyman, *The Abandonment of the Jews: America and the Holocaust, 1941–1945* (New York: New Press, 1984); Richard Breitman and Allan J. Lichtman, *FDR and the Jews* (Cambridge, MA: Belknap Press of Harvard University Press, 2013), 331n1.

37. Jacobs, "A Friend in Need," 394.

38. Breitman and Lichtman, *FDR and the Jews*, 168.

39. Ibid., 168, 368n20.

40. Ibid., 105–7. Attendees at this April 13, 1938, White House conference included James G. McDonald, who became the first chairman of the President's Advisory Committee; Columbia University professor Joseph P. Chamberlain; Steven S. Wise, Henry Morganthau Sr., and Bernard

Baruch representing the Jewish community; Samuel McCrea Cavert and Reverend Michael J. Ready representing the Christian community; Secretary of State Cordell Hull; and Secretary of Labor Frances Perkins.

41. Ibid., 169.
42. Ibid., 168, 368n21. See also Doris Kearns Goodwin, *No Ordinary Time, Franklin & Eleanor Roosevelt: The Home Front in World War II* (Touchstone 1994), 173.
43. Ibid., 173. Steinhardt, the only U.S. ambassador who was Jewish, sent this telegram on October 2, 1940.
44. Ibid., 174. Other attendees at the meeting were George Warren, the executive secretary of the President's Advisory Committee on Political Refugees, and Solicitor General Francis Biddle and Henry Hart from the Justice Department. President Roosevelt also expressed concern about the delays reported by the committee in the State Department's processing of visa applications.
45. Ibid.

## 16.  Help from Eleanor Roosevelt

1. Videotaped interview of Eva Pfister by Kathy Pfister, 1986.
2. Eva Pfister and Otto Pfister, "To Our Children," unpublished memoir (Los Angeles, 1979), 90.
3. Kathy Pfister's 1986 interview of Eva.
4. Eva and Otto Pfister, "To Our Children," 90.
5. Ibid., 91.
6. Summary of Hill's life prepared in her memory upon her death in 1979 and sent to newspapers and to Eva by Hill's close companion, Grace Osgood.
7. Ibid.
8. Not much has been published about the life of Dorothy Hill, this quiet hero who helped so many and would have such a determinative impact on Eva's and Otto's lives. The archives at Wellesley College contain files of the Summer Institute for Social Progress with articles about her long tenure of leadership there.
9. Reference letter for Eva from Dorothy P. Hill dated October 28, 1940.
10. Eleanor Roosevelt, "My Day" column, September 17, 1940.
11. Ibid.

12. Letter dated October 31, 1940, from Eva to the President's Advisory Committee, Att: Mr. George Warren.

13. Letter dated October 31, 1940, from S. M. Levitas to the President's Advisory Committee. Sol Levitas became executive editor of the *New Leader* in 1937, succeeding founding editor James Oneal. The *New Leader* was a publication founded in 1924 to promote the interests of socialist and labor movements. Prominent contributors to the *New Leader* included Eugene V. Debs, Norman Thomas, Conrad Adenauer, Willy Brandt, Albert Camus, Arthur Koestler, George Orwell, and Ignazio Silone. Varian Fry was a contributing editor to the *New Leader* until he resigned in 1945 because of a disagreement with its editorial policy. Twenty years later, Fry wrote an article about the ERC's twenty-fifth anniversary that was published in the *New Leader.* Sheila Isenberg, *Muriel's War: An American Heiress in the Nazi Resistance* (New York: Palgrave Macmillan, 2010), 247–48, 262. The magazine ceased its print publication in 2006 and ceased its online version in 2010.

14. Letter dated October 31, 1940, from F. W. Sollmann "To whom it may concern."

15. Eva's notes introducing her translation from German to English of her November 2, 1940, letter to Willi Eichler.

16. Eva retained a copy of another slightly different version of these summary descriptions with a note in pencil in her handwriting at the top: "Jewish Labor Committee, 11/12/40."

17. The undated memorandum from Stein is titled "A Group of Refugees, Trapped in the Unoccupied Part of France. Some in Switzerland."

18. Letter dated December 9, 1940, from Sumner Welles to Malvina Thompson.

19. For detailed information on Sumner Welles's controversial role in efforts to rescue Jews and political refugees threatened by the Nazis, including his response to the Riegner report on the Nazis' plan for mass murder of the Jews in the fall of 1942, see, e.g., David S. Wyman, *The Abandonment of the Jews: America and the Holocaust, 1941–1945* (New York: New Press, 1984); Richard Breitman and Allan J. Lichtman, *FDR and the Jews* (Cambridge, MA: Belknap Press of Harvard University Press, 2013). See also Gregory J. Wallance, *America's Soul in the Balance: The Holocaust, FDR's State Department, and the Moral Disgrace of an American Aristocracy* (Austin, TX: Greenleaf Book Group, 2012), 91–99, 183–91.

20. Letter dated December 12, 1940, from Eva Lewinski to Malvina Thompson. At the bottom of this letter, Eva listed the names of the persons "for whom Mrs. Roosevelt so kindly intervened: Mr. Pfister, Otto; Mr. Lewinski, Erich and wife Herta; Mr. Kakies, Hans; Miss Blencke, Erna; Mr. Albrecht, Eugen; Miss Block, Nora; Mrs. Walter, Herta; Miss Peiper, Gisela; Miss Timmermann, Frieda; Miss Amelung, Irmgard; Mr. Bertholet, René and wife Johanna."

21. Letter dated December 13, 1940, from Sumner Welles to Eleanor Roosevelt.

## 17. Three Crucial Meetings

1. Eva Pfister and Otto Pfister, "To Our Children," unpublished memoir (Los Angeles, 1979), 92.
2. Videotaped interview of Eva Pfister by Kathy Pfister, 1986.
3. Letter dated December 20, 1940, from Dorothy Hill to Eliot Coulter.
4. Paul L. Benjamin served as president of the American Association of Social Workers, as a member of the Emergency Rescue Committee of Buffalo, and as director of the Buffalo Council of Social Agencies. Benjamin's papers are at the Social Welfare History Archives in the University of Minnesota Libraries. The archive's abstract states: "The Paul L. Benjamin papers reflect his interest in the family, the profession of social work, leisure, and relief measures during the depression."
5. Eva's memorandum is titled "Conference with Mrs. Roosevelt, December 27, 1940, White House."
6. Eva and Otto Pfister, "To Our Children," 93.
7. Letter dated December 30, 1940, from Dorothy P. Hill to Malvina Thompson.
8. Letter dated December 30, 1940, from Dorothy P. Hill to Eleanor Roosevelt.
9. Critical information about the U.S. government's consideration of Otto's visa case was discovered in records obtained pursuant to multiple requests from various agencies under the Freedom of Information Act (FOIA). This process was time-consuming and required persistence. See the Afterword in this volume.
10. Memorandum #2, Department of State, Visa Division, December 28, 1940, titled "Political Refugees," National Archives, Record Group No.

59, Visa Division; General Visa Correspondence, 1940–45, 811.111 Refugees/973, Box 152 (produced on August 22, 2012, in response to FOIA request and administrative appeal).

11. Ibid., 3.

12. Memorandum for the Director, Federal Bureau of Investigation, United States Justice Department, December 31, 1940, from Edward A. Tamm (sent by letter from FBI dated January 24, 2013, in response to FOIA request and administrative appeal).

13. Ibid., 2–3.

14. *Refugees and Rescue: The Diaries and Papers of James G. McDonald, 1935–1945,* eds. Richard Breitman, Barbara McDonald Stewart, and Severin Hochberg (Bloomington: Indiana University Press, 2009), 250–56; Saul S. Friedman, *No Haven for the Oppressed: United States Policy Toward Jewish Refugees, 1938–1945* (Detroit: Wayne State University Press, 1973), 121–24. On June 20, 1941, Congress enacted Senate Bill 913 (P.L. 113) requiring the denial of visas whenever any American diplomatic or consular officer "knows or has reason to believe" that granting a visa would "endanger the public safety of the United States"—providing legislative support for the State Department's application of its "close relatives" rule.

15. Letter dated December 30, 1940, from S. Welles to Malvina Thompson.


## 18. 1940 Correspondence

1. Eva retained these letters, and she translated excerpts of them from French and German into English. We translated additional letters and cards they wrote to each other during this period.

2. When we began our research, we were not certain that the "little blue book" was the diary Eva kept from the time she was interned in the Vel' d'Hiv until she escaped from France—because the cover on that diary was not blue. It was a primarily beige cloth cover with a pattern of blue lines. However, we soon confirmed that this cloth cover was removable (it apparently was put on later for protection), and the diary's actual cover is solid blue. In addition, one of Otto's letters to Eva refers to twelve empty pages at the end of the "little book," and we confirmed that there are twelve blank pages at the end of this diary.

3. Yvonne Oullion was the friend to whom Otto had sent his postcard from the Nazi prisoner-of-war camp and signed it "Paul Bois."

4. René Bertholet used many pseudonyms during the war, including Charles, Pierre, Pierre-Robert, Robert, and Roger.

5. This comment about twelve empty pages helped us confirm that Eva's diary was the "little blue book."


## 19.  Eva's Other Activities

1. Herzog's work included *Die Affäre Dreyfus* (The Dreyfus Affair), which was adapted into a 1931 film in English (*Dreyfus*) and into a play in London in 1937 (*I Accuse!*).

2. Eva retained a copy of this speech she wrote in German, and we translated it. She also gave speeches in English to various other groups seeking support for the rescue of refugees trapped in Europe.


## 20.  Further Pleas

1. Letter dated January 2, 1941, from Sumner Welles to Eleanor Roosevelt.

2. Memo from Visa Division to Mr. Long dated January 3, 1940 (receipt stamped January 3, 1941), National Archives, Record Group No. 59, Visa Division, General Visa Correspondence, 1940–45, 811.111 Refugees/773, Box 151.

3. Ibid. The attached sheet also includes status reports on the visa cases of Nora Block, Herta Walter, Irmgard Amelung, Erhard Konopka, Lise Oppenheimer, René and Johanna Bertholet, Hans Lehnert, Änne Kappius, Max Diamant, Erich and Erna Petzschke, Boris and Rosa Goldenberg, Alfred Stein, Erna Lange, Helene Stoecker, Anita Augsburg, and Lydia Gustava Heymann.

4. The American Friends Service Committee, a Quaker organization devoted to service and peace programs throughout the world, was founded in 1917.

5. Stern signed the letter, identifying himself as "a writer and a worker in adult education, member of the Penclub and former director of the Worker High School in Vienna (Wiener Arbeiter Hochschule). Helped out of Marseille by Department of State cablegrams Nos. 167 and 235, I am at present at the Cooperative College Workshop of the American Friends Service Committee in Haverford, Penna."

6. Letter dated January 13, 1941, from Eva to Paul Benjamin.

7. Letter dated January 22, 1941, from Sumner Welles to Malvina Thompson.

## 21.  Otto's Wait for a Visa

1. This report provides a good sense of the number of people and issues in-volved in Eva's rescue efforts at that time. Eva's correspondence with Willi Eichler (much of which is preserved in the archives of the Friedrich-Ebert-Stiftung in Bonn, Germany) refers to a large number of individuals and groups seeking refuge from the Nazis—in addition to the ISK col-leagues for whom Eva was seeking U.S. visas. The excerpts from this correspondence quoted in this book focus on Eva's efforts to rescue her ISK colleagues, including Otto.
2. Efforts to obtain documents that might answer these questions under the Freedom of Information Act are explained in the Afterword along with information about the apparent destruction of documents.
3. Translated by Eva. The original is in Rainer Maria Rilke, *Werke in Vier Bänden* [Works in Four Volumes], Vol. 2 (Frankfurt am Main: Insel Verlag, 1966), 320.
4. Our Lady of the Guard is a basilica on the highest natural point in Marseille, a 532-foot limestone outcrop on the south side of the Old Port.
5. The Chateau d'If is a fortress, later a prison, on the island of If in the Mediterranean about a mile offshore in the Bay of Marseille.

## 22.  Otto's Escape to America

1. Johannes (Hans) Fittko's wife, Lisa Fittko, described her recollection of her efforts and those of her husband to help guide small groups of refu-gees, including the philosopher Walter Benjamin, in making the crossing over the Pyrenees into Spain. Lisa Fittko, *Escape through the Pyrenees* (Evanston, IL: Northwestern University Press, 1991), first published in German as *Mein Weg über die Pyrenäen, Erinnerungen 1940/41* (Munich: Carl Hanser Verlag, 1985). The trail taken by these refugees, includ-ing Eva and Otto, was later named "Chemin Walter Benjamin" (Walter Benjamin Trail).
2. Eva described in this letter the status of rescue efforts for the following ISK colleagues: Eva's brother Erich Lewinski, his wife Herta Lewinski,

Erika (Mros) Kakies, her husband Hans Kakies, Eugen Albrecht, Frieda Timmermann, Rosa (Erna Blencke), Erhard Konopka, Gisa (Gisela Peiper), Irmgard Amelung, Lise (Konopka), Hanna (Joanna/Jeanne Fortmüller Bertholet), and René Bertholet.

3. Tom Pfister, Peter Pfister, and Kathy Pfister, *Eva and Otto: America's Vetting and Rescue of Political Refugees during World War II* (Los Angeles: Pfisters, 2017), 84–86. See also Helga Haas-Rietschel and Sabine Hering, *Nora Platiel, Sozialistin, Emigrantin, Politikerin: Eine Biographie* (Köln: Bund Verlag GmbH, 1990, printed with the assistance of the Friedrich-Ebert-Stiftung), 113–16.

4. Letter dated April 7, 1941, from Sumner Welles to Eleanor Roosevelt with enclosed memorandum dated April 3, 1941, from Mr. Warren to Mr. Welles, National Archives, Record Group No. 59, Visa Division, General Visa Correspondence, 1940–45, 811.111 Refugees/1274C, Box 155.

5. Ibid.

6. The Emergency Rescue Committee's file on Gisela Peiper includes the following cable that was sent on April 17, 1941: "Advised Mr. Warren that the following people were sailing on the boat 'Nyassa' which left Lisbon on April 15th: Otto Pfister, Lotte Leonard, Mrs. Charlotte Jaeckel, Miss Chane Lerner, Gisela Peiper, Heinz Paechter and family, Dr. Siegfried Kracauer and family."

7. Eva Pfister and Otto Pfister, "To Our Children," unpublished memoir (Los Angeles, 1979), *93*.

8. Ibid., 91.

9. Videotaped interview of Eva Pfister by Kathy Pfister, 1986.

10. Ibid. The organization was known by the Russian acronym "ORT," which stands for "Organization for the Distribution of Artisanal and Agricultural Skills."

## 23. Eva's Defense

1. This correspondence we discovered at the Friedrich-Ebert-Stiftung between Eva and Willi Eichler about her marriage to Otto saddened us. It is difficult to understand how Willi Eichler could criticize Eva for marrying Otto under these circumstances. For further thoughts on the profoundly good and troubling sides of the ISK, see the Afterword in this volume.

## 24. Priorities

1. A review of the early case files of the ERC provides some information about the nature and extent of Eva's work throughout this period. These individual case files are in the German and Jewish Émigré Collection in the M. E. Grenander Department of Special Collections and Archives, State University of New York at Albany.
2. The pending question of the extension of the U.S. visa for "Tegel" (Kakies) is referred to in Eva's letter to Eichler dated August 13, 1941, in which she defended her decision to marry Otto.
3. ERC case file on "Hans Kakies," M. E. Grenander Department of Special Collections and Archives, State University of New York at Albany, Box 1, Folder 32.

## 25. René-Eva Correspondence

1. The declassified OSS documents are in the Operational Records of the Office of Strategic Services, Record Group 226, at the National Archives and Records Administration (hereafter OSS Files, NARA). The declassified SOE documents are available on microfilm at the Cecil H. Green Library at Stanford University in *Special Operations Executive, 1940–1946: Subversion and Sabotage during World War II; Series One: SOE Operations in Western Europe* (from Adam Matthew Publications). Information about the ISK's involvement with the SOE during the war can be found in Part 3: Germany, 1936–1945, reels 28–30 (hereafter SOE Files).
2. Neal H. Petersen, *From Hitler's Doorstep: The Wartime Intelligence Reports of Allen Dulles, 1942–1945* (University Park: Pennsylvania State University Press, 1996), 23 (commentary to Document 1-3).
3. Susan Elizabeth Subak, *Rescue & Flight: American Relief Workers Who Defied the Nazis* (Lincoln: University of Nebraska Press, 2010), 262n18; Christof Mauch, *The Shadow War against Hitler: The Covert Operations of America's Wartime Secret Intelligence Service* (New York: Columbia University Press, 1999); Petersen, *From Hitler's Doorstep.* Susan Subak came closest to identifying the "Eva" in the René-Eva correspondence, noting that she may have been Eva Wasserman, who had worked with the Emergency Rescue and Relief Committee, or Eva Lewinski, who had worked with Toni Sender and Dyno Loewenstein in preparing a memorandum for

the labor division of the OSS. We gratefully acknowledge Susan Subak's assistance in researching the OSS files at the National Archives and locating OSS documents pertaining to the René-Eva correspondence. See the Afterword in this volume.

4. SOE Files, Cecil H. Green Library, Stanford, HS 6/653, 29A.

5. Ibid.

6. Bertholet notes in this letter that "these sums should be enough for today; it is impossible to know how the need will increase if the resistance work spreads further and the purchasing power of the French franc sinks further."

7. The copy of this letter in the SOE's files includes handwritten notations from Willi Eichler to Eva indicating that Bertholet sent it to Eichler before he sent it to her. Eichler's note to Eva crosses out the paragraph describing the proposed method of transferring funds and advises Eva only to use the letter without the portion he crossed out.

8. Léon Jouhaux, who was arrested and imprisoned in Buchenwald, was awarded the Nobel Peace Prize in 1951.

9. January 26, 1942, memorandum from Arthur J. Goldberg to David C. Shaw (declassified authority NND 877092 by EF NARA 10/21/06).

10. Letter dated "15 mai 1942" from Eva to "Très chers amis" (with note "Lewinski an Hanna Fortmüller"), copy obtained from the Friedrich-Ebert-Stiftung in Bonn, Germany.

11. Ibid.

12. Undated document with heading "ADDRESSEE: Mrs. Eva Pfister, 40-40 Ebertson Street, Elmhurst, L.I.," Record Group 226, Stack 190, Row 38, Comp. 18, Shelf 4, Entry 092A, Box 16, OSS Files, NARA, College Park.

13. John C. Hughes to F. Lamont Belin, June 25, 1942, Record Group 226, Stack 190, Row 38, Comp. 18, Shelf 4, Entry 092A, Box 16, OSS Files, NARA, College Park.

14. Undated document with heading "ADDRESSEE: Mrs. Eva Pfister, 40-40 Ebertson Street, Elmhurst, L.I.," Record Group 226, Stack 190, Row 38, Comp. 18, Shelf 4, Entry 092A, Box 16, OSS Files, NARA, College Park.

15. F. L. Belin to Colonel Corderman, July 14, 1942, Record Group 226, Stack 190, Row 38, Comp. 18, Shelf 4, Entry 092A, Box 16, OSS Files, NARA, College Park.

16. Mauch, *The Shadow War against Hitler*, 169. As noted previously, Hagen's real name was Karl Boromäus Frank, but he used the name Paul Hagen in the United States. We refer to him as Hagen in this book.

17. Mauch, *The Shadow War against Hitler*, 170–71.

18. Ibid. Hagen had become the most notorious and controversial figure in the United States among German political refugees. As historian Mauch noted, "No other German exile was the subject of so many reports from American intelligence between 1941 and 1943 as was Hagen, no one else was met with so much mistrust, and no one polarized opinion as much."

19. Ibid., 172.

20. Ibid., 290n27.

21. Late in his life when he was organizing his files for posterity, Hagen still did not know that the OSS had implemented many of his ideas through the work of others, primarily members of the ISK. In Hagen's papers at Stanford's Hoover Library and Archives, a handwritten note dated "1942" was taped on the file containing his memorandum of recommendations to the OSS. The note described the contents of the file: "A plan to make contacts with the German underground movement in order to assist its opposition activities and to gain intelligence for the American forces." It further explained that the plan "was prepared for the U.S. Army . . . in consultation with Lt Col. Julius Klein"; that "mention is made of previous contacts of a similar nature with the OSS, Colonel Donovan, Wallace Deval, and Arthur Goldberg"; and that "there were meetings with Allen Dulles, at one of which I was present and a prospective member of a team in Switzerland." The note concluded: "Neither the OSS nor the U.S. Army was willing to sponsor such a project."

22. Mauch, *The Shadow War against Hitler*, 174.

23. Ibid.

24. Ibid., 174–75.

25. May 7, 1942, memorandum from Arthur J. Goldberg to Allen Dulles and George Bowdon, NARA Rq. 226 190 R.9, Comp. 8, Shelf 1, Entry 168, Box 64 F. 832, Declassified: NND 857168.

26. Record Group 226, Entry 168, Box 66, Folder 832, OSS Files, NARA, College Park (cited in Mauch, *Shadow War against Hitler*, 228n39).

27. Hugh R. Wilson had served in the U.S. Foreign Service as minister to Switzerland (1927–1937) and ambassador to Germany (1938). Petersen, *From Hitler's Doorstep*, 2.

28. The submitters of the Sender Memorandum are described as follows: *Paul Kohn*, Country of Origin Austria, Lecturer on Political Economy, Institute for Workers' Education, Vienna, Research worker in the Economic Statistical Department of the Chamber of Labor in Vienna, and in the Research Department of the Austrian Federation of Labor;

*Dyno Lowenstein*, Country of Origin Germany, son of the head of the Berlin School System who created the Modern Schools in Berlin in 1933, active in Social Democratic Youth Movement in Germany, Secretary, International Federation of Teachers in France, Executive Member, workers' education organization, "Amis de L'Enfance Ouvriere," Paris; *Eva Lewinski Pfister*, Member and Officer, White Collar Workers Union in Western Germany, Member editorial staff of an anti-Nazi publication house in Paris, and Member, French White Collar Workers Union; and *Toni Sender*, 1920–33 Social Democratic member, German Reichstag; member of the Committee on Foreign Affairs and the Committee on Economics during the entire period, Labor member, City Council of Frankfurt, 1919–23, and Editor, Metal Workers Union Magazine, Berlin.

29. Sender Memorandum, 2.

30. Ibid., 3.

31. Ibid., 3–6.

32. Ibid., 7–8.

33. Arthur J. Goldberg to Allen W. Dulles, June 29, 1942, Record Group 226, Stack 190, Row 9, Comp. 8, Shelf 1, Entry 168, Box 64, Folder 832, OSS Files, NARA, College Park; Mauch, *Shadow War against Hitler*, 17.

34. Some officials in the OSS determined that the later reports of the OELR were of limited value. See, e.g., memorandum from John C. Hughes to Major David Bruce, November 18, 1942, Record Group 226, Stack 190, Row 9, Comp. 8, Shelf 1, Entry 168, Box 65, Folder 838, OSS Files, NARA, College Park. Other OSS initiatives to take advantage of the knowledge and connections of German anti-Nazi émigrés in America were hindered by deeply ingrained rifts between the different German political groups in exile. Mauch, *Shadow War against Hitler*, 79–85.

35. SOE Files, Cecil H. Green Library, Stanford, HS 6/653, 12A. The SOE operatives who sent and received memos about Bertholet were designated by initials and numbers to conceal their identities. This memo was from "X" to "DCE/2."

36. SOE Files, Cecil H. Green Library, Stanford, HS 6/653, 18A.

37. Ibid., 33A. This undated document in the SOE's files that remains heavily redacted noted "Robert's desire to have his correspondence passed directly to Willi—without being seen by any of the I.T.F. people. He is insistent on this and I think we ought to obey his wishes." The message explained that Robert "does not think a great deal of the discretion of some of the I.T.F people . . . and [t]he I.T.F. will receive from Willi what they ought

to know." Another heavily redacted document in the SOE's files dated November 18, 1941, confirmed the arrangement about the flow of information from Bertholet to the SOE through Eichler. Ibid., 20A.

38. London Report No. 80/893, February 10, 1943, Source G.400, Country: United States, SOE Files, Cecil H. Green Library, Stanford, HS 6/653.

39. Petersen, *From Hitler's Doorstep*, 23. Correspondence from Eva to the Jewish Labor Committee (JLC) in 1942 and 1943 confirms that the JLC was one source of such funding. See, e.g., letter dated March 15, 1943, from Eva to J. Pat of the JLC marked "strictly confidential" advising that "our friends abroad" had received $3,000 that had been sent at the beginning of February and thanking the JLC for its "generous assistance." Copies of this correspondence were located in files that were graciously provided for us by Jack Jacobs, professor of political science at John Jay College and the CUNY Graduate Center.

40. Petersen, *From Hitler's Doorstep*, 102.

41. It appears that only one biography has been written about Bertholet. It has not been translated into English. Philippe Adant, *Widerstand und Wagemut: René Bertholet—eine Biographie*, translated from French by Susanne Miller (Frankfurt: dipa-Verlag, 1996). A research work by a German student, Sabine Abel, has been cited in various studies, but we have not been able to locate a copy of Abel's work. Others have commented on Bertholet's resistance work. See Jef Rens, "René Bertholet et Otto Pfister," in *Rencontres avec le siècle* [Encounters with the Century], translated from the Dutch by Jean-Pierre Orban (Gembloux, Belgium: Editions Duculot, 1987); Mark Seaman, *Saboteur: The Untold Story of SOE's Youngest Agent at the Heart of the French Resistance* (London: John Blake Publishing, 2018), describing Bertholet's secret work with SOE agent Tony Brooks.

42. Andreas G. Graf, *Anarchisten Gegen Hitler* (Berlin: Lukas Verlag, 2001), 148.

43. Adant, *Widerstand und Wagemut*, 68.

44. Michael R. D. Foot, *SOE in France: An Account of the Work of the British Special Operations Executive in France 1940–1944* (London: Whitehall History Publishing in association with Frank Cass, 2004), 143, 196. See also Seaman, *Saboteur*, 17–18, 96–100.

45. Graf, *Anarchisten Gegen Hitler*, 149n 68, quoting from letter written by Hans Jahn to Eva and Otto dated March 19, 1943 (in MRC, 159/3/C/a/ 106). *See* also Seaman, *Saboteur*.

46. Graf, *Anarchisten Gegen Hitler*, 149n66.

47. Ibid.
48. Adant, *Widerstand und Wagemut*, 70 (quoting Bunzli).
49. Ibid., 48.


## 26. Three Big Decisions

1. Records about the consideration of Eva's application for an extension of her visa were ultimately declassified and released in 2014 after numerous requests and administrative appeals under FOIA. See description in the Afterword.
2. Minutes of Interdepartmental Committee Number II dated March 10, 1943, released by the FBI in response to FOIA request (FOIPA Release No. 253288, February 27, 2014).
3. Ibid.
4. Ibid. Benjamin David Zevin (1901–1984) served as president of World Publishing Company from 1945 to 1962. "Ben Zevin Dies at 88; Leader of World Publishing Company" (Obituaries), *New York Times*, December 29, 1984.
5. An eight-page transcript of this interview was released by the FBI in response to a FOIA request (FOIPA Release No. 253288, February 27, 2014).
6. Ibid.
7. Memorandum from Review Committee A, Mr. W. R. Vallance, to Mr. B. M. Hulley dated May 17, 1945, released by the FBI in response to a FOIA request (FOIPA Release No. 253288, February 27, 2014). The Association of Free Germans, Inc., had been formed in New York in 1941 by a number of prominent political refugees in the United States. The association's purpose was to defeat Nazism and promote the ideals of a Germany free from the dominance of Nazism and all other forms of totalitarianism.
8. Minutes of October 5, 1943, meeting of Interdepartmental Visa Review Committee Division (A), released by the FBI in response to a FOIA request (FOIPA Release No. 253288, February 27, 2014).
9. Ibid. The only alleged communists identified in the majority opinion as being sponsored by Eva while she worked for the ERC were René Bertholet and Boris Goldenberg. René Bertholet had worked for years with the ISK and was at that time providing valuable secret information to the OSS through Eva. The early case files of the ERC during the years

in which Eva worked there do not include a file on Goldenberg.

10. Ibid.

11. These words from Warren Christopher are also in his tribute to Varian Fry in the preface to the most recent edition of Varian Fry's book, *Surrender on Demand* (Boulder, CO: Johnson Books and U.S. Holocaust Memorial Museum, 1997).

12. Minutes of October 5, 1943, meeting of Interdepartmental Visa Review Committee Division (A).

13. Ibid.

14. Ibid.

15. Ibid.

16. Memorandum dated October 22, 1943, with "Excerpt from opinion of the Board of Appeals," released by the FBI in response to a FOIA request (FOIPA Release No. 253288, February 27, 2014). None of the agencies involved in the proceedings pertaining to Eva's application for an extension of her visa released the full opinion of the Board of Appeals in response to multiple FOIA requests.

17. Memorandum dated July 9, 1943, from John Edgar Hoover to "Visa Division, Department of State," produced by the FBI on June 12, 2012, in response to a FOIA request (FOIPA No. 1178379-001).

18. Ibid.

19. Ibid.

20. Ibid.

21. National Archives, Record Group No. 65, FBI file 100-HQ-200123, Serial 4, Box 2921. This document was produced in 2012 in response to our FOIA request and appeal (Case No. NW 38170). Paul Tillich, a well-known German American theologian and philosopher, had been dismissed from his position as a professor of theology at the University of Frankfurt in 1933 as a result of his lectures and speeches in opposition to the Nazis. At the urging of Reinhold Niebuhr, Tillich moved to America in 1933, where he taught for many years at Union Theological Seminary in New York. He later also held academic positions at Harvard University and the University of Chicago.

22. Ibid.

23. Partially redacted memorandum (our emphasis) dated March 22, 1957, to unknown recipient with summary information about "Eva Lewinski Pfister" produced by the FBI on June 12, 2012, in response to a FOIA request (FOIPA No. 1178379-001). We do not know why this

information about Eva was requested from the FBI in 1957.

24. National Archives, U.S. Subject Index to Correspondence and Case Files of the INS, 1903–1959, Record Group 85, Microfilm Publication T458, Index to: Subject and Policy Files, 1893–1957 (ARC ID 559947). In response to our FOIA request and appeal, the document was identified but not found.

25. National Archives, Record Group No. 65, FBI file 100-263362-1, declassified July 24, 2012, and produced on July 27, 2012, in response to a FOIA request and appeal (Case No. NW 38170).

26. Letter dated February 1, 1944, from Otto to Willi Eichler. We were unable to locate the letter from Eichler that is referred to in Otto's letter.

27. National Archives, Record Group No. 226, OSS Personnel Files, Pfister Otto (blue label), Box 601. This personnel file was released in response to our FOIA request. The pages are marked "DECLASSIFIED NND 47589 by MKS, Date 8/13/2012."

28. Memorandum in Otto's OSS personnel file from Lt. (jg) Carl Devoe to Lt. Col. Alan M. Scaife dated July 30, 1945.

29. Memorandum from George O. Pratt to David C. Shaw dated September 12, 1946, re: Extra Compensation for Otto Pfister.

30. Memorandum dated April 13, 1944, from Col. E. F. Connely, chief of the Procurement Branch, to the U.S. surgeon general titled "Otto Pfister, Waiver of Disqualifying Physical Defects (Vision) for Enlistment."

31. Letter dated November 5, 1944, from Eva in New York to Otto in Europe.

## 27.  A Devastating Loss

1. Dr. Karl Kautsky, a well-known Austrian social democrat, was Eva's gynecologist and friend.

2. These individual case files are in the German and Jewish Émigré Collection in the M. E. Grenander Department of Special Collections and Archives at the University at Albany, State University of New York.

3. Emergency Rescue Committee case file on "Dora Jurkat," M. E. Grenander Department of Special Collections and Archives, State University of New York at Albany, Box 1, Folder 29. Dr. Ernest H. Jurkat, born in Germany in 1905, was an economist, sociologist, urban planner, and writer who served as personal economic adviser to Pennsylvania governor

Milton Shapp and was chairman of the Governor's Council of Economic Advisors.

## 28. Otto's OSS Mission

1. Eva Pfister and Otto Pfister, "To Our Children," unpublished memoir (Los Angeles, 1979), 99. Otto apparently received his special OSS training in what is now Prince William Forest Park near Quantico, Virginia. See Dr. John Whiteclay Chambers II, *Bang-Bang Boys, Jedburghs, and the House of Horrors: A History of OSS Training Operations in World War II* (n.p.: An Uncommon Valor Reprint, 2016), describing OSS training facilities in secluded national parks during World War II.
2. Eva and Otto Pfister, "To Our Children," 99.
3. Memorandum from Lt. (jg) Carl Devoe to Lt. Col. Alan M. Scaife, July 30, 1945, Pfister Otto, OSS Personnel Files, Record Group 226, Stack 230, Row 86, Comp. 38, Shelf 4, Entry 224, Box 601, National Archives and Record Administration, College Park. This personnel file was released in response to our FOIA request and marked "DECLASSIFIED" on August 13, 2012.
4. Handwritten chronology in Otto's OSS folder
5. Letter in German from Eichler to Otto, August 1, 1945.
6. Interview of Arthur Goldberg, Persico Papers, Hoover Institution, Stanford, CA.
7. Christof Mauch, *The Shadow War against Hitler: The Covert Operations of America's Wartime Secret Intelligence Service* (New York: Columbia University Press, 1999), 178–80.
8. V-mail (Victory Mail) was a process used by Americans to correspond with soldiers who were stationed overseas. V-mail letters were reviewed by mail censors, photographed and transported as thumbnail images in negative microfilm, and then enlarged and printed at their destination.
9. Marie Juchacz was a prominent anti-Nazi political leader who, as a member of the Reichstag during the Weimar Republic, had been the first woman to make a speech before any German parliament. After Hitler assumed power, she escaped to France and then to America. See *Marie Juchacz, Gründerin der Arbeiterwohlfahrt: Leben und Werk* (Bonn: Arbeiterwohlfahrt, 1979).
10. Pietro Badoglio was an Italian general who was appointed prime minister

of Italy when the king deposed Mussolini in 1943. Badoglio disgraced himself by, among other things, abandoning Rome to the Nazis and fleeing with his government.

11. After Eva's brother moved to England, he began using the English name "John" instead of his German name "Hans." With England at war against Germany and with John being a British soldier, the reason for this name change is clear.

12. The unsuccessful plot by Stauffenberg and other German officers to assassinate Hitler on July 20, 1944, is described in detail in Peter Hoffmann, *German Resistance to Hitler* (Cambridge, MA: Harvard University Press, 1988), 106–25. According to Hoffman, "A 'People's Court' tried and convicted about two hundred people who were involved in the 20 July plot. Most of them were executed within two hours of sentencing. . . . The condemned men were strangled with thin wire. The first few dozen executions were filmed for Hitler to watch" (125).

13. The role of different French resistance groups in the liberation of Paris is thoroughly examined in Robert Gildea, *Fighters in the Shadows: A New History of the French Resistance* (Cambridge, MA: Belknap Press of Harvard University Press, 2015).

## 29. The War Drags On

1. According to historian Rebecca Erbelding, "A reader looking for information [about German extermination camps] could find it, though atrocity stories were usually relegated—due to competition with war news and the fact that they were usually unverified—to the inside pages of the newspaper." Erbelding observed that the Soviet Union had invited journalists to tour the largely abandoned Majdanek concentration camp after it was liberated in July 1944. She also noted that "the ten million subscribers to *Life* magazine could read a description of the crematoriums and mass graves in a September [1944] article, 'Sunday in Poland,' while *PM*, a daily New York newspaper, printed a two-page spread including a life-sized photograph of a child's shoe the reporter had taken from the piles of victim's belongings discovered at the camp and brought home." Rebecca Erbelding, *Rescue Board: The Untold Story of America's Efforts to Save the Jews of Europe* (New York: Doubleday 2018), 219.

2. Eva Pfister and Otto Pfister, "To Our Children," unpublished memoir (Los

Angeles, 1979), 100–101.

3. The Battle of Aachen (October 2–21, 1944) was one of the major battles fought by American forces in World War II. The city of Aachen was the first city on German soil to be taken by the Allies but only after heavy losses suffered by both sides.

4. We do not have further information on the individuals referred to by Otto in this letter.

## 30.  Questions about the Future

1. Emil Kirschmann was a member of the Reichstag in Germany with the Social Democratic Party during the Weimar Republic. He married Marie Juchacz's sister, who died in 1930. After 1933 Kirschmann lived in exile, first in the Saar area and then in France before escaping to America. He and Marie Juchacz later married and lived together in New York.

2. Samuel Estrin, born and educated in Russia, lived in Berlin and Paris before immigrating to the United States in 1939. He began working with the JLC in New York in 1940 and served as its secretary for international affairs for thirty years until he retired in 1970. He was a strong supporter of Eva in New York. Correspondence between Estrin and Eva over many years reveals their continuing friendship and mutual respect.

3. Ernie Pyle was a Pulitzer Prize–winning American war correspondent. The book Eva refers to is *Brave Men* (noted in her December 22, 1944, letter).

4. Eva Pfister and Otto Pfister, "To Our Children," unpublished memoir (Los Angeles, 1979), 101.

5. Ibid., 101–2.

6. OSS document titled "Interrogation Guide" dated November 22, 1944.

7. OSS document titled "Safe Addresses" dated November 30, 1944.

8. Organization Todt was an engineering group founded by Fritz Todt that was initially responsible for the construction of the autobahn network in Germany from 1933 to 1938, drawing on conscripted labor within Germany. After the war began, the organization worked almost exclusively on military and paramilitary projects for the Third Reich. Albert Speer succeeded Todt as head of the organization when Todt died in 1942.

9. OSS "Interrogation Guide," November 22, 1944.

10. Eva and Otto Pfister, "To Our Children," 102.

11. Eva is likely referring here to the death of Emil Kirschmann's wife in

1930.

## 31.  1945: Signs of Spring

1. Friedrich Adler, a well-known Austrian scholar and trade union leader, had given Eva desperately needed money for her ship fare in Lisbon, as described in Chapter 13.
2. Welfare Island (now named Roosevelt Island) is a narrow island in New York City's East River between Manhattan and Queens. When known as "Welfare Island," it was used primarily for hospitals from 1921 to 1971.
3. Regina Kägi (1889–1972), born Regina Fuchsmann, the daughter of a Jewish merchant, was a Swiss humanitarian activist. She assisted Spanish refugee children during the Spanish Civil War and worked on refugee aid and reconstruction in Europe following World War II.
4. "Ruhr Pocket" refers to a major battle in April 1945 in which the Allies encircled and defeated German soldiers in the industrial Ruhr area in Germany.
5. Benedikt Kautsky, son of Karl Kautsky (a famous Czech Austrian socialist, journalist, anti-Bolshevik, and theoretician of Marxism), was secretary of the Viennese Chamber of Labor from 1921 to 1938 and editor of *Arbeit und Wirtschaft* (Labor and Economics). An opponent of Hitler, Kautsky was arrested in May 1938 following the annexation (Anschluss) of Austria by Nazi Germany. He was imprisoned in concentration camps in Dachau, Buchenwald, and Auschwitz (Monowitz camp) and back to Buchenwald, where he was liberated in April 1945. A fellow camp survivor described Benedikt Kautsky, whom he referred to as "Bendl," as "my best friend and mentor from the concentration camps . . . the man to whom I truly owe my life." Burt Linder, *Condemned without Judgment: The Three Lives of a Holocaust Survivor* (New York: S.P.I. Books, 1995), 311.
6. Eva Pfister and Otto Pfister, "To Our Children," unpublished memoir (Los Angeles, 1979), 102.

## Epilogue

1. Eva Pfister and Otto Pfister, "To Our Children," unpublished memoir (Los Angeles, 1979), 106.
2. Memorandum dated April 8, 1946, from the U.S. Department of Justice,

Immigration and Naturalization Service, requesting information from the director of the FBI, Attention: Security Division, and the FBI's response dated June 20, 1946. The U.S. Citizenship and Immigration Services released this document on June 26, 2012, in response to a FOIA request (FBI FOI/PA #1178379-001). The document reflects "File No. 2270-537532 aepu" and "File 40-HQ-40706-4 FDPS pages 313–32."

3. Eva and Otto had known Ola and her family in Europe; Ola's sister Mascha had been with Eva at the Walkemühle. Werner had escaped from Europe, first to Cuba and then to America.

4. Eva and Otto Pfister, "To Our Children," 110.

5. Ibid., 110–11.

6. Letter from Otto to Peter dated September 16, 1984.

7. Felix Adler founded the New York Society for Ethical Culture in 1877. Similar ethical societies later formed in other cities. The following statement has been used by some ethical culture societies to convey their view of ethical humanist religion: "Our faith is in the capacity and responsibility of human beings to act in their personal relationships and in the larger community to help create a better world. Our commitment is to the worth and dignity of the individual, and to treating each human being so as to bring out the best in him or her.'" Edward L. Ericson, *The Humanist Way: An Introduction to Ethical Humanist Religion* (New York: Continuum, 1998), introductory note on secular and religious humanism.

8. The Unitarian Service Committee was one of the few American organizations to provide meaningful assistance to refugees in Europe during World War II. For an excellent account of the remarkable network of Unitarian rescue and relief workers in southern France and Portugal, see Susan Elisabeth Subak, *Rescue & Flight: American Relief Workers Who Defied the Nazis* (Lincoln: University of Nebraska Press, 2010).

9. Relationships were also formed with other families who had emigrated from Europe, including Doro and Fred Odenheimer and their son Michael.

10. Antje Dertinger, *Every Farewell Is a New Beginning: Erich Lewinski, a Biography*, translated by Tom Lewinski from *Die Drei Exile des Erich Lewinski* [Erich Lewinski, Three Times Exiled] (Gerlingen: Bleicher Verlag, 1995), 169; Eva and Otto Pfister, "To Our Children," 103.

11. Ibid., 147–56.

12. Ibid., 120–25. At that time, he observed, "Perhaps it is only my age, I am already forty-four years old and the last ten years have not been easy. In March it will be ten years since we began our wanderings."

13. Eva and Otto Pfister, "To Our Children," 103.

14. Ibid., 115–16.
15. Ibid., 117.
16. Kathy and her husband Neil visited South Africa in 2012, helping to continue the family connection in the next generation. Daughters of Eva's sister Ruth, Yvonne and Charlotte, have also made recent visits in America.
17. We, the authors of this book, each visited Carl-Otto and his family in Munich on our separate trips to Europe during and after our college years, and they visited us on several trips to California. Carl-Otto and Trude have passed away, but our relationship with their daughters continues through correspondence and visits.
18. Eva's diary entry, November 8, 1985.
19. Audiotape of interview of Eva in early August 1986 for a German television documentary about refugees who had escaped from Nazism. The interview was conducted by Karin Alles of Hessischer Rundfunk, which produced a documentary in November 1987 titled *Das Letzte Visum, Fluchtgeschichten anno 1940*.
20. Eva's diary entry, August 6, 1986.
21. Eva's translation of letter from Gaby Cordier following Otto's death in Eva's file "Excerpts of Some Letters Showing How Otto Had Touched People," December 1985.
22. Eva's diary entry, January 28, 1987.
23. Eva Pfister, "Begegnungen mit Marie Juchacz in der Emigration," in *Marie Juchacz: Gründerin der Arbeiterwohlfahrt; Leben und Werk* (Bonn: Arbeiterwohlfahrt, 1979), 143-149.
24. Käthe Kollwitz, *The Diary and Letters of Käthe Kollwitz*, edited by Hans Kollwitz, translated by Richard and Clara Winston (Evanston, IL: Northwestern University Press, 1988).
25. Rainer Maria Rilke, *Sonnets to Orpheus*, translated by M. D. Herter Norton (New York: Norton, 1942).


## Afterword

1. Jef Rens, "René Bertholet et Otto Pfister," in *Rencontres avec le siècle* [Encounters with the Century], translated from the Dutch by Jean-Pierre Orban (Gembloux, Belgium: Editions Duculot, 1987). Peter later learned that the book had been translated into French from the original Dutch.
2. Ibid.

3. Tom Lewinski, "What Happened to the Lewinskis?" (unpublished memoir, 1987), 63.

4. Andreas G. Graf, *Anarchisten Gegen Hitler* (Berlin: Lukas Verlag, 2001), 114 (chapter by Dieter Nelles, "Der Widerstand der Internationalen Transport-Arbeiter-Föderation (ITF) gegen Nationalsocialismus und Faschismus in Deutschland und Spanien").

5. One such bonfire on May 16, 1940, was described by Herbert Lottman in *The Fall of Paris, June 1940* (New York: HarperCollins, 1992), 59:

> Anatole de Monzie was staring up at the sky when the first green objects hurtled down from higher floors. File boxes! From the windows the ministers and their aides watched as the heap of boxes and loose papers grew on the lawn. Then someone poured gasoline over the pile, lit a match. A bonfire that would go down in history had been touched off, as the Foreign Ministry burned its most sensitive records.

6. The declassified SOE documents are available on microfilm at the Cecil H. Green Library at Stanford University in *Special Operations Executive, 1940–1946: Subversion and Sabotage during World War II; Series One: SOE Operations in Western Europe* (from Adam Matthew Publications). Information about the ISK's involvement with the SOE during the war can be found in Part 3: Germany, 1936–1945, reels 28–30.

7. Kathy's husband Neil, Peter's wife Bonnie, and Tom's son Franklin participated in this memorable trip. A friend from our childhood who is also the child of refugees, Natasha Vorster Levine, and her husband Joe joined us for the crossing of the Pyrenees.

8. We had some good fortune in the consideration of our FOIA request on remand: the person employed at the National Archives who was responsible for providing further responses, Mary Kay Schmidt, made meaningful efforts to find the documents we had described in our requests. She contacted us with questions regarding the focus of our requests and made suggestions about other libraries and archives that might have additional information.

9. Mary Kay Schmidt of the National Archives wrote: "We identified the FBI's files on the Inter-Departmental Committee on Political Refugees (100-HQ-17826 and 100-HQ-17826-2) and located serial 100-17826-2-4. . . . We were advised that since the FBI thoroughly 'weeded' the files some years ago, documentation about the Committee is incomplete." July 27, 2012 letter from National Archives re: FOIA Request number NW

38170. One cannot help but wonder what criteria were used, especially by the State Department, in weeding its files about this crucial period when decisions about granting and denying visas were decisions about life and death.

10. Susan Elizabeth Subak, *Rescue & Flight: American Relief Workers Who Defied the Nazis* (Lincoln: University of Nebraska Press, 2010), 262n18. *Rescue & Flight* provides a detailed and moving account of the rescue and relief efforts during this period of the courageous women and men on the Unitarian Service Committee (including Robert and Elizabeth Dexter, Charles Joy, Martha and Waitstill Sharp, Noel Field, and Howard Brooks) and the people in other organizations, including the Emergency Rescue Committee, who helped them (including Varian Fry, Leon Ball, Mary Jayne Gold, Charlie Fawcett, Miriam Davenport, Donald Lowrie, and Rene Zimmer).

11. Bénédite was a former French policeman who worked with Varian Fry at the Centre Américain de Secours in Marseille and continued the rescue and relief work there after Fry's return to the United States at the end of September 1941. See Daniel Bénédite, *Un chemin vers la Liberté sous l'Occupation: Du comité Varian Fry au débarquement en Méditerranée Marseille-Provence, 1940–1944*, edited by Jean-Marie Guillon (Paris: Éditions du Felin, 2017).

12. Subak, *Rescue & Flight, 160.*

13. Ibid., 262n18.

14. Christof Mauch, *The Shadow War against Hitler: The Covert Operations of America's Wartime Secret Intelligence Service* (New York: Columbia University Press, 1999). Allen Dulles was the mission chief of the OSS in Bern, Switzerland, during the war. As explained by Neal H. Petersen, "OSS Bern constituted a virtual Central Intelligence Agency in itself, with operations ranging from the gathering of battle order information, to running espionage networks in enemy territory, to orchestrating unconventional military operations." Neal H. Petersen, *From Hitler's Doorstep: The Wartime Intelligence Reports of Allen Dulles, 1942–1945* (University Park: Pennsylvania State University Press, 1996), 1.

15. Mauch, *The Shadow War against Hitler*, 16–17.

16. Ibid., 228n39.

17. Ibid., 126, 274n102. Mauch noted: "Thus far, it has not been possible to identify Agent 328. He was a Frenchman married to a German woman, and he had excellent contacts to trade unions. In one telegram, 328 is

designated as René; conceivably, this was René Bertholet."
18. Paul Bonart, *But We Said "NO!": Voices from the German Underground* (San Francisco: Mark Backman Productions, 2007).
19. Ibid., 153.
20. Ibid., 162.
21. Ibid.
22. By adopting the Godesberg Program, the SPD adopted a commitment to reform capitalism rather than the goal of replacing it and sought to expand the party beyond its former working-class base by advocating a philosophy of socialism grounded in ethical and moral considerations rather than an attack against capitalism based solely on the economic division between owners/managers and workers.
23. One of the documents Eva retained in her files provides special insight into the ISK's political philosophy and objectives. Written in English and titled "In Memory of Leonard Nelson," it was prepared for a Leonard Nelson Memorial Meeting held in London on July 11, 1942, at Conway Hall, Red Lion Square, commemorating what would have been Nelson's sixtieth birthday. The document includes presentations by Mary Saran, Willi Eichler, Minna Specht, Margaret Henry, Tolle Fryd, and Gustav Heckmann.
24. Other writings about ISK members include *Leonard Nelson Zum Gedächtnis*, eds. Minna Specht and Willi Eichler (Frankfurt, Göttingen: Verlag Öffentliches Leben, 1953); Hellmut Becker, *Erziehung und Politik: Minna Specht zu ihrem 80. Geburtstag* (Frankfurt: Verlag Öffentliches Leben, 1960); Mary Saran, *Never Give Up: Memoirs by Mary Saran* (London: Oswald Wolff, 1976); Helga Haas-Reitschal and Sabine Hering, *Nora Platiel, Sozialistin, Emigrantin, Politikerin: Eine Biographie* (Köln: Bund-Verlag GmbH, 1990); Gisela Konopka, *Courage and Love* (Edina, MN: Burgess Printing, 1988).
25. Rilke's fascination with the nuances and feelings of colors was apparently drawn in part from his friendship with French painter Paul Cézanne. In one of his letters about Cézanne, Rilke spoke further about the color gray:

> I said: gray—yesterday, when I described the background of the self-portrait, light copper obliquely crossed by a gray pattern;—I should have said: a particular metallic white, aluminum or something similar, for gray, literally gray, cannot be found in Cézanne's pictures. To his immensely painterly eye it didn't hold up as a color: he went to the core of it and found that it was violet there

or blue or reddish or green.

Rainer Maria Rilke, *Letters on Cézanne*, edited by Clara Rilke, translated by Joel Agee (New York: North Point, 1985), 76–78.

## Appendix B

1. Memo for O.S.S., Bern, July 31, 1942, Record Group 226, Stack 190, Row 6, Comp. 4, Shelf 3, Entry 92, Box 117, Folder 10, 9A, OSS Files, NARA, College Park.
2. Memo for O.S.S., Bern, August 7, 1942, Record Group 226, Stack 190, Row 6, Comp. 4, Shelf 3, Entry 92, Box 117, Folder 10, 40A. OSS Files, NARA, College Park.
3. Arthur J. Goldberg to David Shaw, March 25, 1943, Record Group 226, Stack 190, Row 6, Comp. 4, Shelf 3, Entry 92, Box 117, Folder 10, OSS Files, NARA, College Park.
4. April 2, 1943 report No. 109, "Material for Eva, 328," "Press Bulletin of Fighting French, No. 78, Mar. 11, 1943."
5. Letter from J.Q. 100 to J.Q. dated May 23, 1942, SOE Files, Cecil H. Green Library, Stanford, HS 6/653, No. 111.
6. SOE Files, Cecil H. Green Library, Stanford, HS 6/654, 24A.

# Bibliography

Adant, Philippe. *Widerstand und Wagemut: René Bertholet—eine Biographie.* Translated from French by Suzanne Miller. Frankfurt: dipa-Verlag, 1996.

Bailey, Christian. *Between Yesterday and Tomorrow: German Visions of Europe, 1926–1950.* New York: Berghahn Books, 2013.

Becker, Hellmut. *Erziehung und Politik: Minna Specht zu ihrem 80. Geburtstag.* Frankfurt: Verlag Öffentliches Leben, 1960.

Bénédite, Daniel. *Un chemin vers la Liberté sous l'Occupation: Du comité Varian Fry au débarquement en Méditerranée Marseille-Provence, 1940–1944.* Edited by Mean-Marie Guillon. Paris: Éditions du Felin, 2017.

Benz, Wolfgang. *Geschichte des Dritten Reichs.* München: Verlag B. H. Beck oHG, 2000.

Bingham, Robert Kim, Sr. *Courageous Dissent: How Harry Bingham Defied His Government to Save Lives.* Greenwich, CT: Triune Books, 2007.

Bingham, Robert Kim, Sr. "Hiram ('Harry') Bingham IV Homepage." http://www.hirambinghamrescuer.com.

Bonart, Paul. *But We Said "NO!": Voices from the German Underground.* San Francisco: Mark Backman Productions, 2007.

Bonelli, Charlotte. *Exit Berlin: How One Woman Saved Her Family from Nazi Germany.* New Haven, CT: Yale University Press, 2014.

Breitman, Richard, and Allan J. Lichtman. *FDR and the Jews.* Cambridge, MA: Belknap Press of Harvard University Press, 2013.

Breitman, Richard, Barbara McDonald Stewart, and Severin Hochberg, eds. *The Diaries and Papers of James G. McDonald, 1935–1945.* Bloomington: Indiana University Press, 2009.

Chambers, John Whiteclay, II. *Bang-Bang Boys, Jedburghs, and the House of Horrors: A History of OSS Training and Operations in World War II.* n.d.: An Uncommon Valor Reprint, 2016.

Dertinger, Antje. *Every Farewell Is a New Beginning: Erich Lewinski, a Biography.* Translated by Tom Lewinski from *Die Drei Exile des Erich Lewinski* [Erich Lewinski, Three Times Exiled]. Gerlingen: Bleicher Verlag, 1995.

Dobbs, Michael. *The Unwanted: America, Auschwitz, and a Village Caught in Between.* New York: Knopf, 2019.

Doerr, Anthony. *All the Light We Cannot See.* New York: Scribner, 2014.

Erbelding, Rebecca. *Rescue Board: The Untold Story of America's Efforts to Save the Jews of Europe.* New York: Doubleday, 2018.

Fittko, Lisa. *Escape through the Pyrenees.* Evanston, IL: Northwestern University Press, 1991. (First published in German as *Mein Weg über die Pyrenäen, Erinnerungen 1940/41.* Munich: Carl Hanser Verlag, 1985.)

Foot, Michael R. D. *SOE in France: An Account of the Work of the British Special Operations Executive in France, 1940–1944.* London: Whitehall History Publishing in association with Frank Cass, 2004.

Friedman, Saul S. *No Haven for the Oppressed: United States Policy toward Jewish Refugees, 1938–1945.* Detroit: Wayne State University Press, 1973.

Fry, Varian. *Surrender on Demand.* Boulder, CO: Johnson Books/U.S. Holocaust Memorial Museum, 1997. (First published by Random House in 1945.)

Gardiner, Muriel, and Joseph Buttinger. *Damit wir nicht vergessen: Unsere Jahre 1934–47 in Wien, Paris und New York* [Lest We Forget: Our Years in Vienna, Paris, and New York, 1934–1947]. Vienna: Wiener Volksbuchhandlung, 1978.

Gildea, Robert. *Fighters in the Shadows: A New History of the French Resistance.* Cambridge, MA: Belknap Press of Harvard University Press, 2015.

Gourd, Andrea, and Thomas Noetzel, eds. *Zukunft der Demokratie in Deutschland.* Opladen: Leske + Budrich, 2001.

Graf, Andreas G. *Anarchisten Gegen Hitler.* Berlin: Lukas Verlag, 2001.

Haas-Rietschel, Helga, and Sabine Hering. *Nora Platiel, Sozialistin, Emigrantin, Politikerin: Eine Biographie.* Köln: Bund Verlag GmbH, 1990 (printed with the assistance of the Friedrich-Ebert-Stiftung).

Hoffmann, Peter. *German Resistance to Hitler.* Cambridge, MA: Harvard University Press, 1988.

Isenberg, Sheila. *A Hero of Our Own: The Story of Varian Fry*. New York: Random House, 2001.

Isenberg, Sheila. *Muriel's War: An American Heiress in the Nazi Resistance*. New York: Palgrave Macmillan, 2010.

Jackson, Michael. "In the Footsteps of Walter Benjamin." *Harvard Divinity Bulletin* 34 (2006).

Jacobs, Jack. "A Friend in Need: The Jewish Labor Committee and Refugees from the German-Speaking Lands, 1933–1945," *YIVO Annual* 23 (1996): 391–417. (Abridged English translation of *Ein Freund in Not: Das Jüdische Arbeiterkomitee in New York und die Flüchtlinge aus den deutschsprachigen Ländern, 1933–1945*. Bonn: Forschungsinstitut der Friedrich-Ebert-Stiftung, 1993.)

Kearns Goodwin, Doris. *No Ordinary Time: Franklin & Eleanor Roosevelt; The Home Front in World War II*. New York: Touchstone, 1994.

Klär, Karl-Heinz. "Zwei Nelson Bünde: Internationaler Jugend-Bund (IJB) und Internationaler Sozialistischer Kampf-Bund (ISK) im Licht Neuer Quellen." *Internationale Wissenschaftliche Korrespondenz zur Geschichte der deutschen Arbeiterbewegung* 18 (1982): 310–60.

Koch, H. W. *In the Name of the Volk: Political Justice in Hitler's Germany*. London: I. B. Taurus, 1989.

Kollwitz, Käthe. *The Diary and Letters of Käthe Kollwitz*. Edited by Hans Kollwitz, translated by Richard and Clara Winston. Evanston, IL: Northwestern University Press, 1988.

Laharie, Claude. *Le Camp de Gurs, 1939–1945, un aspect méconnu de l'histoire de Vichy*. Pau: Société Atlantique d'Impression à Biarritz, 1993.

Langkau-Alex, Ursula. *Deutsche Volksfront 1932–39: Zwischen Berlin, Paris, Prag und Moskau. Zweiter Band; Geschichte des Ausschusses zur Vorbereitung einer Deutshen Volksfront*. Berlin: Akademie Verlag, 2004–2005.

Lemke-Müller, Sabine. *Ethik des Widerstands, Der Kampf des Internationalen Sozialistischen Kampfbundes (ISK) gegen den Nationalsozialismus: Quellen und Texte zum Widerstand aus der Arbeiterbewegung, 1933–1945*. Bonn: Dietz, 1996.

Lévy, Claude, and Paul Tillard. *La Grande Rafle du Vel' d'Hiv, 16 juillet 1942*. Paris: Robert Laffont, 1967.

Lewinski, Erich. "Von der Menschenwürde [Of Human Dignity]." In *Leonard Nelson Zum Gedächtnis*, edited by Minna Specht and Willi Eichler, 271-290. Frankfurt, Göttingen: Verlag Öffentliches Leben, 1953 (translation into English by Tom Lewinski).

Lewinski, Tom. "What Happened to the Lewinskis?" Unpublished memoir, 1987.

Lindner, Heiner. "Um etwas zu erreichen, muss man sich etwas vornehmen, von dem man glaubt, dass es unmöglich sei." In *Der Internationale Sozialistische Kampf-Bund (ISK) und seine Publikationen*. Bonn: Friedrich-Ebert-Stiftung Historisches Forschungszentrum, 2006.

Link, Werner. *Die Geschichte des Internationalen Jugend-Bundes (IJB) und des Internationalen Sozialistischen Kampfbundes (ISK), Ein Beitrag zur Geschichte der Arbeiterbewegung in der Weimarer Republik und im Dritten Reich*. Meisenheim am Glan: Hain, 1964.

Lottman, Herbert R. *The Fall of Paris, June 1940*. New York: HarperCollins, 1992.

Lowrie, Donald. *The Hunted Children*. New York: Norton, 1963.

Marino, Andy. *A Quiet American: The Secret War of Varian Fry*. New York: St. Martin's, 1999.

Mauch, Christof. *The Shadow War against Hitler: The Covert Operations of America's Wartime Secret Intelligence Service*. New York: Columbia University Press, 1999.

May, Ernest R. *Strange Victory: Hitler's Conquest of France*. New York: Hill and Wang, 2000.

McClafferty, Carla Killough. *In Defiance of Hitler: The Secret Mission of Varian Fry*. New York: Farrar, Straus, and Giroux, 2008.

Medoff, Rafael. *FDR and the Holocaust: A Breach of Faith*. Washington, DC: David S. Wyman Institute for Holocaust Studies, 2013.

Meisler, Stanley. *Shocking Paris: Soutine, Chagall and the Outsiders of Montparnasse*. New York: St. Martin's, 2015.

Nelson, Leonard. *Politics and Education*. Translated by W. Lansdell. London: Allen & Unwin, 1928.

Paldiel, Mordecai. *Saving the Jews: Amazing Stories of Men and Women Who Defied the "Final Solution."* Rockville, MD: Schreiber Publishing, 2000.

Petersen, Lilo. *Les Oubliées* [*The Forgotten*]. Clamecy, France: Jacob-Duvernet, 2007.

Petersen, Neal H. *From Hitler's Doorstep: The Wartime Intelligence Reports of Allen Dulles, 1942–1945*. University Park: Pennsylvania State University Press, 1996.

Pfister, Eva. "Begegnungen mit Marie Juchacz in der Emigration." In *Marie Juchacz: Gründerin der Arbeiterwohlfahrt; Leben und Werk, 143-149*. Bonn: Arbeiterwohlfahrt, 1979.

Pfister, Eva, and Otto Pfister. "To Our Children." Unpublished memoir, Los Angeles, 1979.

Pfister, Tom, Peter Pfister, and Kathy Pfister. *Eva and Otto: America's Vetting and Rescue of Political Refugees during World War II.* Los Angeles: Pfisters, 2017.

Prelinger, Elizabeth, Alessandra Comini, and Hildegard Bachert. *Käthe Kollwitz.* Washington DC: National Gallery of Art and Yale University Press, 1992.

Renaud, Terence. "The Genesis of the Emergency Rescue Committee, 1933–1942." Student essay, Boston University, 2005.

Renaud, Terence. "The German Resistance in New York: Karl B. Frank and the New Beginning Group, 1935–1945." Undergraduate thesis, Boston University, 2007.

Renaud, Terence. "'This Is Our Dunkirk': Karl B. Frank and the Politics of the Emergency Rescue Committee." Student essay, Boston University, 2009.

Rens, Jef. "René Bertholet et Otto Pfister." In *Rencontres avec le siècle* [Encounters with the Century]. Translated from the Dutch by Jean-Pierre Orban. Gembloux, Belgium: Editions Duculot, 1987.

Rilke, Rainer Maria. *Letters on Cézanne.* Edited by Clara Rilke, translated by Joel Agee. New York: North Point, 1985.

Rilke, Rainer Maria. *Sonnets to Orpheus.* Translated by M. D. Herter Norton. New York: Norton, 1942.

Rüther, Martin, Uwe Schütz, and Otto Dann. *Deutschland im ersten Nachkriegsjahr, Berichte von Mitgliedern des Internationalen Sozialistischen Kampfbundes (ISK) aus dem besetzen Deutschland 1945/46.* München: K. G. Sauer, 1998.

Ryan, Donna F. *The Holocaust & the Jews of Marseille: The Enforcement of Anti-Semitic Policies in Vichy France.* Urbana: University of Illinois Press, 1996.

Saran, Mary. *Never Give Up: Memoirs by Mary Saran.* London: Oswald Wolff, 1976.

Schramm, Hanna. *Menschen in Gurs: Erinnerungen an ein französisches Internierungslager (1940–1941)* [*Humans in Gurs: Memories of a French Internment Camp, 1940–41*]. Worms: Georg Heintz, 1977.

Seaman, Mark. *Saboteur: The Untold Story of SOE's Youngest Agent at the Heart of the French Resistance.* London: John Blake Publishing, 2018.

Sösemann, Bernd (ed.). *Fritz Eberhard: Rückblicke auf Biographie und Werk.* Stuttgart: Franz Steiner Verlag, 2001.

Struve, Walter. *Elites against Democracy: Leadership Ideals in Bourgeois Political Thought in Germany, 1890–1933*. Reprint ed. Princeton, NJ: Princeton Legacy Library, 2017.

Subak, Susan Elisabeth. *Rescue & Flight: American Relief Workers Who Defied the Nazis*. Lincoln: University of Nebraska Press, 2010.

Varon, Benson. *Fighting Fascism and Surviving Buchenwald: The Life and Memoir of Hans Bergas*. n.p.: B. Varon, 2015.

Wallance, Gregory. *America's Soul in the Balance*. Austin, TX: Greenleaf Book Group, 2012.

Wyman, David S. *The Abandonment of the Jews: America and the Holocaust, 1941–1945*. New York: New Press, 1984.

Young-Bruehl, Elizabeth. *Hannah Arendt: For Love of the World*. New Haven, CT: Yale University Press, 1982.

# Index

# About the Authors

Authors at the Camp de Gurs Memorial in 2011.

The authors are the three children of Eva and Otto.

Tom was a partner at the law firm of Latham & Watkins LLP, where he practiced in its Los Angeles office for over thirty years before retiring. He currently serves on the boards of several nonprofit organizations for which he provides pro bono legal advice. Tom received his AB from Stanford University, where he studied history and German and spent a year of study with Stanford programs in Germany. He received his JD from Harvard Law School.

Kathy is a psychotherapist with a private practice in Amherst, Massachusetts. For many years, she worked as a therapist in the Mount Holyoke College Counseling Service. During that time, she also served as a member of the adjunct faculty at the Smith College Graduate School of Social Work. Kathy received her AB from the University of California at Santa Barbara and her MA in clinical social work from the University of California at Berkeley.

Peter was a partner at the law firm of Morrison & Foerster LLP, where he practiced in its San Francisco office for over forty years. He previously served as chair of that firm, and is currently a senior counsel. As an undergraduate at the University of California at Santa Barbara, Peter spent a year in the Education Abroad program at the University of Göttingen in Germany. He received his JD from Yale Law School.